T0319987

Creating Memories in Late 8th-century Byzantium

# Central European Medieval Studies

The series focuses on the geographical centre of the European continent, but also a region representing various historically changing meanings and concepts. It challenges simplistic notions of Central Europe as a periphery to the medieval 'West', or, equally, a border between barbarity and civilization; an area of a lively convergence of different ethnic groups, and a socially and culturally framed common space; a point where different 'Others' met, or an intermediary 'bridge' between the Roman Catholicism and Latinity of the West, and the Slavic Orthodoxy and Hellenism of the Byzantine East.

# Creating Memories in Late 8th-century Byzantium

*The Short History of Nikephoros of Constantinople*

*Dragoljub Marjanović*

Amsterdam University Press

Cover illustration: Interior part of the dome of the 13th century Sopoćani monastery in Serbia
Source: Author's photo

Cover design: Coördesign, Leiden
Lay-out: Crius Group, Hulshout

Amsterdam University Press English-language titles are distributed in the US and Canada by
the University of Chicago Press.

| | |
|---|---|
| ISBN | 978 94 6298 039 6 |
| e-ISBN | 978 90 4852 965 0 (pdf) |
| DOI | 10.5117/9789462980396 |
| NUR | 684 / 704 |

Printed and bound by CPI Group (UK) Ltd, Croydon, CR0 4YY

# Table of Contents

## List of Tables

# Preface

In essence, this book deals with Iconoclasm in the Byzantine empire. While the core of the dispute remained embedded in a Christological argument about depicting the Word and Son of God – Jesus Christ – in his human likeness, and the struggle to obtain justification for this practice of Orthodoxy, the place and role of the emperor remained an equally significant issue in the controversy. The apologists for icon worship in Byzantium's eighth and ninth centuries consistently insisted upon two crucial points. The first was the undisputed Orthodoxy of displaying God's *oikonomia* of the salvation of humankind through the depicting and revering of his icon, while the second was the *freedom* of the Church to define and propagate its doctrine without pressure and interference from the *basileus*. It was an ancient issue in the Church, reintroduced anew in eighth-century Byzantium with particular strength, bringing quite a few challenges to the Church of Constantinople. The Iconoclasm of the Byzantine emperors inspired various intellectual reactions from the Orthodox party, which proved to be up to the challenge and at the height of its capabilities to repel the attack, which was threatening to undermine the very foundations of Christian doctrine. The political and cultural aspects of Iconoclasm in Byzantium thus step into the forefront of research on this problem, as do equally the ecclesiastical and theological aspects. In fact, these processes were closely connected and intertwined. My aim in this study is to demonstrate that history writing at the end of the eighth century in Byzantium was both shaped and inspired by Iconoclasm. It was summoned to give an original contribution to solving the controversy and the various problems it had initiated. Iconoclasm influenced the Byzantine view of the past and forced an engagement with creative memory-making in order to produce a comprehensible and Orthodox view of the earlier traditions. The *Short History* of Nikephoros of Constantinople in this context presents the earliest example of such an enterprise, and a most original one as well. In this book – a revised Ph.D. dissertation – I shall reveal and demonstrate how Nikephoros wrote history, and how he responded to some of the key issues that brought the Orthodox Church into a dispute with the emperor, burdening their relationship.

This book would not have appeared as it does now without the great inspiration and scholarly support of Professor Vlada Stanković. He directed my understanding of Byzantine historical literature and shaped my interest in Byzantine narrative sources, in a completely new way, when I began my postgraduate studies at the Seminary of Byzantine Studies in the History

Department of Belgrade University. I must reveal here that both of us felt uneasy to a certain extent when Professor Radivoj Radić suggested that I should engage in an analysis of Nikephoros's *Short History* for my Ph.D. thesis. We both occupied ourselves with reading Nikephoros's history, me for the first time, him for the first time after a long time, and in the beginning it seemed to me that, after C. Mango's thorough critical edition of Nikephoros, there remained little to pull out of this remote Byzantine author. However, Nikephoros proved to be quite an interesting and original historian. Where C. Mango left off with the puzzling conclusion that Nikephoros failed to demonstrate the proper consciousness of a historian, I picked up and tried to offer a new outlook on this significant historical figure of late eighth- and early ninth-century Byzantium – a former *asekretis, ptochotrophos,* and, finally, patriarch of the Church of Constantinople. As it turned out, Nikephoros's *mistakes* according to Mango actually reveal his specific and original method for creating a historical narrative and shaping the past in compliance with the Orthodox party's notions of the emperor, his place in the Church, and his relationship with its doctrines.

I express my sincere gratitude to Professor Nada Zečević, from Amsterdam University Press. She patiently led me through multiple phases of preparation of the manuscript for its publication. Her advice and instructions were most valuable in the process of making this book. I convey my appreciation to the peer reviewers who read the draft version of the manuscript and offered very valuable suggestions on how to improve the argument.

Finally, I express my deepest gratefulness to my beloved family. Their steady endurance of the consequences of my research is interwoven with the result of my study of Nikephoros's *Short History*. To them I dedicate this work.

*Belgrade, 1 February 2017*
*St. Makarios the Great*

# Introduction

Due to the influence and historical role of Patriarch Nikephoros of Constantinople at the turn of Byzantium's eighth and ninth centuries, his literary heritage has attracted the attention of modern researchers dealing with various aspects of Byzantine civilization. According to the words of the author of the first monograph dedicated to the epoch and work of Patriarch Nikephoros, the fate of Nikephoros's secular work[1] – the *Short History* and *Short Chronicle* –was somewhat unfavourable,[2] especially when compared to his more numerous theological writings, which gained much wider circulation and use already in the Middle Ages.[3] Likewise, the *Short Chronicle* enjoyed popularity among the Slavic circles familiar with the Byzantine cultural environment and its impact, while the *Short History*, with its two manuscript copies, remained relatively obscure even in the centuries close to the time of its author.

The first explicit reference from the Byzantine era, a sort of review of Nikephoros's *Short History*, occurred only in the second half of the ninth century. It came from the pen of one of the most prominent successors to Nikephoros's patriarchal see: the great Patriarch Photios, who, moreover, presented himself as Nikephoros's relative in the letter addressed to the Roman Pope Nicholas I.[4] Photios's laudatory review of the literary features and qualities of Nikephoros's *Short History*, as displayed in his *Bibliotheca*, resulted from his tendency to connect himself to his predecessor, the

---

1    By referring to the term *secular*, we are implying a literary work different in its character from the literature which predominantly focuses on theological issues, among which also a historiographical work such as a world chronicle can be included when its themes are mostly related to theological or dogmatic interpretations of historical events. Almost contemporary, and by its historical outlook to the past most relevant, is the *Chronicle* of Theophanes.

2    Alexander, *The Patriarch Nicephorus*, pp. 156-157.

3    Nikephoros's literary heritage of theological provenance is more diverse, leading to a greater attention among contemporaries as well as among modern researchers of Byzantine culture and the epoch of the ninth century. For a detailed review of Nikephoros's theological works, see Alexander, *The Patriarch Nicephorus*, pp. 162-188, and O'Connell, *The Ecclesiology of St. Nicephorus*, pp. 53-67. These writings were mostly published in PG 100, whereas one of Nikephoros's most prominent theological works, *Refutatio et eversio*, was edited and published in recent times by J.M. Featherstone. Recently there appeared as well Chryssostalis, *Recherches sur la tradition manuscrite du contra Eusebium*. These, together with the critical edition of the *Short History*, indicate a revival of scientific interest and rounded research on Nikephoros's literary heritage at the end of the twentieth and the beginning of the twenty-first century.

4    Photius, *Epistulae*, ep. 290, 129, 156-158; ep. 133, 310-312.

Patriarch Nikephoros, both *spiritually* and in terms of *kinship*.[5] Still, Photios's account, in which he praised Nikephoros's literary qualities as displayed in his *Short History*, provides valuable testimony concerning the reception and comprehension of the work in the centuries of Byzantine history that followed Nikephoros's demise in 828. In contrast to Photios's open attitude and his reflections on the nature and character of the *Short History*, Nikephoros's historical work appears to have enjoyed a certain degree of attention from the Byzantine historians of a later period such as George the Monk and Symeon Logothete.[6] Could it be that the high appraisal of the *Short History* by Photios presented some impetus for a wider utilization of Nikephoros's work among the aforementioned Byzantine historians?

A valuable critical edition of Nikephoros's *Short History* by C. Mango stands at the end of a lengthy period of mostly secondary studies regarding the features of the work and its character, opening new questions as well. Some of these we shall re-examine in our work on the basis of Mango's edition of the *Short History*.[7] More recent studies devoted to various aspects of Byzantine literature from the eighth and the beginning of the ninth centuries often neglect the *Short History* of Nikephoros in their research, its character, and its status as one of the first historical works of renewed Byzantine history writing from the beginning of the ninth century.[8] However, newer historical overviews of Byzantine literature give an obvious advantage in their research of Byzantine historiography to Theophanes the Chronographer, Nikephoros's contemporary and fellow combatant in their mutual ecclesiastical struggle for the freedom of the Church of Constantinople. It is usually the case in modern literature that the *Short History* is mentioned only regarding specific issues and problems in Theophanes's

5    Photius, *Bibliotheca*, no. 66, 98-99. For the text, see Chapter 2: *Dating of the Short History*.

6    Cf. Липшиц, 'Никифор и его исторический труд', p. 96. In this group of Byzantine historians, who obviously incorporated and transmitted parts of Nikephoros's *Short History*, we are inclined to include Joseph Genesios as a writer in whose work a certain retrospective survey and a reception of style and thought can be noticed. Allegedly, a certain resonance of these ideas can be recognized in Nikephoros's remark on the death of Emperor Leo V, which carries in itself an affirmative retrospect towards some aspects of the reign of this Iconoclast emperor, brought by Genesios into his work.

7    A historical review of the previous editions of Nikephoros's *Short History*, starting from the seventeenth century, can be found in Mango, *Short History*, pp. 29-30.

8    The valuable study of Ljubarskij, 'Man in Byzantine Historiography', can serve as an illustrative example which does not mention Nikephoros's writings in its discussion of Byzantine historical works, among which in a chronological frame the *Short History* certainly belongs. Similarly, not even a marginal mention of Nikephoros's only historiographical work can be found in the volume edited by R. Macrides, *History as Literature in Byzantium*.

*Chronicle*, and even then only in an informal way. This should be viewed as an unavoidable methodological approach in a historical analysis of the work, but in our case we have conducted it in a rather opposite direction, consulting the narration of Theophanes's *Chronicle* in all the places in the text where there exists a mutual correlation with the narration of Nikephoros.[9]

A contribution towards a negative judgment of the *Short History*, or at least towards an underrated view of its nature and character – and, due to this, towards the failure to acknowledge its significance in the reconstruction of the Byzantine literary and cultural revival from the beginning of the ninth century – was given by the editor of the latest critical edition of the text, C. Mango.[10] Contrary to this radically negative outlook from one of the most significant and doubtlessly very proficient researchers of Byzantine past (in which probably lies a partial explanation for the astonishing disinterest of later scholars towards the various problems of the *Short History*, besides those already-mentioned works)[11] stand two older

9    Cf. Kazhdan, *A History of Byzantine Literature*. Although Kazhdan approached the issue of Nikephoros's literary heritage – in particular the literary heritage of his theological works, but also of the *Short History* – he dealt with it only in the context of Theophanes's *Chronicle* and its main characteristics, suggesting in the end that Photios actually had the *Chronicle* of Theophanes in mind when he wrote his description of the *Short History* of Nikephoros (pp. 211-215). Kazhdan, however, limited his evaluation of Nikephoros's literary heritage to a compilation of previously given views and questions concerning the nature and character of the *Short History*. In that sense, his only original contribution to the estimation of these issues was the question regarding the real nature of Patriarch Photios's laudatory words concerning the *Short History*. In contrast, valuable attention concerning the question of which sources Nikephoros could have utilized while writing his only secular work was presented in Howard-Johnston, *Witnesses to a World Crisis*, and Treadgold, 'Trajan the Patrician, Nicephorus, and Theophanes'.

10    C. Mango considered it to be a mediocre work in *The Oxford History of Byzantium*. A similar assessment of Nikephoros as a historian, namely that he was a simple inattentive redactor, was expressed in Treadgold, 'Trajan the Patrician, Nicephorus, and Theophanes', p. 596, n. 31, although this paper presented a new and significant contribution to the complex problem of the sources which make the *Short History*.

11    Howard-Johnston, *Witnesses to a World Crisis*, and Treadgold, 'Trajan the Patrician, Nicephorus, and Theophanes'. See also Treadgold, *The Middle Byzantine Historians*, p. 3 *passim*. Treadgold, however, hypothesized that Nikephoros only rewrote a continuation of the historical work of Trajan the Patrician. He identified this anonymous writer as none other than the Patriarch Tarasios. However, in his analysis Treadgold reconstructed this lost work only on the basis of Nikephoros's *Short History*. We could additionally ask why Nikephoros would then write a new history later, if only to copy the now lost work of his predecessor at the patriarchal see, not contributing anything to its content or manner of presenting past events, especially in the context of Iconoclasm and pro-Iconodule ecclesiastical and political bias, which was obvious around the year 787. Could it be that the qualities of the supposed author whom Treadgold identified as Patriarch Tarasios, but found exclusively through the *Short History* of Nikephoros, actually represent the qualities of Nikephoros as a historian?

but valuable articles which place Nikephoros's *Short History* in the proper chronological and historical context of the Byzantine cultural revival of the beginning of the ninth century.[12] Finally, since it serves as a significant Byzantine narrative source for the history of the seventh and eighth centuries, together with the *Chronicle* of Theophanes, the *Short History* initiated a certain number of studies linked to the problem of its sources, as well as to the narrative information dealing with the so-called 'dark centuries' of Byzantium's history.[13]

For certain data, mainly in our observations on the issues of Nikephoros's life and his career – before, during, and after his active patriarchate – we utilized literature focused primarily on the patriarch's ecclesiology.[14] A structural analysis serves as our main methodological approach in the analysis of the *Short History*, as well as an examination of the manner in which Nikephoros shaped and presented the text. The motivation for such an approach to the research of the text, mainly but also unexpectedly, emerged after our initial examination of the relevant scientific output, which varied in both the cause and the extent of its research. It seems that most previous research into the *Short History* has been rooted in a positivistic approach and, as such, has resulted in a somewhat superficial review of this work, which to a great extent exhausted its own reach of comprehension and gave its uttermost contribution to understanding the work in its proper context. In regard to this observation, we thought that the main direction of our research and our analysis of the *Short History* should be aimed at a historical re-evaluation of the author himself, his place and role in the events of the Byzantine epoch of the late eighth and the early ninth centuries – the time when a new revival of the Byzantine state and culture emerged and developed. In that sense, an attempt towards a total and overall review of Nikephoros's personality, while at the same time knowing that the *Short History* is only one aspect of his multifaceted historical role and his overall efforts, was intended to provide a greater historical context through which, and in accordance with which,

12   Treadgold, 'The Revival of Byzantine Learning', and Ševčenko, 'The Search for the Past'.
13   Speck, *Kaiser Leon III.* Unfortunately, certain titles from the mentioned corpus of studies remained unattainable, especially Speck, *Das geteilte Dossier.*
14   Cf. O'Connell, *The Ecclesiology of St. Nicephorus.* However, works such as Travis, *In Defense of the Faith.* And Lardiero, *The Critical Patriarchate of Nikephoros of Constantinople* remained inaccessible. Accordingly, we have tried to balance this shortcoming by a reference to the theological works of the Patriarch Nikephoros published in PG 100, such as: *Apologeticus Minor, Apologeticus Maior, Antirrheticus* I-III, as well as *Ad Leonem* – a *synodica* of Nikephoros to Pope Leo III from the year 811.

we tried to view and analyse his only secular literary work. From such an approach to the *Short History* new questions emerged, as did different perspectives in reviewing the character and distinctiveness of a text often considered to be a mere abbreviated and incomplete narrative, which, when compared with the more voluminous *Chronicle* of Theophanes, has little to add – a dire approach for a researcher of Byzantine texts of any genre or epoch (who only views such documents as mere sources of information and data).

It is hard to attain even a superficial glance at the scope of political influence, power, and reputation of the imperial *asekretis* Nikephoros from the period of his secular career and his pursuits in the state administration of the Empire. These are blurred by the limited and scant amount of contemporary sources. In contrast, those sources which are explicitly focused on Nikephoros are wrapped in an impenetrably thick veil: the distinctive and characteristic patterns of Byzantine hagiographic literature, which was almost always defined by the rules of its own genre and by the specific interests and intentions of the author. Only after his ascendance to the patriarchal throne of the Church of Constantinople in the first decade of the ninth century does Nikephoros appear to us in a brighter light on the theatre of Byzantium's history. His actions and role in the events are made clearer, although even then certain questions impose themselves on the analysis of a modern researcher. However, some vague evidence does exist. Nikephoros revealed some himself, while other evidence was presented by the acts of the Seventh Ecumenical Council, indicating Nikephoros's very close and friendly relations with some of the most prominent contemporaries of his time even during his secular career.

Some indirect and a few direct pieces of evidence suggest that Nikephoros was close to the highest political and ecclesiastical circles of the Byzantine empire during the first phase of renewed Orthodoxy, shortly before, during, and after the Council of Nicaea in 787. Distant statements from the second half of the ninth century, in the personality of the Patriarch Photios, even suggest that Nikephoros had close family relations to the Patriarch Tarasios of Constantinople. Nikephoros's great successor on the throne of the patriarchs of Constantinople, Photios, built his patriarchal legitimacy and the authority of his ecclesiastical office by underlying both his spiritual and kinship connections to both patriarchs, Tarasios and Nikephoros, thus indirectly demonstrating Nikephoros's later reputation (or building it himself out of his own interest in promoting his legitimacy as patriarch of Constantinople). Conversely, some contemporary evidence from Nikephoros's own era indicates that, while still a secular official, he endured the consequences of his political position as a close accomplice of one of the two sides struggling for imperial power between the Empress Eirene and her son, Emperor Constantine VI. These implications about Nikephoros's deep involvement in the highest political and ecclesiastical events of Byzantium's late-eighth century are a reasonable motif for re-evaluating and analysing his *Short History* in a more serious manner – in accordance with the characteristics of the period in which the author lived and wrote his work.

As a secular work, the *Short History* presented the deeds of Byzantine emperors who reigned over the Empire from the beginning of the seventh century until the second part of the eighth century, portraying the emperors from Herakleios to Constantine V. Although some fourteen emperors and their reigns thematically dominate the text, its narration is, however, closely interwoven with the images of the patriarchs of Byzantium. The patriarchs of the *Short History* are presented infrequently in the narration, thus leaving the impression of a secular work totally oriented in its outlook towards the secular issues of the seventh and eighth centuries. Nevertheless, when analysed more thoroughly, it appears that the history of Byzantine emperors and their reigns as presented in the *Short History* stands in close connection with some of the most important ecclesiastical issues of the time, while some patriarchs are presented as close imperial associates, Sergios and Pyrrhos of Constantinople foremost. From such an examination of the inner composition of the *Short History*, a question arises as to whether a main protagonist exists in Nikephoros's work. Are the predominantly mentioned emperors, in fact, Nikephoros's main characters in his work, or is this role subtly given to the patriarchs of Byzantine Christendom? Nikephoros's dogmatic attitude is clearly Iconophile, and there is no doubt that he made a distinction between the orthodox and heretical patriarchs mentioned in his work. However, some heretical patriarchs in the *Short History* are presented as positive individuals and ecclesiastics, while their heresy is shifted into a second narrative plan. What lies behind such a nonconventional literary approach to the issues of church strife over Orthodoxy and correct ecclesiastical doctrine, which obviously opposes that of his contemporary Iconophile combatant Theophanes and his *Chronicle*? When we analyse the images of Nikephoros's main characters, a compelling question can be asked: who is his main character? Is it Herakleios or Constantine V – the Iconoclast heretic whom Nikephoros managed to represent as a capable statesman, tempering his personality very carefully through the clear separation of his statesmanship from his ecclesiastical policy.

These matters, which mark a principal issue of our study, are answered only and always in the close socio-political and historical context of the time when Nikephoros wrote his work. Thus, the previously dominant issues of the sources which Nikephoros used in creating his work, the relations between the sources utilized, and the question of the originality of his work, which were predominant subjects of past studies, are almost neglected in this book. Such an approach derives completely from our full conviction that the *Short History* of Nikephoros should be read as a finished literary work, since it was read and comprehended as such by its contemporaries. Photios's review of the *Short History* in the *Bibliotheca* spoke of it as an intact literary work with no hint that it was incomplete. The messages that Nikephoros engaged with in this work, and because of which he might even have committed to creating it in the first place, are the main preoccupation of this study.

## On the Methodology and Approach of this Book

This book attempts to re-evaluate Byzantine historical writing at the end of the eighth and the beginning of the ninth centuries, at the very core of its society – the imperial city of Constantinople. As a wider goal, this book also attempts not only to present an analysis of the *Short History* of Nikephoros of Constantinople and his authorial strategies, but also, through an analysis of his narrative techniques, ideological awareness, and engaged interest, to compare the lively ecclesiastical and political issues of his own day with the past that he was shaping and presenting. Thus, our approach was a twofold task: to investigate the inner structure of the *Short History*, especially all the highly engaged passages of the narration, and to compare this narration with the content and manner of representing the same events and processes in the almost contemporary and ideologically very similar *Chronicle* of Theophanes the Confessor (where these historical works are mutually corresponding). Through such an approach, we believe that new paths of analysing the *Short History* can be found and investigated, giving possibly new results.

Nikephoros was a prolific writer and, although he was more productive in the theological apologetics of icon worship, he obviously had an interest in presenting the past events that shaped Byzantium's history during the seventh and first half of the eighth centuries. However, his apologetics written against Iconoclast doctrine, where they touch upon the issue of imperial Iconoclasm, demonstrate a specific historicism in the service of religious dispute. Not only does such evidence present a valuable insight into Nikephoros's overall historical approach, it also uncovers his capability to meet the requirements of both the literary and theological genre he utilized in specific moments of his secular and ecclesiastical career. If we observe Nikephoros as an individual, representative of the Constantinopolitan elite at the turn of the two centuries, such an insight might enable a reconstruction of these elites' doctrinal, intellectual, political, and cultural actions in the specific times and processes which shaped the first post-Iconoclast period between 784 and 815. This template necessarily needs to be combined and analysed with other similar or closely related investigations into Byzantium's eighth and early ninth-century cultural revival. The methodology that we deemed necessary for such a book required that an analysis of the *Short History* and a re-evaluation of the findings of such research needed to be closely interwoven with a personal history of Nikephoros. Thus, such an approach involved a combined literary analysis of the *Short History* and an attempt to reinvestigate Nikephoros's political and ecclesiastical career in the turbulent times between 787 and his downfall from the patriarchal see of the Church of Constantinople.

One other contemporary Byzantine narrative source should be taken into consideration as well. The *Life of Stephen the Younger* inevitably needs to be investigated when dealing with Nikephoros and his historical representation of the first Iconoclasm and its emperors. Composed in the first years of Nikephoros's patriarchal office by Stephen, a deacon of the Great Church, it presented the Orthodox position against the Iconoclasm of the first emperors of the Isaurian dynasty, Leo III and Constantine V. It is indeed a valuable source even when our main task is to attempt an analysis of the *Short History*. The *Life of Stephen the Younger* falls into a different literary genre – thus, a gap between the secular nature of Nikephoros's historical writing and the ecclesiastical and doctrinal nature of the hagiography of Stephen the Younger seems to be an obstacle in our investigation. Nevertheless, a comparison of different literary sources from various genres, such as Theophanes's *Chronicle* and the *Life of Stephen the Younger*, which are all more or less contemporary, might help place Nikephoros's *Short History* in its proper place amongst the Byzantine sources of the period and contribute to a more insightful understanding of its significance. This is an inevitable approach which we follow in our research and try to present in this book.

Where does Nikephoros the historian fall in the long tradition of Byzantine history writing? Can his work be more precisely situated in the aforementioned revival of Byzantine learning and its manifestations at the beginning of the ninth century, as marked and explained in the works of previous researchers? How does he compare to Theophylact Simocatta, the last Byzantine historian before the so-called *dark centuries* of Byzantium? Did Nikephoros have a clear understanding of such a void in the Byzantine tradition of secular literature, or are such questions merely our own preconceived notions? His history ceased this barren period of Byzantine historiography – but what was his overall goal, and was he personally motivated to write in order to continue this tradition, aside from the obvious intention to produce a work with specific ideas and notions that were related to the major issues of his time? An overall conclusion about Nikephoros as a historian at the end of the eighth and the beginning of the ninth centuries based primarily on an analysis of his *Short History* will, where possible, address these subjects as well.

## A Note on Translations and Transliteration of Names

All quotations from Nikephoros's *Short History* and Theophanes's *Chronicle* are according to the English translations by C. Mango in the critical editions of these authors as published in his *Nikephoros Patriarch of Constantinople, Short History: Text, Translation and Commentary* (Washington, DC: Dumbarton Oaks, 1990), and *The Chronicle of Theophanes Confessor: Byzantine and Near Eastern History AD 284-813*, ed. by C. Mango and R. Scott (Oxford: Oxford University Press, 1997). The quotations from the *Life of Nikephoros* by Ignatios the Deacon are according to the translation by Elizabeth A. Fisher in *Byzantine Defenders of Images: Eight Saints' Lives in English Translation*, ed. by A.M. Talbot (Washington, DC: Harvard University Press, 1998). Any departures from these translations are according to my own emendations which I have deemed worthy of introducing into the text. All other sources cited in this book are translated into English by the author.

The transliteration of proper names was impossible in any unified form. I have kept the Greek transcription where it was possible: thus, Nikephoros instead of Nicephorus, Ignatios instead of Ignatius. However, several names of Latin origin which appear in the text of the *Short History* I have kept in their Latin form: Priscus rather than Priskos, Tiberius rather than Tiberios. I have Anglicized personal names where appropriate (e.g. Constantine rather than Constantinos, Stephen rather than Stephanos) and accepted the standard transliteration for foreign names like Chosroes and Shahin.

# 1     Nikephoros the Layman

According to Ignatios the Deacon, the author of the *Short History* was the son of pious parents, Theodore and Eudokia, and he was a born Constantinopolitan.[1] Patriarch Photios, who wrote in the second half of the ninth century, claimed that Nikephoros was related to the Patriarch Tarasios. In one of his letters to Pope Nicholas I, Photios wrote:

> Thus, through us, with us, and because of us, the holy blessed fathers are under threat to be slandered, like Tarasios and Nikephoros, our kin (*οἵ τῆς καθ' ἡμᾶς γενεᾶς*), the perpetual glowing lights. Namely, they became loud predicants of pious ways, stepping on to the highest priestly office in the same manner, from the laity, strengthening the truth by their life and word – I thought that it should be added to this word – presenting these blessed men as better than any condemnation, and higher than any slander [...] such were Tarasios and Nikephoros, stars which glow with justice in this earthly life; they were elected for this sacred service, and they brought forward the rule and model of the Church.[2]

Further, for Patriarch Photios, who himself had to defend his patriarchal ordination before the pope, Tarasios and Nikephoros were not only his kin, as he pointed out in the letter to Nicholas I, but also 'firm guardians of the rules, defenders of piety, torchbearers when the word of godly science and life was attacked in this world' (*οὗτοι γὰρ τῶν κανόνων ἀκριβεῖς φύλακες, τῆς*

---

1    Ignatios, *Life of Nikephoros*, 142.5-11. As one of the most prolific writers of the first half of the ninth century, Ignatios the Deacon is credited with at least three more lives besides Nikephoros's, among them the *Life of Tarasios* is the most valuable, and for our theme it presents a significant additional source for both the reconstruction of the era in which Nikephoros lived and as well for his relationship with the Patriarch Tarasios, whom he succeeded as patriarch. See Efthymiadis, 'On the Hagiographical Work of Ignatius', 73-83, and Pratsch, 'Ignatios the Deacon'. For a historical and literary analysis of Ignatios's literary corpus, see Kazhdan, *A History of Byzantine Literature*, I, 343-366, as well as the comments by Efthymiadis in his edition of Ignatios's *Life of the Patriarch Tarasios*, pp. 3-6 and 38-46.
2    Photius, *Epistulae*, ep. 290; 128, 154-129, 168: 'ἐπεὶ δὲ δι' ἡμᾶς σὺν ἡμῖν καὶ οἱ πρὸ ἡμῶν ἅγιοι καὶ μακάριοι πατέρες συνδιαβεβλῆσθαι κινδυνεύουσιν, ὡς Νικηφόρος καὶ Ταράσιος – ἐκ λαϊκοῦ γὰρ καὶ οὗτοι τοῦ σχήματος εἰς τὸ τῆς ἀρχιερωσύνης ἄκρον προέβησαν, οἳ τῆς καθ' ἡμᾶς γενεᾶς ἀειφανεῖς λαμπτῆρες καὶ τῆς εὐσεβείας διαπρύσιοι γεγόνασι κήρυκες, βίῳ καὶ λόγῳ κρατύναντες τὴν ἀλήθεια –, τὰ λείποντα τῷ λόγῳ προσθεῖναι χρεὼν ἡγησάμην, πάσης αἰτίας κρείττους καὶ πάσης διαβολῆς ἀνωτέρους τοὺς μακαρίους ἐκείνους ἄνδρας ἐπιδεικνύς [...] ἀλλ' οὗτοι – Ταράσιος ἦν καὶ Νικηφόρος – ἐν κοσμικῷ βίῳ ἀστέρων δίκην διαλάμποντες καὶ πρὸς ἱερατικὴν ἀρχὴν γεγονότες ἀπόλεκτοι, παρὰ κανόνα καὶ τύπον τὸν ἐκκλησιαστικὸν τῆς ἐκκλησίας προέστησαν.'

εὐσεβείας ὑπέρμαχοι, τῆς δυσσεβείας κατήγοροι, φωστῆρες ἐν κόσμῳ κατὰ τὸ θεῖον λόγιον λόγον ζωῆς ἐπέχοντες). Photios further emphasized that Nikephoros was not only Tarasios's worthy successor on the patriarchal throne but also his relative, and thus Photios's relative as well.[3]

The exact year of Nikephoros's birth cannot be precisely determined according to his *Life* by Ignatios, although it can be supposed that he was born sometime during the reign of the Emperor Constantine V (741-775).[4] Nikephoros's father Theodore obviously belonged to court aristocratic circles, since at one time he served as a secretary at the court of Constantine V.[5] However, the Iconoclasm of the emperor did not prevent Theodore from firmly confessing his strong adherence to icons in the presence of the emperor himself. As a result of such a confession in the theological dispute over icon veneration, Theodore first lost the lay rank of court secretary, and later on he was even exiled from Constantinople to distant and remote regions of Pimolisa in Asia Minor,[6] and later to Nicaea, where he finally died.[7]

It is uncertain whether Nikephoros followed his father in his two exiles. There are no hints in favour of such interpretation in the *Life of Nikephoros*, although Ignatios did say that Theodore's wife Eudokia, mother of the saint, partook in the hardships of her husband in his banishment, whom she later outlived.[8] There is an entry in the *Life of Nikephoros* that might suggest he lived in Constantinople during the second banishment of his father in Nicaea, which stated that Eudokia lived a short time after Theodore's death together with her son, who acquired a higher education at that time,

---

3    Photius, *Epistulae*, ep. 290; 133, 310-312: 'οὐδὲ Ταράσιον τὸν ἡμέτερον πατρόθειον, οὐδέ γε Νικηφόρον τὸν καὶ τοῦ γένους καὶ τοῦ θρόνου καὶ τῶν τρόπων ἀξίως διάδοχον.' Cf. Афиногенов, *Константинопольский патриархат*, p. 39, who was the first one to notice these statements by Photios.

4    Alexander, *The Patriarch Nicephorus*, p. 54.

5    Ignatios, *Life of Nikephoros*, 142.17-19.

6    Cf. Bryer and Winfield, *The Byzantine Monuments*, pp. 20-22, and the *Dictionary of Greek and Roman Geography*, II, 630. This fortress was situated in the region of southern Pontus, that is, the central part of northern Asia Minor, and it was positioned on the most northern of the three routes which led from Constantinople to the East.

7    Ignatios, *Life of Nikephoros*, 142.17-143.23. The representation of Theodore's firm adherence to icon worship, towards which Ignatios the Deacon showed a certain interest in the introductory part of the *Life of Nikephoros*, actually has a significant role in praising Nikephoros himself, since Theodore's firmness in faith represents a literary development of the idea mentioned earlier about the piety of Nikephoros's parents, in which the author skilfully used the etymology of their names to stress the origins of the main character's virtues.

8    Ignatios, *Life of Nikephoros*, 143.24-144.21.

working as a secretary in the imperial chancery.[9] From such a portrayal of
the course of events, it seems that Nikephoros acquired his secular education
in Constantinople, during the reign of Emperor Constantine V, at the time
when his father died and, moreover, that he inherited his father's office of
imperial secretary at the court of the Iconoclast emperor.[10] However, on the
basis of such an interpretation of the quoted passage, a question necessarily
arises, first about Nikephoros's personal relation and his position regarding
the issue of icon veneration, and second, of the real character of Emperor
Constantine V's policy on Iconoclasm. Namely, if Nikephoros's father experienced banishment and exile due to his firm Orthodoxy, as Ignatios tells
us in the *Life of Nikephoros*, and if his son at the same time administered
the political function of imperial secretary at the court of Constantine V,
this would imply that the emperor himself was far more respectful towards
icon worshipers than their later writings are ready to admit.

Nikephoros offered a particular image of the Emperor Constantine V
and his reign in a complex manner, explicitly disapproving the 'imperial
dogma' of Iconoclasm. However, it is significant that Nikephoros did not
utilize the slanderous term *Κοπρώνιμος* – dung named – in his *Short History*,
a term very common and popular in the later Iconodule literature.[11] This

9    Ignatios, *Life of Nikephoros*, 144.4-8: 'αὕτη μετὰ τὴν τοῦ συνοίκου μακαρίαν τελείωσιν ἐφ' ἱκανὸν
χρόνον τῷ παιδὶ συμβιώσασα, ἄρτι τότε τῆς ἐγκυκλίου παιδείας ἐφαπτομένῳ καὶ τὴν διὰ χειρῶν καὶ
μέλανος τέχνην πονουμένῳ. ᾑρέθη γὰρ ὑπογραφεὺς τοῖς τῶν κρατούντων μυστηρίοις ὑπηρετούμενος.'
The term *ἐγκύκλιος παιδεία* (circular or general education) which Ignatios used implies a higher
level of secular education which Nikephoros acquired while working in the imperial chancery;
cf. Lemerle, *Le premier humanisme byzantin*, p. 130. However, there might be an additional way to
interpret these passages. Namely, it can be suggested that Ignatios here both unconsciously and
even deliberately compressed time and thus presented events separated in real time in the same
chronological level in his narrative. This literary approach is quite common, appearing several
times in the *Life*, in connection to his 'spiritual and secular writings', which were mentioned as
his virtues in the story of his patriarchal election, and also in Nikephoros's role at the Council
of Nicaea in 787. Ignatios later offered a more detailed description of Nikephoros's high secular
education, which he acquired while dealing with lay issues at the imperial court. Cf. Kalogeras,
*Byzantine Childhood Education*, pp. 139-140, who emphasized that the term *ἐγκύκλιος παιδεία* kept
the same meaning in the Iconoclast era of Byzantium's history as it had in the earlier epochs;
accordingly, it was in relation to the higher secular education which integrated the excellence
of both trivium and quadrivium. Additional terms which Ignatios used when speaking about
Nikephoros's education and his writings are quite common for the time when he wrote: *θύραθην
παιδεία*, as well as *τοῖς λόγοις θύραθην*, implying secular, external education or works, as opposed
to theological knowledge and writings. Ignatios, *Life of Nikephoros*, 149.5; 154.12.
10   Alexander, *The Patriarch Nicephorus*, p. 57.
11   Cf. Gero, *Byzantine Iconoclasm during the Reign of Constantine V*, pp. 171-172, 173 n. 27,
who noticed the absence of the term in the text of the *Short History*, while it is present in the
patriarch's theological and apologetic writings.

description of Nikephoros's position at the imperial court, however, could also suggest that he acquired his secular education and his first experience in the imperial chancery at the time of the Emperor Leo IV. In this way, a certain confusion about a seemingly strange inconsistency in the policy of the Iconoclast emperor could be explained, if one takes into consideration that these events as described by Ignatios occurred during the reign of his son, Emperor Leo IV. It is generally accepted that the wave of Iconoclastic persecutions was significantly reduced during his reign, and of the monastic clergy in particular.[12] This interpretation might further imply that Nikephoros took the issue of icon reverence at that time far more moderately than in the later course of his life, during his patriarchate or later, after his abdication from the patriarchal see under the reign of Leo V and Michael of Amorion.[13]

That Nikephoros indeed took a far more nuanced and cautious approach towards the issue of icon worship while serving in the imperial administration is suggested by yet another account of Ignatios. Namely, after he spoke about Nikephoros's high repute which he enjoyed at the court, Ignatios said:

> When he saw that a party of those who adhered to the true faith had suffered a shipwreck, due to those who then controlled the helm of the Roman Empire, he calmed the storm to the best of his ability. For in their arrogance [those rulers] set aside a tradition that the Church had inherited blamelessly from the beginning through apostolic and patristic ordinance, that is, I mean to say, the painting and veneration of the holy icons.[14]

It is significant to notice in this account that Ignatios used the formulation of 'labouring to quiet the tempest' which indicates a specific action by Nikephoros, and even further his relevance in Iconoclast circles, and raises several questions regarding such a reading of the passage from his *Life*.

---

12   Cf. Bury, *A History of the Later Roman Empire*, p. 477; Gero, *Byzantine Iconoclasm during the Reign of Constantine V*, p. 140; Treadgold, *A History of the Byzantine State*, p. 369; and Brubaker and Haldon, *Byzantium in the Iconoclast Era*, pp. 249-250 *passim*.

13   Alexander, *The Patriarch Nicephorus*, p. 59, hypothesized in this direction, concluding from such scarce narrating by Ignatios the Deacon that at the time of Nikephoros's youth his hero, being in the lay service at the court of Constantine V or his son Leo IV, and under *protasekretis* Tarasios in the chancery, he occupied a more moderate posture in regard to icon worship.

14   Ignatios, *Life of Nikephoros*, 145.11-17: 'οὗτος ἐπειδή τι μέρος τῶν περὶ τὴν ὑγιᾶ πίστιν ναυαγίῳ περιπεὸν (εἶδεν) ἐκ τῶν κατ' ἐκεῖνο καιροῦ τὰ τῆς Ῥωμαϊκῆς ἀρχῆς οἰακιζόντων βασίλεια, ὅσον ἐφ' ἑαυτῷ τὴν ζάλην ἔστησε. τὴν γὰρ ἀνέκαθεν ἐξ ἀποστολικῆς καὶ πατρικῆς θεσμοθεσίας τῇ ἀμωμήτῳ ἐκκλησίᾳ παράδοσιν, φημὶ δὴ τῶν ἱερῶν εἰκόνων τύπωσιν καὶ προσκύνησιν.'

Namely, was it possible for him to act as a mediator in this controversy, or is this only a literary form used by Ignatios to additionally highlight Nikephoros's life and his early contribution to the victory of Orthodoxy, even before he was elected the patriarch of the Church of Constantinople?

In his epistle to Pope Leo III, Nikephoros mentioned his court career, though only briefly, leaving out both the name of the emperor under whom he served and the circumstances which occurred in the imperial palace regarding icon worship and his stance in this dispute. His stance was possibly more moderate than would be expected of someone who was later elected patriarch of the Church of Constantinople. A detailed account of this phase of his career to the pope could be linked to the patriarch's fear that these issues might provoke a new dispute with the Church of Rome concerning the relations between the Church and the Empire in Byzantium during the time of Iconoclasm. Thus, perhaps Nikephoros rather limited himself to few passages of a general character. He emphasized that he found himself at the imperial court at the beginning of his adulthood, just as he has passed adolescence. Also, he stressed that he did not perform some minor duty at the palace, but that he held the responsible office of imperial *hypographeus*, that is, of an *asekretis* – a term upon which Nikephoros insisted in his letter to the pope:

> The circumstances of my life followed as such: after I had reached adulthood, after adolescence, I found myself at the imperial court and I received a post neither insignificant nor unworthy, but an office that was fulfilled by hands and pen – becoming namely an imperial *hypographeus*.[15]

This is all the information given by Nikephoros to Pope Leo III about his lay career. Immediately after these introductory remarks about his secular office, he proceeded to narrate the circumstances and causes due to which he left his lay post for a spiritual life, accentuating the advantages and the predominance of spiritual issues over secular ones, and justifying his act of withdrawal with the spiritual concern for salvation.

It is hard to grasp the real nature of the political and ecclesiastical stance of the future patriarch at the time of his secular career based only on such accounts and the way they were presented in his letter to Leo III and in his

---

15    Nikephoros, *Ad Leonem*, col. 173B: 'Ἐμοὶ δὲ οὕτω τὰ τῆς παρούσης βιοτῆς περιέστηκεν. Ἡνίκα τοίνυν εἰς ἄνδρας ἐτέλουν, τὸ νέον τῆς ἡλικίας παραμειψάμενος, ἤδη περὶ τὰς βασιλείους ἐπιχωριάζων αὐλάς, στρατείας τινὸς ἐπεκύρησα, καὶ ταύτης οὐκ ἀεργοῦς καὶ ἀνειμένης, ἀλλὰ τῆς διὰ χειρῶν καὶ καλάμων ἐκπονουμένης· καὶ γὰρ τῶν βασιλικῶν ὑπογραφεὺς ἐτύγχανον ὤν.'

*Life* by Ignatios the Deacon. We can only conclude that these sources leave us far more confused, rather than offering us explanations about this part of Nikephoros's career. Primarily, they do not provide us with circumstantial information concerning under which emperor's reign Nikephoros began his secular career at the court, nor with any valuable details about the nature of his lay education.

## Nikephoros's Secular Education

The matter of Nikephoros's education is of great value for our analysis of the nature and character of his only secular work, the *Short History*. Nikephoros undoubtedly mastered theological knowledge before his election to the patriarchal post, and he entered his new office with all the knowledge needed for this highest ecclesiastical post.[16] In the *Life of Nikephoros*, Ignatios mentioned multiple times Nikephoros's study of the Scriptures followed by the very interesting and valuable remark that secular education did not contradict theological knowledge. Of course, at the time when Ignatios wrote his work, such a remark was almost a commonplace exactly due to the high number of cases where individuals entered the highest ecclesiastical offices from the laity directly.[17] An even more interesting note on Nikephoros's education can be taken from Ignatios's account of the Seventh Ecumenical Council and the role Nikephoros the layman had at this council as a person who actively participated in defining of the Orthodox theology of icon worship.[18]

Nikephoros's high theological education is best evidenced in his several theological, polemical, and apologetic works, which were written mostly during and after his patriarchal career, as a result of the newly arisen Iconoclastic dispute under the Emperor Leo V. Nikephoros himself did not give any particular attention to the issue of his education in his letter to Pope Leo III, since the character and reason for his address to the Roman Pontiff were of a predominantly ecclesiastical nature and in the service of the renovation and the fastening of unity between Constantinople and

---

16   Cf. Lemerle, *Le premier humanisme byzantin*, pp. 100-104 and 131-133. Ignatios, *Life of Nikephoros*, also alluded to Nikephoros's study of the Psalter: 150.4-6 (λυράν τὴν ἑκατονκαιπεντηκοντάχορδον). This might be significant regarding the opinion given by Mango, *Short History*, pp. 11-12, and Treadgold, *The Middle Byzantine Historians*, p. 27, that Nikephoros was unfamiliar with theology and church history when writing his *Short History*.

17   Ignatios, *Life of Nikephoros*, 148.23; 149.5.

18   Ignatios, *Life of Nikephoros*, 147.9-13.

Rome. The only information about Nikephoros's education was given by Ignatios the Deacon in the patriarch's *Life*, but, as noted, this was presented in the most general manner and without specific attention to the clear characteristics of Nikephoros's personal education.[19] Ignatios most probably did not have any actual evidence at his disposal when he wrote about Nikephoros's education. He, however, could not pass over this topos, so he included what he did have at his disposal: a curriculum of secular education most general in its content and probably anachronistic to the time when Nikephoros completed his studies.[20] In contrast, the author of the *Life* was Nikephoros's contemporary and himself a grammarian (γραμματικός), and thus he was probably familiar with the current structure of education at the capital of the Empire at the turn of the ninth century.[21] Ignatios tells us that his hero did not consider lay erudition inappropriate or opposed to Christian virtue and excellence. On the contrary, Ignatios spoke of Nikephoros as the one who managed to gain brilliance both in education and in his striving towards a virtuous life.[22]

But it is Nikephoros's art of rhetoric which is particularly important for our reflection on his education, and it directly relates to his *Short History*. The way Ignatios wrote about Nikephoros's rhetorical skills is very perceptive for the issue of his erudition, and it also provides valuable data on his only secular work, especially concerning the chronology of its composition. Ignatios wrote:

> For it is clear even to those with only a modest knowledge of the art [of rhetoric] how great [an authority Nikephoros] was on grammar, its component parts, and the logical [principles] by which correct and

---

19  Ignatios, *Life of Nikephoros*, 149.3-151.13.

20  Alexander, *The Patriarch Nicephorus*, pp. 57-59, forwarded an assumption that there existed a school for lay officials and their education at the imperial court itself, and that Nikephoros, working under the supervision of Tarasios the *protasekretis*, was under his educational influence as well (p. 59). See also Irigoin, 'Survie et renouveau', p. 290, and Fisher's translation of Ignatios's *Life of Nikephoros*, pp. 25-26.

21  *Suidae Lexicon II*, 607.30-608.3. Da Costa-Louillet, 'Saints de Constantinople', pp. 247-248, hypothesized that Ignatios and Nikephoros studied together under Tarasios, despite the fact that there is no evidence that Tarasios taught. Cf. Treadgold, 'The Revival of Byzantine Learning', p. 1254. Kalogeras, *Byzantine Childhood Education*, pp. 40-41 and 49, thought that Ignatios's personal closeness and familiarity with the Patriarch Nikephoros provided authenticity to his account of Nikephoros's education, which may present an accurate image of Byzantine education in the epoch of Iconoclasm when compared to the accounts of education in Ignatios's *Life of Tarasios*.

22  Ignatios, *Life of Nikephoros*, 151.20-23.

incorrect writing is to be distinguished, by which the [classical] Greek language is governed, and by which metrical elements are brought into harmonious order. It is [no less] easy to see what a reputation he gained for sweet and gracious speech [as a performer] on the rhetoricians' many stringed lyres. For he steadfastly rejected the affected and verbose style that leads to aimless sophistic babble and chatter. He used a sweet and graceful style [observing linguistic] clarity and purity.[23]

This part of Ignatios's display of Nikephoros's education, and more specifically about his rhetorical ability, is very similar and matches with the high appraisal of the *Short History* given by Photios in his *Bibliotheca* later in the ninth century. Namely, Photios had noticed the simplicity and clarity of Nikephoros's expression above all, but also the absence of verbosity in narration and his conciseness, which he considered to be the main features of the *Short History*. According to Photios, Nikephoros lost the full 'prize', albeit he was skilled in speech, to which he added the beauty of narration.[24] Moreover, it is precisely the *Short History* of the Patriarch Nikephoros that remains as the only proof and evidence of his secular education, opposed to his theological writings, which are more diverse and better preserved than his secular work. However, judging by the high estimation given to such a history and its author by the Patriarch Photios, the *Short History*, besides having value for the history of Byzantium during the seventh and eighth centuries, represents a valuable source for research on Byzantine secular learning, and it offers significant insights into the views of the higher echelons of Byzantine society, its Constantinopolitan elites, and its attitudes towards various issues of late eighth- and early ninth-century Byzantium.[25]

---

23  Ignatios, *Life of Nikephoros*, 149.16-26: 'ὅσος γὰρ περί τε γραμματικὴν ἦν καὶ τὰ μέρη ταύτης καὶ ὄργανα, ὑφ' ὧν τὸ τῆς γραφῆς ὀρθὸν, καὶ μὴ, διακρίνεται καὶ ἡ Ἑλληνὶς γλῶσσα εὐθύνεται καὶ ἡ τῶν μέτρων βάσις ῥυθμίζεται, καὶ αὐτοῖς γοῦν τοῖς καὶ μετρίως τῆς τέχνης ἐπῃσθημένοις καθέστηκε γνώριμον. ὅσος τε περὶ τὴν τῶν ῥητόρων ἐφάνη πολύφθογγον φόρμιγγα ἡδυεπὴς καὶ μειλίχιος οὐ χαλεπὸν συνιδεῖν· τὸ γὰρ κατεγλωττισμένον ταύτης καὶ λάλον, καὶ ὅσον πρὸς σοφιστικὴν ἀπονεύει εἰκαιομυθίαν τε καὶ φληναφίαν παρωσάμενος, δι' εὐκρινείας τε καὶ καθαρότητος τὸ τῆς συνθήκης ἡδὺ καὶ χαρίεν ἐπετήδευε.' For comparison with the account of Photios, see Chapter 2 *Dating of the Short History*.

24  Photius, *Bibliotheca*, p. 99.

25  Cf. Treadgold, 'The Revival of Byzantine Learning', p. 1253. Also see Ševčenko, 'The Search for the Past', p. 293 (for learned individuals such as Tarasios and Nikephoros as promoters of the renewed interest of the Byzantines towards the past), as well as Irigoin, 'Survie et renouveau'.

## The Seventh Ecumenical Council and the Patriarchal Office

An almost six decades-long dispute over icons – which had begun during the rule of Leo III, between 728 and 730, with the death of his grandson, Emperor Leo IV – was reaching the first phase of its end, and was officially ended at the council convoked by the emperor's widow, Eirene, together with her son Constantine VI, in Nicaea in 787. Nikephoros's participation at the Seventh Ecumenical Council is confirmed by several different sources. These are the accounts by Ignatios the Deacon given in his *Life of Tarasios* and *Life of Nikephoros*, as well as two short notices in the acts of the Seventh Ecumenical Council.

After writing about the preparations for the Council, carefully planned by the Empress Eirene and Patriarch Tarasios, Ignatios proceeded to depict the very opening of the Council in his *Life of Tarasios*, mentioning its leading participants: the *apocrisiarius* of the pope and the representatives of the eastern patriarchs. Then Ignatios narrated the role of the *asekretis* Nikephoros, who appeared at the Council in the entourage of Patriarch Tarasios and several other lay officials. Nikephoros was mentioned as the imperial secretary who led a life of holiness, being adored with godly virtues and spiritual reasoning (λογικαῖς ἐπιστήμαις), and who would succeed Tarasios to the patriarchal throne of Byzantium after his death.[26]

In the *Life of Nikephoros*, Ignatios the Deacon used this account of Nikephoros's participation at the Council of Nicaea to create a fuller image of his hero as the one who was chosen beforehand and destined to take the patriarchal see and become a holy man and a confessor of the faith. But Nikephoros was also presented as an individual who won his first spiritual battle for Orthodoxy at the Council of 787, highlighting in a specific way his greater and more significant role in the struggle against the Iconoclast heresy in the future. In that sense, Ignatios's imaging of Nikephoros's participation at the Seventh Ecumenical Council has a specific literary role in the narration of this part of the *Life of Nikephoros*. It also raises the question whether such imagery surpassed the real role Nikephoros might have had at the Council, contrary to the one we read in the *Life of Tarasios* – a much more concise description – and especially in the acts of the council themselves.[27]

---

26 Ignatios, *Life of Tarasios*, 103.18-24: 'ὃς ἐν ὁσιότητι βιοὺς καὶ θείαις ἀρεταῖς καὶ λογικαῖς ἐπιστήμαις κοσμούμενος τῆς πατριαρχικῆς τοῦ Βυζαντίου καθέδρας μετὰ τὴν ὁσίαν Ταρασίου τελείωσιν τὴν τιμὴν διαδέχεται.'
27 O'Connell, *The Ecclesiology of St. Nicephorus*, p. 39, considered Ignatios's narration in Nikephoros's *Life* to be exaggerated.

Nikephoros is presented as equal to the patriarchs, although he had not become member of the clergy yet (συγκάθεδρος τῷ ἱερῷ συλλόγῳ καὶ πρὸ τῆς ἱερᾶς ἀμπεχόνης γεγένηται), and his role in the narrative gradually developed from a lay official and a representative of the state at the Council to an active participant through his confession of the Orthodox theology of icon veneration. By such an arrangement of the story about Nikephoros's engagement at the Council, Ignatios managed to promulgate the idea that Nikephoros's contribution in the battle against Iconoclasm placed him among the fathers of the Council headed by the Patriarch Tarasios. Such image and its narrative message are somewhat similar to the account Ignatios offered in the *Life of Tarasios* and its most significant parts: the presence of Nikephoros in Tarasios's entourage, his virtuous life, and finally his succession after Tarasios to the patriarchal throne.[28]

The official acts of the Council mention ὁ λαμπρότατος μανδάτωρ who was sent at the second session by the emperors to escort one of the Iconoclast bishops, Gregory of Neocaesarea, and then, at the end of the account of the second session, a certain Nikephoros who was entrusted to read the letter of the Roman pope, Hadrian, to the Council, calling him the *imperial asekretis*.[29] If these two individuals mentioned are indeed Nikephoros, the future patriarch, it can be concluded that at that time he enjoyed the great confidence of the empress and the patriarch.[30] Moreover, it can be concluded that he sincerely supported the revival of both icon worship and Orthodox ecclesiology in its relations towards the state, which was negated during the rule of the first three Iconoclast emperors, who abolished the freedom of the Church in its relations with imperial power.

The three sources, although not in the same manner, bring relatively short but quite explicit information that the writer of the *Short History*, and the later successor to Tarasios on the patriarchal throne, participated in some of the council sessions in Nicaea in 787, as an imperial secretary and envoy of the emperors. This inevitably leads us to investigate the nature of the relations between the Patriarch Tarasios and the imperial secretary Nikephoros. A short time earlier Nikephoros stood under his supervision in the imperial chancery, before Tarasios was elected patriarch of the Church of Constantinople, and in whose presence Nikephoros came to at least one of the sessions of the Council of Nicaea. It is certain that from the very

28   Cf. Ignatios, *Life of Nikephoros*, 146.18-147.2 and 147.6-15.
29   Mansi XII, 1051E-1055A. Nikephoros, who read the letter of the Pope, is referred to as 'καὶ ἀνέγνω Νικηφόρος ὁ εὐκλεέστατος βασιλικὸς ἀσηκρῆτις'.
30   Alexander, *The Patriarch Nicephorus*, pp. 60-61.

beginning of his patriarchate Tarasios had close associates in this venture of reviving the veneration of icons in Byzantium, both before the Council of 787, during its course, and after.

A convincing hypothesis was brought forward that at least one aspect of the patriarch's policy was conducted through the promotion of his own protégés, whom he included among the clergy of the Church of Constantinople, primarily in order to reaffirm Orthodox icon worship as it was proclaimed in the *oros* of the Nicaean council of 787. The second reason for such a policy was to create a net of close associates which would provide the needed support in the patriarch's relations with state officials and the empress. The third reason was the internal ecclesiastical opposition found in some monastic circles, mainly around the Studion monastery and its abbot Theodore, which would erupt in the near future.[31]

Among the most significant individuals who began their careers in the high clergy at the time of Tarasios's patriarchate, and who received their bishoprics directly from him, were Efthimios of Sardis, Michael of Synada, Theophylact of Nicomedia, Emilian of Kyzikos, and Eudoxos of Amorion. Among them, Theophylact and Michael were the ones who not only had a significant role at the Council in 787, but they also had an important role in the ecclesiastical strife during Nikephoros's patriarchate as well. Michael, bishop of Synada, was the one entrusted to carry the enthronement letter of Nikephoros to the Roman Pontiff in 811, which aimed to ensure the ecclesiastical unity between the two leading church sees in Christendom.[32]

This selection of individuals whom Tarasios entrusted with ecclesiastical responsibility, through their ordination as clergymen and bishops, and whom he thus included actively in the ecclesiastical events that were occurring, is impressive and shows that the patriarch approached his task of reviving the church hierarchy that was loyal to the renewed Orthodoxy very thoroughly. Tarasios exposed both his sense for the organization of church life and also his determination to renew the church structures with bishops and monks, which were significantly thinned by the presence of former Iconoclast bishops, who offered their repentance for the heresy at the Council of 787.

---

31  Cf. the comments of Efthymiadis in his edition of Ignatios's *Life of Tarasios*, pp. 20-21; Hatlie, *The Monks and Monasteries of Constantinople*, p. 318; and Афиногенов, *Константинопольский патриархат*, p. 39. See also Brubaker and Haldon, *Byzantium in the Iconoclast Era*, p. 260 *passim*.

32  Cf. Ringrose, *Saints, Holy Men and Byzantine Society*, pp. 98-115. Ringrose (p. 110), supposed that it was Michael and Theophylact who decisively influenced the Emperor Nikephoros I to elect Nikephoros as the successor of Tarasios after his death in 806.

Concerning our Nikephoros, the question arises: what was the nature of his role at the Seventh Ecumenical Council, and especially after the Council in his relation to the Patriarch Tarasios, with whom he cooperated while they were both lay officials at the imperial court, Tarasios being his superior? Exactly the fact that it was none other than Nikephoros who succeeded Tarasios on the patriarchal see of Constantinople, although he himself in his letter to the pope emphasized that the initiative came from the imperial power, a statement with which even his hagiographer consented, points towards a continuity in the general policy of governance of the Church that was established during Tarasios's patriarchate, in the context of Nikephoros's later ecclesiastical policies and the way he implemented them.

Nikephoros presented a specific image of the events which lead to his election for the patriarch, which is the image of an overall consensus of all relevant ecclesiastical and imperial factors which were gathered in Constantinople for the election of Tarasios's successor. He noted that he was elected patriarch by the will of the emperor and the sacred council and *synkletos*. Such a presentation of the event is significant, particularly in its relation to the previous uncanonical elections of former Constantinopolitan patriarchs during the Iconoclast era: Anastasios, Constantine II, and Niketas, who were elected and consecrated by the will of the emperors Leo III and Constantine V.[33]

Is it possible to conclude that the election of Nikephoros for patriarch after Tarasios's death was prepared in advance, and could it be supported by the narration where the imperial will was decisive in the election of the new patriarch of Constantinople? In other words, was the future Patriarch Nikephoros, already in the time of Tarasios's patriarchate, a member of the aforementioned circle of men – lay and ecclesiastical officials whom Tarasios gathered perhaps even before his patriarchal consecration, and whom he had certainly gathered when he finally became patriarch of the Church of Constantinople?[34] Since there is no explicit information about the events leading to Nikephoros's patriarchal election and

---

33    Nikephoros, *Ad Leonem*, col. 176B: 'ψήφῳ καὶ κρίσει τῶν τηνικαῦτα ἐν τοῖς βασιλείοις ἐνιδρυμένων θώκοις, τοῦ τε κοινοῦ τῆς ἐκκλησίας ἱεροῦ συστήματος καὶ τῆς συγκλήτου βουλῆς.' Cf also Ignatios, *Life of Nikephoros*, 153.24-154.17, where Ignatios gave a more detailed account, which was also more literary in its character and purpose, accentuating at the same time the emperor's personal qualities and also Nikephoros's resemblance to Tarasios, stressing the idea of continuity with Tarasios's specific ecclesiastical policy.

34    Da Costa-Louillet, 'Saints de Constantinople', p. 249, claimed, without providing a source, that it was Tarasios himself, while on his deathbed, who suggested Nikephoros as his successor

consecration, we must pay attention to Nikephoros's narration about his patriarchate, and to the information which Ignatios provides us in the *Life of Nikephoros*.

After he had expressed the opinion that there are often cases when necessity rules and the outcome happens according to God's will, Nikephoros in his letter to Pope Leo III proceeded to explain the events leading to his patriarchal consecration:

> I did not manage to accomplish towards what I had striven (καὶ τῶν κατὰ νοῦν διημάρτηκα), and I do not know by what reason this had happened, God knows. I was taken out of my beloved desert and brought back to the imperial palace. God is my witness. And by the vote and choice of those who at that time held the imperial throne, the sacred council of the Church, and by the will of Synkletos, by the inexorable and firm judgement, since at that time the *proedros* of the imperial city had left this life as it happens with men, I was brought and elevated to this sacred throne, although I relentlessly opposed the force and forceful deed.[35]

Does this last statement about force, which he brings into connection with his election for patriarch, reflect real events, so that it can be taken in its literal sense? Or does it rather present a part of a general idea which extends throughout this introductory part of the letter? That is, namely, that Nikephoros avoided his election as patriarch, stressing his personal unworthiness (which is also a topos and a motif often repeated in similar genres of ecclesiastical literature).

Although a relatively short account, especially in relation to the one which Ignatios brought forward, which was also more complex in its literary style, Nikephoros's narration deserves to be investigated more closely. In accordance with the Christian view of the world, Nikephoros

---

to the Emperor Nikephoros I. Such explicit information we did not manage to find, neither in Nikephoros's enthronement letter to Pope Leo III, nor in his *Life* by Ignatios the Deacon.

35 Nikephoros, *Ad Leonem*, col. 176B: 'συμβέβηκε τοῦτο τοίνυν καὶ ἐπ' ἐμοί. Καὶ τῶν κατὰ νοῦν διημάρτηκα, καὶ οὐκ οἶδα οἷς κρίμασιν ὁ ταῦτα συγχωρήσας, καὶ παριδὼν Θεὸς ἐξεπίσταται, ἀπεσπάσθην τῆς φίλης ἐρημίας, καὶ ἐπὶ τὴν βασίλειον (πάλιν) ἤχθην, ὡς ὑπὸ Θεῷ μάρτυρι, ψήφῳ καὶ κρίσει τῶν τηνικαῦτα ἐν τοῖς βασιλείοις ἐνιδρυμένων θώκοις, τοῦ τε κοινοῦ τῆς Ἐκκλησίας ἱεροῦ συστήματος καὶ τῆς συγκλήτου βουλῆς, συμβραβευόντων ἀπαραίτητά τε καὶ ἀσυγχώρητα ἐπείπερ ἤδη τῆς βασιλίδος ὁ πρόεδρος τὸν βίον μετήλλαξεν, οἷά περ ἄνθρωπος τὸν ἀνθρώπινον, οἵγε καίτοι πολλὰ ὑπερτιθέμενον καὶ ἀπαυθαδειαζόμενον ἐπὶ τὸν ἱερατικὸν τουτονὶ θρόνον προήγαγον, τυραννίδος μᾶλλον ἢ πειθοῦς ἔργον γινόμενον.'

introduced God in the beginning of his narration as the one who directs the circumstances of man's life. Judging by the story of Nikephoros, it was God's will which took him out of his solitary passivity and led him again into the spotlight of state and ecclesiastical events and processes in Constantinople. However, God works through men, and so Nikephoros, in the further course of the narration, said that he was inaugurated to the patriarchal throne (ἐπὶ τὸν ἱερατικὸν τουτονὶ θρόνον) after the death of the former Patriarch Tarasios, whom he did not mention by name (τῆς βασιλίδος ὁ πρόεδρος). Nikephoros emphasized here that his appointment was made by the will of the imperial power, but also with the consent of the church council and senate.

Therefore, Nikephoros offered a simple but clear image of unity and accord that had followed his patriarchal appointment and he incorporated this into his letter to Leo III. There are no clear indications in the manner in which he presented his predecessor Tarasios that he wished to show himself as enjoying a deeper connection with the man. After all, the enthronement letter had as its main purpose the presentation of Nikephoros and his patriarchate to the Roman Pontiff. Or did Nikephoros try to accentuate Tarasios's prominence precisely by such a literary treatment that did not need to stress the mentioning of his name? If we point our analysis in this direction, then we would conclude that there are traces of Nikephoros's intention to highlight his connection with his famous predecessor on the throne of Constantinople.

It is peculiar that Nikephoros seemingly missed mentioning his influential office of *ptochotrophos*, a position which he occupied before his election to the post of patriarch.[36] Ignatios the Deacon is the only one who tells us, somewhat incidentally, about the office of *ptochotrophos*, which Nikephoros had performed before his patriarchate. However, one can notice that Ignatios spoke about the pressure of the imperial power upon Nikephoros to accept this office: 'Thus the grace of God, by a forceful compulsion from the

---

36 Cf. Oikonomidès, *Les listes de préséance byzantines*, noticed the absence of the title of *ptochotrophos* in Byzantine *taktikons* of the ninth and tenth centuries. Cf. ODB III, 1756 (A. Kazhdan) and Constantelos, *Byzantine Philanthropy*, pp. 257-269. In the *Concise Chronicle*, which is also ascribed to Nikephoros, there is a list of patriarchs of Constantinople, and in that list we find one earlier patriarch who was mentioned as a former *ptochotrophos* of Neapolis: 'Εὐφήμιος πρεσβύτερος Κωνσταντινουπόλεως καὶ πτωχοτρόφος Νεαπόλεως', followed by a notice about his relation towards imperial power, accentuating the same problem and the main issue of the day, which was Nikephoros's idea to deal with in his *Short History*: 'τούτου ἐκβληθέντος ὑπὸ τοῦ βασιλέως Ἀναστασίου'. Cf. *Concise Chronicle*, 117.1-3.

side of those who ruled at that time, deemed Nikephoros worthy to govern the largest poorhouse in the city'.[37]

This account might also serve as a means of better understanding Nikephoros's personal story in the letter to the pope, primarily in the context of his narration about his leaving his beloved desert, but also regarding his description of his election as patriarch. Namely, as we shall see, Ignatios failed to mention any kind of force during the patriarchal election after Tarasios's death in 806, especially from the side of the Emperor Nikephoros I over Nikephoros the future patriarch. From Ignatios's account, it seems that Nikephoros was absent from Constantinople at the moment when he was elected. Since Ignatios said that a delegation was sent for Nikephoros summoning him to the capital, this could suggest that the location of the poorhouse was outside the city. Conversely, such a report by Ignatios, which introduced force into the events leading up to Nikephoros becoming *ptochotrophos*, prior to his patriarchal office, might perhaps explain Nikephoros's expression that he 'opposed the force and forceful deed', as he expressed himself in his enthronement letter. In other words, it is possible that Nikephoros merged two different events into one account. Such a story contained references to both his forceful leaving of his beloved desert and his return to the capital and taking up the office of *ptochotrophos*, of which we know from Ignatios that it was due to the pressure from the emperor. This story, however, also included the account of his patriarchal election, which was done without any force on the side of the emperor, as we know from both the narration of Nikephoros and that of his hagiographer.

Ignatios the Deacon portrayed the election and consecration of Nikephoros as patriarch in a more literary manner. First, he accentuated the role of Emperor Nikephoros I much more strongly, although he did not leave out the role of the church council and the senate as well. He showed more attention, however, to the personality of the former patriarch Tarasios in relation to Nikephoros's enthronement, but in a specific way – in accord with the hagiographical nature of his work – by introducing in his narration the image of Tarasios as a holy man who, even after his death, manipulated the preference of the Emperor Nikephoros I in his choice:

And after his death he wished and yearned to see the one who would succeed him in his labour (τὸν ἀντιληψόμενον τῇ αὐτοῦ γεωργίᾳ), and he

---

37 Ignatios, *Life of Nikephoros*, 152.14-18: 'τοῦ μεγίστου πτωχείου τῶν κατὰ τὴν βασιλίδα ἐπιτροπεύειν προτροπῇ βιαίᾳ τῶν κρατούντων.'

was not disappointed indeed in his wish, since God, who always reveals himself to those who seek him, and opens the door to those who knock, and fulfils truthful prayers, by the divine finger and Spirit, clearly showed to the emperor-namesake (τῷ ὁμωνύμῳ βασιλεῖ), who was perfect in the matters of faith, this Nikephoros as worthy of the sacred anointment.[38]

In accord with the laudatory *Life* which he wrote, Ignatios highlighted several significant issues at this point which are worthy of our attention. Regarding the relations between the two patriarchs, Tarasios and Nikephoros, a sort of continuity was emphasized and maintained by the election of Nikephoros, and especially in connection with the struggle for the true faith, which had begun with the patriarchate of Tarasios, who now as a saint provided a worthy successor to the Church of Constantinople over which he himself presided in the past. To stress this idea, Ignatios used a vivid image borrowed from the Gospels, a comparison with a cultivated field, which could serve as a successful symbol in the context of heresy.[39] So, in that context, Nikephoros was a worthy successor to the former Patriarch Tarasios who took over the governance of the Church and continued guiding it in an orthodox manner.[40] Ignatios used the comparison from the Gospels to elucidate the role of God in the whole scene, thus offering the ultimate legitimacy for the election of the new patriarch. It is God who revealed to the emperor, who was perfect in the matters of faith, that Nikephoros was the one destined to take the helm of the Church. From such an introduction to the story about Nikephoros's patriarchal election, it seems that his appointment was not a simple act of force by the emperor towards the Church. Ignatios introduced in his account the personality of the saintly Patriarch Tarasios and the divine intervention which revealed to the emperor the truth concerning Nikephoros's appointment.

---

38   Ignatios, *Life of Nikephoros*, 153.21-28: 'τὸν ἀντιληψόμενον τῇ αὐτῦ γεωργίᾳ καὶ μετὰ τελευτὴν ἰδεῖν ἐπόθει καὶ ἔστεργεν. καὶ οὐκ ἐψεύσθη γε τῆς αἰτήσεως· ὁ γὰρ τοῖς ζητοῦσιν ἀεὶ θεὸς εὑρισκόμενος, καὶ τοῖς κρούουσι θύραν ἀνοίγων, καὶ τὰς ἀληθεῖς αἰτήσεις ἀποπεραίνων δακτύλῳ θείῳ καὶ πνεύματι τὸν τῆς ἱερᾶς χρίσεως ἄξιον Νικηφόρον τρανῶς ὑπεδείκνυε, καὶ τῷ τότε κρατοῦντι ὁμωνύμῳ βασιλεῖ τὰ περὶ τὴν ἀληθῆ πίστιν τελείῳ τυγχάνοντι λευκότερον ὑπεμήνυεν.' In light of the recent Iconoclasm heralded by the emperors, an emperor *perfect in the matters of faith* is indeed an interesting formulation provided by Ignatios.
39   Cf. Matthew, 13.24-30: 'Another parable put he forth unto them, saying, "The kingdom of heaven is likened unto a man which sowed good seed in his field. But while men slept, his enemy came and sowed tares among the wheat, and went his way."'
40   For this and other literary representations of the idea of patriarchal successions in early ninth-century Byzantine literature, see Marjanović, 'Seventh Ecumenical Council'.

Once such an introduction was set up, an image of the emperor-namesake was also given later on. The Emperor Nikephoros was presented as being informed about the secret of the patriarchal appointment from above, and thus he was simply managing the choice of the ecclesiastical council and the senate towards a proper and a God-pleasing choice, which was also in accordance with the ecclesiastical policy of the Patriarch Tarasios:

> In fact, [this emperor] was a most shrewd man, if ever anyone was. After much searching, he was able to install both as bridegroom and also as marriage broker for the widowed [Church] a man competent to hold fast the faithful word as he hath been taught and to walk most prudently in the footsteps of the previous shepherd Tarasios. In order to do this, he consulted with priests, monks, and those members of the senate whom he deemed notable and eminent so that his choice might also accord with the selection of the majority, which is most just and carries certainty through the assent of the Holy Spirit. Now it is impossible for mere humans to escape what is in accord with the divine grace, but [these] men shattered [any] unanimous [decision] by disagreeing among themselves, and in a mosaic of votes for individual candidates, each one drew forth not the person whom Heaven's influence sketched with divine foreknowledge, but rather the person whom each one's individual will fashioned and promoted. But the activity of [divine] intelligence brought to the emperor's mind a picture of Nikephoros as chief shepherd [of the Church] and [the emperor] pressed all [the others] to look to [Nikephoros] [...]. All in all, the [emperor] deluged everyone's ears with a thick snowstorm of those imperial arguments, without any threat of force; he scooped them all into a unanimous vote [like fish] into a net. From that time, on every lip and on every tongue Nikephoros was proclaimed patriarch.[41]

41  Ignatios, *Life of Nikephoros*, 153.29-154.21: "Ὃς (καὶ γὰρ ἦν ἀγχινούστατος εἴ καί τις ἄλλος) δι᾽ ἐρεύνης εἶχε πολλῆς ἐγκαθιδρῦσαι τῇ ἀνάνδρῳ νυμφίον τε καὶ προμνήστορα ἱκανῶς ἔχοντα τοῦ κατὰ τὴν διδαχὴν πιστοῦ λόγου ἀνθέξεσθαι καὶ βαδιεῖσθαι κατ᾽ ἴχνος τοῦ προποιμάναντος λογικώτατα. διὸ καὶ πᾶσιν ἀνεκοινοῦτο ἱερεῦσί τε καὶ μονάζουσι καὶ τῆς συγκλήτου βουλῆς ὅσον ἔγκριτον καὶ προῦχον ἠπίστατο, ὡς ἂν τῇ τῶν πλειόνων ἐκλογῇ δικαιοτάτῃ οὔσῃ, καὶ τῇ τοῦ θείου πνεύματος ἐπινεύσει τὸ βέβαιον λαμβανούσῃ καὶ ἡ αὐτοῦ ἐφέψοιτο βούλησις. οἱ δὲ (καὶ γὰρ ἀνθρώπους ὄντας διαδρᾶναι τὸ πρὸς χάριν ἀδύνατον) τῇ ἀπ᾽ ἀλλήλων διαστάσει τὸ ὁμόγνωμον διαλύσαντες ἄλλος ἄλλον ἐψηφολόγει καὶ εἷλκεν, οὐχ ὃν ἡ τῆς ἄνω ῥοπῆς ὑπέγραφε πρόγνωσις, τὸ ἑκάστου δὲ θέλειν ἀνετυποῦτο καὶ ἔπειθεν. τῷ δὲ βασιλεῖ τὸ τοῦ νοῦ δραστήριον Νικηφόρον ὑπεζωγράφει ποιμνίαρχον, καὶ πρὸς ἐκεῖνον ὁρᾶν πάντας συνήλαυνεν, ὑπομιμνήσκων τῶν ἀρετῶν τοῦ ἀνδρὸς τὰ αὐχήματα, τὸ ἐν λόγοις, τοῖς τε πνευματικοῖς καὶ τοῖς θύραθεν, καίριον, τὸ ἐν ἤθει ταπεινὸν καὶ μειλίχιον, τὸ ἐν συνειδήσει πρὸς πάντας εἰλικρινὲς καὶ ἀπρόσκοπον. καὶ ἁπαξαπλῶς, οἷα νιφάδι τῷ συνεχεῖ τῶν βασιλικῶν ἐκείνων λογίων τὰς πάντων ἀκοὰς κατακλύσας, μηδεμιᾶς ὑπούσης βίας, εἰς μίαν ψῆφον ὡς εἰς σαγήνην τοὺς πάντας ἐξώγρησεν· ἐξ

In this account of Nikephoros's patriarchal election, first, the motif of continuity with the patriarchate of Tarasios came in the foreground. For Ignatios, it was not a great problem that the emperor was the one who directed the ecclesiastical council in the election of the worthy candidate, as long as he was presented in the narrative as *perfect* in divine things, ready to positively reply to both the divine will and Tarasios's wish, and to act in accordance with them. In order to highlight a positive example of the imperial relationship with the Church, and in the issue of installing patriarchs (which was a particularly dangerous issue from the perspective of Iconoclastic heritage), Ignatios made sure that his narrative accorded with the newly established Orthodoxy in both epochs – in 806, but also in the time when he wrote the two *Lives*, after 843 – stressing that the emperor 'made council with the clergymen' and that he 'without force directed all to one voice' in order that they should recognize the worthy candidate Nikephoros, whom they later accepted and proclaimed to be the new patriarch.

In general, it is obvious that the emperor had a significant role in organizing the appointment of Nikephoros as patriarch after Tarasios's death in 806. Both Nikephoros and Ignatios the Deacon tell us that this process included the senate and the synod of the Church of Constantinople. For Ignatios, it was very important to stress that the emperor did not use force to promote his candidate. He managed to acquire the consent of the entire body of the Church. The 'forceful deed' which Nikephoros mentioned in his letter to the pope might represent an allusion to the events which took place prior to his patriarchal consecration, some years before Tarasios's death, when he was brought back to Constantinople from his monastic foundation, and when he was appointed *ptochotrophos* of the largest poor house of the city.

The connection between the emperor and future patriarch thus date back to the period when Tarasios was still governing the Church of Constantinople. It is interesting that the two were namesakes, a point which Ignatios liked to emphasize in his highly literary account of the patriarchal appointment of Tarasios's successor. The relations between the emperor and the patriarch even before his patriarchal election were obviously more complex and profound, since Nikephoros was indebted to the emperor for the revival of his career in Constantinople somewhere at the beginning of the ninth century. In relation to such an opinion, a reference by Ignatios

ἐκείνου τε γὰρ ἐν παντὶ χείλει καὶ γλώσσῃ πάσῃ Νικηφόρος πατριάρχης ἀνηγορεύετο.' See Alexander, *The Patriarch Nicephorus*, pp. 65-67, with specific attention to the *De Ceremoniis*.

that, through the office of *ptochotrophos*, Nikephoros in fact governed over the entire Church, is significant, since it tells us that Nikephoros was back in the centre of political and ecclesiastical events under Patriarch Tarasios, and that the Emperor Nikephoros was the one who made it possible for him to reconnect with the processes in the capital.[42]

## The Patriarchs Tarasios and Nikephoros

Publicly proclaimed for the first time in the Church of Constantinople on the Sunday of Orthodoxy in 847,[43] the *Synodicon of Orthodoxy* established the memory of the final victory of the Orthodox theology of icon worship over the heresy of Iconoclasm. In one of its passages, the *Synodicon* anathematized all the writings which were directed against the Constantinopolitan patriarchs Germanos, Tarasios, and Nikephoros:

> To Germanos, Tarasios, Nikephoros, and Methodios, truthful hierarchs of God, and defenders and teachers of Orthodoxy (τῆς ὀρθοδοξίας προμάχων καὶ διδασκάλων), memory eternal! To all those who slanderously wrote or spoke against the holy Patriarchs Germanos, Tarasios, Nikephoros, and Methodios, anathema![44]

Such position of the Church of Constantinople towards the rigorous *akribeia* of the *hegumenos* of the Studites monastery presents an echo of the ever-simmering strife between the two church orders: the episcopacy, educated

---

42   Cf. Ignatios, *Life of Nikephoros*, 152.14-18. In his description of Nikephoros's appointment to the post of *ptochotrophos*, Ignatios referred to the Emperor Nikephoros I and his son and co-emperor, Staurakios, as τῶν κρατούντων. The term is known to carry a rather negative connotation in Byzantine literature of the period, and might connect to the entire narrative of that part of the *Life of Nikephoros* which Ignatios might have been keen to slightly emphasize since the saint was taken out of his beloved desert and forcefully brought back to Constantinople. Nikephoros himself used the same term twice in his *Short History*, in both cases to describe negative details from the reigns of Herakleios and Constantine V. Cf. Афиногенов, *Константинопольский патриархат*, pp. 40-41. For a different point of view on these issues see Niavis, *The Reign of the Byzantine Emperor Nicephorus I*, pp. 123-142.

43   Cf. Komatina, *Church Policy of Byzantium*, pp. 72-77 (in Serbian) for the new dating of the proclamation of the *Synodicon*. Komatina perceptively noted that the *Synodicon* was proclaimed in the same year that the relics of Patriarch Nikephoros were translated to Constantinople by Patriarch Methodios, in order to weaken the ideological strength of the Studites opposition.

44   *Synodikon*, 51.110-111; 53.114-116: Γερμανοῦ, Ταρασίου, Νικηφόρου καὶ Μεθοδίου, τῶν ὡς ἀληθῶς ἀρχιερέων Θεοῦ καὶ τῆς ὀρθοδοξίας προμάχων καὶ διδασκάλων, αἰωνία ἡ μνήμη. Ἅπαντα τὰ κατὰ τῶν ἁγίων πατριαρχῶν (Γερμανοῦ), Ταρασίου, Νικηφόρου καὶ Μεθοδίου γραφέντα ἢ λαληθέντα, ἀνάθεμα.'

and inclined towards political compromise, and the monks, pious and zealous in regards to the canons of the Church. Both the education of the episcopacy and the scrupulous adherence to canon law, however, should not be taken strictly and verbatim. Education was often a feature of many monks, while their adherence towards canon law in their disputes with the patriarchs and bishops might also be viewed more as an appropriate tool in these internal ecclesiastical divisions. In one way, these verses point to mutual relations and connections between the patriarchs Tarasios and Nikephoros in the first instance, and more widely, with the former and later patriarchs Germanos and Methodios on a more ideological level. The *Synodicon* obviously accentuated this point, in the relations between the patriarchs, building the idea by using their real interconnections where they were obvious, and translating them onto a higher level of Orthodox ideology versus the Iconoclast ecclesiology and theology. The idea of *oikonomia*, which was particularly promulgated in ecclesiastical dealings at the Seventh Ecumenical Council, and performed by the patriarch himself, is obvious in this manner of presentation of the holy patriarchs, and in the anathematizing of the writings against them composed during the period between the two Iconoclasms. Such an ecclesiology met with opposition, mainly from the side of the Studites – monks led by Theodore the Studites – marking the entire forthcoming period from 806 to 843.

Therefore, the relations between Tarasios and Nikephoros are twofold. As the later imagery of the Church tried to shape it into one specific and lasting form based on ideas and ideology, the real characteristics of their patriarchates were not the same in the sense that they were burdened with specific issues which were evolving in time and different political circumstances. The imperial power itself shifted from a somewhat unique case of the rule of Eirene and her son Emperor Constantine VI, and later only Eirene, to the rule of Emperor Nikephoros I, who came to power by deposing Eirene. But there existed a real continuity between the patriarchates of Tarasios and Nikephoros, mainly regarding their relationship with the monks, and with Theodore the Studites. The idea about the *continuity* of the patriarchs and the Orthodoxy of their policy appears later, at the time of the Patriarch Photios, when it was fully developed, with some founding elements present already in the *Synodicon*. So the issue of *continuity* can also be put into the phenomenon of transmitting and shaping the past events later in Byzantium's history.

Although we lack explicit and definite evidence, it is possible with a high measure of certainty to assume that Nikephoros was under the direct supervision of the *protasekretis* Tarasios at the time when both were lay officials at the imperial court. Further, their family background suggests that the two were of the same doctrinal persuasion in relation to icon veneration as well, since they both had relatives who were devoted Iconophiles. Namely, both had prominent individuals among their families who descended from the same highest echelons of Constantinopolitan society and who were staunch supporters of icons. The family of the Patriarch Tarasios was of noble descent, with notable individuals who belonged both to the ecclesiastical and state structures of Byzantine society. More interesting is that some of these persons were in service of the Iconoclast emperors, and later demonstrated similar loyalty to the newly prevailed doctrine of icon worship after 784.[45] Such features of the family of Tarasios offer some striking similarity with the family of Nikephoros, and in particular to the imperial service of his father and his later banishment, as well as Nikephoros's subsequent presence at the Iconoclastic imperial court, where he probably first met Tarasios. That Nikephoros and Tarasios probably had the same overall stance concerning icon worship is confirmed by several sources which give the account of the Seventh Ecumenical Council, where Nikephoros participated as an imperial delegate, but obviously in close connection with the Patriarch Tarasios, with whom he appeared at the council. This was later utilized by his hagiographer to create an image of his predestination to succeed Tarasios at the patriarchal see, and later, to lead the struggle at the beginning of the second Iconoclastic controversy.

The Patriarch Tarasios had built a monastery on the European shore of the Bosporus, which was probably intended to become, among other things, a place where new clergy and monks were prepared for their ecclesiastical duties in the new Constantinopolitan church. Nikephoros also followed a path similar to that of his former superior, imitating his deeds by founding monasteries. It is not possible to identify the precise time of such activity. We can discern a period of some fifteen years during which Nikephoros built and inhabited his first monastic foundation if we recognize from his letter to the pope that, some time after the Council of 787, he left the capital and founded the first of his two monasteries on the opposite shore of Bosporus, in the vicinity of Constantinople. This might be very telling in connection to his later return to the city, and his active social and ecclesiastical life, after 802. Nikephoros described his life away from Constantinople in general terms, not mentioning his monastery explicitly.[46] In contrast, Ignatios the

---

45   Ignatios, *Life of Tarasios*, 4.1-11. See also the comments of Efthymiadis in his edition of Ignatios's *Life of Tarasios*, pp. 6-11.
46   Nikephoros, *Ad Leonem*, cols. 173D-176A.

Deacon narrated in detail the inner structure and some aspects of the organization in Nikephoros's monastery, and in particular, understandably, about the nature of Nikephoros's life there and his zeal to establish a place of spiritual life and worship. However, both brought up the same motives – Nikephoros's pursuit of a spiritual life – which deprived their accounts of any insinuation about the political causes that might have also been responsible for Nikephoros's absence from Constantinople until 802, when Nikephoros I replaced Empress Eirene at the imperial palace.[47]

Since Nikephoros himself did not take monastic vows in his monastery, and since he left Constantinople at a time of internal turmoil and strife for hegemony between the Empress Eirene and her young son Constantine VI, it is hard to offer a reasonable explanation for the main motives which drove him to leave the capital. This is additionally complicated by the obvious involvement of the Church of Constantinople in this friction, probably the Patriarch Tarasios, and the monastic party led by Plato of Sacudion and Theodore of Studium, since the second marriage of Constantine VI with the niece of these two highly influential monks inevitably involved them and gave them a great opportunity to interfere in the relations between the Church and the state, providing for their own party a suitable cause for action. It is notable that the Patriarch Tarasios disappeared from the sources in this period, which was already noted by scholars, and which was taken at least as a sign of his involvement and probably discord with the Empress Eirene, or her son. These are the main issues of that episode, from 790 to 802, which present a bleak period in our understanding of Nikephoros's actions and his place in these events. So Nikephoros's motives for leaving Constantinople lie in these events.[48]

---

47    Regarding the two monastic foundations of Patriarch Nikephoros, see Janin, *Constantinople Byzantin*, p. 439; Janin, 'L'Église Byzantine', pp. 91-92; and Ruggieri, *Byzantine Religious Architecture*, pp. 199-200.

48    Alexander, *The Patriarch Nicephorus*, hypothesized that Nikephoros left Constantinople some time around the year 797, when the clash between Eirene and Constantine VI was at its height. He further justified such reasoning by the fact that Nikephoros returned to the capital due to the insistence of the new Emperor Nikephoros I in 802, after Eirene was deposed. Афиногенов, *Константинопольский патриархат*, pp. 32-33, made his hypothesis that Nikephoros and Tarasios both suffered from the side of the Empress Eirene at that period since they both took the side of the Emperor Constantine VI. Ignatios the Deacon and his *Life of Tarasios* support this thesis in the story of the patriarch's intercession for a certain *spatharios* who was close to the young emperor, and who found refuge in the cathedral of Holy Wisdom and was tended by Tarasios himself for a long period of time. From such an account it can be concluded that Nikephoros might have followed Tarasios's policy and, due to such stance, might have needed to abandon Constantinople, using the time to strengthen himself and his party by founding

In further analysis of this most unknown part of Nikephoros's life, evidence about possible family relations between him and Tarasios, which Patriarch Photios mentioned in his letter to the Pope Nicholas I, additionally lend if not circumstantial evidence of their real political and ecclesiastical connections, then at least a guide for a future analysis of this very interesting issue. However, it is evident that both Nikephoros, in his letter to Pope Leo III, and his later hagiographer Ignatios the Deacon, remained silent and quite vague in their narration of the events between 787/790 and 802. Why the conciseness and preference to promulgate a story about spiritual issues – Nikephoros's monastic life, and his studies of theological and secular sciences and writings – rather than to give evidence about his secular career during that period? Was this deliberate silence due to the conflict between the emperors and the Church, when relations between the secular and ecclesiastical powers were disturbed, which thus presented a reason for Nikephoros to withdraw from contemporary secular and political life in Constantinople? Was that a turning point in his relations with Tarasios, in the sense that it was considered by both that Nikephoros should follow an ecclesiastical career, assuming that it would bring more benefits for the Church in the future, rather than remain in the secular administration of the Empire at a time when possible changes to a better position for their own party were not in close view? The events of 802 were out of sight at that point, when the new emperor invited Nikephoros to return to Constantinople, and when Patriarch Tarasios assumed his former role in Byzantine society, representing a return of the ecclesiastical doctrine which he had tried to elevate to dominance previously.

It is precisely in this section of the *Life* – after the narration about the Seventh Ecumenical Council and the office of *ptochotrophos* – where Ignatios moved on to the issue of Nikephoros's monastic foundation, its internal organization, and his way of life in the desert. Ignatios gave a long and detailed account of Nikephoros's secular education, which, however, does not correspond chronologically with this period of Nikephoros's life. Ignatios promulgated an image of the future patriarch as a person who was totally oriented towards contemplation, spiritual perfection, and cherishing scholarship. Hence, we deal with a story barren of even a minimal level of detail concerning Nikephoros's social surroundings and his relationship with the influential and significant protagonists of contemporary political

---

a monastery, which may have had a purpose of preparing new ecclesiastics for the party of Tarasios.

and ecclesiastical events. This might partially be due to the nature of the genre of Byzantine hagiography.

From such reasoning it could be asked whether Ignatios actually wanted to emphasize the direct or indirect political clash between Nikephoros and the Empress Eirene by accentuating the topic of his spiritual accomplishments and his learning, which also enabled him to present the empress in the later narrative of the *Life* in a favourable light, with no hint of the possible confrontation which might have existed with the work's main character. Such a literary approach would further enable the presentation of a specific ideological image of both Eirene and Nikephoros as joint contributors to the victory of icon veneration over the heresy of Iconoclasm.

It seems that the Empress Eirene's overthrow of her son Constantine VI created the possibility of Nikephoros's voluntary exile from Constantinople, and that such a case was likely anticipated in the letter to Pope Leo III, where Nikephoros brought forward his understanding of the instability of all things as the main reason for his abdication from his secular office:

> Serving for some time in this office tied by human affairs, I came to the comprehension of the instability of this life. I started thinking how it is hard and almost impossible to accomplish such a service for those who are without perfect hope.[49]

It is possible to suggest two hypotheses in regard to the analysis of this interesting passage in Nikephoros's letter. Both concern his relations with the former Empress Eirene, whose status as a leader of the struggle for proper icon worship, even at the time when the letter was written, was significant and could not be questioned on the ideological level among the Orthodox. Nikephoros might have written in accordance with such ideas of Byzantine ecclesiastical and political society. Yet there is a sense that this ascetic disposition serves as the main motif for the future patriarch's leaving Constantinople. In contrast, Ignatios the Deacon utilized an interesting allegory, comparing the future Patriarch Nikephoros to the Old Testament prophet Elijah, whose living in the Judean desert, before his ascent to the Mount Carmel, was in fact caused by the threat of the godless Jezebel, who threatened to kill the prophet. Ignatios wrote in Nikephoros's *Life*: 'He

---

49   Nikephoros, *Ad Leonem*, col. 173BC: 'Ἐν ταύτῃ ἐπί τινας χρόνους ἐπιζυγούμενος, καὶ ἀνθρωπίνοις περιδεσμούμενος πράγμασιν, εἰς συναίσθησιν τῶν ἐν τῷδε τῷ βίῳ ῥευστῶν ἐλθών, βοῦς (νοῦν) ἀνείλιττον, καὶ λογισμοὺς ἀνεκίνουν, ὡς ἄρα χαλεπὸν καὶ δυσκατόρθωτον, τοὺς τῇ δὲ ἐνησχοληημένους τῶν ὑψηλοτέρων ψαύειν, μάλιστά τις ἐπιτυχὼν τῆς κρείττονος ἐλπίδος, οὐκ ἂν διαμαρτήσειν.'

went to some hill, similar to Carmel, opposite the Thracian Bosporus; he chose poverty not taking anything except the cloak of Elijah.'[50] However, what preceded the prophet's act, to which Ignatios alluded in the *Life of Nikephoros*, was written in the Old Testament *First Book of Kings*:

> Ahab told Jezebel all that Elijah had done, and how he had killed all the prophets with the sword. Then Jezebel sent a messenger to Elijah, saying, 'So let the gods do to me, and more also, if I don't make your life as the life of one of them by tomorrow about this time!' When he saw that, he arose, and went for his life, and came to Beersheba, which belongs to Judah, and left his servant there. But he himself went a day's journey into the wilderness, and came and sat down under a juniper tree.[51]

This parable about Elijah, in connection with Nikephoros's withdrawal from Constantinople on the opposite shore of Bosporus and his monastic endowment, in the broader context of Elijah's dispute with the princess Jezebel, and the author's possible allusion to the relations between Empress Eirene and Nikephoros and his likely forced withdrawal from the capital, was not analysed in this context. Ignatios's comparison of Nikephoros's ascetic feats to those of Elijah, as it was described in the Old Testament, accorded with his eulogy of the future patriarch later on in the pages of his *Life*. Did Ignatios actually lay down a subtle critique of Eirene for Nikephoros's abdication from his secular office, and in that way turn his reader's attention to the real cause of Nikephoros's *forced* absence from Constantinople? In other words, is the possible hostility of the Empress Eirene towards Tarasios and his loyal associate, Nikephoros, during her dispute with her son presented in the *Life* through the utilization of the parable story of the princess Jezebel and her animosity towards the prophet, who did not hesitate to denounce her polytheism and other sins, just like the Orthodox were denouncing the imperial heresy of Iconoclasm before the emperors, or possibly Eirene's coup against her son?

This question also involves Ignatios's own tendency to compare himself, a disciple of Nikephoros, to the prophet Elisha, the disciple of prophet Elijah, who, according to the Old Testament story, inherited Elijah's cloak and

---

50   Ignatios, *Life of Nikephoros*, 147.30-32: 'ἐπί τινα λοφιὰν ἀντικρὺ τοῦ Θρᾳκικοῦ Βοσπόρου μεταναστεύει οὐδὲν πλέον τῆς Ἡλιοῦ μηλωτῆς, τῆς ἀκτησίας φημί, πρὸς τὸν ὅμοιον ἐπιφερόμενος Κάρμηλον.' Cf. Stephen, *Life of Stephen the Younger*, § 20.12-14, where a similar imagery of Stephen the Younger is made in comparison with St. Auxentios at the place of his ascetic feats: 'ἔνθα οὗτος ὁ νέος Ἐλισσαῖος τοῦ παλαιοῦ Ἡλίου ὡς ἐν ὄρει Καρμηλίῳ τὴν στενοτέραν μηλωτῆς σκηνὴν ἔπηξεν.'
51   I Kings, 19.1-4.

performed miracles with it. This opens up a new route in the analysis of Ignatios's literary techniques in his hagiographies and his self-perception, which he tended to display and incorporate in his narration about the saints. After all, Ignatios's subtle and skilfully-emphasized idea of his spiritual relations with the holy patriarch, which he placed in the introductory part of his work, has several narrative levels and carries in itself several different messages. It is understandable that Ignatios, as a repentant Iconoclast who wrote the *Life of Nikephoros* (among other things) as an act of personal remorse for adhering to the heresy of Iconoclasm, had strong reasons to include himself anew in the group of Orthodox Christians, even through a specific literary presentation of himself as a spiritual relative of Nikephoros. In this context, the spiritual relationship presented a strong connection to the Orthodoxy of the patriarch. This spiritual familiarity with the holy patriarch, or rather spiritual adoption, was possible through Ignatios's consecration as a deacon by the hands of Nikephoros, and thus through his participation in the sacramental life of the Church of Constantinople.

Ignatios's central motif in his encomium dedicated to Nikephoros – which featured an appropriate wordplay where Nikephoros was the one who carried victory in his name but was also the one who carried God in his heart as a God-bearing father (Νικηφόρος ὁ θεοφόρος / θεοφόρος πατήρ), and as the one who 'lifted everyone to the true faith' – found its explanation in the epilogue of the *Life* where the author professes his sin and downfall, hoping at the same time that he might find forgiveness and intercession from the holy patriarch before God.[52] In that sense, it is clear that the description of Nikephoros's struggle for Orthodox icon worship presents the main theme and literary motif for Ignatios's writing of the *Life*.

After the political downfall of Empress Eirene in 802, when the former *logothete* Nikephoros assumed the imperial power, our Nikephoros found himself again in the centre of political and ecclesiastical processes, becoming *ptochotrophos* by the insistence of the emperor and his co-emperor Staurakios. In his portrayal of the future patriarch, Ignatios the Deacon turned his attention to vivid descriptions of Nikephoros's patriarchal election and its process, when his character was discussed alongside contemporary political and ecclesiastical individuals in Constantinople. The function of *ptochotrophos*, an office which Nikephoros occupied after his return to Constantinople, is probably one of the most puzzling in the case of Nikephoros, since it was by its nature inclined towards the care for the poor and thus equally rooted in the philanthropic activity of the

---

52  Ignatios, *Life of Nikephoros*, 215.13-217. 27.

Church (in connection with the idea transmitted in the Scriptures and in Christ's Sermon on the Mount). In contrast, there existed a clear secular and imperial tradition of philanthropy by the ruler, which was passed from an even older and deeper pre-Christian tradition of Hellenistic imperial philosophy. Perhaps Nikephoros's new office of *ptochotrophos*, with its ambivalent essence, in the connection of secular and sacral, and in the interweaving of the prerogatives of ecclesiastical and secular ideas of power and service, portrays most successfully Nikephoros's life and his past path – a career of a lay official who was actively involved in events of ecumenical importance for the Empire, but who was also involved in the Church through his participation in the Council of Nicaea in 787, under the clear and obvious patronage of the Patriarch Tarasios.

Conversely, Nikephoros's later career fully developed rather quickly and reached its utmost peak with his election as patriarch of the Church of Constantinople following Tarasios's death – although it was not without its many various tribulations. These mostly concerned Nikephoros's relationship with imperial power, including his final downfall from this highest ecclesiastical position and one of the two highest offices in all of Byzantine society, which testifies to the continuity between the tightly interwoven secular and sacral aspects of the personality of Nikephoros. However, Nikephoros had to confirm the strength of his own position and promote the idea of *oikonomia* to resolve both the difficulties in dealing with the state and internal ecclesiastical strife (which was seldom without political dimensions) in parallel with the struggle to preserve Tarasios's ideological legacy regarding the guidance of the Church of Constantinopole, which he upheld as an equal and powerful pole and counterbalance to imperial power.

## The Patriarch Nikephoros and the Studites Opposition

After his rise to the patriarchal throne of the Church of Constantinople, Nikephoros found himself at the peak of his career and at the highest point of the ecclesiastical see over which he now presided. This was at the time of a relatively short period of renewed Orthodoxy, with just under two decades separating it from the long heritage of the Iconoclast epoch when the emperors demonstrated their highest power over the Church. In contrast to this, the revival of icon worship began a new life, with new strength, by building on the foundations laid at the Ecumenical Council of Nicaea in 787. However, this was also the time of new struggles amid the

Iconophiles, and especially regarding the treatment of former Iconoclasts, an issue which highly influenced Nikephoros's patriarchal policy. The new patriarch, as a former lay official with considerable political experience, was involved in many significant events which had shaped the last twenty years of Byzantium's ecclesiastical and political history. The Patriarch Tarasios and the Empress Eirene, as the bearers of secular power, both followed their own interests and used the newly arisen events to gain authority for the institutions over which they presided. At the Nicaean council in 787, the Church had re-established its old traditional idea of autonomy in relation to the Empire, an idea and a system which was fully destroyed during the rule of the first Iconoclast emperors, and which at times took the shape of a full-scale persecution.[53] For the first time in the long history of the ecumenical councils, it happened that the Constantino-politan patriarch presided over the council sessions – a significant point that demonstrates the newly founded aspirations of the new leaders of the Church. Previously, the successors of the first Christian emperor, Constantine the Great, presided over the council sessions and were accepted in such a role with no objections. By supporting the new patriarch and giving her imperial support to the Council in 787, the Empress Eirene managed to include herself in the sacred line of Byzantine emperors, headed by Constantine the Great, the patron of the First Ecumenical Council in Nicaea in 325. On such foundations, the Empress Eirene managed to gain legitimacy for her power and rule, which was jeopardized by the fact that it was the first instance in Byzantium's history that a woman held the sceptre of the realm.

As for the Constantinopolitan church, the changes which had emerged after the death of emperor Leo IV, and with the short-lived triumph of Orthodoxy in 787 with Patriarch Tarasios at its head, marked the beginning of a lengthy process which might be defined as a struggle of the Church to secure and strengthen its own specific position in the Byzantine Empire in relation to imperial power. This process can be traced from the patriarchates of both Tarasios and Nikephoros, which is very valuable for our analysis, and all the way to Patriarch Photios's introduction to the *Eisagoge* and the clear attempt by the Patriarch Michael Kerularios to finally impose the supremacy of sacral over imperial power in the mid-eleventh century.[54]

---

53  Афиногенов, *Константинопольский патриархат*, pp. 15-16.

54  For a completely different view, and a different conceptual approach to the history of the patriarchs of the Constantinopolitan church from the ninth to the mid-eleventh century, see Stanković, 'The Path toward Michael Keroularios'.

Nikephoros was patriarch for little less than a decade, and his ascent to this office marked the beginning of the ninth century in Byzantium. His patriarchal office faced three shifts in the imperial throne for the period from 806 to 815. In these political developments, Nikephoros was not a passive observer of events. If he was enthroned to the patriarchal see under the influence and will of the Emperor Nikephoros I, his patriarchal activity gives evidence that the successor to Tarasios managed to continue, to some extent, the policies of his predecessor: to establish and confirm a certain authority of the Church in Byzantine society following the Iconoclastic era after 787. Major events which had marked the era of Nikephoros's patriarchal career were, in many ways, a continuation of the affairs which had marked the time of Tarasios and his patriarchal office. Thus it is not strange that Ignatios the Deacon later used the vivid image of Nikephoros as a worthy successor to Tarasios in his patriarchal office, by which he managed to introduce continuity in dealing with the issues which had marked the processes and events at the end of the eighth century.

As patriarch, Nikephoros had to face the firm opposition of the monastic party inside the Church, led by the influential monks Plato of Sacudion, his nephew Theodore, and Sabbas the Studites. This monastic opposition opposed the practice of *oikonomia*, which was used at the Council in 787 by Patriarch Tarasios and his bishops. It can be said that a similar strife marked Nikephoros's patriarchal office, at moments even passing to open conflict and confrontation between the two leaders, the Patriarch Nikephoros and Theodore, *hegumenos* of Studion. Certain moments from the history of these ecclesiastical disputes were interpreted as evidence of Nikephoros's weakness towards imperial power, or as a manifestation of subordination of the Church towards the state.[55]

In this respect, the first step launched by the Patriarch Nikephoros aiming to emphasize the authority of the patriarch in his ecclesiastical boundaries was a council in 806, which confirmed the integrity of Tarasios's policy of *oikonomia*, which was applied in the case of the second unlawful marriage of the Emperor Constantine VI in 797. This local council of the Patriarchate of Constantinople under Nikephoros's presidency reveals the great energy and readiness of the patriarch to promulgate his policy towards the Studites, even more strongly than had been the case with Tarasios. Also, the initiative in the convening of these local synods should be attributed to Nikephoros, rather than to the Emperor Nikephoros I. This is supported by the *Synodicon Vetus*, which narrated that the patriarch convened these councils with the

---

55   See, for example, Niavis, *The Reign of the Byzantine Emperor Nicephorus I*, p. 123 *passim*.

help of the emperor, which further points to their cooperation on these ecclesiastical issues than to imperial force towards the patriarch.[56] Nikephoros reinstated the formerly deposed priest Joseph, who at the time of Tarasios presided over the emperor's adulterous marriage, but who was later deposed by Tarasios (who was pressed by the monks to act in such a manner after the emperor was deposed by his mother). At the Synod of 806, Nikephoros managed to affirm and promote the ecclesiastical policy of Tarasios and in a way terminate the previous victory of the Studites monastic party over Tarasios. In this way, Nikephoros also managed to establish the authority of the institution of church councils and synods, and of the patriarchal office and dignity, over the monks who had pretensions to impose their decisions and authority over the entire Church of Constantinople, and even regarding secular power.[57]

Four letters of Theodore Studites to the Patriarch Nikephoros nicely present the nature of their relationship. The patriarch was obviously facing a strong adversary and an ambitious ecclesiastical faction from the monks. At moments, Theodore openly demonstrated a hostile attitude towards the patriarch and his policies, with his main argument focusing on the adulterous marriage of Emperor Constantine VI and the case of the deposed and restored priest Joseph, to put pressure on the patriarch to yield to the monks' view on Church doctrines. Theodore was ready to acknowledge patriarchal authority, however, when the second Iconoclasm was reinstated in 814.[58] In the early phase of their relations, the Patriarch Nikephoros

---

56 Афиногенов, *Константинопольский патриархат*, pp. 42 and 45-52. Cf. *Synodicon Vetus*, § 153.1-11: 'ὁ τρισμακάριστος Νικηφόρος πατριάρχης, Ταράσιον τὸν ἐν ἁγίοις διαδεξάμενος, θείαν καὶ ἱερὰν μερικὴν συνάρσει τοῦ βασιλέως ἐν Βυζαντίῳ συνήθροισε σύνοδον.' Further it was emphasized in the *Synodicon* that 'some men', alluding to the Studites, managed to fall out of Christ's Church *recklessly* and later returned to unity with the Church.

57 Beside the Synod of 806, the Synod from January of 809, and three subsequent synods from the same year under the presidency of Patriarch Nikephoros where, it should be noted, Theodore, his uncle Plato, and his brother (the archbishop of Thessalonica, Joseph) were convicted and defrocked. The main reason for such condemnation was the refusal for co-celebration with the patriarch and the restored priest Joseph, whom Nikephoros returned to the priesthood. By such activity, or rather inactivity, the Studites in essence managed to deny the decisions of the Synod in 806. Cf. Grumel, *Les Regestes des actes du patriarcat de Constantinople*, pp. 24-25.

58 In the two letters from 814 and 821, Theodore praised Nikephoros's struggle for the proper and Orthodox veneration of holy icons and for the true faith. The persecution of the Iconophiles obviously erased all previous issues between the *hegumenos* and the patriarch, and no mention of these problems can be found in these two late letters. Both the patriarch and Theodore were at that time living in exile, but obviously they maintained friendly contact through letters, the former *hegumenos* of the Studion monastery calling himself most humbly *the smallest son* of the patriarch. Cf. Theodore Studites, *Epistulae*, epp. 286 and 423.

obviously considered Theodore's attitude and posture to be schismatic,[59] while the influential *hegumenos* attempted to accuse the patriarch and the bishops of heresy on the basis of canon law (and its neglect) through the idea of *oikonomia*, which Theodore described in his letter to Pope Leo III, as a violation of the rules.[60] This leads us to the second point, namely, Theodore's readiness to address the Pope, inviting him to interfere in the internal ecclesiastical strife of the Church of Constantinople, after he was exiled from the capital in 809. The renewed Iconoclastic persecutions left the Church of Constantinople with a small number of Orthodox bishops who had not succumbed to the pressure of the imperial power and its Iconoclast doctrines. If this led Theodore, in the second phase of Iconoclasm, to address the pope and ask for his authoritative interference in the matters of doctrine of the Church of Constantinople, then his address to Pope Leo III in the time of Nikephoros I's reign and the patriarchate of the Orthodox patriarch Nikephoros regarding canonical disputes brought the Constantinopolitan see into a dangerous position in its ecclesiastical relations with Rome.

Theodore was obviously ready to acknowledge papal primacy and the pope's right to meddle in the affairs of the Church of Constantinople, in order to win his personal battle with the Patriarch Nikephoros, skilfully utilizing the idea of the apostle Peter's primacy and Leo III's pretensions to exercise such authority in Christendom and the East.[61] And in his two letters to Leo III, Theodore openly accused his patriarch and the synod of the Church of Constantinople of heresy for the uncanonical practice of the adulterous marriage of the former Emperor Constantine VI and the

---

59   Theodore Studites, *Epistulae*, ep. 25. Theodore began his letter with astonishment regarding the patriarch's message uttered to the Studites that they are in schism with the Church (ἀποσχίσται γάρ ἐστὲ τῆς ἐκκλησίας), which the Studites later disapproved by confirming his adherence to all the ecumenical councils and the Orthodox canons of the Church – however, he warned the patriarch that the restoration of the priest Joseph, who had officiated at the emperor's adulterous marriage, would provoke a great schism in the Church. Later on, Theodore developed a view that the patriarch and all those who were in communion with the priest Joseph were, in fact, heretics who were destroying the faith of the Church and the Gospels.

60   Theodore Studites, *Epistulae*, ep. 34.100-109.

61   Theodore Studites, *Epistulae*, ep. 33. Theodore addressed his letter 'To the most holy and the supreme father of fathers Leo, my lord, apostolic pope. As Christ gave to Peter the keys of the Heavenly Kingdom and the dignity of the first shepherd, it is necessary to inform his successor about all the innovations in the Catholic Church which lead astray from the truth.' Theodore further wrote that he addressed the pope as being learned by the Holy Fathers from old, thus in fact accepting the Roman idea of supremacy as an established practice from the early Church fathers. Theodore even called the Synod of 809, convened by the Patriarch Nikephoros, a heretical one, disputing its legitimacy since it was not convened with the blessing and participation of the Roman Pope.

restoration of the priest Joseph to the priesthood, which happened in 806. Theodore here repeated all the arguments which he previously presented to Nikephoros in his two letters from 806 and 808, but now in a more hostile manner, since he was writing from banishment and without any of the authority that he previously exercised as the *hegumenos* of the Studion monastery. Theodore's argumentation was entirely made of ecclesiastical citations from the Scriptures and the Epistles of the Apostles, as well as of some sayings of the fathers – Gregory the Theologian and Basil the Great. But we may ask ourselves whether this insistence upon such a matter – the inappropriate restoration of the priest Joseph, who had previously officiated at the adulterous marriage of Constantine VI and was deposed and restored to priesthood by Nikephoros – was a plain and straightforward issue for Theodore, or rather a point on which he could build his more complex and more serious struggle against the authority of the patriarch, who was elected from a secular and not a monastic milieu? His willingness to admit the right of the pope to interfere in this matter obviously had to be adequately dealt with by the patriarch himself. Thus the *Synodika* of Nikephoros to Leo III in 811 presented a valuable proof of his own ecclesiology, which could suitably be presented to the Roman Pontiff in the form of an official letter.

As for Nikephoros the patriarch and Theodore Studites, their relationship seems to have changed for the better in the years of the renewed persecution of Iconophiles under Leo V in 814. In the letter from 814, Theodore honoured the exiled patriarch in such words: 'Rejoice O great sun of Orthodoxy whose rays of confession enlighten the *Oikoumene*'.[62] And in 821 it seems that Theodore finally gave up the Roman path of his ecclesiology, designating Patriarch Nikephoros as the 'godly *coryphaeus* and highest peak of the sacred heads'.[63] Thus it may be concluded, regarding the *oikonomia* which he so strongly denounced in his letters to the Pope in 809, that he condemned it in his struggle with the patriarch but, when the second Iconoclasm had burst out, he was convinced of the patriarch's Orthodoxy and his firm adherence to the same principles of the Church autocephaly in relation to the imperial power, as Theodore himself had promoted in his own teachings. However, it is ultimately evident that the Church of Constantinople, in the beginning of the ninth century, had two great but different ecclesiastics – who stemmed from various spiritual milieux of Byzantine society and whose paths could

---

62    Theodore Studites, *Epistulae*, ep. 286.7-8 *passim.* 'χαῖρε ὁ μέγας ἥλιος τῆς ὀρθοδοξίας, οὗ ταῖς ὁμολογητικαῖς ἀκτῖσι φωτοβολεῖται ἡ οἰκουμένη.'

63    Theodore Studites, *Epistulae*, ep. 423.5-6 *passim.* 'ἀυτὸς δέ, ὦ θεία καὶ κορυφαία τῶν ἱερῶν κεφαλῶν ἀκρότης.'

not always be complementary. In relation to the murdered Emperor Leo V, Theodore had acclaimed his murder in the very altar of the church as a symbolic and righteous act, while the exiled Patriarch Nikephoros had rather separated the emperor's Iconoclastic heresy from his firm and successful secular policy in keeping the Byzantine realm a victorious Empire, an accomplishment of Leo V which he knew to praise.

## Patriarch Nikephoros and Pope Leo III

The *Synodika*, the enthronement letter of Patriarch Nikephoros to Pope Leo III, presents a valuable source both for the analysis of ecclesiastical relations between Constantinople and Rome at the outset of the ninth century, and also for the reconstruction of several issues in connection with Nikephoros, foremost concerning his relations with secular power in Byzantium at the time. The letter sparked a controversy regarding the long delay with which it was sent to Rome, raising a question about the nature of the relations between the patriarch and Emperor Nikephoros I. Namely, the *Synodika* was sent to Pope Leo III in 811 just after the emperor's death, and five years after Nikephoros's patriarchal enthronement. Theophanes the Confessor, who generally presented the entire reign of Nikephoros I in a predominantly negative manner, laid the blame for this delay upon the emperor (thus remaining firm and consistent in his attitude towards Nikephoros I) while accentuating the patriarch's holiness.[64] Previous interpretations of the delayed enthronement letter of Nikephoros, and the blame placed on the emperor for its postponement, can and should be re-examined, primarily through an analysis of the relations between the two hierarchs based on Nikephoros's creed, which he professed in his *Synodika*, from which follows a revision of the previous interpretation that this signalled the patriarch's submission to the will and power of the emperor. In this sense, even the words of Patriarch Nikephoros on this issue should be placed into their proper context – the time and relations of the two most prominent sees in Christendom.[65]

---

64  Cf. Theophanes, *Chronicle*, 494.22-25: 'καὶ Νικηφόρος ὁ αγιώτατος πατριάρχης ἀπέστειλε συνοδικὰ πρὸς Λέοντα τὸν ἁγιώτατον πάπαν Ῥώμης, πρὸ τούτου γὰρ ἐκωλύετο ὑπὸ Νικηφόρου τοῦτο ποιῆσαι.'

65  Афиногенов, *Константинопольский патриархат*, pp. 39-58, devoted great attention to the analysis of the patriarchal office of Nikephoros, and in particular with regard to secular power and the nature of their mutual relations. Although he himself openly questioned the previously accepted opinion that the patriarch was subordinated to Emperor Nikephoros I, and

The patriarch's justification for the long delay in exercising ecclesiastical relations, at the moment when the Emperor Nikephoros I passed away, as well as the entire context of the strife inside the Church of Constantinople between the patriarch and Theodore Studites (who did not hesitate to appeal to papal authority in settling church matters), should direct our analysis of the letter and its content in a different course.[66] In fact, Nikephoros's struggle for the continuity and succession of Tarasios's patriarchal policies against the opposition was confronted by the Studites, which can be seen in the letter to Pope Leo III:

> Later, I have seen the envy of the slanderers who were perpetually and maliciously trying to blame us in all things whether we act well or bad. The ones who do not see the plank in their own eye, and do not wish to cleanse the dirt which is in their eyes, dealing with the particles of others, worthless things and trifles, and arm their tongues dishonourably against the head, attacking sharply and most unlawfully.[67]

The *Studites question* should be taken into consideration in the analysis of this problem, since the Church of Constantinople confronted itself with the Roman church exactly and among other ways through the opposition of the Studites towards the patriarchs Tarasios and Nikephoros. Namely, Plato's and Theodore's resistance to Nikephoros's accession to the patriarchal throne from the laity, ἀπὸ λαικῶν, seems to have been on the same line with the aspirations of the Roman church towards its own primacy over the entire Church, since earlier it was Pope Hadrian who criticized Tarasios's patriarchal appointment from the laity before the Seventh Ecumenical Council.[68] Theodore's letter to Pope Leo III from 809, however, might well be considered to be referenced in these words of Patriarch Nikephoros. So the issue of Nikephoros's *Synodika* to Pope Leo III, which was sent five

---

managed to a great extent to revise such stance, yet he did not raise the issue of Nikephoros's *Synodika* to Leo III and his statement about imperial force that casts a shadow on their mutual relations, which were presented as good in the *Life of Nikephoros* by Ignatios the Deacon.

66  Cf. O'Connell, *The Ecclesiology of St. Nicephorus*, pp. 206-227, for Theodore's petitions to the Roman Pontiff.

67  Nikephoros, *Ad Leonem*, col. 176 CD: "Επειτα δὲ ἰδὼν καὶ τῆς ἀρχῆς τὸ ἐπείσακτον καὶ ἐπίφθονον τῶν βασκαινόντων ὑπείδομαι τὸ δολερὸν καὶ κακόηθες οἳ πάντη ἐπιτηρεῖν σπουδάζουσι τὰ ἡμέτερα εὖ τε καὶ ὡς ἑτέρως ἔχοντα. Τὰς μὲν δοκοὺς τοῖς ἑαυτῶν ἐπικειμένας οὐ βλέποντες ὄμμασιν. οὐδὲ τὴν λήμην ἀπὸ τῶν ὀφθαλμῶν προκαθαίρειν αἱρούμενοι, ἀλλότρια δὲ κάρφη περιεργαζόμενοι, καὶ σμικρῶν ἄγαν καὶ εὐτελῶν ἕνεκεν, καὶ τοῦ μηδονος λόγου ἀξίων τὰς γλώσσας τὰς ἑαυτῶν κατὰ τῶν προεχόντων ἀνοσίως ὁπλίζουσι, καὶ ἀμφοτέρωθεν πικρῶς καὶ ἀδικώτατα βάλλουσι.'

68  Theophanes, *Chronicle*, 481.20-25.

years after his enthronement, asks for a more complex investigation into the broader context of the epoch and ecclesiastical relations between Constantinople and Rome.[69] In that sense, Nikephoros's stance towards the idea of Roman primacy arises as a crucial issue, one that should be investigated in his creed as displayed in his letter to the Pope.

When he defined his faith, Nikephoros accentuated the teaching of the Holy Apostles and the prophets, which were the foundation of the faith expressed by the Church of Constantinople, but with a particular emphasis that Christ himself was the cornerstone of the faith of Constantinople, contrary to the words of the apostle Peter and the words of the Gospel of Matthew, which are exactly the words that were often quoted by Theodore Studites in his letters.[70] Further, in the same passage, Nikephoros concluded that those who bore the name of *New Rome* did not fall behind the *Old Rome* in any way, and subsequently glorified the apostle Paul, who united new with old:

> Adhering to their teaching and faith we establish ourselves, strengthening ourselves with the confession of our faith, in which we stand and with which we laud ourselves, and our confession of the most glorious and most pure faith we announce loudly with bright faces.[71]

69   O'Connell, *The Ecclesiology of St. Nicephorus*, pp. 68-78 and 160-194, gave significant attention to the issue of Nikephoros's relationship with the Roman church, as it was expressed in his letter to the Pope Leo III and in his theological writings. However, it seems there was no awareness of the time or the major events in which the issue of the correspondence with Rome took place. The topic of Roman primacy and Nikephoros's alleged compliance with such ecclesiology seems to have been the central focus of this research, and thus its consequent conclusions. A totally different view on the same topic was given in Dvornik, *Byzantium and the Roman Primacy*, who saw, in the proclamations and thrust which the Byzantine defenders of images had towards the Roman Pontiff, a new phase in Byzantine perceptions of the primacy of Rome. But Dvornik also called for caution, pointing to the firm devotion and adherence of Constantinople towards its own ecclesiastical traditions, which can nicely be seen in the Greek translation of the letter of Pope Hadrian in 787 with all of its changes (which had to comply with Byzantine ecclesiology, while also neglecting certain matters viewed by Byzantines as a Roman intrusion into their own tradition).

70   Nikephoros, *Ad Leonem*, col. 181A. 'Τεθέντος ἀκρογωνιαίου λίθου τοῦ πάντων ἡμῶν Σωτῆρος Χριστοῦ καὶ Θεοῦ', and then emphasizing: 'κατ' οὐδὲν ἐν πίστει τὰ δεύτερα τῶν πρεσβυτέρων ἀποφερόμεθα.' 'And I say also unto thee, That thou are Peter, and upon this rock I will build my church; and the gates of hell shall not prevail against it. And I will give unto thee the keys of the kingdom of heaven: and whatsoever thou shalt bind on earth shall be bound in heaven: and whatsoever thou shall loose on earth shall be loosed in heaven.' (Matthew, 16.18-19)

71   Nikephoros, *Ad Leonem*, col. 181B. Cf. Dvornik, *Byzantium and the Roman Primacy*, who noticed this emphasis on the apostle Paul in Nikephoros's ecclesiology and especially in defining the faith of the entire Church, and of Constantinople as well.

However, it is notable as well that when he spoke about the faith of the
*Romans*, that is, the Roman church, he avoided mentioning the apostle
Peter, but emphasized the significance of the apostle Paul, who 'taught in
faith the Christians of old'. At that place Nikephoros introduced a quotation
from Paul's sermon to the Romans (Rom., 1.8.), adding that the faith to which
the Church of Constantinople adhered, and he as patriarch, did not limit
itself to the domains of Rome, thus indirectly promulgating the ecumenical
character of faith and authority professed by the Church of Constantinople.
Further, it is significant to mention that in the designation of his letter
Nikephoros left out the title *ecumenical* from his patriarchal title. However,
in the letter itself he proceeded to develop the very idea of the ecumenical
pretensions of Constantinople, and at the same time he associated the
apostolic succession of the Roman church with the apostle Paul, and its faith
in Paul's profession and his apostolic exposition of the Gospel. Contrary to
the epistolographic and ecclesiological method of Theodore Studites, the
absence of the apostle Peter from this exposition of faith by Nikephoros is
quite remarkable, and particularly as it was addressed to Pope Leo III.[72]

Nikephoros's ecclesiology as presented in his enthronement letter actually dealt with the issue of the pretensions towards primacy by the papacy,
which was already addressed during the time of the Patriarch Tarasios at
the Seventh Ecumenical Council, and which found its expression in the
two letters by Pope Hadrian delivered to the Council. For the Byzantines,
it was without a doubt inappropriate to accept this idea of the primacy of
the apostle Peter and the authority of the Roman Pontiff as the head of all
Churches. At that time, the Church of Constantinople solved the issue by
simply leaving out in their Greek translation all those unpleasant parts,
including the objections towards Tarasios's accession to the patriarchal
throne from the laity, which were remarks not in accordance with the
Byzantine view of church unity and its catholicity. Paul's name was added
in all the places where the apostle Peter was mentioned as the sole source
of papal authority. In his *Synodika* to Pope Leo III, Nikephoros used the
advantage which he had as the author of the letter to simply leave out the
name of Peter and, contrary to him, to emphasize the significance of Paul.

---

72   In 817 Theodore Studites addressed Pope Paschal, informing him about the reintroduction
of Iconoclasm in Byzantium, since, as he stated, 'our head [e.g. Patriarch Nikephoros] is in
captivity'. He then continued to espouse the Petrine authority of the Pope of Rome: 'Give ear
apostolic head, shepherd of Christ's sheep brought forth by God, keeper of the keys of Heavenly
Kingdom, rock of faith upon which the Catholic church is founded. For you are Peter, adorning
and governing the throne of Peter.' See Theodore Studites, *Epistulae*, ep. 271.17-20.

In most of his theological writings issued in the defence of icons, Patriarch Nikephoros displayed the proper place, role, and significance of Peter both in the Scriptures, in relation to the other Apostles, but also in the context to the primacy of the Roman see, though always exclusively in the sense of a primacy and championship in honour. Contrary to Nikephoros, Theodor Studites utilized the argument of Petrine authority with much less restraint, often openly acclaiming the primacy of the Roman church. However, while investigating the Byzantine notion and utilization of the idea of Petrine primacy, and even the primacy of honour of the Roman church, and of its competency to deal with and solve various theological disputes which shaped the history of the Christian East, it should be considered that the Roman church, beginning with the fourth century and the emergence of the Arian heresy, and later during Monophysitism and Monothelitism in the fifth and sixth centuries, always safeguarded the Orthodox teachings in relation to the Eastern Churches. This was not due to its own theological experience and practice, or due to its tendency towards resolving theological issues – the intellectual and cultural centres of the Christian world, such as Alexandria and Antioch, were in the East – but more due to its own isolation and conservative and traditionalist approach, deprived of any deeper aspiration concerning theological and philosophical reflection, which in the East flourished and had its own rich tradition, due to which heresies were not infrequent. In context of such circumstances, in which the keeping of Orthodox doctrines was almost always reserved for the Western Church, due to its own theological inactivity (the last great theologian of the Western Church, Augustine of Hippo, had died in the fifth century), only one Roman bishop, Honorius I, was anathematized by an ecumenical council.

Contrary to many patriarchs of Constantinople and Eastern bishops, the Roman church had come to a position where its own role in solving Christological and Iconoclastic disputes became of seminal importance, often decisive in promulgating victory for Orthodoxy, since its theology was a starting point for the Eastern Churches, and the Church of Constantinople in defining the Orthodox dogmas. However, these professions of Constantinople were always new and presented an innovative confirmation of the original Christian tradition and its *oikonomia* of salvation.[73] Adding to such

---

73  The letters of Theodore Studites to popes Leo III and Paschal should be read precisely in this context, together with his insistence on the Petrine authority of the Roman church, since the Church of Constantinople was neither free nor Orthodox under the Iconoclast Byzantine emperors. Thus it was impossible for Theodore to reach the support of the Orthodox from any other see than from Rome. It should be noted that Theodore, by means of such rhetoric, also pressured the Iconoclasts, bishops, and emperors alike, forcing upon them the idea of

a stance toward the place and role of the Roman church in the early history of the ecumenical councils and of the establishment of the key points in Christian dogma, the Byzantines obviously accepted such *Orthodoxy* of Rome as a result of its *freedom* in regard to the secular pressure of the imperial power, which ceased to execute its direct right and control over Rome already in the fifth century.

After such consideration, at least we can comply with the conclusion that Patriarch Nikephoros did not care about the possible implications which Emperor Nikephoros's policy towards the Roman church might provoke.[74] However, we would suggest a step forward in this analysis. Namely, both the emperor and the patriarch had their own interests, political and ecclesiastical, to postpone their relations with the Roman see. In other words, the aforementioned delay in sending of the patriarchal *Synodika* to the pope by Emperor Nikephoros I – while we should not forget that the letter was written after the emperor's death and that, as such, Nikephoros's argument for the delay may have a relative character – was in the interest of the Church of Constantinople, since the events which had burdened her relations with the Studites had promulgated the issue of Rome's primacy, contrary to the status and authority of the patriarch of Constantinople, Theodore Studites being its most frequent abuser. Thus the tradition of sending enthronement letters as a sign of ecclesiastical unity was broken on the side of Constantinople with the possible intention of minimizing the Petrine argument used by Theodore. Such a stance of Constantinople was developed in relation to the rising ambitions and pretensions of Rome, not only towards total primacy in the entire Church but also towards political manoeuvrings, as was the coronation of Charlemagne by Pope Leo III. These were all issues leading to the questioning of the imperial ideology promoted by Constantinople.

Ignatios the Deacon ended his evaluation of Nikephoros's letter to Leo III by imposing a rhetorical question whether Nikephoros's exposition of faith simply ended with the words written in the *Synodika*. However, Ignatios concluded that Nikephoros added to his pious confession of faith the deeds of his fervent opposition towards those who had carried out tyranny over the matters of faith. It is clear that such a remark by Ignatios was directed towards the Emperor Leo V, and not towards the alleged tyranny of Emperor

---

Roman primacy in matters of faith, since Rome at that time was Orthodox – and so binding the Iconoclasts to be in obedience to such a Church, which was anti-Iconoclastic in its exposition of faith.

74    Cf. Alexander, *The Patriarch Nicephorus*, p. 110.

Nikephoros I over his namesake patriarch.[75] From a strictly ecclesiastical point of view, at the time when both patriarchs, Tarasios and Nikephoros, fought to strengthen the authority of the Church in her relation to secular power, but also in relation to certain monastic groups led by Theodore Studites in their leaning towards the authority of Rome, Nikephoros's letter to Pope Leo III carried signs of this strife. These are evident first in his undermining of Roman ecclesiology based on the supposed authority of the apostle Peter, and through highlighting the role and contribution of the apostle Paul in his apostolic office, upon which both sees, Rome and Constantinople, based their faith and authority. Thus, while the local church councils that were convened by Patriarch Nikephoros in 806 and 809 reaffirmed patriarchal authority in the Church of Constantinople, and the idea of *oikonomia*, contrary to the monastic party, Nikephoros's letter to Leo III also asserted the renewed freedom of the Church of Constantinople, which appeared with new authority after decades of forceful subjection to the heresy of Iconoclasm. The Church of Constantinople finally managed to restore its Orthodoxy and thus its own authority, reaffirming her dignity on a wider ecclesiological plan, in relation to Rome, challenging its argumentation related to the primacy of the Western Church over the Church of Byzantium.

## The Patriarch in Exile

After the great defeat of the Byzantine army against the Bulgarians in 811 and the death of the Emperor Nikephoros I, Theophanes the Chronographer wrote that the son of the deceased emperor, Staurakios, remarked to the patriarch that he would not have a better friend in the personality of the new Emperor Michael I than he had in him.[76] And, truly, the year 811 and the defeat of Byzantines announced a new era, a certain upheaval in political and religious processes in the life of the Empire. For the first time since the defeat in 378 in the battle of Adrianople, the Byzantine emperor lost his life on the battlefield, and it came as an event in the time marked by the recent, significant, and great military victories of Constantine V. From the perspective of this relatively close past, and the three accomplished

---

75　Cf. Ignatios, *Life of Nikephoros*, 162.2-10: 'ἀλλὰ σὺν ὁμολογίᾳ καὶ ζήλῳ καὶ κινδύνοις λόγος αὐτῷ βιωφελὴς μαχαίρας τομώτερος ταῖς φρεσὶν ἀπηώρητο, τῶν τὰ θεῖα τυραννεῖν ᾑρημένων ἐκκόπτων ἐπιεικῶς τὰ φρονήματα.' After this Ignatios proceeded to narrate the events of the reign of Leo V.
76　Theophanes, *Chronicle*, 493.20-30: 'φίλον αὐτοῦ κρείττονα οὐχ εὑρήσεις.'

reigns of Leo III, Constantine V, and his successor Leo IV, this hard defeat of the Byzantines led by the nominally Orthodox Emperor Nikephoros I presented a strong cause for the social processes in Byzantium to turn again in favour of the Iconoclastic heresy and the revival of its religious and political doctrines.[77] The successful rule of Leo III and Constantine V, and most of all their military feats, did not leave even the icon worshipers indifferent, from the higher strata of Byzantine government and from the Church of Constantinople as well. It was the future patriarch Nikephoros who managed to deploy a subtle image of the Emperor Constantine V in his *Short History*, making a distinction between his Iconoclasm and his successful policy and military victories.

However, before the final phase of Iconoclasm ensued, almost parallel with the rise of Leo V to the imperial throne in 815, a short interim period of four years brought the patriarch to the very centre of major political events in the Empire. It is telling that the patriarch sent his *Synodika* to the Pope exactly at such a time. In light of Staurakios's statement, it can be suggested that Nikephoros tried to reaffirm ecclesiastical unity with Rome after losing the firm support which he had enjoyed from the late Emperor Nikephoros I. Did Nikephoros perhaps anticipate the possibility of an Iconoclastic revival and its new ascent as an official imperial doctrine after the military defeat in 811? Certainly one indication of future events occurred when several soldiers entered the church of the Holy Apostles, at the time when the patriarch was celebrating the Eucharist, and cried to the late Emperor Constantine V: 'rise and help the perishing state!'[78] At the beginning of the ninth century, sympathies towards Iconoclasm were actually very strong in Byzantine society, and it was Nikephoros who faced its revival in 815 and confronted it in his dispute with the Emperor Leo V. There are infrequent signs in the sources that the Church of Constantinople had Iconoclasts in its ranks, although the struggle for establishing Orthodoxy by the patriarchs Tarasios and Nikephoros was strong. The monastic ranks again step into the spotlight. Theophanes the Confessor mentioned one 'wandering pseudo-hermit' who desecrated the icon of the Virgin in the

77   Brubaker and Haldon, *Byzantium in the Iconoclast Era*, pp. 366-367.
78   Cf. Theophanes, *Chronicle*, 501.3-27, who gave a significant remark about the essence of this event, namely, that the soldiers blamed icon veneration and Orthodox doctrine, which were the official dogma of the Byzantine empire since 787, for the military catastrophe in 811. Alexander, *The Patriarch Nicephorus*, pp. 111-125, noticed that the revival of icon worship in 787 was not as much a result of a weakening of the Iconoclastic party, but more a result of happy circumstances, first of all Emperor Leo IV's short reign. See also Brubaker and Haldon, *Byzantium in the Iconoclast Era*, p. 261.

time of Emperor Michael I, while Skylitzes left a remark that the council of a monk called Sabatios led the Emperor Leo V towards Iconoclastic doctrine.[79] Although in both cases the hermits were the ones who advocated the heretical doctrine, these examples give evidence that the monastic clergy can in some of its ranks be labeled as Iconoclastic, more than later icon worshipers were ready to admit after 843.

In these new circumstances, after the military defeat in 811 and the shift in the imperial throne, while the presence of Iconoclast adherents in the Byzantine society was still very strong, Patriarch Nikephoros found himself in a new situation and in a position allowing him the possibility to influence to some extent political processes in Constantinople. The new emperor, Michael I, ascended the throne partly due to Nikephoros's mediation, but also with the oath that guaranteed his devotion to Orthodox dogma, which was an act enforced by the patriarch. Namely, the emperor guaranteed that he would keep firm to the Orthodox creed, that he would not defile his hands by the blood of Christians, and that he would not persecute the clergy of the Church of Constantinople.[80] This event by itself gives evidence of the authority which the patriarch of Constantinople had at that point. This act of the patriarch towards the emperor and later his attempt to enforce the same oath upon Leo the Armenian prior to his coronation testifies to the renewed authority of the patriarch of Constantinople after the first Iconoclastic crisis, which, however, did not pass without a reaction from the side of secular power, and the struggle for the confirmation of such authority during the second phase of Iconoclasm.

However, in the new order which had been established during the rule of Michael I, the Studites opposition seems to have managed to re-establish its influence, most importantly towards the new emperor. While the Studites were persecuted and even imprisoned during the reign of the previous Emperor Nikephoros I, and particularly in connection with Nikephoros's election as patriarch, now they secured free access to the imperial palace and managed to significantly influence some aspects of imperial politics, first of all in regard to several heretical groups which were present in the Empire.[81] Their influence on the foreign policy of the Empire, and especially

---

79 Cf. Theophanes, *Chronicle*, 496.27-30. John Skylitzes, *Synopsis of Histories*, 14.55-72.

80 Theophanes, *Chronicle*, 493.10-14.

81 Cf. Alexander, *The Patriarch Nicephorus*, p. 99, and Grumel, *Les Regestes des actes du patriarcat de Constantinople*, pp. 26-27. These were Jews, Paulicians, and Phrigian dualists, whose doctrines Nikephoros had described to the emperor, criticizing them and asking for imperial action against them. Theodore Studites interfered actively and stopped the possible persecution of heretics. In regard to Theodore's position concerning this issue and his relation to Nikephoros,

towards Bulgaria, was also achieved through the religious dimension which had a certain significance in these events.[82]

The Bulgarian question, which emerged drastically and with great strength after the Byzantine defeat of the armies and the death of the emperor in 811, became the largest political issue in the Empire in its relations with neighbouring states, but it soon started to be reflected in the internal Byzantine political and ecclesiastical processes. A balance in relationships, with a somewhat strengthened and confirmed authority of patriarchal power, which was established between 787 and 811, was compromised again from within by the reinforcement of the political role of the Studites inside the monastic party. Faced with the menace of the Bulgarian neighbour, the Emperor Michael I lacked determination, and in a military context failed to offer victory for which Byzantine society and military officials in particularly yearned.[83] As a consequence, a pretender emerged from the military ranks, the commander of the Anatolian theme, the *strategos* Leo the Armenian, who managed to peacefully take the Byzantine imperial throne after yet another military defeat of the Byzantine army against the Bulgarians in 813.[84] In these events, Patriarch Nikephoros again had his place and role.

According to the writing of Theophanes, Patriarch Nikephoros had supported the initiative of Michael I to renounce the throne in favour of a more competent individual, mostly for reason of his safety and the safety of his family. Then the *strategos* Leo had written and delivered a letter expounding his Orthodoxy to the patriarch, asking for his prayers and consent to take the imperial throne. Everything seemed to be in accordance with the tradition that the Church of Constantinople wished to impose in the relation to the emperors, and a proper procedure was seemingly established. Theophanes's account of these events, and especially Leo's letter to the patriarch in which he accepted the patriarch's authority, informing

see Theophanes, *Chronicle*, 497.28-30, who designated the Studites as 'wretched counsellors' (κακοσυμβούλοι), obviously taking the side of the patriarch and opposing the Studites.

82   Alexander, *The Patriarch Nicephorus*, pp. 99-101.

83   Cf. Theophanes, *Chronicle*, 500.10-501.3, who noted that in 813, facing the Bulgarians on the battlefield at Versinikia, the Emperor Michael I refused to step into battle against Krum, listening to 'evil councelors' (τῶν κακῶν συμβούλων) despite the readiness of two *strategoi* of the Anatolian and Macedonian themes, Leo and John, to wage battle. Theophanes then shifted his narration to the events in Constantinople, and to the incident which took place in the church of Holy Apostles, and the invocation of the Iconoclast Constantine V, who was buried there.

84   Alexander, *The Patriarch Nicephorus*, p. 123, thought that the *legend* about the Emperor Constantine V not only influenced the revival of Iconoclasm, but also that the future Emperor Leo V himself was to a great extent inspired by these stories, which were in public circulation.

him about the actions he was to take and asking for acceptance for these actions, shows a certain image of authority on behalf of the Church and patriarch and of Nikephoros's active role in the process of a peaceful shift in secular power which took place in 813.[85] It is, however, in contradiction with the description of events as displayed by Ignatios the Deacon in the *Life of Nikephoros*. The greatest and most significant difference is exactly Leo's refusal to deliver an oath to adhere to Orthodox doctrines, which Nikephoros unsuccessfully tried to oblige him to provide before his imperial coronation.[86] Ignatios offered another story, an anecdote concerning the sole act of coronation – an omen which announced to the holy patriarch the forthcoming revival of heresy – appearing from the side of the emperor himself. Nikephoros became the first confessor and martyr in the new struggle for the freedom of the Church and its Orthodoxy.[87]

How can this remarkable difference in the portrayal of the Emperor Leo V on the pages of the *Chronicle* and the *Life of Nikephoros* be explained? Theophanes, who was as much a stern icon worshiper as the repentant Ignatios the Deacon, managed to portray Leo V in a positive light, designating him as *pious* and characterizing his ascension to the throne as a result of an agreement with the patriarch Nikephoros. Ignatios the Deacon, who conversely wrote the patriarch's *Life* in a laudatory manner (beside being inclined towards a negative approach in depicting the image of the emperor by the hagiographical genre), wrote after the death of the Iconoclast emperor and after living memory of the persecution led by the emperor against the Church and the patriarch.[88] Theophanes's account should be trusted as more objective and relevant, since he was chronologically closer to the events he described – Theophanes had finished his work before he was destined to carry the weight of persecution himself for his Iconophile belief. Theodore Studites recorded a part of a dialogue which Theophanes led with the later Iconoclast patriarch John the Grammarian in the presence of the emperor, and which depicted his harsh character in a nice manner – which is also evident in the pages of his *Chronicle* concerning various heretical emperors of the Byzantine past. John the Grammarian, obviously keen for a theological debate, had asked Theophanes where Christ's divine nature

---

85 Theophanes, *Chronicle*, 502.1-503.5.

86 Cf. Codoñer, *The Emperor Theophilos*, pp. 14-20, and Brubaker and Haldon, *Byzantium in the Iconoclast Era*, p. 268 *passim*.

87 Cf. Ignatios, *Life of Nikephoros*, 164.8-19, and John Skylitzes, *Synopsis of Histories*, 15.17-20.

88 Codoñer, *The Emperor Theophilos*, p. 16: 'This version of events [e.g. by Ignatios] was probably concocted by the patriarch after his exile in order to prove Leo's duplicity and justify his initial support of the emperor.'

abided while his body lied in the grave. And Theophanes answered to him from the litter where he was laid with a vehement reply that had enraged Leo V himself, namely, that divinity abides everywhere except in the heart of the Iconoclast patriarch, since he was the enemy of God.[89]

Nikephoros's creed of Orthodox faith, which was a part of the enthronement letter to Leo III, was utilized by Ignatios the Deacon as a sort of introduction to his narration about the greatest feat of the patriarch, which was the inspiration for the *Life*. That was Nikephoros's firm stand against the Iconoclast Leo V, which as a consequence brought him persecution, and death in exile, but which brought him recognition for his victory over the imperial heresy, and therefore holiness.

In the third year of Leo V's reign, and in the tenth year of his patriarchal office, Nikephoros decided to abdicate the patriarchal throne of Constantinople due to his firm and persistent opposition to the revival of Iconoclasm promulgated by Leo V. He lived his exile first in a monastery near Constantinople, on the opposite shore of Bosporus, and some years later he moved to a more distant monastery, possibly his second monastic foundation.[90] In exile, the Patriarch Nikephoros wrote almost all his theological writings in defence of the holy icons and the Seventh Ecumenical Council.[91] Following their patriarch, many bishops and monks (being firm opponents of the 'imperial dogma') headed into exile as well. Some of them, like Theodore Studites with his monks, were resolute adversaries of the patriarch and his ecclesiastical policy, which was inspired by *oikonomia* in matters not concerning the essence of faith. In his opposition to the Iconoclasm of Leo V, Nikephoros pronounced that there should be no compromise on crucial issues – matters of dogma and the theology of icons, which substantiated the main teaching of Christ's plan for salvation through his incarnation, which can be represented and revered in images. Through his resistance towards the Iconoclast emperor, ultimately, Patriarch Nikephoros defended the authority and freedom of the Church in relation to secular imperial power.

Shortly after Nikephoros, a firm adherent of icon worship, Theophanes the Chronographer, headed into exile as well. John Scylitzes, who wrote his

---

89   Cf. the introduction to the *Chronicle* of Theophanes by Scott and Mango, p. xlvi.

90   Ignatios mentioned two monasteries which he designated as Nikephoros's foundations. The first one is the μονή τοῦ Ἀγαθοῦ, which was perhaps closer to the capital. It is possible that Ignatios was describing this monastery when narrating Nikephoros's leaving Constantinople and his return by the will of Emperor Nikephoros I in 802. Nikephoros was later transferred to the more remote monastery of the martyr Theodore, which was also his foundation. Cf. Ignatios, *Life of Nikephoros*, 201.1-7.

91   Brubaker and Haldon, *Byzantium in the Iconoclast Era*, pp. 371-372.

*History* in the second half of the eleventh century, recorded the moment of the parting of the two firm Iconophiles. In the time when the ship with the exiled patriarch passed the shores of Asia Minor, where the monastery τοῦ Ἀγροῦ was situated, whose founder and *hegumenos* was Theophanes, he followed the passing of the patriarch from a distance standing on the shore with lighted candles and incense burning. The patriarch, standing in the direction of Theophanes's monastery, replied with bowing and with the sign of blessing. The pinnacle of this remote account offered by Skylitzes is the conclusion that neither of the two men saw the other one, but, watching each other with spiritual eyes, they offered the appropriate honour to one another.[92]

This description of the mutual farewell greeting of Nikephoros and Theophanes, concerning which one cannot exclude the possibility that it was made up after the victory of Orthodoxy in the time of Empress Theodora and the Patriarch Methodios, brought the two authors into a direct relationship, in a way, while their works, each in its own specific way and in accordance with the place and personal characters of its author, present an indication of the renewal of Byzantine culture and the written word, which began with renewed strength in the second half of the ninth century.

---

92 John Skylitzes, *Synopsis of Histories*, 15.20-16.27.

# 2　The *Short History* in the Byzantine Historiographical Tradition

How can we judge Nikephoros as a historian, in the long line of Byzantine historiographical tradition? What criteria should we use in shaping of such an outlook?

The value of his *Short History* becomes clear when viewed in the context of the significant data it provides for the history of the Byzantine empire from 610 to 769. Some of the information Nikephoros presented is unique – not attested in any other source. However, such an evaluation of his work is not relevant when judging him as a historian in the context of the time when he wrote, which presents more of our subjective preferences. Thus, a more suitable question is: what kind of literary work did Nikephoros present to his contemporaries? Patriarch Photios from the late ninth century provides us with a not very contemporary glance at the *Short History*. Nevertheless, it represents the view of an important successor to Nikephoros at the patriarchal see of Constantinople and thus it demonstrates the specific ecclesiastical ideology promoted by Photios, who placed the *Short History* in the composition of his *Bibliotheca* right after his description of the *History* of Theophylact Simocatta. So, did Nikephoros have a plan to create a secular historical work that aimed to continue the last great history of the early Byzantine epoch, and did he seek to legitimize himself as a historian through such an ambition?

It has already been noted that the *Short History* started with the very same topic with which the *History* of Simocatta abruptly ended. In our opinion, this is a strong argument that Nikephoros was at least conscious of the lack of historical works, which were rarely written in Byzantium during the seventh and first half of the eighth century, and which did not reach the turn from the eighth to the ninth century. Alternatively, was his aim much simpler but more conceited – to present himself as a continuator of such historiographical and rhetorical skilfulness that even Theophylact brought to the level of bad taste? The *Short History* does not approve of such a pretension on the side of Nikephoros, but these questions raise the important issue of the place, significance, and possible influence of the *Concise Chronicle* of Trajan the Patrician, which both Theophanes and Nikephoros obviously utilized, and which appears to have been a historical work of a certain quality and value. The decision to connect himself to Theophylact Simocatta speaks strongly of Nikephoros's historiographical outlook and his historical method. This is an issue worth a more detailed assessment.

By starting his narration where Theophylact had ended, Nikephoros seems to have silently told his contemporaries about a historiographical tradition that was part of the heritage of Byzantine culture, and in a more profound and deeper way a link to the classical past, which was abruptly ended after the reign of Emperor Herakleios and which obviously had to be restored. Nikephoros's time, and especially when he wrote his history, at the end of the eighth century, was an epoch of great restoration. The Seventh Ecumenical Council had restored Orthodoxy in the Empire, and the Empire itself in the personality and acts of Eirene and Constantine VI was restored in its relation to society, the Church, and the true faith. This age of specific renewal could have included the idea of the renewal of culture as well, which was neglected by the Iconoclast emperors since Iconodule propaganda wanted to appropriate it. Thus, the renewal of history writing formed an integral part of the renewal of the Orthodox Empire. It was the Iconodules, Nikephoros of Constantinople in the first place, who managed to reconnect Byzantine historiography with the past tradition of distinguished historians and their histories. It has been suggested that the Patriarch Tarasios himself wrote historical treatises during his secular career.[1] It was as if they wished to proclaim that, after such an extended period, the Orthodox icon worshipers themselves were the ones who restored the culture of the secular written word, previously neglected by the Iconoclast emperors. For them, this great tradition was also an important medium for transmitting various ideological messages and ideas, shaping the true image of a proper state order, its *taxis*, and its relationship with the Church.

We believe that Nikephoros's desire to reconnect with Simocatta, and not with Trajan the Patrician, and to do so in a most obvious way, rested upon this understanding of a restoration of the culture of the secular written word by Orthodox icon worshipers. Trajan's *Chronicle* could not compete for acceptance as part of the great epoch of previous times since, chronologically, his work was closer to the epoch of Iconoclasm, which had to be denounced in such a way by the historians of the new Iconodule circle. Additionally, and equally importantly, Nikephoros deliberately made a new connection to the older tradition, undermining Trajan the Patrician (even if he was with great certainty an Orthodox author) by deciding to write a new continuation of Simocatta. Thus, later in the ninth century,

---

1    Treadgold, *The Middle Byzantine Historians*, pp. 22-25.

Photios placed Nikephoros as Simocatta's successor in history writing. Nevertheless, Trajan's *Chronicle* must be considered in the further evaluation of Nikephoros's historiographical method and his utilization of the historical genre.

The inclusion of the historical work of Trajan, of whom we do not know much except for the short entry in the *Suda* lexicon, actually makes it harder, rather than easier, to judge Nikephoros as a historian. The *Concise Chronicle* of Trajan remains lost and must be evaluated by the works of Nikephoros and Theophanes, who probably utilized parts of it. This remains a problematic approach involving great uncertainties and presumptions. All issues regarding Nikephoros's historiographical relationship with the work of Trajan the Patrician can only be given in a hypothetical manner. Nevertheless, it seems that Nikephoros managed to interpolate Trajan's material so that it fit the general manner of storytelling in the *Short History*, without interrupting his main levels of narration and the ideas he transmitted. These parts of the *Short History*, even if they depended on Trajan's *History*, still conform to the historical depiction of the Iconoclast era with which Nikephoros ended his work. If we accept that Nikephoros might have used Trajan's material to present the history of Justinian II's reign and that of his immediate successors, Philippikos Bardanes in the first place, then these sections of the *Short History* seem to be complementary both with the previous parts of the work – the reign of Herakleios – and some parts of the narration about the reigns of Leo III and Constantine V. In this part of Nikephoros's narration, one can find several significant references to the nature of imperial reigns that stand in relation to both the reigns of the age of Herakleios and the reigns of the Iconoclast emperors. The inactivity and passive conduct of Emperor Philippikos in the face of Bulgarian raids in the vicinity of Constantinople stands in contrast to Herakleios's *parrhesia* and his struggle for the benefit of the Roman state. While Justinian II undid the measures of his father concerning the peace and order in the Byzantine empire, the following emperors, Leo III and Constantine V, managed to settle these matters in the interest of the Roman state. In contrast, Philippikos Bardanes is portrayed as the one who convoked a synod to vindicate the Sixth Ecumenical Council and to reaffirm the Monothelite doctrine, just as Constantine V had summoned an illegitimate Iconoclast council, which could not pretend to be ecumenical by installing Iconoclasm as official imperial doctrine imposed upon the Church as well.

It is our opinion that Nikephoros did more than just paraphrase Trajan's *Chronicle*, as Warren Treadgold suggested. If we accept that he utilized

Trajan's work even for the events after Herakleios's death, which led the Empire into political strife, involving Patriarch Pyrrhos of Constantinople, we suggest that he managed to adjust his source in order to comply with his main idea that extended throughout the work. The best example would be the role of the Patriarch Pyrrhos of Constantinople in the events that ensued after Herakleios's death and the discord which broke out in the Empire with the political pretensions of Empress Martina. In Theophanes's *Chronicle*, which Treadgold suggested was written under Trajan's influence, Pyrrhos and Martina were the ones who poisoned and thus murdered Herakleios's son and first heir to the throne, Herakleios Constantine. Nikephoros gave a radically different story, namely, that the patriarch himself was a victim of the turmoil that had prevailed in Constantinople, and was thus forced to abdicate. In the overall narration of the *Short History*, this image conformed to the later depictions of patriarchal abdications of Germanos of Constantinople and of the Patriarch Constantine II (in the part of the *Short History* which was not influenced by Trajan's work).

Another example of Nikephoros's possible revision of Trajan's *Chronicle*, which attached a very different meaning to it in the *Short History*, is the portrayal of Constantine IV's peace agreement with the Bulgars. While Theophanes, who might have copied Trajan the Patrician literally, wrote that the Byzantine defeat was due to their sins (and thus a divine punishment), Nikephoros used the account of the peace to introduce the idea of the 'peace and tranquillity' that had settled throughout the Empire, both in the East and in the West. It is obvious that the two accounts derived from the same source, probably Trajan's *Chronicle*. What reveals Nikephoros's discernible rearrangement of his source material, including significant alterations to the narrative, is the story about the Sixth Ecumenical Council. While Theophanes, or rather Trajan, openly blamed the patriarchs Sergios and Pyrrhos for the introduction of Monothelitism in the Empire, Nikephoros avoided mentioning them at all, possibly hinting at their responsibility in a much-generalized manner.

| Theophanes, *Chronicle*, 359.28-33 | Nikephoros, *Short History*, § 37.1-10 |
|---|---|

| His particular concern was to unite God's holy churches which had been everywhere divided from the days of the Emperor Herakleios, his great-grandfather, and of the heretical Sergios and Pyrrhos, who had unworthily presided over the see of Constantinople and had taught one will and one energy in our Lord, God, and Saviour Jesus Christ. Being anxious to refute their evil beliefs, the same most Christian Emperor convened at Constantinople an ecumenical council of 289 bishops. | The Roman Empire being thus at peace on all sides, the impious heresy of the Monothelites (which had begun in the days of Emperor Herakleios) was gaining in strength and a schism prevailed in the Catholic church. On perceiving this, Constantine convened an ecumenical council which confirmed the five preceding ecumenical synods as well as the dogma of the two wills and two natural energies of our Lord Christ, whom it proclaimed perfect in His divinity and in His manhood while condemning to anathema the leaders of the heresy. |

| σπουδὴν ἔχων ἐξαίρετον ἐνῶσαι τὰς ἀπανταχῆ διηρημένας ἁγίας τοῦ θεοῦ ἐκκλησίας ἀπὸ τῶν χρόνων Ἡρακλείου τοῦ βασιλέως καὶ προπάππου αὐτοῦ, καὶ Σεργίου τοῦ κακόφρονος καὶ Πύρρου, τῶν ἀναξίως ἡγησαμένων τοῦ θρόνου Κωνσταντινουπόλεως, μίαν τε θέλησιν καὶ μίαν ἐνέργειαν ἐπὶ τοῦ κυρίου καὶ θεοῦ καὶ σωτῆρος ἡμῶν Ἰησοῦ Χριστοῦ δογματισάντων, ὧν τὰς κακοδοξίας ἀνατρέψαι σπουδάζων ὁ αὐτὸς χριστιανικώτατος βασιλεὺς σύνοδον οἰκουμενικὴν συναθροίσας ἐπισκόπων σπθ' ἐν Κωνσταντινουπόλει. | Οὕτω τοιγαροῦν εἰρηνευούσης πάντοθεν τῆς Ῥωμαίων βασιλείας ἡ τῶν Μονοθελητῶν δυσσεβὴς αἵρεσις ἐκρατύνετο, ἤδη τῶν ἀφ' Ἡρακλείου τοῦ βασιλέως χρόνων λαβοῦσα τὴν ἀρχήν· καὶ σχίσμα ἦν περὶ τὴν καθολικὴν ἐκκλησίαν. ταῦτα διαγνοὺς Κωνσταντῖνος σύνοδον οἰκουμενικὴν συγκροτεῖ, ἣ τὰς μὲν προλαβούσας πέντε ἁγίας οἰκουμενικὰς συνόδους ἐκύρωσε καὶ τὰ δύο ἐπὶ τοῦ σωτῆρος Χριστοῦ θελήματα καὶ δύο φυσικὰς ἐνεργείας, τέλειον αὐτὸν ἐν θεότητι καὶ τέλειον ἐν ἀνθρωπότητι διατρανώσασα καὶ τῷ ἀναθέματι τοὺς τῆς αἱρέσεως ἄρξαντας παραπέμψασα. |

Nikephoros utilized Trajan the Patrician and his *Concise Chronicle*, but nevertheless chose to create a new continuation of Theophylact Simocatta, the last great *History* of early Byzantium. Trajan the Patrician wrote a work of which we do not know the beginning, nor its end. Warren Treadgold suggested that Nikephoros utilized a partial copy of Trajan's *Chronicle*. However, more serious reasons might have induced Nikephoros to start his *Short History* where Simocatta left off. Theophylact was a prominent imperial official, familiar to the Emperor Herakleios and the Patriarch Sergios, to whom he dedicated his *Ecumenical History*, which could be a detail of particular interest for Nikephoros, clearly alluding to a parallel with the new historians of the renewed Iconodule circles of late eighth-century Constantinople. At the time when Simocatta wrote his *History*, he was a senior imperial secretary.[2] The title of his work – *Ecumenical History* – alluded to both the extensive nature of his historical narrative, and to Patriarch Sergios of Constantinople, to whom it was dedicated, who assumed the title *ecumenical* during his patriarchate. Another detail that might have been of interest to Nikephoros is the remark of Theophylact in his preface that the historiographical discipline 'was dead for a long time'.[3] This idea of a breach in continuity in history writing presented an interesting motif which might have inspired Nikephoros to create his continuation of Simocatta. In other words, to reproduce a similar renewal of historical writing at the end of the eighth century, after the 'second age' of the *death of history* had passed with the first wave of Iconoclasm, and furthermore as an additional way to build his credibility as a historian. In a more general sense of his historical plan, it is evident that Nikephoros as a historian utilized the secular historical genre for considerable and significant ideas that tightly connected to the political and ecclesiastical issues of the day.

Where does Nikephoros's *Short History* fall in the long line of Byzantine historiography? A starting point for answering this question could be the significance of Nikephoros being a part of a circle of men who recognized the value of historiography for the renewal of Byzantine culture and Orthodox

---

2    Treadgold, *The Early Byzantine Historians*, p. 332. Beside Nikephoros, who was Tarasios's subordinate during their secular careers, George Synkellos was another important figure of this group. Synkellos was close to the Patriarch Tarasios by the very nature of his position in the ecclesiastical hierarchy. His role and contribution in history writing at the beginning of the ninth century, especially as the possible author of the *Chronicle* ascribed to Theophanes, is significantly reconsidered and thus elevates him to a greater prominence at the expense of Theophanes's authorial credibility. Cf. Treadgold, 'The Life and Wider Significance of George Syncellus', but also Kompa, 'In Search of Syncellus', and Zuckerman, 'Theophanes the Confessor'.
3    Theophylact Simocatta, *History*, 24.1-5.

tradition. These men viewed the process of writing histories as a valuable tool for shaping the ideas of their own time through a specific presentation, or rather creation, of the past. Interesting references to the writing of books are present even in the hagiographies of the saints, with a most interesting example being the *Life of Stephen the Younger*, written in the early years of Nikephoros's patriarchal office, where icons, and books as well, were described as tools for elevating the mind of the viewer and reader towards the ideal prototypes they protrayed.[4] In the context of book writing and composing histories, this provides a valuable insight into understanding history writing and the significance of properly shaping of the past and its image.

As a literary work with secular features, the *Short History* has as its main narrative focus the personalities of Byzantine emperors. In a concise way, these descriptions were limited to a narrative of political processes in the Empire, centred on Constantinople. The emperor's person was usually presented in the primary narrative plan, as when Nikephoros described the peoples living in Byzantium's vicinity. In a chronological range from the year 610 to 769, fourteen emperors received mention in the *Short History* – a work much more concise than the almost-contemporary *Chronicle* of Theophanes. These portrayals are neither of equal length, nor are they alike in their literary approach. Therefore, it is possible to encounter a short description of the future Emperor Leo IV only in the last chapter of the work – in a brief passage on of his wedding with the future Empress Eirene. In contrast, it is possible to read complex and lengthy narratives describing the reigns of the two most significant imperial personalities on the pages of the *Short History*: the emperors Herakleios and Constantine V (which, in fact, constitutes almost half of the entire work).

Although primarily a secular historical work, at least in terms of its main and most obvious features, the *Short History* offers a unique description of imperial personalities when analysed with a view to the ecclesiastical and dogmatic controversies of the time, while the fundamental character of what is a politically and ecclesiastically engaged work remains hidden under the layers of its structure and manner of narration. The Iconoclastic and Monothelite controversies are dominant themes in the *Short History*.[5]

---

4    Cf. Stephen, *Life of Stephen the Younger*, 2.5-15

5    Although Iconoclasm was not a classical Christological dispute in the manner of earlier heresies such as Arianism and Monothelitism in the earlier centuries of Byzantine history, nevertheless it is our opinion that the main doctrinal problem raised by Iconoclastic theology was fundamentally a crucial problem of Christ's Incarnation, or, of the so called *oikonomia* of man's salvation according to which the incarnation of God the Son was theologically expressed,

Emperors of both epochs certainly played significant roles in these disputes, embedding them in political issues in addition to their particular ecclesiastical aspects. Within the manner in which Nikephoros represented these issues lies the core of the portrayals of Byzantine emperors in the *Short History*. Here we shall only briefly point to two examples, which we will investigate in detail in the forthcoming chapters. Namely, both Emperor Herakleios and Constantine V, each in his own time, exerted influence upon the development of key ecclesiastical events and contemporary Christological disputes. They were not, however, given equal treatment in a literary sense within the pages of the *Short History*. The Iconoclast Constantine V was portrayed according to his ecclesiastical policy towards the Church of Constantinople, and his harsh measures towards lay individuals, clerics, and monks of Iconodule disposition, which tarnished the image of the emperor.[6] Emperor Herakleios was vested in more nuanced imagery. While Herakleios significantly directed the flow of ecclesiastical events of his own time, by pushing the two confronted parties – Chalcedonians and Monophysites – towards unity, he was given a completely different image, despite his real involvement in the Monothelite dispute and his personal relations with this heresy. In fact, Nikephoros did not raise the issue of Herakleios's responsibility for the rise of the Monothelite heresy. Neither did he raise the issue of the responsibility of the two foremost advocates of Monothelitism among the Constantinopolitan high clergy – the patriarchs Sergios and Pyrrhos of Constantinople. In contrast, as we shall see, Nikephoros openly blamed Constantine V for his Iconoclasm – 'the imperial dogma', as Nikephoros identified it in the *Short History* – and his persecution of the patriarch and pious Christians. And although Nikephoros placed this blame strongly at the feet of Constantine, he did not do so concerning his father, Leo III. Indeed, he presented his image of Leo III as an Iconoclast much more

professed, and defended exactly through painting icons of the Son of God and the reverence through which the main dogma of Christian theology was affirmed. Cf. Mansi XII, 1014C, where a repentant Iconoclast bishop, Theodosios of Amorium, declared: 'the icon of the Saviour and the Theotokos should be painted foremost so that the *oikonomia* of the salvation can be accessible to all.' And Nikephoros himself, in his first *Antirrheticus* against the wicked Mammon, meaning the Emperor Constantine V, emphasized in the title of his letter the emperor's 'irreligion against the salutary [incarnation] of God Logos', later emphasizing that all Constantine's deeds 'were made from the beginning to the end in order to insult the *oikonomia* of Christ the Saviour and Christ himself in the end.' Cf. Nikephoros, *Antirrheticus* I, cols. 224D-225A.

6    This nuanced image of the emperor was given in the context of a parallel statement emphasizing the emperor's successful war against Bulgars and Arabs, together with a criticism of his Iconoclasm that was not, however, literary and ideologically developed, as in Nikephoros's later theological works.

weakly, especially regarding his relationship with the Patriarch Germanos. The same idea regarding his successor, but with stronger emphasis, was displayed through anecdotes used in the narrative to describe natural catastrophes and omens, which were literary motifs Nikephoros particularly deployed in his theological and apologetic works to portray the heretical character of Iconoclast emperors, above all Constantine V.

In relation to everything said above, a direct question arises concerning Nikephoros's perception of the past and his representation of it. This is one of the greatest issues regarding the *Short History* as a whole, which concerns the choice of the author to deal almost entirely with the distant epoch of the seventh century, while more contemporary events, like the Iconoclasm of the eighth century, received much less attention and space. If the imperial Iconoclasm of the eighth century presented an important theme for modelling the image of emperors, and likewise, Monothelitism for the emperors of the seventh century – Herakleios in particular –, then it seems that the heresy of Monothelitism did not assume a significant role in shaping the picture of the Emperor Herakleios, to whom the largest amount of attention was given. In contrast, the Monothelitism of the Emperor Philippikos Bardanes, as well as the question of the Orthodoxy of Constantine IV, were not specifically stressed in the narrative. This connects to Nikephoros's message regarding the Sixth Ecumenical Council and his parallel narrative about the relations between the Church of Constantinople and the Empire, and the idea of the authority of ecumenical councils. All this points to a different approach in Nikephoros's process of modelling the image of the emperors, his conscious and sensible use of data, and his approach to the material he drew upon while writing his work. Nikephoros wrote with a clear purpose and outlook regarding those issues which were accentuated in the *Short History* more or less explicitly.

As Nikephoros's *Short History* represents a concise work, its narration is deprived of any excessive details. This evaluation becomes more clear alongside a parallel reading of the *Chronicle* of Theophanes and an analysis of the same or similar parts in his narration, which is often more detailed in facts, and which includes the open observations of the author himself, especially regarding the religious stance of the person described (by which means the author actually professed his own doctrinal views). There are no such manners of narration in Nikephoros's work. This, however, does not mean that he was without his personal observations about certain aspects of the reigns of the emperors described, nor that his opinions are not present in his work. Instead, understanding Nikephoros's views requires an analysis of the *Short History*'s structure and narration, that is, the manner by which Nikephoros managed to deliver his stories, which again directs us towards an analysis of the amount of attention he showed towards various aspects of each imperial reign, as well as, conversely, the way in which he undermined other aspects of imperial governance. In this respect, a basic analysis shows the amount of space given to the aforementioned Herakleios and Constantine V, as well as to the rule of Justinian II, whose Orthodoxy, as it seems, was not even hinted, while other emperors, like the Orthodox Constantine IV and the Iconoclast Leo III, appear to have received only incidental or casual attention – an image which will prove to be misleading in understanding Nikephoros's historiographical method.

The absence of a classical introduction to the *Short History*, like the one encountered at the beginning of the *Chronicle* of Theophanes, leaves us without the author's explanation for the circumstances and conditions which lie in the foundation of his literary work. This would be valuable for our understanding of the motifs and approaches Nikephoros deployed in his narration about the emperors of the seventh and eighth centuries. But would this prologue, if it existed, instead lead us astray in our attempt to gain a total comprehension of Nikephoros's *Short History* and his place among the Byzantine historians of the late eighth and early ninth century, as is the case with the modern studies in Theophanes and his *Chronicle*?

Nikephoros composed a history, which is clearly indicated by its official title. In the context of genre, it would appear that his secular work stands opposite to the chronicles of George the Synkellos and Theophanes, which were composed at the same time or in the years close to Nikephoros's work. Nikephoros avoided mentioning years in dating events, which could imply that his primary intention was to write a history according to the rules of that genre, possibly in compliance with the earlier Byzantine histories. After all, he seems to have intended to connect back to the *Ecumenical History* of Theophylact Simocatta and the older tradition which it transmitted. Yet Nikephoros's *Short History* in many ways failed to answer the basic requirements of the historical genre. This has often been proposed to present the author as suffering from an inadequate education or failing to meet the demands of the genre he presumed to follow. Compared with both previous and later historical works, the *Short History* cannot compete with the high reaches of their style and narration. However, we cannot say that Nikephoros failed to utilize his sources, both in his historiographical treatment and in his making of specific imagery for the past which could be received in his own time. This inevitably brings him forth as an author who knew how to utilize the genre for his specific and subtle purposes. In this specific context, he certainly managed to follow previous historians in their treatment of the historical narrative and genre for specific political objectives. Several cases in the *Short History* clearly display such ability. For instance, both patriarchs Sergios and Pyrrhos were presented as Herakleios's 'friends' and 'brothers' and his close associates in the political events of the first decades of the seventh century, while their Monothelitism was tacitly omitted from the narrative. In this way, Nikephoros managed to create an image of the past relationships in almost perfect accord with the ideal notions of the two poles of power in Byzantium as restored in his own time by Eirene and Tarasios around 787.

Another feature of the work, which is a literary act of the author, should be considered. Namely, Nikephoros used various allusions and anecdotes with a specific literary value to stress more strongly his narratological message when he wished to promulgate a specific evaluation of the nature of a reign of a particular emperor – the Iconoclast Constantine V. It is remarkable that such literary sections are absent from the part of the *Short History* before the reign of Emperor Leo III, in the first fifty-one chapters of the work, yet is present in the remaining thirty-six chapters, which cover the reigns of the two Iconoclast emperors. This might indicate Nikephoros's specific approach in portraying the reigns of Leo III and Constantine V. Such an approach is further corroborated by an analysis of the similar use of anecdotes in connection to these emperors in his works on the theological refutations of Iconoclasm and the Iconoclast councils. Thus, through utilizing such literary techniques, Nikephoros managed to put forward a more subtle critique of the reigns of these two emperors within the pages of his historical work, pretending to follow the basic requirements of the genre.[7] Some of these scenes were given in specific chapters that either preceded or followed his account of imperial acts, while others formed part of wider narratives. In both ways, these passages found their particular place in the shaping of the overall image of emperors in the *Short History*.

---

7    Nikephoros, *Short History*, § 59: a volcanic eruption in the vicinity of the islands called Thera and Therasia, in the Aegean sea; § 62: a mention of an earthquake in Constantinople and as a consequence the destruction of many public buildings in the city, with a particular and very meaningful and suggestive mention of the destruction of Hagia Eirene in Constantinople; § 67: a description of a plague which ravaged the capital of the Empire as a consequence of Constantine V's ungodly Iconoclasm; § 69: a mention of a destructive earthquake in Syria in the context of the birth of the future Emperor Leo IV; § 71: a mention of celestial omens; § 74: a description of an unusually strong winter in Constantinople. Many of these passages can also be found in Nikephoros's theological writings and need to be evaluated in the context of his idea, both in secular and sacral contexts, of his literary heritage.

If we seek to give a final evaluation of Nikephoros's historiographical and historical outlook as displayed in his *Short History*, then we can suggest one further scheme which he managed to present. Byzantine history, from Herakleios to Eirene, developed in irregular periods of state order and the breaking of the *taxis*, which Nikephoros always tended to link to the religious issues of every period which he portrayed. Therefore, the *Short History* began with the complete disorder that had set in during the reign of Phokas, which Herakleios then ended by restoring internal order and after defeating the Persian empire. The order, however, diminished in its external political relations with the Arabs at the end of Herakleios's reign, but Nikephoros tended to minimize the unsuccessful actions of Herakleios and blamed the second occurrence of disorder which broke out in the Byzantine Empire on his immediate descendants. The peace and tranquillity of the Empire was then restored during the reign of Constantine IV, but diminished immediately during the reign of his son Justinian II and his successors. It was Leo III who restored the fallen order in the Empire and established peace with the Arabs after successfully defending Constantinople in 717. However, the responsibility for the outbreak of Iconoclasm was shifted to Leo's successor and son, Constantine V, who managed to continue the policies of his father but introduced a new disorder in ecclesiastical relations between the Empire and the Church. Ending his *Short History* with the marriage of Leo IV and Eirene, Nikephoros hinted at a new restoration of order during her successive reign, which he did not portray, but his historiographical portrayal of historical periods is clearly distinctive and, moreover, it ended with a victory of state order, which set in with the accession of the empress whose name suggests peace, both in the context of Orthodox icon worship and in her relation to the Church.

In such an approach it is evident that Nikephoros tended to use the historiographical genre to evaluate and promote the Byzantine state order of his own time as the new period of restoration of both political *taxis* and ecclesiastical Orthodoxy, contrary to the Monothelite and Iconoclast heresies which had previously prevailed in the Empire in the periods of friction and internal strife. His portrayal of the past in a historical manner produced an engaging narrative fully in the service of promoting new agendas and ideas from his own time, and from the reign of the Empress Eirene. It would appear that Nikephoros wrote almost as an independent historian, not serving the interest of the ruler of the time, but adhering more to the ideas of the circles to which he belonged during his secular career, when he was under the authority and influence of the future patriarch, Tarasios.

## The Structure of the *Short History*

The *Short History* is not a work of significant volume. It is comprised of eighty-eight chapters of various and unequal length, without any formal introduction. The narration begins with Emperor Maurice's execution and Phokas's accession to the imperial throne in 602 and ends with the story of Eirene's marriage to the Iconoclast Emperor Leo IV in 769. The structure of the work is determined by the chronological approach, to which the future Patriarch Nikephoros adhered in his narration of the history of the Byzantine Empire from Herakleios to Constantine V. In that sense, his narration is straightforward, without any attempts to review the aforementioned issues or themes, but with a significant tendency, when dealing with the Iconoclast Constantine V, to raise several issues in advance, before his main narration completely passes to the description of the reign of this emperor, and to set up the narrative of his reign by mentioning several details from his life prior to his official imperial rule, thus shaping an original image of Emperor Constantine V on the pages of the *Short History* in a specific literary way.

The structure of the work is evidently influenced by the open Iconophile bias of the author. This bias is, however, presented only in the ending parts of the work, in the narration of the reigns of the first two Iconoclast emperors, Leo III and his son Constantine V. Not a small portion of the work is dedicated to these two emperors, almost a third of its content – thirty-seven out of eighty-eight chapters.[8] The theme of icon worship is normally raised in these chapters and the arrangement of episodes where Nikephoros narrated about icons in various contexts is done accordingly in order to present a specific image of the rulers Leo III and Constantine V, although it is apparent that the main account about the first phase of Iconoclasm really begins in the part of the *Short History* where the reign of Constantine V is presented. Through ten chapters, Nikephoros presented *his* history of the first Iconoclasm, openly writing from the position of an Iconophile and criticizing this aspect of the reign of the first two emperors of the Isaurian dynasty, against which he equally stressed the motif of their successful rule in secular issues and particularly military campaigns. These two motifs, the Iconoclasm of the emperors but also their successful rules, are mutually interwoven, thus forming a complex and a specific narratological structure. A short overview of chapters where Nikephoros dealt with issues related to Constantine V's Iconoclasm or his impious actions would look as such:

8    Nikephoros, *Short History* § 52-§ 88.

§ 60 and 62 are related to the Iconoclasm of the Emperor Leo III; § 67 and 72 explicitly tell about the Iconoclasm of Constantine V; § 80 is dedicated to describing the persecutions Constantine V inflicted upon monks and all the citizens who adhered to pious life (where only incidentally it is mentioned that some of these were martyred by being hit with holy icons). In § 81, Nikephoros narrated the martyrdom of St. Stephen the Younger, which he described oddly with no connection to Iconoclasm, but in this chapter and the next (§ 82) an oath of the Patriarch Constantine II that he shall not revere icons is mentioned. § 83 gives an account of the persecution of monks, and although no connection with icon worship whatsoever is made, here and in § 84 the execution of the Patriarch Constantine II is described. Iconoclasm is mentioned for the last time in the *Short History* in connection with the Patriarch Niketas of Constantinople (§ 86). Nikephoros thus narrated the impiety of Constantine V, his persecution of monks, and the martyrdom of St. Stephen the Younger without connecting it to the issue of icon worship or placing it close in narration with the execution of the Iconoclast patriarch of Constantinople Constantine II. The emperor's Iconoclasm was mentioned explicitly only in five chapters out of the twenty-six chapters (§ 62-§ 88) dedicated to his rule.

Monothelitism, which is the second significant heresy mentioned in the *Short History* and which chronologically preceded Iconoclasm, is mentioned almost in passing. In the structure of the *Short History*, Monothelitism seems to receive a secondary value in the narratives about the first emperors described in the work, if viewed in the sense of the author's value system, which was influenced by the time when he lived and the historical context of the epoch when he wrote. Thus, Monothelitism is placed in the chronological context of Nikephoros's narrative about the government of Emperor Herakleios, and his successors, first in the reign of Constantine IV, but also in relation to the short account about the reign of Philippikos Bardanes. In comparison with the theme of Iconoclasm in the *Short History* (with two full chapters dedicated to the issues around that dispute), the two chapters and one incidental mention in the account of Patriarch Pyrrhos's forceful abdication, which were not entirely dedicated to Monothelitism but at least placed some importance in the issue, actually point to the disproportion evident in the portrayal of these two heresies in the *Short History*. It cannot be said, however, that Monothelitism in connection to *emperor-patriarch* relations in the first part of the work, and Iconoclasm in the same context in the second part of the work, lack the same ideological function on the level of the entire work. Likewise, Nikephoros displayed his own stance regarding the *emperor-patriarch* relations in both of the historical periods with which he dealt in his work – in the pre-Iconoclast era of the seventh century, and in the Iconoclast era of the second half of the eighth century.[9] It is hard to speak about a completely disproportionate description of the two heresies, even if Iconoclasm was the heresy of the day at the time when Nikephoros wrote his secular work. And this *secular* character of his work, if even formal, has to some extent influenced the structure of the *Short History* in which both theological disputes were almost casually mentioned, they maintained their role in the overall narrative and the message delivered by Nikephoros, whose connections with the Iconodule group of Tarasios were evident, as well as his family's publicly displayed Iconophile preferences.

As we shall demonstrate in the next chapters, the content of the *Short History* is divided into three parts when viewed from the perspective of the ideas implemented in the work. This is, however, just a provisional division which derives from our approach and the methodology of analysis of the work. The work is made out of the first introductory part in which twenty-seven chapters provide a history of Herakleios's lengthy reign.[10] To this part of the *Short History*, a group of ten chapters should be added in which the reigns of Herakleios's successors are narrated, ending with the Emperor Constantine IV, while the reign of Justinian II, as the last descendant of Herakleios's lineage, should be analysed with additional attention to its background in the sources and their nature (due to its specific content and the ideological context attached to it).[11]

According to the criterion of quantity and the amount of space given to the personalities, and in particular to the rulers, in the *Short History*, it would appear that the next significant section of the work, both by its length and the details embedded in the manner of narration, is the account of the reign of Justinian II. The reign of this highly controversial Byzantine emperor, as displayed in the two Byzantine sources – the *Short History* and the *Chronicle* of Theophanes – is presented in Nikephoros's work in eight long chapters.[12] These eight sections are placed in the wider context of a particular and specific idea of the author which is manifested in his

---

9    Nikephoros, *Short History*, § 62, which narrated Germanos's abdication from the patriarchal office and his successor, Patriarch Anastasios; § 72 described the Iconoclast council of 754. In the remaining chapters in which Iconoclasm was mentioned, it was embedded into a wider narrative. Thus, it cannot be said that more than two chapters were dedicated to Iconoclasm. Monothelitism also received attention in two full chapters and one mention in passing in the account of Pyrrhos's forceful abdication: § 37.1-14; § 46.1-7; § 31.28-33.

10   Nikephoros, *Short History*, § 1-27.

11   Nikephoros, *Short History*, § 28-37.

12   Nikephoros, *Short History*, 38-45.

aspiration to present both ideal and unsuccessful reigns of emperors. Thus
the chapters dedicated to Emperor Justinian II present a valuable section
of the entire work, a specific transition in the narration of the *Short History*, with Nikephoros's authorial intention to connect and highlight all
the good features of the rulers as presented in the reigns of Herakleios and
Constantine V, whose reigns stand at the opening and the ending parts
of the *Short History*. Within this section of the work, two reigns, those of
the emperors Leontios and Tiberius,[13] who ruled between Justinian's two
downfalls, and a group of emperors who reigned over the Empire prior
to Leo III's ascendancy to the throne – Philippikos Bardanes,[14] Artemios
(Anastasios II),[15] and Theodosios III[16] – should be viewed as an integral
part of this section of the *Short History*. These chapters, in fact, narrate
the downfall of imperial political organization – the idea of *taxis*, which is
present although not explicitly mentioned in work, and which leads to the
establishment of order with the reign of the first Iconoclast Emperor Leo
III. At first glance, this is odd when coming from the pen of an Iconophile
author such as Nikephoros, who later even became patriarch of the Church
of Constantinople. The third and the last part of the *Short History* is in fact
an image of the reestablishment of order in the Byzantine state, as displayed
in the reigns of Iconoclasts Leo III and his son Constantine V, who received
the most attention in Nikephoros's historical perspective of the second half
of the eighth century, with a total of twenty-five chapters,[17] which, when
compared with the twelve chapters dedicated to his predecessor Leo III,[18]
clearly indicates the essential importance of the image of Constantine's
rule for the overall message of the work. Even in the context of the author's
personal Iconophile orientation, and in his literary presentation of the first
two Iconoclast emperors Leo III and his son Constantine V, their images are
not equal in the context of the religious strife that their reigns produced.
In that sense, it can be said that Nikephoros did not depict them equally as
heretical emperors, obviously excluding Leo's reign from the true context
of Iconoclasm.

In general, a conclusion can be made that the *Short History* is, in fact, a
work which, according to its content, or rather its lack of predominantly
doctrinal matters or entire chapters dedicated exclusively to ecclesiastical

13   Nikephoros, *Short History*, § 40-§ 42.
14   Nikephoros, *Short History*, § 46-§ 48.
15   Nikephoros, *Short History*, § 48-§ 51.
16   Nikephoros, *Short History*, § 50-§ 52.
17   Nikephoros, *Short History*, § 64-§ 88.
18   Nikephoros, *Short History*, § 52-§ 63.

disputes, by far contrasts the later monastic chronicles and histories where theological disputes and polemics had a significant place. The closest example is certainly the *Chronicle* of Theophanes, in which a predominant interest towards doctrinal issues from the history of Christological disputes is evident, as is the ideological and dogmatic bias and favouritism of the author himself. Such an approach to writing a history of ecclesiastical disputes continued to flourish in later works of different literary genres as well. Such were hagiographies and theological works of a polemical nature, thus breaking out of a strictly historiographical concept, which as a consequence created an almost impenetrable and totally uniform image of events during the history of Iconoclasm as shaped by the Iconodules. Although he certainly had experience and knowledge of ecclesiastical and doctrinal matters, even familiarity with monastic practice, Nikephoros managed to write his history in a secular manner and under secular influences which had shaped his personality and his views on historiography. Nikephoros thus presented accordingly the two topics and their interrelationship – the emperors and the relationship between the emperors and the patriarchs.[19]

Nikephoros's relation and attitude towards the problems of theology and faith, Monothelitism, and Iconoclasm, especially in the context of the role which the state had (and applied in the examples of some Byzantine emperors), is ambivalent and totally different in method from Theophanes. When he wrote about the history of Christological disputes, Nikephoros was rather reserved and avoided involving himself in an open alignment with the Orthodox party – to which he belonged and to which he adhered in every particular example, including the case of Monothelitism. However, in the case of Patriarch Pyrrhos's forceful abdication, Nikephoros was almost mysterious in his open and positive attitude towards this renowned protagonist of the Monothelite heresy. This had led several researchers to a puzzling conclusion within their classic positivistic approach: the future Patriarch Nikephoros simply was not properly educated in the history of the past Christological disputes when he wrote about Pyrrhos of Constantinople. From such an approach stems the hypothesis that the *Short History* was written in Nikephoros's youth, long before his patriarchal career, and even before his secular career in the imperial administration.[20]

---

19    The levels of narration in the *Short History* can actually be multiply diverse, depending on our ability to properly apply essential questions, through which new directions of research may develop. The work itself is open to evaluation in many aspects according to the historical context of the epoch in which it was made.

20    Both assumptions concerning Pyrrhos and the dating of the *Short History* were brought by Mango, *Short History*, pp. 11-12, and Mango, 'The Breviarium', pp. 544-545. Such a hypothesis

## The Reign of Emperor Constans II (641-668): An Omitted or Encircled Historical Narrative?

Certainly one of the greatest questions, when it comes to the structure of the *Short History* and Nikephoros's historiographical approach, concerns a disruption in the narration that appears at the end of § 32, in which Nikephoros described the circumstances of succession for Herakleios's heirs, events in which the controversial Empress Martina had a significant role. Seemingly, Nikephoros continued his narration in § 33, with a short notice about the death of Emperor Constans II, but a chronological (and thus historical) gap between the years 641, which is the year of Herakleios's death, and the year 668 appears in the *Short History*. The entire reign of Herakleios's grandson, Emperor Constans II, is omitted in Nikephoros's work.

The editor of the latest critical edition of the *Short History*, C. Mango, seems not to have assumed a definite standpoint towards this problem when he stated that there is a possibility that several sheets simply fell out of Nikephoros's original manuscript, which then in such state reached its first modern researchers.[21] Mango, however, did not reject entirely the possibility that Nikephoros was forced to pass over the reign of Constans II due to a lack of historical sources for this part of Byzantium's history, which might seem plausible since Theophanes utilized only sources of near eastern origin for the same period in his *Chronicle*.[22] Mango, however, noticed the account of the meeting which took place in Africa between the abdicated Patriarch Pyrrhos of Constantinople and Maximos the Confessor and their dialogue about Monotheletism, which is present in the *Short History* – an event dating exactly to the middle of the controversial gap in narration.[23]

The only known reference to the *Short History* that originates from the time of Byzantium is the one given in a concise form by the Patriarch Photios, later in the ninth century. Photios emphasized in the very beginning that the history covered the period from after Emperor Maurice's death until the marriage of Emperor Leo IV with Eirene. Can this remark be understood

---

opens a new issue linked to the possibility that Nikephoros might have written his work under the Iconoclast regime, in the epoch of Constantine V or Leo IV, which is a significant and an interesting question especially for the last part of the *Short History*, in which the ecclesiastical aspects of Constantine V's reign were presented with a highly critical tone on behalf of the emperor's *impiety* towards the patriarch and the entire Church of Constantinople.

21   Mango, *Short History*, p. 15.

22   See the introduction to the *Chronicle* of Theophanes by Mango and Scott, pp. lxxxii-lxxxvii; cf. Howard-Johnston, *Witnesses to a World Crisis*, pp. 256-257 and 298-299.

23   Mango, *Short History*, p. 11, and Mango, 'The Breviarium', pp. 544-545.

as if the Patriarch Photios read the *Short History* in its complete form, which included the years 641 to 668 and the reign of Constans II? In other words, would Photios in his time praise the *Short History* and its author as he did in his *Bibliotheca* if there existed in its narration such a long chronological and thematic gap – an entire reign of Constans II being omitted? He eulogized Nikephoros as an author of a perfect literary style who adhered to classical role models, being somewhat concise and thus losing the complete prize, but he never mentioned the incompleteness of the *Short History*. However, the fact that Photios did not mention Theophanes's *Chronicle* at all would imply that he did not read it, and thus perhaps he did not notice the absence of the reign of Constans II in Nikephoros's work. Or rather, he did not deem it necessary to mention the absence of a historical account for the period between the years 641-668 after giving such high praise to Nikephoros's literary style.

In the introduction to the critical edition of the *Short History*, a hypothesis was suggested that one would expect the author to have challenged the lack of relevant narrative sources, if that was indeed the real reason for the gap in the historical image of Herakleios's successors, and to attempt to present a comprehensive and *finished* narrative about the strife and dynastic turmoil inside Herakleios's lineage which occurred after his death. And further, concerning the reign of Constans II, we would add that if Nikephoros did not utilize adequate narrative sources for that period, he would probably have at least tried to shape his narrative as a rounded and finished story, without leaving an impression that there existed some preceding text or content which might allude to the detailed description of Constans II's reign. However, the aforementioned section follows as such: 'Then, after a reign of twenty-seven years, Constantine [e.g. Constans II] was treacherously killed by his own servants in his bath in Sicily and so ended his life.'[24] The presence of the adverb οὖν in this short notice about the Emperor Constans II led some researchers to assume that one or several pages of Nikephoros's original work, which contained the description of this emperor's accession to the throne and his rule, at some point fell out from the codex.[25] As C. Mango already noted, such a proposal immediately asks for another question: Since the gap exists in both available copies of the *Short History*, it would follow

---

24  Nikephoros, *Short History*, § 33.1-3: 'Κωνσταντῖνος οὖν ἐν Σικελίᾳ ὑπὸ τῶν ἰδίων ὑπηρετῶν δόλῳ φονευθεὶς ἐν τῷ λουτρῷ, ἤδη ἐν τῇ βασιλείᾳ εἰκοστὸν ἔβδομον ἀνύσας ἔτος, ἐτελεύτα.'
25  For an overview cf. Mango, *Short History*, p. 15; he personally does not consider that such a strong emphasis should be placed on the adverb, which Nikephoros also used in other places throughout his work, where other writers could use instead the particle δέ.

that the barren period in Byzantium's seventh-century history existed in the manuscript from which they both originate, which at least hypothetically stemmed from Nikephoros's autograph. Such a hypothesis would imply that Nikephoros did not notice such a lacuna in his own text when finally sorting out his final draft of the *Short History*, which then reached us as it is in the two extant manuscripts of the work.[26] Such reasoning nevertheless raises doubts. Could Nikephoros fail to notice the absence of a part of his manuscript? This is a doubt which we are ready to accept as well. In contrast, C. Mango was more inclined to accept the viewpoint that Nikephoros simply did not utilize relevant historical sources for the specified period of Byzantium's history, which was a problem that Theophanes managed to overcome by utilizing sources of Syrian provenance.[27]

After this summary of previous hypotheses and assumptions connected to the section which until now was only regarded as lost, or as a lacuna in Nikephoros's narration due to the absence of relevant sources, we would suggest a different approach to the problem and in particular to the previously quoted account of Constans II's death in Sicily. This will be done solely in the context of its narratological connection to the preceding § 32, and, in a wider sense, in the context of Nikephoros's narration about the events which ensued after Herakleios's death (§ 28-§ 32).

In connection with the problem of the structure of the *Short History*, and the narratological lacuna, we will suggest a hypothesis that Nikephoros did not lose the pages dedicated to the history of Constans's reign, nor did he pass over it due to a lack of sources. His specific narration in § 28 to § 33 is in fact connected with his specific idea in presenting the disorder in the Byzantine state that ensued after Herakleios's death due to the imperial ambitions of his *unlawful* wife, Empress Martina. In that sense all that was written by Nikephoros has in fact a strong meaning and carries a specific idea, which might have surpassed the lack of information regarding the details of Constans II's reign. In regard to the assumption that the narration in § 32 ends, as C. Mango concluded, *in media res* – without specific mention of Empress Martina's final downfall and Constans II's final accession to the imperial throne – we will try to show that in fact we are dealing with a finished narrative which fits into a wider idea of state order which Nikephoros

---

26   Cf. Mango, *Short History*, p. 15.

27   Howard-Johnston, *Witnesses to a World Crisis*, pp. 298-299, is inclined towards such an interpretation of the problem, while Treadgold, 'Trajan the Patrician, Nicephorus, and Theophanes', p. 595 and further pp. 607-608 had expressed a more nuanced assumption that both Nikephoros and Theophanes utilized the same source, but probably Theophanes had at his disposal a more complete version which Nikephoros was not able to consult.

developed throughout his work. Therefore, Nikephoros seemingly did not finish his account of the political turmoil and struggle for power which ensued after Herakleios's death, which occurred as a consequence of the political aspirations of Empress Martina and her striving to secure imperial power for her sons. In that sense, Nikephoros at least seemingly did not finish his narration, not mentioning that Empress Martina and her son, Heraklona, were finally overthrown from power and that Herakleios's descendant from his marriage with the lawful Empress Eudokia, his grandson – the future Constans II – assumed power by being designated to the imperial throne, as Theophanes mentioned in his *Chronicle*.[28]

Nikephoros certainly knew that Constans II ruled the Empire, since he mentioned a plot against him in Sicily, and since he provided chronological information about the length of his reign, which by itself indicates that he utilized some source for his reign, but in which state we do not know. However, he did not mention Constans's accession to power, or at least not explicitly, leaving contemporary researchers under the impression that either he did not have sources or that several pages of his manuscript fell out of the codex. Is such reasoning, however, appropriate, since it derives from our personal preconceptions about what should be the author's logical literary and historical procedure, and what kind of an end to his narration he should have provided? Nikephoros, in fact, had a different intention in this part of his work. When he narrated the unstable period filled with conflict inside Herakleios's family, he intended to finish a specific section of narration which was started in § 28, in which the image of Empress Martina is dominant but from a negative aspect – in the context of her immoral marriage with Herakleios. Due to this, Nikephoros presented the struggle of Herakleios's lawful descendants of Eudokia to keep their legal right to rule the Empire in the aforementioned chapters. A survey of this § 28 and the following three chapters, finishing with § 31, would follow as such:

–   In § 28 Nikephoros narrated Empress Martina's efforts to secure imperial power for herself and her sons, in the presence of the Patriarch Pyrrhos and court officials, before the citizens of Constantinople. The gathered citizens refuted Martina's imperial pretensions, and they demanded that Herakleios the New Constantine – Herakleios's first son – be elected emperor. In this chapter, a narrative about the forthcoming disorder and political turbulences in Constantinople, in the imperial family and in the Church of Constantinople, began.

28  Theophanes, *Chronicle*, 341.24-28.

The initiative came from Martina. It is significant that Nikephoros mentioned the patriarch in this political context. A plot, which had its beginning set in this chapter, developed in the next one.

– § 29 narrated that Herakleios's first son, Herakleios Constantine, took imperial power. Since the emperor was ill, and his death was expected, but fearing that Empress Martina would do him harm, Philagrios, imperial treasurer, admonished the emperor to announce to the army that his death was approaching and that the soldiers should help his own children not to be excluded from imperial power (e.g. the grandchildren of Herakleios and Empress Eudokia). Among the sons of Herakleios Constantine were the future Emperor Constans II and his brother, Caesar David – Tiberius. The emperor accepted the counsel of Philagrios and confided the task to the general Valentinos, who instructed the army to oppose Martina and her children after the emperor's death. The emperor then died. Empress Martina was already presented in this narrative as a person who might threaten the order which had been introduced in the Empire with the legitimate accession to the imperial throne of the late Emperor Herakleios Constantine. The emperor's descendants should further keep such order with the proper successions at the imperial throne. Such a narrative which Nikephoros built in these chapters obviously carries the idea of the legitimacy of the descendants of Eudokia, contrary to those of Herakleios's second wife, Martina. However, in the next chapter, just the opposite happened, and the order which was established by the imperial rule of Herakleios Constantine became endangered. In this way, the narration which Nikephoros built around the events after Herakleios's death implied that the original balance (which was embedded in the idea that only the older branch of Herakleios's dynasty, which proceeded from his marriage to Eudokia, had the right to rule over the Empire) was now disturbed and the entire forthcoming narration was directed towards the reestablishment of the disrupted order, which culminated in § 32, which has been regarded as unfinished until now.

– § 30 narrated the proclamation of Martina's son Heraklonas as emperor, a dignity which he shared with his mother. Philagrios and his close associates were banished from Constantinople. The result was a rebellion of the army under Valentinos against Martina and her son. In the presence of Pyrrhos, Emperor Heraklonas, son of Martina, gave an oath that the children of the late Emperor Herakleios Constantine would not be hurt in any way. However, he also revealed that Valentinos was attempting to usurp imperial power, and the citizens of Constantinople cursed Valentinos. On a narratological level, here and in the next chapter, the disturbance of order as described in this part of the work reached its peak. The son of Empress Eudokia, Herakleios Constantine, together with Philagrios and Valentinos, tried to secure the imperial power. Martina, however, managed to usurp the throne after Herakleios Constantine's death, and thus caused a rebellion of the army under general Valentinos, which had the instructions of the former emperor to prevent such events and to safeguard the sovereignty of Herakleios's and Eudokia's lineage. Nevertheless, disorder was introduced in Constantinople, and consequently in the Empire.

–   In § 31, Patriarch Pyrrhos stepped to the forefront. It should be kept in mind that Pyrrhos was previously presented as the one who was involved in the political turmoil that occurred in Constantinople after Emperor Herakleios Constantine died and Empress Martina ascended the throne. At the same time, the citizens of Constantinople began to express disapproval, since the rebellious army of Valentinos ravaged their vineyards around Chalcedon. They demanded that the son of the late Emperor Herakleios Constantine – the future Constans II – be crowned. In that sense, they pressured the patriarch. The future Constans II (mentioned simply as Constantine) received the crown from Pyrrhos. Thus, the initial idea about the primacy of Eudokia's descendants was renewed in the narrative, and the order in the state was also partially restored by such a political outcome. However, in the further course of this narrative, the patriarch was forced to abdicate, an account which plays a significant role in Nikephoros's overall approach to shaping an image of the patriarchs mentioned in the *Short History*. However, in the framework of the entire analysis of § 28 to § 32 and of the characteristically concise account of Constans II's reign, the description of Pyrrhos's forced abdication introduced an additional narratological context. Namely, the peace which was established in the capital with Constans II's imperial coronation was not completely restored, since the patriarch had left Constantinople, and the Church remained without its first hierarch. The next chapter has a crucial role in the overall analysis of this entire section of the *Short History*, in the sense that it completed the entire narrative about the history of the Empire, here reduced to the events which were happening in Constantinople and its surroundings. It also led to order, and in context of the narrative it brought the story to its logical ending, with all things set to their proper and original balance.

- § 32 narrated the attempts by Empress Martina and her son Heraklona to achieve an agreement with Valentinos, who was still in the vicinity of Chalcedon and still ravaging the properties of the Constantinopolitans. Valentinos then received the dignity of *comes excubitorum*, while his soldiers received financial revenues. The second son of the late Emperor Herakleios Constantine – Cesar David, Eudokia's grandson – was crowned and renamed Tiberius. He obviously received the recognition of his imperial rights and dignity, which was expressed by his new imperial name (which was a part of the Roman imperial tradition), and, finally, the new patriarch was elected. Nikephoros concisely tells us that it was the former *oikonomos*, Paul of Hagia Sophia – who was also a Monothelite (a detail not mentioned by Nikephoros). In this way, an entire narrative about the eruption of disorder caused by Empress Martina was finished and completed in § 32. The rebellion which had resulted from the clash between the two lineages of Herakleios was calmed, and all the individuals who were of importance received their rounded treatment in the narration: first of all, imperial rights and imperial dignities of Herakleios's son Herakleios Constantine and his children were restored and preserved. Constans II was crowned emperor, while the other son, David, was proclaimed emperor as well and assumed the imperial name Tiberius. Moreover, the disarray, which affected the Church of Constantinople, when the patriarch abdicated and left the capital, was resolved as well, by the election of the new Monothelite patriarch Paul the *oikonomos*. By mentioning the affirmation of the imperial rights of Herakleios's lineage through Empress Eudokia, which culminated in § 32, not only did Nikephoros manage to close his entire account which began in § 28, but he also succeeded in stressing that Martina and her sons were finally removed from their participation in imperial power and governance over the Empire. Nikephoros obviously mentioned that Herakleios, son of Herakleios Constantine, the future Constans II (here in the *Short History* simply mentioned as Constantine), was in fact crowned as emperor. However, he did not mention this event in § 32 of his work, where C. Mango would have expected it, but in the previous § 31. Mango's remark that it is odd that Nikephoros did not mention Constans II assuming power is contradicted by this detail about Constans's imperial coronation by the Patriarch Pyrrhos in the account of Empress Martina's attempt to secure imperial power for her own lineage. In addition, another detail in Nikephoros's work implies that the author had such a viewpoint regarding the rulership of the emperor, namely that he considered that the emperor's rule began when he received his imperial consecration. Nikephoros said in § 29 that Emperor Herakleios Constantine ruled twenty-eight years, together with his father, Emperor Herakleios, that is, he was his father's co-ruler but not an independent ruler in full extent.[29]

J. Ljubarskij identified a similar literary technique in the *Chronicle* of Theophanes. He explained such a mode of narrativity as a narration which begins with the disturbing of the equilibrium, which is further directed towards the building of a narrative, or rather a plot which is finally resolved by restoring the equilibrium, thus forming a specific narratological circle through which the author presents his story.[30] Thus, Nikephoros did not remain partial or even concise. His narration in § 32 ended abruptly only seemingly, and only when viewed through our notion regarding the issue of how the material should be organized with its literary structure and displayed. Based on an overall presentation of the whole event, it is evident that Nikephoros chose a different narrative path in the literary shaping of his material, which he had at his disposal. Nikephoros had the main objective to highlight the history of Herakleios's lineage which proceeded from his marriage with the lawful Empress Eudokia, opposed to Empress Martina, which was an ambition he successfully managed to fulfil. A description of Martina's final downfall was not essential for such an account, since the obvious favouring of the history of Eudokia's lineage was more significant, and this was completely presented in an overall picture, in § 28 to § 32.

In light of such considerations, it remains for us to conclude the concise account of the reign of Emperor Constans II. The end of his reign was presented in § 33. However, here we read that he ruled twenty-seven years, which implies that there existed some kind of narrative source which Nikephoros had at his disposal. Nevertheless, what remained unnoticed until now, or was not considered as significant in the analysis of the image of this emperor in the *Short History*, is the mention of his coronation in § 31. It seems that Nikephoros managed to identify chronological boundaries and events which marked the beginning and the end of Constans II's rule – his

---

29   Nikephoros utilized here (and later) a Greek term, συμβασιλεύσας, stating that he was *remaining*, or literally *living*, in *imperial dignity* (καὶ ἐπιβιοὺς εἰς τήν βασιλείαν) another one hundred and three days. Cf. Nikephoros, *Short History*, § 29, 24-26.
30   Ljubarskij, 'Concerning the Literary Techniques', p. 320.

coronation and his assassination. To this Nikephoros added chronological information about the length of his rule and an accurate account of his downfall, which he placed in a geographical and spatial context of the region and location where this emperor was murdered. Compared with the description of later emperors Leontios, Tiberius Apsimar, and Theodosios III, Nikephoros offered a significantly detailed image of Constans II.

At first glance, a sudden disruption in the narration in § 32, when analysed in a broader narratological context, is rather an encircled image of a specific account about the events which ensued in 641 after Herakleios's death. In contrast, Nikephoros told us about Constans II as much as it was at his disposal in his sources. After all, the account of the eight-year reign of Emperor Phokas, which stands at the very beginning of the *Short History*, was reduced to a few remarks about his rise to power after the murder of Emperor Maurice, and to the account of his downfall during Herakleios's revolt in 610.

## Dating the *Short History*

The question of when Nikephoros wrote the *Short History* is of great importance for a proper understanding of its content and the message it carries in its narration. It is our opinion that a fitting analysis of this work can be successful only if is based on the study of the author and of the *Short History* itself within the wider historical context of the time when Nikephoros wrote his work. An overall judgement of the work certainly has a different weight depending on whether Nikephoros wrote his work as a patriarch of the Church of Constantinople, or as a lay person. If the work appeared under the pen of a state official, then we need to know the particular phase of his secular career during which Nikephoros wrote, since various cultural, ecclesiastical, and political processes were mutually interlaced and, as such, influenced the character of the author and his historical work.

All previous analyses and attempts at the dating of the work were justifiably based on the analysis of the *Short History*. Thus, Bury suggested that the work was written before the year 796, that is when Pannonia was under Avar rule, since this was mentioned in the work itself.[31] Some, like Ohnsorge and Speck, took the words of critique towards Empress Martina by the citizens of Constantinople (that it is not proper for a woman to rule the Empire) as a projection from Nikephoros's own time and as an allusion to the possible

---

31    Bury, *A History of the Later Roman Empire*, p. 450, n. 1, (cf. Nikephoros, *Short History*, 35.17-18).

feelings of Constantinopolitans towards Empress Eirene, thus suggesting that the work might have been written after the year 790.[32]

In the introduction to his critical edition, C. Mango had offered a detailed review of the different propositions for solving the problem of the dating of the *Short History* with a remark that there does not exist evidence to conclusively answer the question. Mango suggested several phases in Nikephoros's life as the possible time when the *Short History* might have been written. These were the time of Nikephoros's secular office in the state apparatus of the Empire, between 780 and 797, or possibly after his withdrawal from the capital to the opposite shore of the Bosporus between 797 and 802, when he returned to Constantinople, or perhaps when he held the office of *ptochotrophos* and administered the greatest poorhouse in Constantinople, from 802 to 806. Mango assigned the lowest possibility to the period after the year 815 and Nikephoros's exile from the Patriarchate, and certainly not during his patriarchal office between 806 and 815.[33] C. Mango concluded that the *Short History* was most probably 'an *oeuvre de jeunesse*', datable to the 780s, since he noted Nikephoros's positive attitude towards the heretical Monothelite patriarch Pyrrhos of Constantinople, which is evident in his work. In this regard, Mango suggested that Nikephoros the layman obviously was not familiar with the past of the Constantinopolitan church and the heretical views of Pyrrhos, which then opened the possibility for Pyrrhos to enter the *Short History* as a positive character, contrary to his negative image in the *Chronicle* of Theophanes.[34]

While writing his history, Nikephoros adopted the style and literary characteristics of the historical genre, which then influenced him as a writer to take an unbiased attitude, which obviously contributed to the lack of any explicit expressions which might by their presence in the text contribute to a closer dating of his work. A critical overview of several distinctive pieces of information given by Ignatios the Deacon, judged in their value by the striking similarity with the later appraisal of the *Short History* and Nikephoros by the Patriarch Photios, seems to contribute to some extent to defining a

---

32   Cf. Nikephoros, *Short History*, § 28.1-18; Ohnsorge, *Konstantinopel*, pp. 57-58; Speck, *Kaiser Konstantin VIII*, p. 638, n. 233; Mango, *Short History*, p. 8; and Tinnefeld, *Kategorien der Kaiserkritik*, p. 57.

33   Mango, *Short History*, pp. 8-12. Alexander, *The Patriarch Nicephorus*, p. 162, preferred the year 787 or earlier as the date when the work was written, since Nikephoros seemed to be unaware of the revival of Orthodox icon worship at the Seventh Ecumenical Council.

34   Mango, *Short History*, pp. 11-12; Mango, 'The Breviarium', pp. 544-545. Treadgold, *The Middle Byzantine Historians*, p. 27, argued for the year 790, adopting Mango's conclusions regarding the work.

somewhat closer time span in which the work might have been written. The fact that the hagiographer himself was a slightly younger contemporary of the patriarch, and that he probably even started his own ecclesiastical career during the patriarchal office of Nikephoros, directs us to the assumption that the two instances when the patriarch's education and his secular writings were mentioned in the *Life* are actually traces of historical truth which might contribute to the attempt to identify the time when the *Short History* was written.[35] It was C. Mango who already noted that, in the introductory part of the *Life of Nikephoros*, Ignatios the Deacon called himself a 'son' of the late patriarch, and that the entire *Life* indicates a personal awareness of the author to the events which had forced the patriarch to abdicate in 815.[36]

The first piece of information presented in Nikephoros's *Life* by Ignatios which directs us to a closer dating of his *Short History* is the narrative about Nikephoros's withdrawal from the capital to the opposite shore of Bosporus and the description of the monastic life which he lived there, during which Nikephoros also found time for his secular studies. Thus this seems to be a valuable account which raises several questions, among which the most crucial is the issue of Nikephoros's absence from the capital and the reasons which led to this event, which is again connected to the problem of the dating of his *Short History*. Namely, feeling a mystical appeal towards ascetic life dedicated only to God, Nikephoros left the capital and its turmoil, settling himself on the Asian side of Bosporus, which was harsh for life:

> Then he appointed the place a monastery of holy men, [dedicated] to the unceasing praise of the Almighty. Together with them, he himself persisted day and night in prayerful and holy speech and in taking delight in a most excellent degree of temperate conduct. For he devoted himself to reading the Scriptures and to [secular] studies [...].[37] But since I have mentioned his studies, I consider it without neither charm nor a redundant digression also to remark upon both his exactitude and his

---

35   Cf. Pratsch, 'Ignatios the Deacon', pp. 89-94, for the hypothesis that Ignatios the Deacon actually started his career in the Church of Constantinople during Nikephoros's patriarchal office.

36   See Mango's comments on the *Correspondence* of Ignatios the Deacon, p. 23, n. 92 (cf. Ignatios, *Life of Nikephoros*, 140.5-8). For the character and literary features of Nikephoros's *Life* by Ignatios, see Efthymiadis, 'On the Hagiographical Work of Ignatius', p. 80.

37   Ignatios, *Life of Nikephoros*, 148.25-30: 'τοιγαροῦν σεμνεῖον ἱερῶν ἀνδρῶν τὸν χῶρον διώρισε πρός, ἄληκτον ὑμνολογίαν τοῦ κρείττονος, μεθ᾽ ὧν καὶ αὐτὸς ἀδιαστάτως νύκτωρ τε καὶ μεθ᾽ ἡμέραν ταῖς εὐκτικαῖς ἱερολογίαις ἐγκαρτερῶν καὶ τῷ ἀρίστῳ μέτρῳ τῆς ἐγκρατείας κατεντρυφῶν τῇ ἀναγνώσει τῶν θείων προσεῖχε καὶ τοῖς μαθήμασι, τράπεζαν.'

excellence in these matters. For as well as studying Holy Scripture, he also acquired familiarity with secular – τὴν θύραθην [rhetorical education], partly out of a desire to expose the implausibility of [heretical] error.[38]

Although these words could have the features of a *topos* and of a commonplace characteristic of the hagiographical literary style, in their essence they possibly transmit a trace of historical truth. This passage provides a basis for the presumption that Nikephoros, after he left Constantinople, among other things, began his task of preparing or even writing his history which, by its content, structure, and manner of narration, was directed towards exposing the Iconoclast error in the reigns of the emperors Leo III and Constantine V.

Judging the position of this passage in the structure of the hagiography, which appears right after the narration about Nikephoros's participation at the Seventh Ecumenical Council, we could conclude that his withdrawal took place after the Council in 787, which may have influenced Nikephoros to disregard his secular career and to turn to a life of contemplation, mimicking the monastic way of life. Alternatively, if we are to view these motifs in their correlation to the political events of the day, the strife between Eirene and her son Constantine VI and his final downfall might point to the year 790 as the moment when Nikephoros left the capital, and consequently began his work on the *Short History*.

The second passage, which could be designated as somewhat more explicit, although still an indirect hint, refers to the already quoted story about the election of Nikephoros to the office of patriarch, after Tarasios's death in 806. Namely, after he had described the diversity in attitudes among lay clergy, monks, and the members of the senate, and while each one of them was proposing his own candidate, Ignatios narrated that the emperor, bearing in mind all the virtues of Nikephoros, managed to persuade the multitude of those taking part in the election to one-mindedly accept Nikephoros as the new patriarch: 'Recalling [to them] the glorious accomplishments of his virtues, his crucial [contribution] in both spiritual and secular writings, his humble and gentle character, and his purity of conscience, void of offence toward anyone.'[39]

---

38  Ignatios, *Life of Nikephoros*, 149.3-7: 'Ἀλλ' ἐπειδὴ μαθημάτων ἐμνήσθην, οὐκ ἄχαρι οὔτε μὴν παρέλκον ἡγοῦμαι καὶ τῆς περὶ ταῦτα τοῦ ἀνδρὸς ἐπιμνησθῆναι ἀκριβείας τε καὶ ἀκρότητος. πρὸς γὰρ τῇ τῶν θείων λογίων μελέτῃ καὶ τὴν τῆς θύραθεν (παιδείας) εἰσεποιήσατο μέθεξιν· τῇ μὲν τὸ ἐν διδαχαῖς καταπλουτίσαι θέλων πειθήνιον, τῇ δὲ τὸ τῆς πλάνης διελέγχειν ἀπίσθανον.'
39  Ignatios, *Life of Nikephoros*, 154, 11-16.

The explicit mention of 'secular writings' as part of Nikephoros's oeuvre is valuable for the evaluation of the problem connected with the dating of the *Short History* – the only known secular work of the future patriarch. In favour of the proposed view about the significance of the 'secular writings' is the fact that this is the only known 'virtue' of such kind placed within the narrative clearly in order to provide additional praise for the person who was to become a patriarch, obviously with the author's message that *secular* excellence was not in contradiction to Nikephoros's spiritual virtues. However, caution should be taken because the plural utilized in the account of Ignatios points to several of Nikephoros's secular works. Since Nikephoros is also credited with writing the so-called *Short Chronicle*, although this work appears as an anonymous text in its two later copies. This additional work, a world chronicle attributed to Nikephoros, may have been written at the same time or close to the period when the *Short History* was written, in order to supplement it with additional historical material and a chronology for the period of Byzantine history which it covered.[40]

The explicit reference to 'spiritual writings', parallel with and corresponding to the secular ones – 'in writings, spiritual as well as secular' (τὸ ἐν λόγοις, τοῖς τε πνευματικοῖς καὶ τοῖς θύραθεν) – might seem to instil uncertainty or doubt about the value of such a passage, since all known theological writings by Nikephoros were written in the later part of his patriarchal office or even during his life in exile. Yet in this place in the *Life of Nikephoros*, the passage might have a literary value but might also carry a subtle message or understanding of the *Short History* itself, if it is viewed in the context of the Iconophile ecclesiology and the manner of representing Byzantine emperors and patriarchs of the past. In that context, it would seem that Ignatios, a follower of both patriarchs, Tarasios and Nikephoros, was aware of their ecclesiological stances in relation to the Empire, and the idea and ideology of such features which Nikephoros managed to embed in his secular work (and basically impose a specific ecclesiastic idea and a message through the genre of history). The *Life of Nikephoros* by Ignatios was specifically focused on glorifying Nikephoros's struggle for Orthodoxy during the second outbreak of Iconoclasm, but it also sought to re-establish the author himself in the Orthodoxy of the Constantinopolitan church as proclaimed in 843. It was a means of distancing himself from his own Iconoclastic past. The 'spiritual writings' mentioned in Nikephoros's *Life* have a deep and profound meaning, both in a strictly literary sense, in relation to the hagiographical genre of the work, but also a practical

40  Mango, *Short History*, p. 4.

one, which might be viewed through the prism of ecclesiastical relations with the Roman church and the dispute which existed between the two sees in regard to the issue of the primacy of Rome and the autocephaly of Constantinople. Such was Pope Hadrian's negative stance towards Tarasios's assumption of the patriarchal dignity directly from his secular office, which the Roman Pontiff tended to view as contrary to common canonical practice, as well as his appropriation of the title 'ecumenical patriarch'. In that sense, the spiritual writings of the *future* Patriarch Nikephoros had to be mentioned in his *Life*. Moreover, another possible explanation for why this argumentation was embedded in the narrative about those virtues of Nikephoros which recommended him for the patriarchal office might be offered, one that connects to the time when the *Life* was written, and to the person who commissioned its writing. Namely, at the time of Methodios's patriarchal office, when he also struggled against the opposition of the Studites towards the official ecclesiastical authority of the higher clergy, the patriarch in particular deemed it worthy and necessary to translate the relics of Nikephoros back to Constantinople – an ideological act which also aimed to crush the firm opposition of the Studites, which was weakened after Theodore's death.[41]

This might then be a proper place to point to and analyse the two corresponding accounts by Ignatios and Photios concerning Nikephoros's *Short History*, in which the first mentioned Nikephoros's literary style in general, and the second spoke admirably of the *Short History*, leaving a concise remark regarding Nikephoros's literary style. Namely, in the *Bibliotheca* of Photios, the *Short History* is the only literary work of Patriarch Nikephoros that was mentioned, and here we shall point to this interesting fact that Photios did not mention Nikephoros's apologetic and theological works, but rather preferred to speak about his secular work. The learned patriarch said that he read the *Short History* and he praised its literary qualities – its clearness of phrase. According to Photios, Patriarch Nikephoros adhered to classical models, since he was perfect and skilful in rhetoric. His narration is characterized by simplicity and the clearness of speech, while his storytelling is eloquent, neither too lengthy nor too concise:

41    As we have already mentioned, at the time of Photios, the ecumenical authority of the former patriarchs Tarasios and Nikephoros became so important that their successor on the patriarchal see of Constantinople called upon and pointed towards their example in his own dispute with Pope Nicolas I, when the issue of Photios's uncanonical consecration to the patriarchate as a lay person was raised.

It is of simple and clear speech, devoid of everything superfluous, and by its gentleness in speech and in the structure of narration nor is it long-winded or too brief. But if it was necessary he would appear indeed as a man perfect and skilful in speech. Namely, he avoids innovation and completely adheres to the old customs. Additionally, he unites pleasure with the splendour of narration. And he would have completely surpassed the historical works of his predecessors if he was not too much concise, thus losing the full prize.[42]

Ignatios spoke in a very similar manner about Nikephoros's education, that Nikephoros was a great authority in grammar, distinguishing correct from incorrect writing, bringing into a harmonious order all the metrical elements of the Greek language. Nikephoros gained a reputation for a 'sweet and gracious speech by steadfastly rejecting the affected and verbose style', concluding that he used 'a sweet and graceful style'.[43] If we compare Ignatios's portrayal of Nikephoros's literary style with the remark left later by Photios, we can easily see that both authors praise the future patriarch's rhetorical skill in a similar way, his temperance in speech, and clearness of narration, as well as his devotion to classical literary models. The only difference in these two accounts is that Photios mentioned the *Short History* when speaking about Nikephoros's literary skilfulness, while Ignatios, adhering to the hagiographical genre of his work, avoided mentioning the *Short History* by name, of which he certainly knew (and perhaps even read) before writing the patriarch's *Life* after 843.

The two reports found in the *Life of Nikephoros* by Ignatios can be viewed in terms of their interconnections. The first remark that Nikephoros devoted himself to secular studies in his monastic foundation can be understood as an indirect hint about the time when he may have committed himself to writing the *Short History*. Since we do not have a precise date when Nikephoros renounced his secular career, but since his role as an imperial

---

42  Photius, *Bibliotheca*, cod. 66, 99: Ἀνεγνώσθη ἱστορικὸν σύντομον Νικηφόρου τοῦ ἐν ἁγίοις Κωνσταντινουπόλεως ἀρχιερέως. ἄρχεται ἀπὸ τῆς ἀναιρέσεως Μαυρικίου καὶ κάτεισι μέχρι τῆς εἰς γάμον κοινωνίας Λέοντος καὶ Εἰρήνης. ἔστι δὲ τὴν φράσιν ἀπέριττός τε καὶ σαφής, καλλιλεξίᾳ τε καὶ συνθήκῃ λόγου οὔτε λελυμένῃ οὔτε αὖ πάλιν συμπεπιεσμένῃ περιέργως κεχρημένος, ἀλλ' οἵᾳ ἂν χρήσαιτο ὁ ῥητορικὸς ὡς ἀληθῶς καὶ τέλειος ἀνήρ· τό τε γὰρ νεωτεροποιὸν ἐκκλίνει, καὶ τὸ ἀρχαιότροπον καὶ ἐξησκημένον οὐ παρατρέχει. ἔτι δὲ καὶ ἡδονὴ κέκραται αὐτοῦ σὺν χάριτι τοῖς λόγοις. Καὶ ὅλως πολλοὺς ἔστι τῶν πρὸ αὐτοῦ ἀποκρυπτόμενος τῇδε τῆς ἱστορίας τῇ συγγραφῇ, εἰ μὴ τῳ τὸ λίαν συντετμημένον οὐχ ὁλόκληρον δόξει διαπεραίνειν τὴν χάριν.' For the characteristics of Photios's literary theory, see Afinogenov, 'Patriarch Photius'.

43  Ignatios, *Life of Nikephoros*, 149.16-26.

secretary and imperial envoy to the Seventh Ecumenical Council is well attested, the year 787 or several years after might serve as a *terminus post quem* for the writing of the *Short History*. Or, if we are to accept the presumptions of some earlier researchers that the conflict between the Empress Eirene and her son Constantine VI was the true reason why Nikephoros left Constantinople – allusions to which might exist in the very *Life of Nikephoros*, in which his hagiographer compared Nikephoros to the prophet Elijah, who was forced to escape the wrath of the impious Jezebel – then the year 797 could present the starting chronological entry for dating the *Short History*. In connection to this is the other account, according to which the Emperor Nikephoros I had in mind Nikephoros's secular writings as virtues which brought this notable Constantinopolitan, former imperial *asekretis*, and later ascetic and *ptochotrophos*, to the attention of the *basileus*. Thus we obtain the year 806 as the *terminus ante quem* for the writing of the *Short History*.

The years between 787/797 and 806 were a critical time in which the Church of Constantinople, after the first phase of Iconoclasm, made every effort to revive its influence and status in Byzantine society, mostly in relation to imperial power. For Nikephoros himself, and his contemporaries as well, the *Short History* had a far more complex role, transmitting on a narratological level specific and significant messages and ideas, which were linked to the ecclesiastical and political issues of the day. It is precisely toward such aspects of the *Short History* that we wish to turn our attention in further research of the work and its author.

## 3  Herakleios: Model of an Emperor

### Setting a Pattern

In the year 614, the Persian king Chosroes II sent an army against the Romans under the command of Shahin, who after capturing Jerusalem proceeded to raid imperial territories in Egypt and then returned closer to Constantinople, besieging Chalcedon in 615.[1] Nikephoros illustrated in his *Short History* the total disorder which had settled in the Byzantine Empire as a result of the Persian raids. He then proceeds to narrate a meeting between Herakleios and the Persian general near Chalcedon, and it is in this scene that Shahin delivered a specific oration, emphasizing several crucial points which established a specific idea of *peace* that subtly dominated the entire narrative of the *Short History*.[2] This oration brought to the forefront specific ideas. The Persian promoted 'friendship and concord' (φιλία καὶ σύμβασις) promoting these ideals in the presence of Herakleios, stressing that these virtues were opposed to 'mutual hostility' and 'enmity' (μήτε διίστασθαι ταῖς γνώμαις μηδ' ὁπωστιοῦν ἀλλήλοις ἀντικαθίστασθαι).[3] Further, 'good mutual relations and friendship' (εὔνοια καὶ φιλία) were achieved by 'wisdom and prudence' (ἐπιφροσύνη καὶ εὐβουλία). As opposed to these virtues stood the

---

1    For a survey of literature and relevant historical sources for the period, see Haldon, *Byzantium in the Seventh Century*, pp. 42-45; Reinink and Stolte, *The Reign of Heraclius*.

2    See Howard-Johnston, *Witnesses to a World Crisis*, pp. 244-250, who tended to view this section of the *Short History* as a separate unit, opposed to the rest of the work, in which he identified one additional part that covered the late seventh and the early eighth centuries (ending with the year 717) and corresponded to the description of the period of the fall of the internal organization of the Empire and the crumbling of the order/*taxis* as it was narrated in the *Short History*. However, all this Howard-Johnston hypothesized in the context of those sources which Nikephoros utilized, seeing in the aforementioned segment a contemporary or almost contemporary report that was, according to Howard-Johnston, one of the most significant aspects of the *Short History* – its value and contribution – since it preserved a lost work, the so called (second) continuation to the *History of John of Antioch*, which covered the period between the years 610-641. Cf. Фрейберг, *Традиционное и новое*, pp. 50-51, who noticed this multi-layered and multi-faceted image of Emperor Herakleios in her review of ninth-century Byzantine literature and its characteristics, including Nikephoros's *Short History* as well.

3    Nikephoros emphasized that such ideals where considered worthy and desirable both by people in remote antiquity and by 'everyone today' (ὅπερ ἥδιστόν τε καὶ εὔχαρι ἀνθρώποις τοῖς πάλαι καὶ νῦν τυγχάνει ἅπασιν) – which might be viewed as the author's personal attitude and a desire to link his own epoch with the values of Herakleios's time, which then serve as a role model for the Byzantine state of his own time. Cf. Tinnefeld, *Kategorien der Kaiserkritik*, p. 58, who concluded that both Theophanes's and Nikephoros's criticism of the reign of Justinian II arose from the general attitude of 'a generation tormented by wars'.

distress and disorder in the states of the Romans and Persians, and detriment for all the subjects of both states (κακοῦν τὸ ὑπήκοον), since Shahin also asserted that: 'This concord should be as profound as our empires are great, for we know that no other state will ever appear to rival these our empires'. From 'like-mindedness and peace' (εἰ μὲν τὸ ὁμόγνωμον καὶ εἰρηνικὸν θήσεσθε) stems 'happiness' (εὐδαιμονία) and those who adhere to it become worthy of envy and admiration (ζηλωτούς τε καὶ ἀξιαγάστους ἐς τὸν ἅπαντα βίον δείκνυσθαι). 'Hardships' (πόνοι) become 'painless' (ἄμοχθος), and 'worries' (φροντίς) yield to 'joy' (εὐθυμία). In contrast, hostility and hatred lead to many wars which are 'unpleasant and hateful' (δυσμένεια καὶ ἔχθος), and the consequences of war is great distress (μέγα κακοῦ τὸ τοῦ πολέμου ὑμῖν πέρας ἥξει), and the states fall into a 'miserable and piteous' (οἰκτρότατος καὶ ἀθλιώτατος) condition. The oration ended with the Persian promising that Chosroes II would establish a firm and long lasting peace with the Byzantines (τὴν εἰρήνην τὸ λοιπὸν εἰς τὸν ἅπαντα χρόνον βεβαίαν τε καὶ ἀκραιφνῆ καταστήσεσθαι).[4]

The place of Shahin's oration in the structure of the opening account of Herakleios's Persian campaign pointed, in fact, to the Byzantine emperor, who was the one who adhered to all the desired features of an appropriate reign as pronounced in the oration. Namely, after the oration, we read that the same general took the Byzantine envoys to Chosroes II and bound them in fetters as soon as they entered Persia. In contrast, it was Herakleios with the Patriarch Sergios who gladly accepted all the proposed ideas from the oration and decided to send envoys to discuss peace with Chosroes II, who actually hoped to capture Herakleios. Nikephoros presented a specific image of the emperor's reaction to the words of the Persian general. 'Rejoicing' (συνηδόμενος) and 'being enchanted' (κατακηλούμενος) by what he heard, he promised that he would act in accordance with the proposal 'most readily and most quickly' (ἑτοιμότατος τε καὶ σπουδαιότατος), while his views were 'supported' (συμπράσσω) and 'approved' (συναινέω) by the patriarch and the state officials. The ambassadors were chosen 'swiftly' (τάχιστα).[5] In such a way, Herakleios's forthcoming war against Chosroes II, which Nikephoros proceeded to depict, became an exploit in accordance with the proclaimed ideals in the oration, and in fact, Nikephoros managed to ascribe the merit for keeping peace and order to the Byzantines and their emperor, who were destined to bring these ideals into fulfilment.

The oration of Shahin with its highly ideological theory of state order, its relations with the foreign empires, and the threats which should be

---

4    Nikephoros, *Short History*, § 6.16-43.
5    Nikephoros, *Short History*, § 7.1-5 *passim*.

avoided in every occasion, presented a specific program, an ideal imperial policy which should be desirable for every reign of every Byzantine emperor in the history of such a state. Obvious the prospects of such a reign, with its positive outcome and results, evidently have a significant place in a Byzantine historical narrative. Its position in the structure of the work, in the opening chapters of Herakleios's reign, obviously shaped the ideal of his imperial policy. This, however, went beyond the account of Herakleios's reign in Nikephoros's display of later Byzantine history. The oration of Shahin, readily accepted by the Byzantine emperor and subsequently pursued throughout Herakleios's reign, strongly suggests that Nikephoros created a specific introduction to his work, although not a typical one. He set a pattern according to which he wrote his *Short History*. It was a pattern of an absolutely ideal imperial reign, according to which he later shaped his successive historical narrative. This is also a very specific approach in the shaping of a historical narrative, which Nikephoros decided to follow and achieve. He clearly needed a firm foundation on an ideological level in order to build his historical storytelling in the following chapters. However, the *Short History* really began with a description of a total disaster which befell Byzantium in the reign of Emperor Phokas.

## Restoring Order

> After the murder of Emperor Maurice, Phokas, who had committed this (deed), seized the imperial office. When he had assumed power the situation of the Christians came to such a pitch of misfortune that it was commonly said that, while the Persians were injuring the Roman state from without, Phokas was doing worse (damage) within. This the Romans could not bear.[6]

With this remark begins the narration of the *Short History*. It is a scene of complete disorder in which Herakleios rose to the imperial office. The

---

6    Nikephoros, *Short History*, § 1.1-8: ʻΜετὰ τὴν Μαυρικίου τοῦ βασιλέως ἀναίρεσιν Φωκᾶς, ἐπεὶ ταύτην διειργάσατο, τῆς βασιλείου ἀρχῆς ἐπιλαμβάνεται· οὗ δὴ ἄρξαντος ἐπὶ τοσοῦτο κακώσεως Χριστιανοῖς ἤλασε τὰ πράγματα ὡς παρὰ πολλοῖς ἄδεσθαι ὅτι Πέρσαι μὲν τὴν Ῥωμαίων ἀρχὴν ἐκτὸς κατεπήμαινον, Φωκᾶς δὲ ἔνδον χείρω τούτων ἔπραττε. ταῦτα οὐκ ἀνεκτὰ Ῥωμαίοις ἐγίνετο.ʼ Cf. Kaegi, *Heraclius*, pp. 37-38. Haldon, 'The Reign of Heraclius', p. 2, thought that the dislike on behalf of the Emperor Phokas which existed in Constantinople, but not in the entire Byzantine society, actually contributed to the unfavourable picture of Phokas, which later mislead modern researchers.

causes for the rebellion against Emperor Phokas were many, but one of the main motifs was the transgression of assuming imperial power after murdering Emperor Maurice and his children. In Nikephoros's portrayal of Phokas's rule, this led to other misfortunes which had befallen the Romans. This idea was stressed by the reference that 'the Romans could not bear' these misfortunes. Following this, Herakleios was introduced in the narration as acting with the consent of the two governors of Libya. Their action was portrayed as legitimate since the former Emperor Maurice appointed these two governors of Libya to their post. Subsequently, Herakleios was presented as the one who punished Phokas for the murder of Maurice and his children.

Nikephoros gave not only a brief but also a rather simplified presentation of the act of rebellion led by Herakleios and the members of his family. The literary technique displayed here demonstrates his main idea of presenting Herakleios as a central figure in the narration. The portrayal of Herakleios's accession to power was given without a detailed description of the military operations led in Egypt under the command of Herakleios's first cousin Niketas.[7] On the contrary, Nikephoros provided a different image, namely, that both Herakleios and Niketas were sent to Constantinople, by the agreement of two brothers – Herakleios (the older) and Gregorios (father of Niketas). Herakleios led a fleet and Niketas led an army by land. The narrative concluded by stating that Herakleios was 'greeted by fortune' (δεξιᾷ δὲ τύχῃ χρησάμενος) and 'carried by favourable winds' to Constantinople before Niketas.[8] This emphasis on luck and favourable occasions promoted the role of Herakleios in the events and indicated his dominant presence in the approaching narrative. It is important to notice that the other persons mentioned in this opening chapter of the *Short History*, Herakleios the older, Gregorios, and Niketas, who all had their significant role and contribution to the downfall of Phokas, were significantly side-lined in the narration, while the future

7    Kaegi, *Heraclius*, p. 44, provided a full description of the military operations led by Niketas in Egypt, as part of a wider action on taking the Empire by the family of Herakleios.

8    Nikephoros, *Short History*, § 1.17-20. In Theophanes, *Chronicle*, 297.5-10, we encounter the same story about the agreement. Obviously both authors utilized the same or a similar source, although Theophanes provided further details regarding the ground expedition of Niketas, emphasizing that he later reached Constantinople through Alexandria (298.19-21), while he provided more details about the events in Constantinople under Phokas's rule that were omitted by Nikephoros. Cf. Mango, *Short History*, p. 173, for a detailed review of sources on these events. However, Butler, *The Arab Conquest*, pp. 4-5, already pointed to the naivety of the story given by Nikephoros, pointing to the simple fact that an army approaching Constantinople by land from North Africa could not reach the capital before the navy lead by Herakleios.

Emperor Herakleios received all the attention from the beginning. In contrast, it appears that Nikephoros wanted to stress the fact that the *coup d'état* was indeed an act of the entire Herakleian family. This we can deduce from the manner according to which Theophanes wrote about the same events, mentioning the agreement of Herakleios *the older* and Gregorios but avoiding to mention that the two were brothers, a remark which was emphasized in the *Short History* twice. Thus, we can point to a gradual development of the image and cause of Emperor Phokas's downfall. First, it was the Romans who could not bear the misfortunes imposed on them as a result of Phokas's disastrous rule, then two military commanders from Carthage, who were previously given the military command by the late Emperor Maurice, decided to rebel against the emperor. From these events, guided by fortune, Herakleios managed to reach the capital first and overthrow Phokas due to his transgressions.

The further course of the narration developed the idea of Phokas's poor governance and consequently, the causes of the coup and his overthrow, which received its logical ending in a short dialogue between Herakleios and Phokas, who was brought before Herakleios. 'On seeing him, Herakleios said "Is it thus, O wretch, that you have governed the state?" He answered: "No doubt, you will govern it better."'[9] A crucial motif reveals itself in this short dialogue. The deposed emperor and the rebellious Herakleios discussed the issue of state governance. From the results of Phokas's rule, it appears that he was a 'wretch' (ἄθλιος), while in a very specific manner, Nikephoros emphasized that the rebel Herakleios governed the state of the Romans in a better manner.

The account of Herakleios's rise to imperial power continued with narrative elements brought forward to accomplish the idea that Herakleios coup was a legitimate act. The elements that made this message were Herakleios's entrance in Constantinople. It was emphasized that the Patriarch Sergios of Constantinople and citizens greeted him with great honour (σὺν πάσῃ εὐγνωμοσύνῃ). The motif of revenge for the unlawful murder of Emperor Maurice and his family is the second element, which was presented as the main cause of the rebellion by Herakleios when he tried to deliver the imperial power to the city eparch Priskus, who would not accept it.[10] Only

9    Nikephoros, *Short History*, § 1.41-43: 'ὃν ἰδὼν Ἡράκλειος ἔφη "οὕτως, ἄθλιε, τὴν πολιτείαν διῴκησας"; ὁ δὲ "σὺ μᾶλλον" εἶπε "κάλλιον διοικεῖν μέλλεις".'
10   Mentioned by Nikephoros in the *Short History* as Krispos, Priscus was a significant imperial official in the Byzantine military and administrative system both in the time of Herakleios and the former Emperor Phokas. However, Nikephoros did not expand the account of his previous offices, only mentioning him in relation to the new Emperor Herakleios and the specific

after describing these events, which are not attested in other sources, did Nikephoros proceed to narrate that Herakleios received imperial power after being proclaimed emperor by the senate and the people, while the patriarch invested him with the imperial crown.[11] This opening arrangement of events, which stand at the beginning of Herakleios imperial rule, presented an introduction to a plot by which Nikephoros delivered the idea of the authority of the imperial dignity. This was accomplished through the account of Herakleios's public dispute with the aforementioned prefect Priscus, who was Emperor Phokas's brother-in-law.

The sequences of events which unfolded after Herakleios was invested with the imperial power are as follows: Priscus refused Herakleios's offer to receive the imperial crown after which he was appointed the commander of the Byzantine troops in Cappadocia. Previously Nikephoros already laid the foundation of the image of Priscus as disloyal and astute by mentioning his participation in a plot against Phokas and his crossing to the side of the rebels. Meeting with Priscus later in Caesarea, Emperor Herakleios revealed the true character of Priscus when the commander received the emperor in an inappropriate manner 'with displeasure and unwillingly'. Nikephoros described this scene as τὸ δρᾶμα but in fact, considers it an insult (ἡ ὕβρις). It is clear from the sequel that Nikephoros implied the insult of the imperial dignity. Herakleios understood the play, bore the insult, and bade his time. Then Nikephoros brought forward a significant detail, namely how Priscus 'as if in mockery' (οἷα ἐπιτωθάζων) stated that it was improper for the emperor to abandon the capital 'and to tarry among distant armies'. In a wider context of Nikephoros's ambition to present the character of Emperor Herakleios as a successful warrior, specially against the Persian enemies of the Empire, this phrase presented a significant association which already at the beginning of the work announced the true character of Herakleios, which was directly opposed to Priscus's remark and to the image of the former Emperor Phokas, an image of a bold emperor which Nikephoros proceeded to develop.

The climax of this narrative contained the description of yet another play (τὸ δραματούργημα) being conducted in order to finally display both the insult of Priscus and his deception, and the divine nature of the imperial dignity and its authority:

---

narrative he wished to build: the story about Herakleios's reign. See the *Prosopography of the Later Roman Empire*, IIIB, 1052-1057.

11    Cf. Mango, *Short History*, p. 174.

Krispos too came to Byzantium so as to join in celebrating the arrival of Niketas. Now Herakleios pretended that he was about to purify his son in the sacred font and would have him adopted by Krispos. On this pretext, Krispos entered the palace. After assembling all the members of the Senate and the remaining people of the city together with their bishop Sergios, Herakleios is reported to have asked them: 'When a man insults an emperor, whom does he offend?' They answered: 'He offends God who has appointed the emperor.' And he urged Krispos also to express his honest opinion. The latter, not understanding the play (τὸ δραματούργημα) that was being acted, said that a man convicted of such a daring deed (ἐπὶ τοιύτῳ ἁλόντα τολμήματι) should not even have the benefit of a lenient sentence. The emperor reminded him of his feigned illness at Caesarea, and how he thought of degrading the imperial dignity (τὸ τῆς βασιλείας κατευτελίζειν ἀξίωμα), and how he had offered him the Empire. And picking up a book, he struck him on the head and then said: 'You have not made a [good] son-in-law. How will you make a friend?' And straight away he directed that his head should be shorn in the manner of a clergyman and that the bishop should recite the customary [prayers] over the act of tonsure.[12]

This account presented a culmination in describing the relations between the emperor and the city prefect Priscus, who was treacherous towards the previous emperor. His guilt was the insult done to the imperial dignity, which he had refused, as Nikephoros accentuated, thus supporting the usurpation of the imperial throne in 610 by Herakleios. The deposition of Priscus from among the emperor's closest associates and allies was presented in such a way as if Herakleios himself had acted in accordance with the opinion of the guilty one, since Priscus opted for the most severe punishment in the case of insulting of the imperial dignity, which he professed before

---

12  Nikephoros, *Short History*, § 2.28-47: 'καὶ Κρίσπος δὲ εἰς Βυζάντιον ἦκεν ὡς τῇ εἰσόδῳ Νικήτα συνησθησόμενος. σκήπτεται δὲ Ἡράκλειος τῷ θείῳ λουτρῷ τὸν υἱὸν καθαγνίζειν, υἱοθετεῖσθαι δὲ αὐτὸν ὑπὸ Κρίσπου. ὁ δὲ ἐπὶ τούτοις εἰσέρχεται εἰς τὰ βασίλεια. Ἡράκλειον δὴ ἀθροίσαντα τοὺς ἐκ τῆς συγκλήτου βουλῆς ἅπαντας καὶ τὴν ἄλλην πληθὺν τοῦ ἄστεως ἅμα τῷ προέδρῳ Σεργίῳ εἰπεῖν λέγεται πρὸς αὐτούς "ὁ βασιλέα ὑβρίζων τίνι προσκρούει;" τοὺς δὲ φάναι "τῷ θεῷ τῷ ποιήσαντι αὐτὸν βασιλέα". καὶ Κρίσπον προτρέπειν, καὶ αὐτὸν ἀποφαίνεσθαι τὸ δοκοῦν ὀρθῶς· τὸν δὲ οὐκ εἰδότα τὸ δραματούργημα λέξαι μηδὲ φιλανθρώπου τυχεῖν δίκης τὸν ἐπὶ τοιούτῳ ἁλόντα τολμήματι. καὶ τὸν βασιλέα ἀναμιμνήσκειν αὐτὸν οἷα ἐν Καισαρείᾳ ἐπὶ τῇ νόσῳ κατεσχηματίσατο, καὶ ὡς τὸ τῆς βασιλείας κατευτελίζειν ἀξίωμα ᾤετο, καὶ ὡς εἰς τὴν βασίλειον ἀρχὴν προύτρεπε. καὶ ἅμα λαβόντα τόμον κατὰ κόρρης τοῦτον παίειν, καὶ εἶτα λέγοντα "ὡς γαμβρὸν οὐκ ἐποίησας, φίλον πῶς ἂν ποιήσειας;" εὐθὺς δὲ ἐπιτρέψαι εἰς κληρικοῦ σχῆμα τὴν κεφαλὴν ἀποκείρασθαι, καὶ τὸν ἱεράρχην τὰ νενομισμένα ἐπὶ τῇ ἀποκάρσει ἐπιφθέγξασθαι.'

the patriarch of Constantinople and members of the senate in the play (τὸ δραματούργημα) staged by the emperor. As an introduction to the account of Herakleios's play, which had to expose Priscus's unfaithfulness, Nikephoros also inserted the motif of mutual accord and respect between the two brothers, Herakleios and Niketas, which seems to have played a role in highlighting Priscus's deceitful attitude towards the emperor and his insolence toward the imperial dignity. In that sense, Nikephoros emphasized the firmness of accord and mutual trust between Niketas and Herakleios, as opposed to the deceit of the city eparch towards the new emperor.[13] From the entire passage then proceeds that Herakleios had nothing left than to bring to a close this plot and conclude that the eparch's offence testified to his unfitness to remain the emperor's *friend*, an idea which seems to have had a special notion in Nikephoros's portrayal of emperors and their relationships with their close associates.

The entire episode of Herakleios's relationship with the former emperor's son-in-law and the former city eparch Priscus fit within the overall idea of restoring proper state order which was lost during Phokas's rule. Nikephoros portrayed the events that had taken place at the imperial court or around the new emperor with significant details, in order to present the image of the restoration of the lost order and the dignity of imperial power which Phokas by his illegitimate rule had brought to a very low status. In that sense, the story about Priscus was crucial to Nikephoros's setting of the model that presented his notion of a worthy emperor. In the scene about Priscus's mocking of Herakleios's active rule, and his tarrying amongst the distant armies, Nikephoros promoted the ideal of a bold ruler who was committed to administering the Empire with responsibility, an image that was opposed later in the account of Philippikos Bardanes's weak and unsuccessful rule. In contrast, in the scene of Priscus's final downfall, Nikephoros established the idea of the sovereignty of the emperor who abided by the main prerequisites of proper imperial governance. While Herakleios had every right to engage in rebellion against the disastrous rule of Emperor Phokas, since his neglect of the imperial duties had brought the Roman state into disorder, Priscus's attack against Herakleios's imperial dignity and, more importantly, his attack against Herakleios's manner of governing the Empire, was an act that threatened to return disorder in the Byzantine state. Thus, in the first chapters of the *Short History*, Nikephoros portrayed Herakleios as an emperor who managed to restore the order in the Byzantine empire that had been diminished during Phokas's rule. This

13    Cf. Nikephoros, *Short History*, § 2.24-28.

restoration, however, could not be possible without Herakleios's personal virtue of *boldness*, which was fully displayed in the lengthy and complex account of his Persian war against Chosroes II.

## A Courageous Emperor

The war against Persia and Herakleios's personal act of valour in leading the Byzantine army against Chosroes II (which displayed the personal qualities of the two rulers in Nikephoros's account) presented the lengthiest and most complex narrative in the entire account of Herakleios's rule in the *Short History*. Parallel narrative messages were also embedded in this part of the work, such as the image of the Constantinopolitan patriarchs Sergios and Pyrrhos. The patriarchs were presented in light of their political role related to the emperor. The image of Herakleios was fundamentally shaped exactly in the narrative about his relationship with the two hierarchs and in the entire section dedicated to his wars against Persia. While the opening narration about his rebellion, taking the imperial dignity, and his personal conflict with Priscus, had to provide imperial legitimacy and to justify the dynamic manner of his rule. It was in the section about the war against Persia that Nikephoros first accentuated Herakleios's readiness to conclude peace with Chosroes II, adding to this image his personal act of courage in battle.

The report about Herakleios's Persian war began with a mention of how Chosroes II waged war against the Romans (ἐπιστρατεύει κατὰ Ῥωμαίων), thus attaching the responsibility to the Persian ruler. The Persian troops were under the command of the general Shahrbaraz: 'He devastated the entire eastern region taking from the Holy Land the life-giving tree of the Saviour's Cross (τὰ ζωποιὰ ξύλα τοῦ σωτηρίου σταυροῦ), while Modestos was the bishop of Jerusalem'.[14]

---

14   Nikephoros, *Short History*, § 12.1-6: 'ὃς κατεδῄου πᾶσαν τὴν ἀνατολικὴν χώραν. καταλαμβάνει δὲ τῶν ἁγίων τόπων τὰ ζωοποιὰ ξύλα τοῦ σωτηρίου σταυροῦ, Μωδέστου τηνικαῦτα Ἱεροσολύμων προεδρεύοντος.' Cf. Russell, 'The Persian Invasions', pp. 49-51. Concerning those archaeological findings which connect to this part of Nikephoros's narration about Herakleios's war with Persia, Russell (pp. 41-71) called attention to the great uncertainty concerning in the precise archaeological identification and dating of particular findings in such a narrow chronological period as the seventeen-year-long Persian presence in Syria and Palestine – findings which also, in relation to that, indicate disagreement with contemporary and later Byzantine narrative sources. Cf. also Stoyanov, *Defenders and Enemies*, pp. 11-24.

The subsequent commentary about Herakleios's Persian campaign was reduced to several significant units with following narratological moments:

- Herakleios's invasion of Persia. The narration began in § 12, just after the account of the meeting between the emperor and the Lord of the Turks, with whom an alliance was established, and Herakleios entered the Persian kingdom.

- The description of the siege of Constantinople in 626, which was a separate story embedded in the narration about Herakleios's Persian war. However, in the account of the siege of 626, the main protagonists in the narration were the Patriarch Sergios of Constantinople, the Patrician Bonos, and the young Emperor Herakleios Constantine, son of Empress Eudokia.[15]

- Herakleios's duel with the Persian general Razates, which actually presented an introduction to the detailed account about the reasons and circumstances surrounding the political downfall of Chosroes II and his death. This § 14 had a significant place in the overall approach of depicting the two rulers, the Byzantine and the Persian emperor. Namely, Chosroes sent an experienced and a brave warrior against Herakleios: 'When Chosroes had been informed that Herakleios was close to the Persian royal residence he sent out against him a brave and experienced in fighting general named Razates'.[16] The Persian general's courage and the experience of his adversary, whom he managed to defeat personally, made Herakleios's victory even more glorious: 'When Herakleios became aware that none of his men would volunteer, he went forth himself against the barbarian', and the emperor's personal *boldness* had inspired the Roman army to decidedly defeat the enemy.[17] Through such a narrative Nikephoros placed the Persian emperor Chosroes II in opposition to Herakleios. The positive characteristics given to Herakleios in this account were the ones of which Chosroes II was deprived. His action in connection to the same event, Herakleios's approach to the vicinity of the Persian imperial residence, was opposite to the victory of the Byzantines. Nikephoros developed this idea in § 15: 'When the Persian archons became aware that the Roman emperor had made light his own life for the sake of his state, they plotted with

---

15   Nikephoros, *Short History*, § 13.1-42.
16   Nikephoros, *Short History*, § 14.1-3: 'Μαθὼν δὲ Χοσρόης Ἡράκλειον πλησιάσαντα τοῖς βασιλείοις Περσῶν ἐκπέμπει κατ᾽ αὐτοῦ στρατηγόν τινα Ῥαζάτην ὄνομα, γενναῖον ὄντα καὶ ἔμπειρον τὰ πολέμια.'
17   Nikephoros, *Short History*, § 14.6-7: ''Ηράκλειος δὲ ἐπεὶ οὐδένα τοῦ οἰκείου στρατοῦ προθυμούμενον ἐπεγίνωσκεν, αὐτὸς ἐξήει κατὰ τοῦ βαρβάρου.'

Chosroes's son Seiroes to slay Chosroes inasmuch as he had shown great neglect towards his own state.'[18] Howard-Johnston saw a trace of a hypothetical source in this description of the duel, which was of Persian origin, now lost, and which was directed towards discrediting Emperor Herakleios, since he actually cheated his adversary (one of the emperor's bodyguards helped him defeat Razates).[19] However, Howard-Johnston did notice the phrase τὴν τοῦ βασιλέως παρρησίαν, which Nikephoros used in the description of Herakleios's duel, but considered it unexplainable in the context of a negative portrayal of Herakleios in the source of Persian origin. What he did not notice or consider possible was that Nikephoros as author even utilized a source of anti-Byzantine posture, and adjusted it to a narrative in accordance with his own idea of a desirable image of Herakleios, which later on he developed further in mentioning Herakleios neglecting of his own life for the sake of the Empire, a virtue which Chosroes II did not demonstrate and which finally brought him to his downfall. Thus, the personal boldness of the emperor highlighted in this chapter yet another personal virtue of Herakleios. Waging war for the welfare of the state of the Romans was Herakleios's greatest virtue, and stood in direct relation to the previous scene of his clash with Priscus, who deemed it unworthy of an emperor to reside with his army in the distant provinces. Nikephoros here actually displayed the results of Herakleios's policy, which was not only placed in contrast to internal Byzantine opposition portrayed in the personality of Priscus, but also in the personality of the Persian emperor Chosroes II. These scenes also comply with the main ideas as professed and accepted by Herakleios in the oration of Shahin.

– The downfall of Chosroes II, his imprisonment, and demise, which presented a significant detail in the narration shaping the main tendency of the author, namely to highlight the nature of Herakleios's government over the state, its qualities, and in contrast to the Persian state order and the ruler himself. § 14 and § 15 mutually connected to one another in the sense that they together accentuated the notion of Herakleios's personal bravery and his selfless dedication, while Chosroes II demonstrated the opposite features. Nikephoros proceeded to present Chosroes II as a gold-loving king who neglected the affairs

18  Nikephoros, *Short History*, § 15.1-5: 'Οἱ δὲ Περσῶν ἄρχοντες ἐπεὶ διεγνώκεσαν ὡς ὁ τῶν Ῥωμαίων βασιλεὺς ὑπὲρ τῆς ἑαυτοῦ πολιτείας τῆς οἰκείας ζωῆς κατεφρόνησε, μετὰ Σειρόου τοῦ υἱοῦ Χοσρόου βουλεύονται Χοσρόην ἀνελεῖν, μέγα περὶ τῆς οἰκείας πολιτείας καταφρονήσαντα.'
19  See Howard-Johnston, *Witnesses to a World Crisis*, pp. 247-248.

of the state, which was the reason why he lost both his empire and his life. A similar image of the Emperor Phokas here seems to be plausible for comparison. In such a portrayal the image of the Persian emperor was similar to the mythic King Midas, especially since Nikephoros later on openly designated Constantine V as a 'new Midas'. It is reported that the conspirators against Chosroes II offered him gold, silver, and precious stones, sarcastically inviting him to take pleasure in the things which he 'loved immensely and mindlessly'.[20] In this story, Nikephoros accentuated the idea of the unworthiness of earthly riches compared with virtuousness and a good rule, since they cannot keep a man in life. A negative concept embedded in this report is obvious with the intent to denounce avarice in relation to emperors, even in general. And exactly in such a relation, befitting the idea about a public and state interest and in the context of the matters of the state, we encounter a philosophical treatment of the tendency towards avarice in Aristotle's work on state matters. In his *Politics* one can find the same motif of starvation in front of vast amounts of gold, in the story of the mythic King Midas, and further treatment of the relation between wealth and the governing of the state. Namely, Aristotle wrote that a large amount of money was considered as wealth since trade and other business was implemented with money. But there is a contrary notion that money is nonsense (λῆρος εἶναι δοκεῖ τὸ νόμισμα) and according to its nature nothing (φύσει δ' οὐθέν). Since it does not benefit basic living – even a man with large amounts of money can also die from starvation, as a consequence of his avarice, like the mythic Midas.[21]

–   With the description of Chosroes II's political downfall, which emerged as a result of Herakleios's heroic act displayed in the duel with Razates, but also in the overall image of his statesmanship, a short account followed concerning state disorder in Persia. In addition, at the end of this section of the work, the author again emphasized the idea of peace and quietude (ἐφησυχάζειν) which should be introduced in both states. Namely, after Chosroes II's death, his son had written a letter

---

20   Nikephoros, *Short History*, § 15.8-10.

21   Cf. Aristotle, *Politics*, 42.16-44, 17. (καθάπερ καὶ τὸν Μίδαν ἐκεῖνον μυθολογοῦσι διὰ τὴν ἀπληστίαν τῆς εὐχῆς πάντων αὐτῷ γιγνομένων τῶν παρατιθεμένων χρυσῶν.) Cf. Lemerle, *Le premier humanisme byzantin*, pp. 133-135, who argued that the study of ancient philosophy did not disappear even in the so called *dark centuries* of Byzantium, and that Aristotle's philosophy, to which the hagiographer Ignatios the Deacon alluded in his standard description of Nikephoros's education when describing his knowledge in philosophy, was in fact known in the epoch of Patriarch Nikephoros.

to Herakleios, committing himself to the task of introducing peace between the Persians and the Romans.[22] The emperor was emphasized in this story, particularly since he was uniquely compared to the Biblical person of Symeon the God-Receiver through a paraphrase of the letter sent to Herakleios from Persia. This comparison made Herakleios's personality in the *Short History* even more complex, in a very original way, providing yet another element in the literary shaping of his image as part of a wide and varied mosaic of his character: 'Just as you claim that your God was delivered into the arms of an old man [called] Symeon, so I am delivering into your hands my son who is your slave. May the God whom you worship watch how you treat him'.[23] Other attributes attached to Herakleios's image in the subsequent narration were: his ignominious flight from the Avars,[24] and his incestuous marriage with

---

22 Nikephoros, *Short History*, § 15.10-14.

23 Cf. Nikephoros, *Short History*, § 16.1-10: 'ὃν τρόπον λέγετε τὸν θεὸν ὑμῶν δοθῆναι γηραιῷ τινι ἀνθρώπῳ Συμεὼν εἰς τὰς ἀγκάλας, οὕτως καὶ τὸν δοῦλόν σου τὸν υἱόν μου δίδωμι εἰς τὰς χεῖράς σου. γνοίη δὲ θεὸς ὃν σέβῃ, ὡς ποιήσεις αὐτῷ.' For the biblical story about St. Symeon the God-Receiver, see Luke 2.25-35; *Synaxarium ecclesiae Constantinopolitanae*, 439-442. Also see Болотов, 'Къ исторіи императора Ираклія', p. 86, who took this letter to be authentic.

24 The Avar account with the portrayal of Herakleios's 'unmanly flight' and his appearance as 'an ordinary man' introduced yet another 'negative' image of Herakleios in the overall positive account on his reign. The Khagan of the Avars, according to Nikephoros, assumed a mask of friendship and spoke alluring and tempting words pretending to be a friend of the Romans (*Short History*, § 10.1-2 *passim*). Nikephoros then proceeded to describe the details of the plot against Herakleios planned by the Khagan, who was presented as a man of perfidy – all the more so since Herakleios was in this story presented as somewhat naïve. Namely, the emperor prepared for his meeting with the Avar by organizing equestrian races and selecting presents which he would offer to the Khagan when concluding the peace treaty. This is the repeated image of Herakleios from the beginning of the *Short History*, when he was presented as the one who readily accepted peace offers of the Persian general Shahin. While the emperor was preparing to meet the Avar, the latter was busy as well, and Nikephoros tells us that he was engaged in organizing a raid by placing his men on proper places in the wider vicinity of the City from where they could seize the emperor, who was unaware of such preparations. The Avars 'secretly' (κρύβδην) make an ambush in the high and wooded regions above the Long Walls with the intention to 'easily stalk' the emperor and his retinue. The emperor, who did not suspect such preparations, reached the appointed meeting place and only then became aware of the plot prepared by the Avar. Nikephoros then proceeded to describe Herakleios's consternation brought upon him by the suddenness of the Avar attack, depicting his ignominious escape with his imperial crown under his arm, and in the dress of a simple man, his imperial robes discarded in an attempt to escape to Constantinople. Nikephoros used vivid terms in his description of this act of Herakleios, telling us that the emperor had taken simple and poor clothes (οἰκτρὸν δέ τι καὶ πενιχρον) in order to appear as a simple man (ὡς ἂν ἰδιώτης) – (a characterization similar to that of the Emperor Theodosios III in the later part of the *Short History*), and then run in an unmanly manner (εἰς ἀγεννῶς φυγὴν). Cf. Nikephoros, *Short History*, § 10.24-30.

his niece, opposed by the patriarch of Constantinople, his unsuccessful defence of Egypt and his illness and death, connected directly to his personal moral transgression due to the incestuous marriage with Martina. All this made a very complex image of Herakleios with an intricate message of the author on behalf of his work and the individuals which he treated in other parts of the *Short History*.

## Holy War

Although it cannot be said that in his historical representation of the war against Persia Nikephoros placed emphasis on the idea of *holy war* against the Persians, several significant events which carried a certain notion of sacral imagery were placed in the narrative. It appears that Nikephoros, who probably placed these sections in his narrative utilizing his sources, managed to promote a specific religious idea, which was more close to his own time and the dispute over Iconoclasm than to the historiographical portrayal of the past. Some of these narratives linked to the personal acts of imperial rule demonstrated by Herakleios, such as the account of the baptism of the Huns,[25] while others indeed carried a strong notion of Iconodule doctrines promoted during the eighth- and ninth-century disputes in the Byzantine state and Church. Such is the account of the meeting between Herakleios and the Lord of the Turks, at the outset of Herakleios's Persian campaign. Nikephoros mentioned Herakleios's skill in providing new allies against the Persians among the Turks of the Eastern Turkic Khaganate.[26]

25　Nikephoros, *Short History*, § 9.1-9. These events are not attested in any other narrative source of Byzantine provenance. Cf. Howard-Johnston, *Witnesses to a World Crisis*, p. 255, who viewed this account as an echo of a contemporary court report. For an analysis of the nation in question, and named Huns in the account of Nikephoros, see Mango, *Short History*, pp. 177-178, who provided a survey of the literature which dealt with this issue and two theories about the identity of the nation which Nikephoros refers to as the Huns.

26　For the history of the Turkic peoples, see Golden, *An Introduction to the History of the Turkic Peoples*, pp. 127-136 and 235-237; Golden, *Khazar Studies*, pp. 37-42; ODB III, 2129-2130; and more specifically, of Khazars and their relations with Byzantium: Zuckerman, 'The Khazars', who gave an overview of this episode by Nikephoros, attempting to determine the exact identity of the mentioned Turks and the time of their first encounter with Byzantium, arguing that these are in fact a Turkic ethnicity from the so called Turkic khaganate under whose rule were also local Khazars. Thus, Nikephoros's ethnic identification proves to be more exact than that of Theophanes, who called the ethnicity with whom Herakleios made alliance 'Turks, also known as Khazars' (Theophanes, *Chronicle*, 315.15-16). Cf. Zuckerman, 'The Khazars', pp. 411-412. Later on Nikephoros will write about Khazars in the account of Emperor Justinian II's reign and the events which led to his second rule in Constantinople, and in the story about Constantine V's

A relatively large amount of space was dedicated to the description of the meeting with the Lord of the Turks (κύριος τῶν Τούρκων). This was, in fact, a significant moment in Herakleios's offensive against Persia, when the role and contribution of the Turks to the final victorious outcome for the Byzantines was of great significance.[27] However, this significance and the role of the Turks in the Persian campaign were not additionally developed as a story in the *Short History*. Nikephoros provided only the account about the initial meeting between Herakleios and the Lord of the Turks, where he presented the nature of their relations, which underlined the high dignity of the emperor, and in relation to this motif a sincere loyalty and devotion of the Turkic leader towards the emperor.[28] Nikephoros's literary act in his description of Herakleios's Persian campaign thus appeared as apparently engaged and accordingly arranged to stress a specific message. This image of the Turks as loyal allies of Byzantium and the emperor, with all the rich elements which made its narrative structure, was in the function of the making of a statement that it was Herakleios's merit for the victory over the Persians in his personal act of endeavour and feat.[29]

An analysis of the structure which we encounter in the account of Herakleios's meeting with the Lord of the Turks highlights one particular idea which may carry a notion of Iconodule argumentation embedded in the Herakleios narrative, thus shaping the past in accordance with Iconophile notions of history. 'From there he sent gifts to the chieftain of the Turks, whom he urged to enter into an alliance against the Persians. The later accepted [the gifts] and promised to be an ally.'[30] To reaffirm this alliance Herakleios offered to the Lord of the Turks the hand of his daughter Eudokia: 'Fearing, however, lest he suffer the same faith as with the Avar, and with a

marriage with the Khazars princes (*Short History*, § 42.1-77; § 45.1-105; § 63.1-4). For a summary of Byzantine sources about the Khazars and a review about the narration of the *Short History*, see Howard-Johnston, 'Byzantine Sources', p. 168.

27 Cf. Kaegi, *Heraclius*, pp. 98 and 142-145.

28 Howard-Johnston, *Witnesses to a World Crisis*, p. 251, assumed that this description and several others as well were Nikephoros's deliberate act made in the process of summarizing his source, which he placed in the text with the goal of emphasizing the superiority of the Romans over the Persians.

29 Contrary to Nikephoros, Theophanes, who himself wrote rather concisely about the Turks, mentioned what would be proper in that context, namely, that they had contributed to the Roman victory in Persia. It seems that for Nikephoros, unlike Theophanes, what was of most interest was to provide an image of Herakleios's relations with the Lord of the Turks, and to present the image of the Roman-Persian war as a single feat of the emperor. Cf. Theophanes, *Chronicle*, 315.11-316.16.

30 Nikephoros, *Short History*, § 12.16-19: 'ἐντεῦθεν ἀποστέλλει δῶρα πρὸς τὸν Τούρκων κύριον, ἐπὶ συμμαχίᾳ τῇ κατὰ Περσῶν συγκαλούμενος· ὁ δὲ δεξάμενος ὑπέσχετο συμμαχήσειν.'

view to making the agreement more binding, he showed him the portrait (εἰκόνα) of his daughter Eudokia.' Nikephoros then explained: '[The Turk] was so struck by the beauty of the picture and its adornment that he fell in love with the person represented (ἔρωτι τοῦ ἀρχετύπου) and held fast to the alliance all the more.'[31] The terminology which Nikephoros adopted in this account is very interesting from the aspect of icon worship and the Iconodule apologetics. In such a time when icons were presented not as idols but as a medium in the religious practice of worshiping Christ, such a presentation of this event in the political milieu of the seventh century and Herakleios's Persian campaign raises the question whether Nikephoros had more subtle and more contemporary notions which he embedded in his history. However, as patriarch, Nikephoros promoted a proper relationship towards image worship, claiming that the icon was an image of the archetype (εἰκών ἐστιν ὁμοίωμα ἀρχετύπου) and that the icon had the quality of the archetype, thus presenting the external aspect of the likeness which was painted on the icon.[32] In the account of the meeting between Herakleios and the Lord of the Turks, and the manner of historical representation of this meeting, by applying specific Iconodule terminology, Orthodox semantics become obvious in Nikephoros's shaping of the past.

Another very interesting section of the account which dealt with Herakleios's war against Persia is the story of the True Cross, which gained its separate history, portraying Herakleios's reign as influenced by the Cross. The account of Herakleios's successful struggle against Persia and Chosroes II ended with the same motif which can be found in the structure of narration at the outset of the story. Namely, in the narrative about the return of the Cross from Persia to Jerusalem, the relic was presented to the patriarch and the pious citizens with the notice that the eyes of barbarians did not see it in Persia and that it was kept undefiled and in one piece all the time in captivity. A naïve story, but it is interesting that actually the most negative representation of the Persians in the entire *Short History* was

31   Nikephoros, *Short History*, § 12.32-40: 'εἶτα δεδιὼς μὴ τὰ αὐτὰ τῷ Ἀβάρῳ καὶ παρ' ἐκείνου πείσεται, ἐπικρατέστερα δ' αὐτῷ καὶ τὰ τῆς συμβάσεως ἀπεργάζεται, παραδείκνυσιν αὐτῷ τῆς θυγατρὸς Εὐδοκίας εἰκόνα ἔφη τε πρὸς αὐτὸν ὡς "ἥνωσεν ἡμᾶς ὁ θεός, σὲ τέκνον ἐμὸν ἀπέδειξεν. ἰδοὺ δὴ αὕτη θυγάτηρ μού ἐστι καὶ Ῥωμαίων Αὐγούστα. εἰ οὖν συναίρεις μοι καὶ βοηθεῖς κατὰ τῶν ἐχθρῶν, εἰς γυναῖκα δίδωμί σοι αὐτήν". ὁ δὲ τῷ κάλλει τῆς εἰκόνος καὶ τῷ περὶ αὐτὴν κόσμῳ τρωθεὶς ἔρωτι τοῦ ἀρχετύπου ἔτι μᾶλλον ἐπὶ τῇ συμμαχίᾳ ἐπέκειτο.' Cf. Zuckerman, 'La petite augusta', who managed to prove the historicity of this story and the Turkic (rather than Khazar) origins of the *Lord of the Turks*, which adds to the historical background of this new, until the unattested Byzantine practice of marrying in-purple-born princesses to foreign rulers.

32   Cf. Nikephoros, *Antirrheticus* I, col. 277A. And: 'ὅτι ἡ εἰκὼν σχέσιν ἔχει πρὸς τὸ ἀρχέτυπον' (col. 277D). On Nikephoros's theology, cf. Alexander, *The Patriarch Nicephorus*, pp. 189-213.

given in connection with the Cross – 'their ungodly and murderous and profane hands did not touch' the Holy Cross – and that the Persians were not even worthy of seeing it.[33]

The narrative about the Cross is significant since the account about its history in the early seventh century is the only such account in the *Short History* which narrated the story of a Christian relic. The references to the Cross were particularly accentuated, not in relation to the rather small amount of places where references to icons dominate the text of the *Short History*, but with the idea of worshiping icons in Byzantine society in the late eighth and early ninth centuries. This is an interesting circumstance since the reverence of the Cross presented a significant argument of the Iconoclasts in their dispute against icon worshipers, where they presented the Cross as the only acceptable relic in Christian worship. In that sense, it can be said that the use of such an idea of the domination of the Cross over icons in literary works of Iconoclast provenance had for its main goal the suppression of the cult of icons both in practical spirituality and in the theological sense.[34] Considering this, Nikephoros's comprehension of the idea of the Cross, which was embedded in the Herakleios narrative, presented a significant authorial approach in depicting the epoch of Byzantium's war with Persia. This event marked the reign of Herakleios in his time significantly, but also in the eyes of later Byzantine historians, and in a literary sense regarding the chronological framework and the prevailing ideology of social structures of the society from which Nikephoros stemmed.[35]

The mention of the Cross and its place in the overall narration about the reign of Herakleios was placed in the narrow historical context of the seventh century, so a possible hypothesis that Nikephoros might have used it to transform the Iconoclast idea about the Cross into an Iconophile

33  Nikephoros, *Short History*, § 18.8-21: 'ὡς ἀνέπαφα καὶ ἀθέατα βεβήλοις καὶ μιαιφόνοις χερσὶ τῶν βαρβάρων'. Drijvers, 'Heraclius', p. 177, noticed that, despite various contemporary sources and several earlier sources, the historical reality of the return of the Cross is actually hard to reconstruct (p. 177, n. 8 list of sources). Болотов, 'Къ исторіи императора Ираклія', p. 78 n. 4, noticed that such an account as presented in the *Short History* of Nikephoros points to the circumstances in which an educated Byzantine of the early ninth century trusted such stories which did not have an elementary basis in truth. The naivety of such a story points towards a different understanding of the outlook which the Byzantines might have had in relation to history writing and the reading of historical texts.

34  About these aspects in Iconoclast disputations and the place of the Cross in the development of the conceptual system of the Iconoclast theology, see Kazhdan, 'Constantine Imaginaire'.

35  Compare the feast established for the commemoration of Constantine's vision of the Cross and of the finding of the True Cross by his mother Helen, but not the memory of the return of the Cross from Persia under Herakleios: *Synaxarium ecclesiae Constantinopolitanae*, 43-45.

context seems plausible. However, with the absence of a more significant mention of icons in the work, the story about the Cross stands out from the predominant narrative about the political events of the seventh and eighth centuries as the only sacral motif in the entire narration of the *Short History*.[36] In contrast, the entire history of the Holy Cross as it was formed during Herakleios's reign, and as presented in the Byzantine literature of the seventh century, certainly found its reflection in the unknown sources which Nikephoros utilized. A particular tradition of literature on the Cross, especially among the writers of Herakleios's epoch, made the event a significant element in the narrative of Herakleios's history, and equally, this idea intruded into new literary genres, entering the narratives of later Byzantine literature, and Nikephoros's *Short History* as well. Nevertheless, Nikephoros clearly portrayed the Cross in his narrative as a significant motif of Herakleios's reign, and of his victory over the Persians. Herakleios indeed transferred the relic to the imperial city and gave a certain amount of his attention to this event. After the Cross was brought from Persia to Jerusalem, and after the patriarch of Jerusalem had verified that the Cross was indeed the True Cross, Herakleios 'immediately sent it to Byzantium. Sergios, the archpriest of Byzantium, received it in procession at Blachernai, which is a church of the Mother of God, and, after bringing it to the Great Church, he elevated it.'[37]

The possible Iconodule allusions in the narrative of Herakleios's Persian campaign are not exhausted with these references about the True Cross or the image-archetype allusions in the Turk account. Namely, in his narrative about Herakleios's victorious intrusion into Persia, Nikephoros made an interesting description of Herakleios's reaction to Chosroes II's personal deification:

> [Herakleios] invaded Persia, and set about destroying cities and over-turning the fire temples. In one of these temples it was discovered that Chosroes, making himself into a god ($\theta\epsilon o\pi o\iota\dot\eta\sigma\alpha\varsigma$), placed on the ceiling [e.g. a picture of] himself as if he were seated in heaven, and had fabricated stars, the sun and the moon, and angels as standing round

---

36   Such is the poem *Restitutio Crucis* written by Herakleios's contemporary George Pisidas, which may represent a central literary work that contributed in a literary and historical sense to the further development and spreading of the narrative about the Cross in a historical presentation under Herakleios's rule.

37   Nikephoros, *Short History*, § 18.16-20: ʽὑψωθέντων δὲ αὐτῶν ἐκεῖσε εὐθὺς ἐς τὸ Βυζάντιον ὁ βασιλεὺς ἐξέπεμψεν. ἃ δὴ Σέργιος ὁ τοῦ Βυζαντίου ἱεράρχης ἐκ Βλαχερνῶν (ἱερὸν δὲ αἱ Βλαχέρναι τῆς θεομήτορος) λιτανεύων ὑπεδέξατο καὶ πρὸς τὴν μεγίστην ἐκκλησίαν ἀγαγὼν ταῦτα ἀνύψωσε.'

him, and a mechanism for producing thunder and rain whenever he so wished. Upon seeing this abomination, Herakleios threw it down and ground it into dust.[38]

Here it is significant to mention that Nikephoros avoided the use of any Greek term which could imply a religious image and thus be understood as an icon, clearly making a difference from the narration about the Turk's devotion to the image of Herakleios's daughter, a narrative in which he not only used the term εἰκόν but also developed the Orthodox idea of the relationship between the archetype and the image. In the account of Chosroes's deification through an image which was placed in the temple, the image was understood only through the context of the description of the entire scene. As if Nikephoros was careful not to apply to this section of Herakleios's account an Iconoclastic argumentation which was at his time regular in disputes over icon veneration.

In the entire *Short History*, there are not many direct comparisons of its protagonists with the personalities from the sacred history of the Old and New Testament. The comparison of Herakleios with Symeon the God-Receiver presents a valuable literary act, and together with the later association of Emperor Constantine V with the Phrygian king Midas, presents the only such examples in the making of the *Short History*.[39] St. Symeon and his role in the New Testament narrative about Christ assumed a significant place, mentioned in the alleged appeal of the Persian new ruler Hormizdas, which, if accepted as authentic, could give evidence about a developed cult of St. Symeon in Persia, where a significant Christian community existed since the earliest, almost apostolic times, as reported in the Acts of the Apostles (where among other nations present at Pentecost in Jerusalem, Parthians, Medes, and Elamites were mentioned as well.)[40] In contrast, if this comparison of the emperor with St. Symeon is viewed as Byzantine political propaganda formed and launched by the emperor, it would imply

---

38 Nikephoros, *Short History*, § 12.41-49: 'σὺν αὐτοῖς τε εἰς τὴν Περσικὴν εἰσβαλὼν τάς τε πόλεις καθῄρει καὶ τὰ πυρεῖα διέστρεφεν. ἐφ' ἑνὸς δὲ τούτων εὕρηται, ὡς Χοσρόης ἑαυτὸν θεοποιήσας ἐν τῇ τούτου στέγῃ ἑαυτὸν καθήμενον ὡς ἐν οὐρανῷ ἀνεστήλωσεν, ἀστραπὰς καὶ ἥλιον καὶ σελήνην συγκατασκευάσας, ἀγγέλους περιεστῶτας αὐτῷ, καὶ βροντὴν διὰ μηχανῆς ποιεῖν καὶ ὕειν ὁπότ' ἂν θελήσειεν. τοῦτο τὸ βδέλυγμα θεασάμενος Ἡράκλειος εἰς γῆν κατέρριψε καὶ ὡς κονιορτὸν διέλυσε.' The similarity of this description to the story in the homily on the return of the Cross composed between 826 and 844 by Rabanus Maurus is evident. The learned bishop of Mainz (776/784?-854) was a contemporary of Patriarch Nikephoros. Cf. Rabanus Maurus, *Reversio sanctae atque glorissime Crucis*. Cf. McCarthy, 'Rabanus Maurus'. Cf. Drijvers, 'Heraclius', p. 179, n. 13.
39 Nikephoros, *Short History*, § 85.12-13: 'ὁ μισόχριστος νέος Μίδας Κωνσταντῖνος.'
40 Acts, 2.1-9.

that the saintly cult of St. Symeon was indeed significant in the Byzantine society of Herakleios's epoch. From this then a clear attempt by the emperor to connect himself in the idealistic image of the saint would arise and thus additionally build the legitimacy of his power. In that sense, one should bear in mind that Herakleios had carefully built his authority and the right to imperial power, among other things, by connecting with contemporary notable ascetics like Theodore of Sykeon, whose relics were transferred to Constantinople after his passing.[41] In connection to this, and in relation to emphasizing Herakleios's connection to St. Symeon, it should be noted that the tradition of celebrating Christ's circumcision in the Temple according to the Old Testament tradition of Moses – in which at one moment St. Symeon stepped into the centre of the history of God's providence for mankind and His *oikonomia* of salvation – began to be celebrated officially in Byzantium for the first time during Justinian I's reign.[42] From a chronological perspective, this was an event relatively close to the people of Herakleios's time. In such circumstances, it was possible for the personality of St. Symeon to be utilized in the forming of the imperial idea of a connection between emperors and certain persons from sacred history. Nikephoros, who obviously took this detail from his source, interpolated it into his text, thus providing yet another suitably positive image of Herakleios in his narrative, promoting an image of the emperor in connection to the saint who at one time held Christ in his arms. Byzantine authors often resorted to invoking Old Testament figures with the aim of accentuating their stories and their moral or ethical messages, and the emotional response of their audience.[43] This reference to St. Symeon the God-Receiver presented a unique and a somewhat specific case, one which did not fit the classical model of an Old Testament character, since he stood at the boundary between the Old and the New Testament eras, being included in the Old Testament era by the tradition of the Church and connected to that era by the story of his task of translating the Scriptures, and through the story in Luke's Gospel where he assumed a significant role in the shaping of the New Testament idea of Jesus Christ as the Son of God and God-Man. Such a comparison of Herakleios with St. Symeon is not attested in other Byzantine sources, not even in the *Chronicle* of Theophanes.

41  Kaegi, *Heraclius*, pp. 75-76.
42  Cf. Theophanes, *Chronicle*, 222.22-25: 'In the same year, on February 2nd, the feast of the Presentation (ἡ ὑπαπαντὴ τοῦ κυρίου) was celebrated for the first time in Byzantium.'
43  Cf. Rapp, 'Old Testament Models', p. 180. The author however notes that the *Short History* of Nikephoros, unlike Theophanes's *Chronicle*, is without reference to Old Testament figures (p. 187).

Some of the significant features of the image of St. Symeon the God-Receiver which were attested either in the Scriptures or in the tradition of the Church as expressed in the hagiographies and theological literature of the Byzantine period are his work on translating the Old Testament in the time of Ptolemy II Philadelfos among the seventy translators, a story which included a prophecy about the birth of Christ from the Virgin. But the only mention of him in the entire Scripture was in the Gospel according to Luke, where he was depicted as receiving Christ in his arms with a prophetic song about God's *oikonomia* of salvation, which took a central place in this account. St. Symeon thus assumed a place at the boundary between the two Testaments, Old and New, and so united in a way two histories, the history of the Old Testament Israelites and its fulfilment in the New Testament. Herakleios's epoch knew also comparisons of this emperor with another Old Testament personality – the king and prophet David.[44]

Several questions arise as part of our analysis of the *Short History* and this particular section of the work. First, from which source did this detail enter Nikephoros's work? According to older research, this comparison formed part of an authentic letter of the Persian emperor to Herakleios. A further question arises, taking into consideration the historical and chronological boundaries in which Nikephoros wrote, whether by interpolating such a motif he actually wanted to make an allusion to the issues and topics of his own time. Iconoclastic disputes and the relation between the Church and the emperors presents itself as a possible motif. Namely, Nikephoros could have left out this comparison of Herakleios and St. Symeon; after all, he was following a concise style of writing. There is, however, one point in which both the author's ideas embedded in his work and the narrative about St. Symeon have something in common. Namely, that is the idea of *peace* present in both the narrative about Herakleios's Persian war (his struggle to introduce peace between the two empires through victory over Chosroes II) and St. Symeon's words present in Luke's Gospel (where the idea of peace was also present, although in a different context.) 'Lord now lettest Thou Thy servant depart in peace, according to Thy word, for mine eyes have seen Thy salvation, which Thou hast prepared before the face of all people, a light to enlighten the Gentiles, and the glory of Thy people Israel'.[45]

Herakleios's victorious war against Persia obviously had certain religious elements primarily through the place and role of the Holy Cross, its capture,

---

44  Cf. Alexander, 'Heraclius', and for new and different hypotheses, see Leader, 'The David Plates'; also cf. Drijvers, 'Heraclius'.

45  Luke, 2.29-32.

its later return to Jerusalem, and the role of the emperor in these events. These elements can be placed in the context of St. Symeon's verses spoken before Christ. In that case, a comparison of Herakleios and St. Symeon is obvious. It was he who was guided by God in his victorious campaign against Persia and the *barbarians* and returned the Cross from captivity.[46] The idea of peace was also present in the narration about St. Symeon meeting Christ the child, just as peace was introduced after victory over Persians, and with the return of the Cross – in St. Symeon's speech, *for mine eyes have seen Thy salvation* – the Cross certainly served as a sign of salvation. Thus, the idea and mission of saving not only the Cross but also the entire Roman nation – *New Israel* – was finally achieved. In a more historical analysis of the Byzantine-Persian relations in the context of the Christianity of Herakleios's time, C. Mango brought forward several hypotheses regarding the ending period in the war against Persia and establishment of allied relations between the two states, noting several crucial details which point to the validity of his approach. Namely, after analysing several sources of Byzantine provenance (Nikephoros and Theophanes) but also several eastern writers like Michael the Syrian and an anonymous chronicle of Nestorian origins, Mango suggested that there existed in Persia a crypto-Christian group among the civil and military elite which included the general Shahrbaraz. Mango emphasized that his children had Byzantine dignities and Roman names, like the Patrician Niketas. And through the marriage of his daughter Nika to Herakleios's son, Theodosios, Shahrbaraz became a member of the Byzantine reigning family. The mention of St. Symeon the God-Receiver was taken as an additional argument by Mango to his hypothesis about cooperation between Herakleios and Shahrbaraz even during the Persian campaign, and especially after the defeat of Chosroes II. As a consequence, a new conclusion arose. Namely, Herakleios pursued a Christianization of Persia, guided by eschatological sentiments characteristic for his epoch, and the expectation of the imminent approach of the *Parousia* – the Kingdom of God and, in connection to it, the need for spreading the word of the Gospels among the barbarians.[47]

The story about Herakleios's duty to safeguard the young Persian prince in a manner which invoked parallels from the sacred history of the New Testament, then, echoed his attempt to 'enlighten' Persia with the Christian faith. Thus, the account of Herakleios's Persian war in the end received its eschatological and Christianized identity. Together with the mention of

---

46  Nikephoros, *Short History*, § 18.8-21.
47  Cf. Mango, 'Deux études sur Byzance', pp. 105-118.

the significant point in the war, as presented in the short account about the history of the Cross and its return to Jerusalem and translation to Constantinople, the account fit into the wider narrative of salvation, both political – of the order and peace in the Roman Empire and in its relations with the new Persian elite – and in a more profound, spiritual way. This was not without further development as an idea in the *Short History*, with more literary elaborations in the account of Constantine V's reign.

## Emperor – *Friend* and *Brother* of the Patriarchs

The career of the imperial *asekretis*, the later patriarch Nikephoros, as of his predecessor Tarasios, but also of his later successor Photios, demonstrate the ability of the Byzantines to establish a more-or-less successful *symphony* between the secular and ecclesiastical domains of life, between the issues of imperial and church order. However, this feature, or aspiration, was not without its opponents in Byzantine society itself – in the post-Iconoclastic period among the lower structures of the Church of Constantinople which endured periods of concealed or open conflict between the episcopate and the lower clergy, particularly monks. However, in such conceptions of internal ecclesiastical relations, one should try to avoid simplification since every church group – monks, lay clergy, higher clerics – each in its specific circumstances of a particular period, entered into quite specific mutual relations and strife. Nikephoros's conflict with Theodore Studites is particularly indicative, however, again in a specific manner. This conflict to some extent also originated from the unsolved relations of the two parties inside the Church of Constantinople.[48] The tight interweaving of the secular and the spiritual remained significant for the ecclesiastical structure of the Church, however, and her affairs with the state did not support stable and peaceful relations among the churches of Rome and Constantinople. Let us suggest just one aspect of a doubtlessly more complex and multifaceted nature of this phenomenon: namely, the Roman Pontiffs considered these relations in a juridical context, from which a conflict with the Church of Constantinople arose. Such was, for example, the conflict from the time of Photios, where the patriarchal election of Photios was the main accusation of the Western Church in the troubled relations between the two sees and their long-lasting disputes in the ninth century.

---

48   See Ringrose, *Saints, Holy Men and Byzantine Society.*

As a secular work, Nikephoros's *Short History* was nevertheless interconnected with the ecclesiastical issues of Byzantine history during the seventh and eighth centuries. Alternatively, in a historian's perception, these two processes cannot be separated. In that sense, Nikephoros himself could not separate sacred history from the political issues with which he predominantly dealt in his work. Thus, the events which represented the history of the Church in the seventh and eighth centuries – Christological disputes and their relations to the state in Byzantium – could not be neglected in the *Short History*, since the relationship endured not only a crisis but also a theoretical shaping of its dogmas in the post-Iconoclastic period of Byzantine history. These issues were mentioned in specific places in the narration, as the structure and composition of the work permitted, or rather, as it was suitable to the author's idea and his conception of his own literary presentation of the historical material. If we have in mind that Nikephoros wrote a concise history of the Empire – a work meant to represent a classical model of historiography, which thus focused primarily on the political processes of the Empire's past –, then his approach to a concise presentation of the ecclesiastical problems of the specified period becomes more understandable. Nevertheless, a reasonable question can be asked whether even such concise reports and the mentions of the patriarchs had their place and role in the wider narrative of the work, and in a more specified sense a precise role of representing a characteristic image of the patriarchs in accordance with the author's own attitude and his Iconophile perspective.

Concerning everything said, it seems that such reasoning is not without grounds and that a work such as the *Short History* was written under the pen of an author who, at the time when he wrote, was a lay official and a dignitary in the structures of the Empire, undoubtedly educated, familiar and involved in the events and political processes of the Byzantine empire at the end of the eighth century. In other words, Nikephoros wrote his work as an imperial secretary, or as a former imperial secretary, and thus a certain secular manner of writing reveals itself in the structure and the content of the *Short History*. The most prominent feature of this is the interest which Nikephoros demonstrated towards the interdependence between the proper governance or a state order on one side, and the character of the imperial office of a certain ruler on the other. Aside from other things, this is what led him to present the details from sacred history as passing details in his primary narrative, but underneath to attach significant and valuable messages and to embed and promulgate some of the most crucial ideas in his entire work. Nikephoros's authorial work should be viewed in the context of an idea that the narration which is built in the *Short History* around the personalities of the patriarchs had a clearly defined goal and that these mentions only seemingly belong to the wider narratological flow, bypassing the attention of the author. However, a different image and understanding of Nikephoros's accounts from the history of the religious disputes of Byzantium's seventh and eighth centuries reveals itself, in which the patriarchs were exclusively presented in relation to the emperors and in their mutual interaction, which was presented in the *Short History* in a highly nuanced manner. In that sense, including certain moments from ecclesiastical history that entered into the narrative Nikephoros highlighted the place and significance of the Church of Constantinople and its patriarchs and their role in Byzantine society. In this context, there exists a similarity to the events of Nikephoros's own time, which is of a certain value when dealing with his *Short History*. This was also often overlooked in past research, and thus it was a case that several narratives of his work were considered at least odd, as was the case with the account of the abdication of Patriarch Pyrrhos.

This parallel narration about the events of ecclesiastical provenance in the *Short History* began with the depiction of a political role which the Patriarch Sergios assumed during the reign of Emperor Herakleios. It is a portrayal which revealed their mutual striving in the governance of the Empire at a time full of tempests, with a turning point faced during the wars against Persia and the Arabs. The narration then continued with the image of the Patriarch Pyrrhos, Sergios's successor, whose inheritance of the patriarchal dignity from Sergios was especially emphasized in the narration as a significant topic in the reimaging of Pyrrhos's relationship with Herakleios. Their relationship was elevated in the narrative to a higher level by portraying the emperor and Pyrrhos according to the notion of *spiritual brotherhood*. Such an image of Patriarch Pyrrhos later developed in the narration into a seemingly puzzling description of his forceful abdication, which was transformed into a favourable account by Nikephoros in depicting this patriarch's removal from the patriarchal see.

Sergios occupied the patriarchal see of the Church of Constantinople in the period between 610 and 638, and as is apparent, his patriarchal office almost entirely corresponded chronologically with the reign of the Emperor Herakleios, although Sergios was elected patriarch somewhat earlier, before the coup against Emperor Phokas. This enabled him to receive and crown Herakleios as new emperor in Constantinople.[49] The political role was

---

49   See van Dieten, *Geschichte der Patriarchen*, pp. 1-56. For the history of theological disputes in the epoch of Monothelitism, see Hovorun, *Will, Action and Freedom*.

emphasized in such wording and narration and was further displayed by using other appropriate events which connected to Sergios's role in Herakleios's rise to power. Such were his coronation παρὰ τοῦ προέδρου, and the mention of the patriarch in the secular political context of an imperial official, together with other imperial dignitaries in a specific anecdotal story about the relationship between Herakleios and Priscus. The patriarch was portrayed as the one who equally participated in the meeting, and his was the voice that spoke out, together with others who condemned the unlawful act of insulting the imperial dignity. In a way, this might imply the patriarch's subordination to the emperor and imperial secular power. However, the proclamation of the members of the senate and the patriarch that it was God who was insulted, since he was the one who made men emperors, maintained a sacral and ecclesiastical context for imperial power. The patriarch's presence in such a meeting underlined such reasoning, while his participation in the event also emphasized his own political role.

A significant role of the Patriarch Sergios in the political life of the Byzantine Empire was emphasized in the *Short History* in several places. When all the news about Sergios is analysed, we can see that it was the patriarch of Constantinople who was the closest person to Herakleios and almost his only associate. At least that is what Nikephoros tended to present in his history. His presence in the text dominated when compared to the personality of the city prefect Priscus or the Patrician Bonos, who was mentioned only once in the context of a regency that followed Herakleios's departure from Constantinople in order to lead a military campaign against the Persians. Even during this regency, alongside Bonos, it was the Patriarch Sergios who took a significant part in leading the regency during the siege of Constantinople by the Avars and the Persians. Thus, Sergios of Constantinople received the second place, after Herakleios, in the narration of the Byzantine-Persian war.

Such display of the patriarch's influence and his active role in making decisions concerning state matters is best portrayed in the episode about Herakleios's talks with the Persian general Shahin. After Herakleios had expressed his readiness to act according to the ideals promoted in the oration, Nikephoros proceeds to inform us that Herakleios enjoyed the support of the patriarch: 'His views on these matters were supported and approved by the one initiated into sacred things (ὁ ἱερομύστης) and the dignitaries.'[50] The presence of the patriarch in these talks, together with other dignitaries,

---

50    Nikephoros, *Short History*, § 7.1-5: 'Βασιλεὺς δὲ Ἡράκλειος, ἐπεὶ τοῦτ᾽ οὖν ἐπέπυστο, τῷ προσηνεῖ καὶ θελκτηρίῳ τῶν λόγων συνηδόμενός τε καὶ κατακηλούμενος, ὑπέσχετο εἰς ἄπαντα πράσσειν

similar to the story about the meeting when the city eparch Priscus was forcefully pressed to abdicate his office, further shaped this *political* role of the patriarch. Nikephoros additionally stressed his presence and his support for the emperor by applying a specific terminology, namely, by using a term which was very specific in its meaning, emphasizing the patriarch's not only political but also sacral role and prerogatives. The term ὁ ἱερομύστης points towards a more profound understanding of Nikephoros's depiction of Sergios in this account.

First, it is very strange that he applied such a term to the patriarch when narrating the secular and political issues of the state, and not the sacral topics over which the patriarch certainly had authority.[51] Second, a question arises concerning the meaning of the term applied in such a context. To translate it simply as 'high priest'[52] would call to mind a deeper meaning of the phrase, implying a more general notion of the patriarch. Of course, from the translation 'high priest' it is clear that it was the Patriarch Sergios who was meant under this term. However, we are more inclined to see in this term a complex idea which Nikephoros decided to apply in his narrative with a specific intention. The meaning of the term also carried a notion of sacredness or even holiness, which might be directed towards the idea of *peace*, which was the main topic in this part of the work. Both the Persian general and the Byzantine emperor strove towards establishing peace in their states, and the patriarch supported the emperor. But 'the one initiated into sacred things' carried additional sacral meaning, pointing to the specific ecclesiastical and liturgical notions of the one who had been appointed to offer the sacred mysteries of the Eucharist in the church.[53] This might be yet another path in viewing this term applied only to the Patriarch Sergios in the entire *Short History*, as a tool designated to highlight the patriarch's active contribution towards the embellishment of the Divine Liturgy and the holy and sacred mystery of the Eucharist.[54]

---

ἑτοιμότατά τε καὶ σπουδαιότατα. καὶ οἷς ἐβουλεύετο τούτων πέρι συνέπραττόν τε μάλιστα καὶ συνήνουν ὁ ἱερομύστης τε καὶ οἱ ἐν τέλει.'

51  See, for example, a similar term ὁ μυστιπόλος applied to Patriarch Germanos of Constantinople in Stephen, *Life of Stephen the Younger*, § 5, 94.6-18, at the time of Nikephoros's patriarchal office.

52  Translation by Mango, *Short History*, § 7.

53  Cf. Sophocles, *Greek Lexicon*, p. 594; Liddell and Scott, *A Greek-English Lexicon*, p. 822; and in *Suidae Lexicon II*, 101: which interpreted the term simply as ἅγιος.

54  Cf. *Chronicon Paschale*, I, 714, 9-20: 'May our mouths be filled with your praise o Lord that we may sing of your glory since you have made us worthy of participating in your sacred mysteries (τῶν ἁγίων σου μυστηρίων). Guard us in your sanctification so that all day long we may be taught in

Such liturgical poetry, which was ascribed to the patriarch already in the seventh century, might have echoed in the time when Nikephoros wrote his *Short History*. Nikephoros obviously thought it fit to apply it to the patriarch as he was portraying him in his work. Nothing similar can be found in Theophanes's account of the patriarch, and it is our opinion that such an application of a term to the personality of the Monothelite patriarch presents another seemingly inappropriate portrayal of a heretical patriarch, together with the account of the Patriarch Pyrrhos. The patriarch's role in counseling the emperor to accept the peace proposal of the Persian general was seemingly appropriate for Nikephoros to attach the ἱερομύστης term at that particular place in his narration. After all, the idea of peace is most profound in his entire system of political values and probably was considered appropriate to be made equal to the more sacral meaning of the term attached to the patriarch in that context, thus additionally pointing to his action and presence in a moment of such significance for the Byzantine state.

Such shaping of the patriarch's image, however, received a somewhat unexpected turn with the negative imagery of Herakleios's incestuous marriage, which Nikephoros not only openly excoriated, but also presented through a specific story about the condemnation of such an unlawful deed by the patriarch. In such an image of patriarch-emperor relations, a new characteristic was given to the patriarch and his public service. This time Nikephoros was critical of the imperial office, thus stressing not only the unity between the two poles of power but also attaching to the ecclesiastical and sacral authority of the patriarch the right to judge the emperor in his unlawful deeds. The account of Herakleios's illicit marriage to his niece Martina strongly emphasized the authority of the patriarch, who openly condemns the marriage and denounces it as an 'unlawful deed' that was contrary even to the Roman custom.[55] Nikephoros then once more pointed out that the marriage of Herakleios with his niece was an 'unseemly mar-riage' (τὸ ἄσεμνον συνοικέσιον) that was denounced even by the partisans of the Green and the Blue colours, who managed to unite in this instance over the emperor's transgression. However, the largest denunciation was

your righteousness.' For the historical context of Sergios's liturgical poetry, see Kaegi, *Heraclius*, pp. 124-125.

55    A certain correlation can be seen between such a description of the emperor's second marriage and the statement from the opening of this account: 'Even though matters of state had come to such a sorry and abnormal pass, [Herakleios] did not even take care to put his private affairs in order.' The matters of state and the *private affairs* of the emperor are here clearly placed in the same level of significance.

by Sergios of Constantinople in which Nikephoros gave a compelling image
of the patriarch, placing the praise of the patriarch's status in the reply of
the emperor:

> Sergios, the archpriest of Byzantium, also put earnest pressure on him
> by letter and admonished him to repudiate his connection with this
> woman, but he excused himself as follows: 'What you say is very well.
> The obligation you owe me as high priest and friend (ὡς ἀρχιερεῖ καὶ φίλῳ)
> you have already paid. For the rest, the responsibility shall lie on me.'[56]

The refutation of the emperor's unlawful marriage by the patriarch was only
mentioned in this scene, presented in the form of a letter. The patriarch's
view regarding this problem was simply brought into the narrative. Nevertheless, the emperor's reply offered a more complex image of their relations,
involving proper wording, which carried a significant message and image
of the patriarch. First, we are not aware in what form the emperor gave
his reply to the patriarch. Was it a reply also in the form of a letter or in a
direct meeting between Herakleios and Sergios? The emperor's reply to the
patriarch was straightforward and carried a notion of their mutual close and
sincere relations. However, the act of the patriarch, his open denunciation
of the emperor's immoral act, is evident in this account. This narrative
considered it to be the patriarch's duty to enforce upon the emperor those
modes of conduct acceptable to Roman custom. From such a construction
it followed that the patriarch enjoyed certain prerogatives which might
exceed the authority of the imperial office. If so, then such admittance of the
patriarch's right to act according to such authority, and being pronounced
as it was displayed in the text – by the emperor himself – emphasized the
emperor's readiness to abide according to such norms. Herakleios then
pronounced Sergios to be his 'friend'; thus, the patriarch's *friendship* with
the emperor set a precedent for patriarchal relations with secular power in

---

56  Nikephoros, *Short History*, § 11.16-23: 'Σέργιος δὲ ὁ τῶν Βυζαντίων ἱεράρχης γράμμασιν αὐτὸν
λιπαρῶς ἐγκείμενος ἐνουθέτει τὴν πρὸς τὸ γύναιον τοῦτο κοινωνίαν ἀνήνασθαι. ὁ δὲ αὐτῷ ἀπελογεῖτο
ὡς "εὖ μὲν ἔχει τὰ παρὰ σοὶ λεγόμενα· ὃ γάρ σοι χρέος ὡς ἀρχιερεῖ καὶ φίλῳ, ἤδη ἀποδέδωκας· ἐφ ἡμῖν
δὲ τὸ λοιπὸν κείσεται τὰ τῆς πράξεως.' For the history of Empress Martina, see Garland, *Byzantine
Empresses*, pp. 61-72. Contrary to Nikephoros, who placed this marriage after the unsuccessful
attempt of the Avars to catch the emperor in 623, and before Herakleios's Persian campaign,
Theophanes placed this event closer to the first years of his reign, in the years 612/613. Cf.
Howard-Johnston, *Witnesses to a World Crisis*, pp. 281-282, who saw, in such a layout of material,
Nikephoros's attempt to separate Herakleios's sinful marriage together with his later successful
military actions against Persia.

Byzantium, which is specifically significant for the later account of imperial pressure applied to the Church and its patriarchs during the time of Iconoclasm. Nikephoros actually set an ideal image of the patriarch-emperor relations in his account, which then remained a cornerstone of analysing and depicting ecclesiastical relations with the state in the next part of the *Short History*, where direct relations between Leo III and the Patriarch Germanos of Constantinople were portrayed, as well as the disgrace and execution of the Iconoclast patriarch Constantine II.

If we compare all the places in the *Short History* with the corresponding ones in the *Chronicle* of Theophanes where Sergios assumed a certain role, we can conclude that the *Chronicle* considerably differed from Nikephoros in its approach to portraying this patriarch. Theophanes mentioned Sergios in several places of his narration, but always in connection with the ceremonies of an imperial coronation, wedding, or baptism of the members of the imperial family. We encounter a total of five such instances: the story about the wedding of Herakleios with Eudokia and her coronation,[57] which is followed by the account of the birth and baptism of Herakleios's daughter Epiphaneia,[58] further, in a short narration about the imperial coronation of Epiphaneia and Herakleios New Constantine,[59] in a short report about Herakleios's marriage to Martina and her coronation by the patriarch,[60] and in the report about the baptism of Herakleios's second son Constantine.[61] The sixth mention in some extent transferred the patriarch from the context of a high priest and placed him in a more political role, in the story about his appointment by the emperor as a guardian to his young son, Emperor Constantine.[62] Regarding Herakleios's marriage to Martina, Theophanes did not mention the unlawful and scandalous nature of the marriage, upon which Nikephoros insisted, but he did mention the patriarch's participation in the ceremony, which in contrast was suppressed by Nikephoros in his account of the event. By mentioning Sergios's blessing

---

57   Theophanes, *Chronicle*, 299.8-14.
58   Theophanes, *Chronicle*, 299.18-20.
59   Theophanes, *Chronicle*, 300.12-18.
60   Theophanes, *Chronicle*, 300.25-28.
61   Theophanes, *Chronicle*, 301.6-7.
62   Theophanes, *Chronicle*, 303.3-6. Here we must point out that Theophanes attached a significant role to the Patrician Bonos, for whom he emphasized that he was a prudent man, experienced and wise in everything: 'He left his own son at Constantinople in the care of the Patriarch Sergios to conduct the business of state (διοικεῖν τὰ πράγματα) along with the Patrician Bonosos, a man of prudence, intelligence, and experience.' Such praise for Bonos is not present in Nikephoros's *Short History*, and conversely it seems that Theophanes gave an image of the patriarch in contrast to the praiseworthy features of the patrician's character.

of the unlawful marriage of Herakleios and Martina, Theophanes might have wanted to link the patriarch with yet another transgression adding to his heretical image in the *Chronicle* – another sin beside his Monothelitism, which was often mentioned in the work.[63]

In this aspect, Nikephoros's portrayal of Sergios of Constantinople represents a more complex and a meaningful approach, especially if viewed in contrast to the image of Sergios in the *Chronicle* of Theophanes. While Theophanes limited the image of Sergios to a strictly ceremonial role of a high priest, who officiated baptisms, marriages, and who crowned Herakleios and members of his family, and while such an approach might stem from his negative attitude towards the heretical patriarch, Nikephoros demonstrated a different, more historiographical, and more realistic approach. Notable is the portrayal of Sergios of Constantinople which Nikephoros placed in the account of the Avar siege of the City in 626, when Sergios acted as a guardian of Herakleios's children.[64] Such an approach to shaping an image of a historical figure did not leave a possibility for a re-evaluation of his personality from a doctrinal perspective. Instead, it placed the focus on the patriarch's political role as the emperor's close associate and collaborator in the matters of state affairs. For example, Nikephoros avoided mentioning that the unlawful marriage of Herakleios and Martina was officiated by the patriarch, as Theophanes wrote in his *Chronicle*. He rather shifted the meaning of the event and the patriarch's role towards a more political context and a position of the patriarch as opposing the scandalous marriage. Thus, he even managed to promote a specific image of their relations in the context of the idea of their mutual friendship, while he did not forget to point out in the end that the emperor's illness was due to this unlawful marriage. However, the image of the patriarch in this account, unlike in Theophanes's account, was nuanced and closer in emphasizing the political role of the patriarch than in emphasizing his strictly ecclesiastical and sacerdotal role as a priest who officiated the marriage of the imperial couple.

If we compare Nikephoros's image of Patriarch Sergios in the aforementioned accounts as we have analysed them to the narration of Theophanes in his *Chronicle* about the same events, an even more precise picture of the place of the Patriarch Sergios in the *Short History* comes into view. Namely, in his description of the siege of Constantinople in 626 by the Avars, Theophanes did not mention the patriarch whatsoever. In his account, unlike in Nikephoros's, we encounter an explicit mention of divine providence

---

63   Theophanes, *Chronicle*, 329.21-32 and 330.1-29.
64   Nikephoros, *Short History*, § 12,7-14.

and protection of the City, which Theophanes ascribed to the Mother of God – a treatment which he applied later on in his description of Leo III's successful defence of Constantinople against the Arabs in 717, where all the credit for the saving of the City was shifted from the successful emperor to the protection by the Theotokos. Nikephoros, in contrast, did not mention divine intervention in defence of Constantinople in 626 in the same manner as Theophanes, only mentioning 'a divine energy' – θεία δύναμις – which had destroyed the siege engines that the Avars had brought with them to Constantinople. In such a way, he offered a more realistic description of the events which took place, barren of religious details which Theophanes introduced into his text.[65] What Nikephoros wanted and managed to accomplish was to set the archpriest of the Church of Constantinople in a political milieu, as a close associate of the two emperors in the crucial events in the history of Constantinople and the entire Roman Empire.

Nikephoros's counterpart in history writing, Theophanes the Confessor, demonstrated a different approach in transmitting history and a certain disinterest towards this nuanced approach in depicting the institution of ecclesiastical autonomy in relation to the state. This is telling in the context of the different conceptions of the two authors concerning their task of writing history, especially since they both wrote almost at the same time – certainly in the same epoch, marked by same ideas and interests of the new Byzantine society which emerged with Empress Eirene. This indicates that each historian wrote more according to his secular or ecclesiastical position which he assumed at the time of writing – Nikephoros being an imperial secretary, or a former secretary, and Theophanes being a monk and a *hegumenos* of a renowned monastery, which he built himself and supported largely by his own economic means.[66]

---

65   Theophanes wrote that after a ten days siege the Avars were defeated 'by God's might and help and by the intercession of the immaculate Virgin, the Mother of God' (*Chronicle*, 315.18-21), while Nikephoros did not mention this detail in his own account of the event, which significantly described his overall approach. In relation to this, the manner in which he portrayed Leo III's defence of Constantinople in 717 becomes more understandable. Nikephoros's account also disagrees with Theophanes, being again more objective, and it further poses a general question regarding his stance towards icon worship, since the siege of Constantinople in 626 was already vested in the Iconodule narrative by Theophanes in his account of the procession with the icon of the Mother of God on the city walls lead by Patriarch Sergios, which remained absent in Nikephoros's account. Lastly, it poses a wider question whether his *Short History* was written in the manner of Iconodule apologetics or as propaganda. Cf. Speck, 'Byzantium', p. 78.

66   Theophanes's monastic philosophy is reflected in the fact that he was a founder and a *hegumenos* of a monastery which he built with his own financial funding, and he revealed a certain zealous monastic interpretation of the historical role of Iconoclast emperors which

Nikephoros also demonstrated such an approach in portraying emperor-patriarch relations during the reign of Herakleios in the case of the Patriarch Pyrrhos of Constantinople. References to the Patriarch Pyrrhos of Constantinople are significantly shorter than those concerning Patriarch Sergios. Nevertheless, the significance of the image of Pyrrhos in the context of his forceful abdication is almost equal to the entire context of Sergios's patriarchal office. The image of the Patriarch Pyrrhos was reduced almost to his election and abdication, but these were the two key aspects of the idea about the representation of patriarchs which Nikephoros embedded in his work.[67] After Sergios had died, Pyrrhos was brought to the patriarchal see by the direct advocacy of the emperor. It is of significance to note here, that in such a display of Pyrrhos's accession to his patriarchal office, Nikephoros pointed out that he was chosen because he was known as a close associate of the former patriarch:

> In the twelfth indiction Sergios, bishop of Byzantium died. Since Herakleios was devoted to Pyrrhos, whom he called his brother (because when he was being baptized in the holy bath the emperor's sister had received him in her arms) and knew him, furthermore, to have been on friendly terms with Sergios (whose quarters he had shared), he appointed this man archpriest of Byzantium.[68]

There are several interesting and significant points in this statement about Pyrrhos's appointment to the patriarchal office. The first is the spiritual

---

is similar to the monastic line of Theodore Studites, which is again specific in its own way. Conversely, and very importantly at the same time, Theophanes's monastic philosophy was not very close to the one which Theodore tried to enforce and impose upon the entire Church of Constantinople and upon the patriarchs Tarasios and Nikephoros. In this intra-ecclesiastical strife among the Iconodules, Theophanes aligned himself with the learned patriarchs Tarasios and Nikephoros, who both entered the Church from a secular and political milieu. In this Theophanes was obviously standing in opposition to Theodore and his excessively zealous approach in resolving church matters, which was not without political impurity, and which had brought him several times into open schism with the Church and the aforementioned patriarchs. Theophanes's divergence and disagreement with Theodore Studites found its expression in his *Chronicle* as well. Cf. Komatina, *Church Policy of Byzantium*, pp. 62-80, who analysed the issue of the Studites schism and its implications for the unity of the Church in the later period, after 843.

67  On Pyrrhos of Constantinople, see van Dieten, *Geschichte der Patriarchen*, pp. 57-75 and 104-105.

68  Nikephoros, *Short History*, § 26.1-6: ʽΚατὰ δὲ τὴν δωδεκάτην ἰνδικτιόνα ἐτελεύτα Σέργιος ὁ τοῦ Βυζαντίου πρόεδρος. Καὶ ἐπειδήπερ προσέκειτο Ἡράκλειος Πύρρῳ, ἀδελφόν τε ἐκάλει, ὡς ἡνίκα τῷ θείῳ λουτρῷ ἐφωτίζετο ἡ τοῦ Βασιλέως ἀδελφὴ χερσὶν ἐδέξατο, καὶ ἅμα ᾠκειωμένον Σεργίῳ καὶ συνδιαιτώμενον ἐγίνωσκε, τοῦτον ἀρχιερέα τοῦ Βυζαντίου ἀνηγόρευσεν.ʼ

brotherhood between the emperor and the new patriarch, since Nikephoros pointed out that it was the emperor's sister who acted as his godmother at his baptism. This also points to a deeper and more profound connection of Pyrrhos to the imperial family, assuming that the story is not fictional. This account is not present in the *Chronicle* of Theophanes, perhaps because he omitted such details on purpose, since he took a different approach and portrayed Pyrrhos as a heretical patriarch while depicting Herakleios as a pious emperor.[69] However, the next significant information we encounter in this passage is the connection between the patriarchs. Namely, Nikephoros stated that the emperor knew Pyrrhos as Sergios's friend, whose quarters he had shared. Clearly, an idea of succession was emphasized here. Nikephoros presented it as being recognized and maintained by the emperor. It is very significant to point out these facts since they correspond to the later emphasis of a similar succession to Tarasios by Nikephoros, with the intervention of Nikephoros I, but in a strictly historical context of Nikephoros's work they also point to continuity in the emperor's policy towards the Church of Constantinople. From the specific terminology which Nikephoros applied here, it proceeded that Pyrrhos was, in fact, Sergios's *synkellos*.[70] Nikephoros presented this patriarchal succession from Sergios to Pyrrhos in a strictly political sense, since it was the emperor who appointed the later knowing the former and respecting him as his close associate in the political affairs of the state. The idea of his *friendship* with Sergios, who was his φίλος, upgraded to the *brotherhood* between the emperor and the new patriarch.[71]

Theophanes, in contrast, displayed a preference for stories of a doctrinal character, in this case of succession from Sergios to Pyrrhos in the context of their Monothelitism. He gave a short account of the nature of Pyrrhos's patriarchal office, while at the same time he dropped out all the details which were narrated by Nikephoros, making his story about Pyrrhos only a part of the account of the history of Sergios's patriarchal office:

> After the death of Sergios, Pyrrhos succeeded him in the see of Constantinople and impiously confirmed the doctrines of Sergios and Kyros.

---

69   See, for example, Theophanes, *Chronicle*, 299.5-7, where Herakleios *defeated* 'the usurper Phokas by the grace of Christ', or 303.17-23, when the emperor placed his trust in the icon of Christ and began his war with Persia – an obvious Iconodule context which Theophanes embedded into the narrative about Herakleios's Persian campaign.

70   'ᾠκειωμένον Σεργίῳ καὶ συνδιαιτώμενον.' Cf. Mango, *Short History*, p. 190; ODB III, 1993-1994.

71   On the idea of the succession of patriarchs in late eighth and early ninth-century Byzantium, see Marjanović, 'Seventh Ecumenical Council'.

When Herakleios had died and his son Constantine became emperor, Pyrrhos along with Martina killed him by poison, and Heraklonas, Martina's son, was made emperor. But the senate and the City drove out Pyrrhos for his impiety together with Martina and her son. And so Constans, Constantine's son, became emperor, while Paul who was also a heretic, was ordained bishop of Constantinople.[72]

Here we will just point to one key difference from the account which was left by Nikephoros: the expulsion of Pyrrhos by 'the senate and the City', which carried a certain notion of legality of the act, while in Nikephoros's version of the event, the patriarchal abdication was a forceful act done amidst great turmoil in the City as a result of the aggressive rampage of the 'boorish citizens' against Pyrrhos.

If we turn back now to the initial mention of Patriarch Pyrrhos in the *Short History*, we must first analyse the significance of addressing the patriarch as a 'brother' – ἀδελφός – of the emperor, due to the spiritual bond which was founded in the event of his baptism. It seems that a personal notion had directed the emperor to choose Pyrrhos to be patriarch. The *brotherhood* of the emperor and the patriarch was a specific and very meaningful representation of their relations, one which left no doubt that the patriarch in such a context enjoyed great authority and possibly political influence as well. This might be the author's preoccupation presented as a historical truth, since this is the only such story in known Byzantine narrative sources and since it stands in sharp contrast to the account and overall image of Pyrrhos provided by Theophanes.[73]

The term 'brother' with which Pyrrhos was designated left no doubt about the level of his distinction and relation to emperor, while later mentions of the patriarchs from the epoch of Iconoclasm – of Germanos, Anastasios, and Constantine II – stand in sharp contrast to the previous examples as portrayed in the personalities of Sergios and Pyrrhos. This later relationship with the patriarch was an image of absolute imperial power over the patriarchs and the Church. In this respect, such an address to Pyrrhos by

---

72 Theophanes, *Chronicle*, 330.29-331.6: 'μετὰ δὲ τὴν τελευτὴν Σεργίου Πύρρος τὸν θρόνον Κωνσταντινουπόλεως διεδέξατο, ὅς τις τὰ δογματισθέντα ὑπὸ Σεργίου καὶ Κύρου ἀσεβῶς ἐκράτυνεν. τοῦ δὲ Ἡρακλείου τελευτήσαντος, καὶ τοῦ υἱοῦ αὐτοῦ Κωνσταντίνου βασιλεύσαντος, Πύρρος σὺν τῇ Μαρτίνῃ φαρμάκῳ τοῦτον ἀνεῖλεν, καὶ βασιλεύει Ἡρακλωνᾶς, ὁ τῆς Μαρτίνης υἱός. ἡ δὲ σύγκλητος καὶ ἡ πόλις Πύρρον ὡς ἀσεβῆ σὺν τῇ Μαρτίνῃ καὶ τῷ υἱῷ αὐτῆς ἐξέωσαν· καὶ βασιλεύει Κώνστας, ὁ Κωνσταντίνου υἱός, καὶ χειροτονεῖται Παῦλος ἐπίσκοπος Κωνσταντινουπόλεως, καὶ αὐτὸς αἱρετικός.'
73 However, Mango, *Short History*, p. 190, did not comment on such addressing of the patriarch in his relation to the emperor.

the emperor presented a significant role model on which later assessment of such relations were evaluated by Nikephoros.

## Disorder Sets In Again

In the chapter dedicated to the structure of the *Short History* and the narration about the reign of Constans II, we have summarized Nikephoros's account about the events which ensued after Herakleios's death caused by Empress Martina's aspirations to imperial power. We have noted that it was a complete reintroduction of disorder which had occurred in the Byzantine state after Herakleios's reign and that the Patriarch Pyrrhos's abdication was one of the consequences of such turmoil. In these events, Nikephoros portrayed Pyrrhos as a supporter of Heraklonas. Martina's son, however, offered his oath to respect the imperial rights of the late emperor Herakleios Constantine in front of the patriarch. Also significant is the fact that Empress Martina was not presented as someone who was close in her relations with the patriarch. This same motif was present also in the narration about the patriarch's abdication later on, where Pyrrhos transmitted the idea that the rebellion of the citizens and their demand that Herakleios's grandson – the son of Herakleios Constantine – be crowned was, in fact, an attempt of Valentinos to assume power. In the *Chronicle* of Theophanes, Pyrrhos was directly accused of the death of Emperor Herakleios Constantine together with Empress Martina. In contrast, Nikephoros wrote that the emperor died due to his illness, without mentioning the plot of Pyrrhos and Martina.[74] He also indicated that a possible plot against him was organized by the empress, which might have been the cause of emperor's illness and his death. Notably, he avoided mentioning Patriarch Pyrrhos in such a context, thus excluding him from this possible sin, unlike Theophanes. However, Nikephoros gave an account of Pyrrhos's abdication as a result of the turmoil, a story which also displayed the break-up of the established status of the patriarch as displayed in the relationship with Herakleios during his rule. It is a highly significant account both from the aspect of Nikephoros's idea about the desired order in the Empire, and in the context of the place and role of the patriarch in the Byzantine state:

> When vintage time had come, the citizens saw that the army accompanying Valentinos was destroying their vineyards and not allowing them to

74    Nikephoros, *Short History*, § 29.9-11: 'ἐπεὶ δὲ νόσῳ χρονίᾳ Κωνσταντῖνος συνείχετο.'

cross thither, and so they urged Pyrrhos by their clamours that he should crown Constantine's son Herakleios. On beholding the disturbance and uprising (τὴν ταραχὴν καὶ τὴν στάσιν) of the people, Pyrrhos excused himself on the grounds that the insurrection had a different purpose, namely, to gain imperial office for Valentinos; but as the mob was insisting, he laid the whole matter before the emperor. The latter, taking along his nephew Herakleios, proceeded to the church and mounted the ambo together with Pyrrhos, whom he invited to crown Herakleios; and as the crowd was pressing him to accomplish the deed, he took from the church the crown of his father Herakleios and performed the ceremony. And straightaway the mob renamed the crowned one Constantine. Now the more ruffianly and boorish part of the people armed themselves against Pyrrhos and came to the church, but did not find him; so at the time of vespers, they entered the sanctuary, accompanied by a group of Jews and other unbelievers. They tore the altar cloth, shamefully defiled the holy spot and, having seized the keys to the door, affixed them to a pole and so went round the City in a lawless fashion. When Pyrrhos had been informed of this, he came to the church the following night and, after embracing the sacred objects, took off his pallium and placed it on the altar table, saying: 'without renouncing the priesthood I abjure the disobedient people.' So he went out quietly and found a secret refuge with a pious woman; then, seizing a favourable occasion, he sailed away to Chalcedon.[75] When some of the monks there heard of his arrival, their leaders were Maximos and Theodosios, who dwelt in Africa, they interrogated him concerning the Exposition made by the former Emperor Herakleios and by Sergios, archpriest of the City, regarding the two wills and energies of Christ our Saviour. So much for Pyrrhos.[76]

75  Mango, *Short History*, p. 83, n. 17, noticed the obvious permutation of places, although it is clear that the event took place in north Africa, in Carthage in 645, it should be noted that, beside such cases being often in Byzantine texts, it should be considered that maybe Nikephoros here utilized a play in words, or rather names of the cities, alluding to Carthage as *new Chalcedon* since Pyrrhos was met by Maximos and other bishops who were obviously *Chalcedonians* in the context of their theology and Orthodox doctrines, toward which they tended to draw Pyrrhos the Monothelite.

76  Nikephoros, *Short History*, § 31.1-33: 'Τῆς τρύγης δὲ ἐπιλαβούσης, οἱ τῆς πόλεως αἰσθόμενοι ὡς ὁ μετὰ Οὐαλεντίνου στρατὸς τούς τε ἀμπελῶνας αὐτῶν διαφθείρει κἀκείνους οὐ συγχωρεῖ ἐκεῖσε περαιοῦσθαι, συνίστανται Πύρρῳ βοῶντες στέφειν Ἡράκλειον τὸν Κωνσταντίνου υἱόν. Πύρρος δὲ τὴν ταραχὴν καὶ τὴν στάσιν τοῦ λαοῦ περιαθρήσας ἀπελογεῖτο ὡς οὐ διὰ τοῦτο αὐτοὶ στασιάζουσιν, ἀλλ' Οὐαλεντίνῳ τὴν βασιλείαν περιποιοῦνται. ἔτι οὖν ἐπικειμένου τοῦ ὄχλου δῆλα ποιεῖ βασιλεῖ ἅπαντα. ὁ δὲ συλλαβόμενος τὸν ἀνεψιὸν Ἡράκλειον εὐθέως ἐπὶ τὸ ἱερὸν ἐχώρει καὶ ἀνέρχεται ἅμα Πύρρῳ ἐν τῷ ἄμβωνι καὶ προτρέπεται στέφειν Ἡράκλειον. οἱ δὲ ὄχλοι τὸν βασιλέα ἐβιάζοντο τὸ ἔργον ἐπιτελεῖν.

This is the most detailed account about Pyrrhos in the *Short History*. It focused on the events which lead to his downfall, as a consequence of the political turmoil that had broken out in Constantinople after Herakleios's death. The description of Pyrrhos's abdication is more detailed than the portrayal of another patriarch's abdication also described in the *Short History* – that of the Orthodox and Iconophile patriarch Germanos of Constantinople. The entire story about Pyrrhos's downfall was vested in a political milieu of his patriarchal office and his connections to the imperial family and the court. The patriarch was portrayed as the advocate of the young Emperor Heraklonas, Martina's son, whose legitimacy and the right to the imperial office he defended, although this was not the main motif of the account and it was certainly not emphasized in the text as it was in the *Chronicle* of Theophanes. This motif was emphasized by the statement that Pyrrhos accused Valentinos of attempting to usurp the imperial rights of Heraklonas, which consequently led to the rebellion of the citizens, since their interests were affected by the military coup. From such events, Nikephoros drew consequences which later resulted in Pyrrhos's downfall.

Nikephoros utilized several terms in this account which carry a strong notion of disorder and iniquity: *ἡ ταραχή, ἡ στάσις, στασιάζω* as well as *ἡ κακοδοξία/κακόδοξοι*. By using these terms, Nikephoros stressed the opposing ideal of order and legitimacy was threatened, leading to negative results. A clear distinction between Pyrrhos and the impersonal multitude of citizens is evident in the account, since they were characterized as 'boorish and ruffian' (*ἀγυρῶδες καὶ ἀγροικωδέστερον*) as they desecrated the holy altar of the church, probably the Hagia Sophia, in their search for the patriarch. Who were these boorish citizens, who, according to Nikephoros, were followed by Jews and other unbelievers, searching for Pyrrhos after he had accomplished the coronation of Herakleios's grandson, who stemmed from

---

ὁ δὲ λαβὼν ἐκ τῆς ἐκκλησίας τὸν τοῦ πατρὸς Ἡρακλείου στέφανον τὸ ἔργον ἐπλήρου. εὐθὺς οὖν τὸν στεφθέντα Κωνσταντῖνον οἱ ὄχλοι μετονομάζουσι. τὸ οὖν ἀγυρῶδες καὶ ἀγροικωδέστερον τοῦ λαοῦ κατὰ Πύρρου τὰς χεῖρας ὥπλιζον, καὶ πρὸς τὸ ἱερὸν γενόμενοι αὐτὸν μὲν οὐχ εὗρον, κατὰ δὲ τὸν καιρὸν τῆς τοῦ λυχνικοῦ συνάξεως εἰσέρχονται ἐπαγόμενοι Ἑβραίων καὶ ἄλλων κακοδόξων ὅμιλον ἐν τῷ θυσιαστηρίῳ. καὶ τὴν μὲν ἐνδυτὴν διαρρηγνῦσι, καὶ τὸν ἱερὸν χῶρον αἰσχρῶς κατερρύπαινον, τάς τε κλεῖς τῶν πυλῶν λαβόντες ἐπὶ κοντοῦ ἀνήρτων, καὶ οὕτω τὴν πόλιν ἀθέσμως περιῄεσαν. Πύρρος δὲ ταῦτα μαθὼν τῇ ἐπιούσῃ νυκτὶ ἐν τῷ ἱερῷ παραγίνεται καὶ πάντα τὰ ἱερὰ ἀσπάζεται καὶ τὸ περικείμενον αὐτῷ ὠμοφόριον περιελὼν τῇ ἱερᾷ ἀποτίθεται τραπέζῃ, φήσας "τῆς ἱερωσύνης μὴ ἀφιστάμενος ἀποτάσσομαι λαῷ ἀπειθεῖ". ἐκεῖθεν ἡσυχῇ ἐξελθὼν παρὰ μιᾷ θεοσεβεστάτῃ γυναικὶ κρυφῇ κατήγετο καὶ καιροῦ εὐθέτου λαβόμενος πρὸς τὴν Χαλκηδόνος ἀπέπλει. οὗ τὴν ἔλευσίν τινες τῶν μοναζόντων ἐκεῖσε ἀκηκοότες περὶ τῶν ἐκτεθέντων παρὰ τοῦ πάλαι Ἡρακλείου τοῦ βασιλέως καὶ Σεργίου τοῦ τῆς πόλεως ἱεράρχου, ἕνεκεν τῶν δύο ἐπὶ τοῦ σωτῆρος Χριστοῦ θελημάτων καὶ ἐνεργειῶν ἀνηρεύνων, ὧν προασπισταὶ ἐτύγχανον Μάξιμος καὶ Θεοδόσιος ὄντες ἐν Ἀφρικῇ. καὶ τὰ μὲν κατὰ Πύρρον οὕτω πως ἔσχεν.'

Eudokias's lineage? Since the crowd pressed Heraklonas and the patriarch to accomplish the coronation, no alternative was left but the conclusion that these 'boorish and ruffianly' citizens who searched for Pyrrhos were, in fact, the more staunch supporters of Empress Martina and her son, who refused to accept the coronation of Constans II. In this aspect, the very term κακόδοξοι should be read not in a doctrinal, theological manner, but in the context of the political idea and the notion of the legitimacy of Herakleios's lineage stemming from Eudokia, and not from the *unlawful* marriage with Martina, which ultimately had consequences for the Church and the patriarch. These citizens, however, managed to seize the keys to the church doors and carried them around the city on a pole. The sharp image might allude to a deeper idea of the pressure and attack against the Church and its patriarch 'in a lawless manner' (ἀθέσμως).

Certain citizens, the 'unbelievers' in a specific context, had armed themselves against the patriarch; they exerted their anger on the holy sanctuary of the Church since they did not find the patriarch. Then they seized and carried the keys to the church door 'in a lawless manner' around the city. Patriarch Pyrrhos, upon learning these events, rather than renounce his priesthood, 'renounced the disobedient people' and withdrew from the patriarchal office. Since Pyrrhos was not connected to the heresy of the Monothelites in the previous narrative, the result is that the Church of Constantinople had lost its archpriest, without stressing that it was a heretical patriarch who abdicated. There were no theological implications in connection to Pyrrhos's Monothelitism. The 'unbelievers' were not mentioned in the context of Orthodoxy versus Monothelitism, but in the political context of Martina's supporters who were ready to attack the patriarch for having crowned as emperor the son of Herakleios from his first *lawful* marriage to the Empress Eudokia. In other words, they were referred to as κακόδοξοι since they disapproved of the imperial lineage of Eudokia, and, in a more specific context, those who participated in the desecration of the holy altar of the church and the *unlawful* carrying of the church keys through the streets of Constantinople.

It is evident that the account of Pyrrhos's abdication from his patriarchal office lacked any theological perspective in connection with the disputes over Monothelitism of the time, but that it was vested completely in the political context of the events which appeared at the imperial court. Nikephoros's main idea was to present the consequences of Martina's imperial ambitions to rule the Empire after Herakleios's death together with her descendants. In that context, and in the context of Nikephoros's open rebuke of Herakleios's unlawful marriage with her, the main message of these chapters was to point out the legitimacy of Herakleios's sons from his first and lawful marriage with Eudokia. Theological context of the phrase ἄλλων κακοδόξων would suggest either that Nikephoros here utilized a source of Monothelite provenance and that such a phrase was directed against the Orthodox, Chalcedonian opposition, or that Nikephoros was not aware of the consequences and the result of utilizing such a phrase in his narrative.[77] However, the account itself was not vested in the theological context of polemics over Monothelite disputes. Nikephoros demonstrated elsewhere his high awareness of the essence of this Christological clash of the seventh century. In a wider context, the 'unbelievers' were the citizens of Constantinople who armed themselves against Pyrrhos, as much as Emperor Constantine V was *impious* in his persecution and execution of the Patriarch Constantine II, who supported Iconoclasm.

The abdication of Pyrrhos corresponds with the description of Bishop Martyrios of Antioch in one aspect. The patriarch's words of renouncing his patriarchal office are similar to what Theophanes in his *Chronicle* ascribed to Martyrios of Antioch, who struggled against the Monophysites during the reign of Emperor Leo I. Bishop Martyrios went to Constantinople to negotiate with the emperor against the Monophysite reaction in Antioch. When he returned to his bishopric, he found Zeno, the emperor's son-in-law, aiding the heretics:

> After returning to Antioch and finding the people in revolt and Zeno lending them aid, he resigned from his bishopric in front of the congregation, saying: 'With the clergy insubordinate, the people disobedient, and the Church polluted, I resign, keeping for myself the dignity of the priesthood.'[78]

The essence of this report was present in the account of Pyrrhos's abdication. The 'disobedient people' were in fact the same referenced in both stories, and both bishops renounced them, rather than renounce their priesthood. In the case of Martyrios of Antioch, the Monophysite dispute was the main cause, while in the case of Patriarch Pyrrhos, who was a Monothelite – the heresy stemming from Monophysitism – the cause was of a political

---

77   Cf. Mango, *Short History*, pp. 11-12. Cf. Mango, 'The Breviarium', pp. 544-545.
78   Cf. Theophanes, *Chronicle*, 113.32-34: 'ἐπανελθὼν δὲ εἰς Ἀντιόχειαν καὶ εὑρὼν τοὺς λαοὺς στασιάζοντας καὶ Ζήνωνα τούτοις συμπράττοντα ἐπ ἐκκλησίας τῇ ἐπισκοπῇ ἀπετάξατο εἰπών· κλήρῳ ἀνυποτάκτῳ, καὶ λαῷ ἀπειθεῖ, καὶ ἐκκλησίᾳ ἐρρυπωμένῃ ἀποτάττομαι, φυλάττων ἑαυτῷ τὸ ἀξίωμα τῆς ἱερωσύνης.' Cf. Mango, *Short History*, p. 193.

nature, or at least Nikephoros transferred this narrative into a political context. However, the Patriarch Pyrrhos was in a way compared to the Bishop Martyrios, who obviously was a Chalcedonian in term of doctrine and Orthodoxy. In this context, Nikephoros's mistake of making Pyrrhos leave Constantinople for Chalcedon instead of Carthage seems even more suspicious and maybe not so spontaneous or misleading after all.

From the perspective of the epoch between the two Iconoclasms, disobedience (or rather obedience) as a motif in the Church of Constantinople was a significant issue. It is apparent concerning the disobedience of the monks, led by the Studites opposition to the patriarchs Tarasios and Nikephoros, which was caused by the Studites having ambitions to influence Church policy. In contrast, there was the issue of obedience towards the Church's autonomous status in the Empire, which was in fact diminished and almost totally cancelled during the first Iconoclastic period, under the emperors Leo III and Constantine V. Nikephoros later stressed this same motif in his account of Patriarch Germanos's abdication under Leo III, citing exactly his compliance to the ecclesiastical tradition of submission to the ecumenical councils in doctrinal matters and matters of faith. Thus, his refusal to accept Iconoclasm as proposed by the emperor was, in fact, his remaining in the tradition of the Orthodox understanding of the place and role of the bishop regarding doctrinal matters, and, of course, in these issues emperors did not have any authority.

The imposition of an oath of loyalty to Orthodoxy as professed by the Church of Constantinople after 787, which Emperor Michael I had sworn before Patriarch Nikephoros, and later the patriarch's attempt to impose a similar oath to the Emperor Leo V, which (according to Theophanes) Leo offered in advance of his coronation, testifies to the commitment of the imperial power to remain in obedience to the Church in matters of faith. Leo V's refusal to admit such relations before his coronation testifies to the intention of the Church to finish what was started in 787 and to impose such a practice as a canon in the ninth century as well. In such a context, the words of the Patriarch Pyrrhos from the account of his abdication as a consequence of the disobedience to the Church fit this proposed concept.

## The Advancement of the Arabs

In order to acquire a complete understanding of Nikephoros's literary method in the process of creating of the image of Herakleios, it is necessary to turn our attention to the last part of the account on his rule and the representation of the Arab conquests of Byzantine territories in the Near East and Egypt.[79] Herakleios's policies concerning the Arabs were unsuccessful. He failed to preserve those regions which he had recently liberated from the Persian conquerors. The intrusion of Arabs in Palestine, Syria, and Egypt was not stopped, and these territories were lost for the Empire during Herakleios's life.[80] Such events, however, were presented in a particular manner in the *Short History*. After a successful military campaign against Persia, which was introduced in the work as Herakleios's personal virtue (thus forming a positive image of the emperor, who was unselfishly devoted in decisive moments for the state), a different period ensued with completely opposite results for the emperor's reign. In this second part of Herakleios's narrative, the emperor was mostly mentioned in the context of his personal moral transgression and fall, finally ending with the description of his death caused by illness, which was mentioned as a consequence of his personal sin.[81]

The section of Herakleios's rule that was described in the context of his affairs with the Arabs is more concise in comparison with the account of his Persian war. In the first eighteen chapters of Herakleios's history, nine were dedicated to various aspects of the war against Chosroes II, that is, more than half of these eighteen chapters dealt with Herakleios's successful war with Persia. In the remaining ten chapters, only four were dedicated to the issue of the Arab conquests and the Byzantine military defeats. Furthermore, the 'Arab episode' was significantly deprived of literary elements and of the arrangement of narration in the context of the structure of the text, which had its purpose in the previous Persian account to highlight Herakleios and his accomplishments. In the description of lost battles and defeats which the Byzantines had suffered from the Arabs, all the narratological elements present in the oration of Shahin (and similar literary elements of the text in the history of Arab incursions into Egypt) are not visible in this part of the *Short History*.[82] By such features in the last part

79  A certain chronological confusion in Nikephoros's account of the Arabic conquests was noted already by Butler, *The Arab Conquest*, pp. 207-209. See also Mango, *Short History*, pp. 188-189.
80  Cf. Kaegi, *Byzantium and the Early Islamic Conquest*; Kaegi, *Heraclius*, pp. 229-264 and 281-289.
81  The famous image of Herakleios's fear and depression which had almost isolated him from his imperial duties and the capital city of the Empire is placed in this second part of the account of his reign (Nikephoros, *Short History*, § 25.1-10). However, Kaegi, *Byzantium and the Early Islamic Conquest*, pp. 63-65, believed that even after the year 630 Herakleios was indeed at the height of his power and reigning abilities.
82  Judging by the hypotheses brought forward by Howard-Johnston, *Witnesses to a World Crisis*, p. 251, regarding the nature of the *Short History* and its relation to the sources utilized

of Herakleios account, it seems that Nikephoros deliberately presented this part of Herakleios's reign in a more concise manner.[83]

In this section of the *Short History*, a structural aspect is evident, having for its purpose a desire to shape the message about the character of Herakleios's rule – a crossover and pervasion of two elements of narration. Although Nikephoros has already introduced Arabs in the narrative as a new factor in the description of Herakleios's rule, he inserted the narrative of Herakleios's triumph and the celebration of his victories over the Persians, which were celebrated in Constantinople, parallel to telling a story about how Byzantium lost its territories in the Arab attacks. The story about the Cross and its elevation by Patriarch Sergios of Constantinople was mentioned in this place in the narration. At first glance, it could be difficult to notice these events, arranged to fit into the very beginning of the account about the defeats inflicted upon the Byzantines by the Arabs. Thus, § 18 began with a short remark how the 'Saracens' began to appear from the region known as 'Aithribos' and attempted to sack neighbouring regions. Further, the narration in this chapter shifted to Herakleios's policy concerning the Turks, emphasizing Herakleios's readiness to fulfil his promise of marriage between the Lord of the Turks and Eudokia, an agreement which was not implemented due to the Turk's death. Additionally, through the mention of his children's deaths and with more details about the bringing of the Cross from Jerusalem to Constantinople (with the patriarch meeting the emperor and the relic), Nikephoros promulgated the idea about the need for guarding the relic by the Byzantines and their attempt to keep it from falling into the hands of the Arabs, the new adversaries of the Empire. However, in the pages of the *Short History*, the description of the elevation of the Cross in Constantinople was placed in the account of Herakleios's victory over the Persians and the celebration of the results of his successful past imperial policies. In the following § 19, Nikephoros placed the story about Herakleios's triumphal return to the City, and in § 20 he proceeded to

by the author, it is reasonable to presume on the basis of this evident difference in the manner of portrayal of the Arab section of the *Short History* that Nikephoros probably summarized his sources, which might have been considerably more comprehensive than they seem to be according to Nikephoros's narration in his text.

83  Липшиц, 'Никифор и его исторический труд', pp. 85-105, was inclined towards such a hypothesis. She also noticed that George the Monk followed Nikephoros in his own account of the Persian war lead by Herakleios. She, however, regarded Nikephoros as a selective author who was ready to pass over negative aspects of certain emperors portrayed in his history. In contrast, Mango, *Short History*, p. 9, expressed doubt towards such an understanding of Nikephoros's authorial approach in shaping the images of emperors.

a more detailed account of the raids conducted by the Arabs in the region of Antioch.

Through such an arrangement of his material and historical events, a considerable literary attempt of the author reveals itself, possibly to reduce the actual failure of Herakleios's policy towards the Arabs. In that sense, it is interesting to make a comparison between the two stories which carry almost identical narrative elements but which have mutually different contexts and thus different purposes. Namely, in the aforementioned episode of Herakleios's meeting with the Lord of the Turks and the making of a military alliance in the wake of his Persian campaign, the agreement and alliance itself was to be secured by the marriage of the Turkic Khagan and the Byzantine princess. What should be emphasized here is the unmentioned but an obvious fact that the Khagan of the Turks was not a Christian like the Lord of the Huns, whose baptism Nikephoros described as well. However, in § 19 immediately after the first introduction of Arabs into the narration, Nikephoros mentioned almost in a passing that Herakleios had the intention to fulfil the agreement about marriage as he promised earlier to the Khagan of the Turks. In contrast, in the Arab section of his account about Herakleios's reign, we encounter a story about the attempt by the Patriarch Kyros of Alexandria to make peace with the leader of the Arabs by proposing a similar marriage, this time between the emperor's daughter and Ambros, leader of Arabs who had invaded Egypt. However, Nikephoros here informs us that Herakleios acted furiously, and that he rejected such a proposition by the patriarch with clear disapproval, calling the Arab leader godless and an enemy of Christians. Possibly because he was a foe and not an ally of the Byzantines? So the idea of Ambros as a heathen now became accentuated in the story, while in the previous narrative about the alliance with the Turkic leader this was not mentioned. The emphasis was rather placed on his readiness to make friendship with Herakleios.[84]

However, by arranging such terms in Egypt, Kyros of Alexandria fell into disgrace and earned only Herakleios's disapproval and criticism. These are two distinct but similar events with obviously different narrative messages. In the portrayal of Patriarch Kyros, who was directly blamed for the fall of Egypt under the Arabs, an image of Herakleios was formed,

---

84  Nikephoros, *Short History*, § 18.4-7: 'Herakleios had ordered that his daughter Eudokia, whom he had betrothed to the lord of the Turks, should be sent from Byzantium, but when it became known that the Lord of the Turks was slain, he ordered that she should return.' ("Ἡράκλειος δὲ τὴν θυγατέρα Εὐδοκίαν τοῦ Βυζαντίου ἐξιέναι ἐπέτρεψεν ὡς τῷ Τούρκῳ ταύτην κατεγγυήσας· καὶ ἐπειδὴ ἔγνωστο ὅτι σφαγῇ ὁ Τοῦρκος ἀνῄρητο, ταύτην ὑποστρέφειν ἐκέλευεν.')

and that image excused the emperor to some extent for the loss of such an important province. In the case of the Patriarch Kyros, this was not the final representation of his person in the Byzantine historical events of the seventh century. Nikephoros later explained that the patriarch of Alexandria, who was deposed from his see by Herakleios, enjoyed respect among the Arabs and their leader Ambros. Kyros was later also rehabilitated in his patriarchal office by Herakleios's successor – Emperor Heraklonas. However, the esteem which Kyros enjoyed among the Arabs implied that his political strategy of making an alliance with the Arabs in Egypt in order to preserve this province under Byzantine rule would have proved useful if Herakleios had not rejected it.[85] If this detail can be ascribed rather to the source Nikephoros utilized in the course of his writing, it remains undisputed that he introduced these literary elements into his work with a plan to create a certain image of Emperor Herakleios and the character of his reign.

Nikephoros, however, did not avoid mentioning several military defeats of the appointed Byzantine generals, whom Herakleios sent to confront the Arabs.[86] These accounts present the only explicit mention of Byzantine defeats in relation to the Arabs in the part of the *Short History* dedicated to Herakleios. However, in one of just two mentions of Byzantine military defeats in the war against the Arabs, Nikephoros pointed out that the army commander acted according to his own initiative, in pursuit of war, despite Herakleios's clear orders to avoid open battle with the Arabs. The emperor's stance that the war with the Arabs in Syria should be avoided connected with the Byzantines refusing the Arabs a right to trade on Byzantine territories. Therefore, Nikephoros mentioned and described the manner of death of a Byzantine dignitary, Sergios ὁ κατὰ Νικήταν who was personally responsible for such an outcome, and further in the course of this story Nikephoros added that 'due to such reasons' Herakleios had ruled out the possibility of conflicts with the Arabs:[87]

> The charge against him [e.g. Sergios ὁ κατὰ Νικήταν] was that he had persuaded Herakleios not to allow the Saracens to trade from the Roman country and send out of the Roman State the 30 lbs. of gold which

85  Butler, *The Arab Conquest*, pp. 213 and 306 – a historical evaluation of these events which assumes that Kyros might have been inspired towards such policy of making an alliance with the Arabs in order to free the Patriarchate of Alexandria from the influence of Constantinople.
86  Cf. Nikephoros, *Short History*, § 23.1-4 and 19-21.
87  Cf. Howard-Johnston, *Witnesses to a World Crisis*, p. 261, identified three different clashes of Byzantines with Arabs in Nikephoros's accounts of Byzantine defeats.

they normally received by way of commercial gain, and for this reason they began to lay waste the Roman lands. On this account [Herakleios] ordered Theodore not to join battle with the Saracens. But his subordinate commander did not act according to the emperor's wishes because he had rebellion in his mind (ἐπεὶ νεώτερα αὐτῷ βουλευσάμενος ἦν) and [the men] were induced to fight so as to overcome the enemy unexpectedly: they believed that victory would be on the side of the insurgents against the emperor. And so he joined battle with the Saracens at a place called Gabitha. But they, having set ambuscades beforehand and skirmished with a few men, advanced on the Romans. The ambushed men fell suddenly on the latter and, having surrounded them, slew many soldiers and officers.[88]

This story was placed in a account which focused on the plot against the emperor, but which also included the mention of his unlawful marriage, with allusion to the king and prophet David and his sin through the expression ἡ ἁμαρτία αὐτοῦ ἐνώπιον αὐτοῦ διὰ παντός, which accentuated Herakleios's constant unlawful position due to his unlawful marriage with his niece.[89] In such a complex context, the detail about the defeat of Byzantine army against the Arabs at Gabitha appeared in the narrative, as well as the motif of treachery. The emperor's *strategos* Theodore acted contrary to Herakleios's orders, thus justifying the Arabs and their attack, while conversely alluding that the Byzantines were responsible for their own defeat. The emperor thus clearly wanted to evade such an unjust war, or rather, that might be a notion the author wished his audience to adopt. In that sense, it seems that the author's opinion about the plot against the emperor has appeared – it is as if Nikephoros's irony is visible in the statement: '[the men] were induced to fight so as to overcome the enemy unexpectedly: they believed that victory would be on the side of the insurgents against the emperor', but in fact, we read further that they suffered a grievous defeat. From such a narration, a message appears, namely, that the emperor did not have trustful associates when dealing with the Arabs. And as a second

---

88    Nikephoros, *Short History*, § 20.15-31: 'αἰτίαν δὲ αὐτῷ ἐπῆγον ὡς αὐτὸς παρεσκεύασεν Ἡράκλειον μὴ συγχωρεῖν Σαρακηνοῖς (ἐκ τῆς Ῥωμαίων γῆς ἐκπορεύεσθαι) τὰς συνήθως παρεχομένας αὐτοῖς τριάκοντα χρυσίου λίτρας δι' ἐμπορικῆς ἀμοιβῆς ἐκ τῆς Ῥωμαϊκῆς πολιτείας ἐκπέμπειν· ἐντεῦθέν τε αὐτοὺς ἄρξαι τῇ Ῥωμαίων λυμαίνεσθαι χώρᾳ. ἐκ τούτου παρήγγειλε Θεοδώρῳ μὴ συμβάλλειν πρὸς μάχην Σαρακηνοῖς. οἱ δὲ προλοχήσαντες καὶ ὀλίγοις τισὶν ἀκροβολισάμενοι Ῥωμαίοις ὑπήγοντο. εἰσπίπτουσι δὲ αὐτοῖς οἱ ἐκ τῶν ἐνέδρων ἐξαπιναίως, καὶ μέσον ἀπολαβόντες πολλοὺς ἔκτειναν στρατιώτας τε καὶ ἄρχοντας.'
89    Nikephoros, *Short History*, § 20.6-7.

conclusion, it becomes obvious from the author's point of view, that not all attacks from the side of the Arabs were considered in a negative context. This same attitude was shown towards the Byzantine defeats, which were sometimes a result of their misbehaviour in relation to the emperor or the state. In other words, in the case of the initial defeat in the battle of Gabitha against the Arabs, the Byzantines were justly defeated, since they denied the Arabs their right to trade in the territories under Roman rule, which was contrary to Herakleios's policy. Later on, Nikephoros emphasized a similar point in the reign of Justinian II and his war against the Arabs, which he portrayed as a result of neglecting the peace treaty which was established with the Arabs during the reign of his father Constantine IV. Of course, this account also promoted the idea of rebellion against a righteous emperor, which in its essence was an attack upon the state order, which brought defeat and other grave consequences to the Byzantine state. From that aspect, Nikephoros could not approve such actions. This account fit into his general idea of the crumbling of order when imperial power was weak or neglected, or even opposed in an attempted coup.

In light of our analysis of the image of Herakleios as Nikephoros portrayed him in this second part of the account of his entire reign, it appears as a conclusion that it was not the emperor who was responsible for at least some of the Byzantine defeats which were inflicted upon them in Syria. However, when dealing with Egypt, Nikephoros seems to praise the initiative of the patriarch of Alexandria, also portraying a certain inconsistency in Herakleios by highlighting his failure to accept the political strategy of the patriarch. In § 23 Nikephoros wrote that Herakleios had conferred to a certain Marianos the *cubicularios* the command over Byzantine troops in Egypt,[90] after a series of defeats against the Arabs:

> And [he] dispatched him with instructions to consult with Kyros, arch-priest of Alexandria, that they might take joint action with regard to the Saracens. Now Kyros had informed the emperor that he was going to conclude an agreement with Ambros, *phylarch* of the Saracens, and [pay him] tribute which, he stated, he would raise by a commercial levy, while the imperial taxes would not be affected. [He also recommended] that the Augusta Eudokia or another of the emperor's daughters should be offered in marriage [to Ambros] with a view to his being consequently baptized in the holy bath and becoming a Christian, for Ambros and his

---

90   Howard-Johnston, *Witnesses to a World Crisis*, p. 262, regarding the name and identity of this dignitary.

army had confidence in Kyros and regarded him with great affection. But Herakleios would have none of that. So Marianos, too, was aware of these matters, he rejected the advice (γνώμη) of Kyros,[91] and having attacked the Saracens, fell in battle as did many of his soldiers.[92]

Here it is significant to notice that Nikephoros utilized a more general term τὰ πρὸς τοὺς Σαρακηνοὺς διάθοιντο, which left space for different policies, including peace arrangements versus open warfare. Later, in § 26 when Nikephoros again told the story about Patriarch Kyros and his strategy of peaceful integration of Arabs in Egypt, he presented the patriarch's defence, highlighting his words that, in the event that his proposal of paying tribute to the Arabs was accepted, the Arabs would remain calm (ἡσυχάζω).[93]

Nikephoros only accentuated Herakleios's attitude towards Kyros's strategy in one short sentence, as if stressing his reluctance to accept the proposed tactic for the defence of Egypt and his carelessness to grasp the idea. Thus he emphasized the emperor's rashness in dismissing the advice of the patriarch. By placing the contrary story of Herakleios's readiness to remain committed to the Lord of the Turks in his promise to betroth his daughter Eudokia for the Khagan in a relatively close place in the text, Nikephoros promulgated the idea of the emperor's inconsistency and maybe a fault in the defence of Egypt.[94] Further, in the same section of the story, the

---

91  Nikephoros utilizes the term γνώμη, which might imply *judgement* or *reasoning*, which again has almost a tone of praise for Kyros's suggested measures, and a critique of the emperor's act of refusal.

92  Nikephoros, *Short History*, § 23.6-21: 'μετ᾽ ἐκεῖνον προβάλλεται στρατηγὸν Μαριανὸν κουβικουλάριον παρὰ Ῥωμαίων τὴν ἀξίαν καὶ πέμπει ἐκεῖσε, παραγγείλας ὡς ἀνακοινοῦσθαι Κύρῳ τῷ Ἀλεξανδρείας ἱεράρχῃ, καὶ ὡς ἂν κοινῇ (βουλεύσοιντο) τὰ πρὸς τοὺς Σαρακηνοὺς διάθοιντο. Κῦρος δὲ ἦν δεδηλωκὼς βασιλεῖ σπείσεσθαι ἐπὶ τελέσμασιν Ἄμβρῳ τῷ τῶν Σαρακηνῶν φυλάρχῳ, ἃ δὴ καὶ ὑπέχειν δι᾽ ἐμπολαίου συνεισφορᾶς ἐσήμαινε, τὰ δὲ τῷ βασιλεῖ παρεχόμενα ἀδιάπτωτα μένειν· κατεγγυηθῆναι δὲ αὐτῷ Εὐδοκίαν τὴν Αὐγούσταν ἢ μίαν τῶν θυγατέρων τοῦ βασιλέως ὡς ἐντεῦθεν καὶ τῷ θείῳ λουτρῷ βαπτισθησομένῳ καὶ Χριστιανῷ χρηματίσοντι. ἐπείθετο γὰρ Ἄμβρος τῷ Κύρῳ καὶ ὁ τούτου στρατός· καὶ γὰρ ἠγάπων αὐτὸν λίαν. καὶ τούτων Ἡράκλειος οὐδενὸς ἠνείχετο. ἐπειδὴ δὲ καὶ Μαριανὸς ταῦτα ἐξηπίστατο, διίστατο τῆς τοῦ Κύρου γνώμης, καὶ συμβαλὼν Σαρακηνοῖς πίπτει τε αὐτός καὶ σὺν αὐτῷ στρατὸς ἱκανός.' Cf. Butler, *The Arab Conquest*, pp. 207-209, who identified the chronological inconsistency in Nikephoros's account and who also expressed doubt towards this entire story since it is not present in the oriental sources. However, Mango, *Short History*, p. 189, noted that similar stories are present in Theophanes's *Chronicle* and in the *History* of Michael the Syrian, but pointed out that the origins of this account still remain to be determined.

93  Nikephoros, *Short History*, § 26.11-15.

94  Howard-Johnston, *Witnesses to a World Crisis*, p. 263, remarked that Herakleios himself had already set a precedent in his diplomatic activity with the Turks, so that there exists a foundation to express trust towards the narrative about Kyros's strategy as Nikephoros presented it.

consequences of such a policy by the emperor were described. Namely, the commander who had shared Herakleios's distrust towards the patriarch's diplomacy was decisively defeated on the battlefield. Thus the military disaster came as an outcome of incompetent Byzantine politics.

If we accept that the main theme around which the entire narration in § 26 was based was the proposed strategy of Kyros in defence of Egypt and its capture by the Arabs, then it follow that the rest of the narration about the failure of the military commanders appointed by Herakleios to win victory over Arabs was directed towards a positive image of the Patriarch Kyros of Alexandria. However, this part of the *Short History* can be viewed in a different way. Namely, the main narrative described Herakleios's relation to the Arabs and their invasion of Byzantine territories, and his failure (or rather his commanders' failure) to win victory over the enemy brought the patriarch of Alexandria into the main focus of the story. Thus, it seems that two different narratives arcs are present in the story, so that the main one, which described the emperor's policy, becomes replaced by the account regarding Kyros's proposal about making peace with the Arabs, which was rejected, and it finally ends with the mention of the final Byzantine failure in Egypt. Nikephoros, therefore, brought to a close his presentation of Herakleios's policy towards the Arabs with the conclusion that his policy was unsuccessful. He then turned his attention in the next four chapters to Herakleios personally and again mentioned Kyros's proposed policy towards the Arabs, Herakleios's refusal, the patriarch's defence, and his unwilling-ness to accept the emperor's accusations. This is a motif of considerable significance in the later shaping of the image of emperor-patriarch relations in the time of the Iconoclastic Emperors Leo III and Constantine V, but which also corresponds to the image of Patriarch Sergios of Constantinople, who directly criticized Herakleios's unlawful marriage.

# 4 The Dark Century

## The 'Peace and Tranquillity' of the Emperor Constantine IV

In the reign of Emperor Herakleios, Nikephoros had set the model of an ideal emperor, of a desirable state order, and of a relationship between the emperor and the patriarch in Byzantium. The reign of Herakleios was portrayed as an age of order which had been established in contrast to the previous state of affairs during Phokas's rule, and according to the ideal notions as they were expressed in the oration of Shahin. Herakleios managed to restore the Byzantine state in the face of the threats coming from Persia. He established friendly and brotherly relations with the patriarchs of Constantinople. However, his unlawful marriage was a cause of internal disorder, which had first taken root in the imperial family after his death, and later in Constantinople, causing the abdication of Patriarch Pyrrhos. Regarding the further historical narration in the *Short History*, Nikephoros continued by narrating the reign of the Emperor Constantine IV, whose reign is the last accomplished rule according to the previously established models which were presented in Herakleios's reign. The inner turmoil of the Dark Century of Byzantium set in with the reigns of Justinian II and the emperors who ruled until the restoration of state under the Isaurian dynasty.

In the chronological frame between the years after Herakleios's death and the assumption of power by Leo III, ten emperors in total were mentioned, with more or less space dedicated to several of these emperors. In this part of his work, Nikephoros gave most of his attention to the government of Emperor Justinian II, his first downfall, his return to power, and his execution. In the context of an overall narrative, his rule can be viewed as central to this part of the *Short History*, since it connected the two periods of rules by Herakleios and the later emperors Leo III and Constantine V, and since it accentuated the establishment of state order in the Empire. The account of Justinian II's reign and his subsequent successors, in the form in which it was presented, thus formed a prelude to the final part of the *Short History*, but it also accented the previous reigns of Herakleios and Constantine IV. The problem presented by the portrayal of Justinian II in a strictly negative manner requires a wider examination of this issue in its narratological context and in its links to other significant ideas within the *Short History*, among which the connection between the descriptions of state order and the images of emperors is the key theme.

The narrative about the reign of Justinian II would not be so striking in its illustration of this emperor's cruel and indecent manner of rule, in which peace was utterly diminished both in the internal and external affairs of the Empire, if it was not for the preceding image of Constantine IV and his reign, which was characterized by the phrase 'peace and tranquillity', which he managed to introduce during his reign. This is a rather short but a significant part of Nikephoros's work.

Immediately after Constantine IV 'was invested with the imperial office [...], the leader of the Saracens built many ships and sent them against Byzantium under the command of Chaleb, a man most loyal and experienced in war'. Nikephoros then wrote that, during the next seven years, many naval battles took place in the vicinity of Constantinople, starting in spring and ending in winter, and the Arab fleet made no success. On the contrary, since they were 'harshly hurt' and 'severely defeated', they suffered a great shipwreck during their retreat, so: 'On hearing of the disaster of his fleet, the emperor of the Saracens (τῶν Σαρακηνῶν βασιλεὺς) sent ambassadors to Constantine with a view to concluding a treaty on payment of an annual tribute.' The emperor had sent an experienced and wise patrician, who had to conclude peace with the Arabs (ὡς τὰ ἐπὶ τῇ εἰρήνῃ διαλεχθησόμενον):

> He reached an agreement with them and confirmed by oath a peace treaty for thirty years (ὅρκοις τὴν εἰρήνεν βεβαιωσάμενος). When this news had reached those who inhabited the West, the leader of the Avars, and the archons of neighbouring nations who were living further West, they [too] sent ambassadors to the emperor bearing gifts and asked for peace (εἰρήνην ἐξῄτησαν). The emperor consented to this, and from then peace and tranquillity (εἰρήνη καὶ γαλήνη) prevailed in both West and in the East.[1]

---

1    Nikephoros, *Short History*, § 34.1-36: 'Μεθ' ὃν Κωνσταντῖνος ὁ υἱὸς τὰ τῆς βασιλείας ἐγχειρίζεται σκῆπτρα. καὶ τούτου ἀρξαμένου εὐθὺς ὁ τῶν Σαρακηνῶν ἡγούμενος ναῦς πλείστας κατασκευάσας κατὰ τοῦ Βυζαντίου ἐκπέμπει, ἡγεμόνα τούτων ἐπιστήσας, ἅτε πιστότατον καὶ τὰ πολέμια ἔμπειρον, κατὰ τὴν ἑαυτῶν διάλεκτον Χαλὲβ ὀνομαζόμενον· ὃς ἀναχθεὶς προσωρμίζετο ἐν προαστείοις τοῦ Βυζαντίου, κατὰ τὸν παραθαλάσσιον τόπον τὸν καλούτοῦ Βυζαντίου, κατὰ τὸν παραθαλάσσιον τόπον τὸν καλούμενον Ἕβδομον. τοῦτον αἰσθόμενος Κωνσταντῖνος ἀντιπαρατάττεται καὶ αὐτὸς στόλῳ μεγάλῳ. ὑφ' ὧν πλεῖσται ναυμαχίαι ἑκάστης ἡμέρας ἐγίνοντο, τοῦ πολέμου συγκροτουμένου ἀπὸ τοῦ ἐαρινοῦ μέχρι φθινοπωρινοῦ καιροῦ. χειμῶνος δὲ ἐπιγινομένου ὁ τῶν Σαρακηνῶν στόλος διαπεραιωθεὶς ἐν Κυζίκῳ διεχείμαζε, καὶ πάλιν ἔαρος ἀρχομένου ἐκεῖθεν ἀντανάχθεὶς ὡσαύτως τοῦ διὰ θαλάσσης πολέμου εἴχετο. ἑπτὰ οὖν ἔτεσι τοῦ πολέμου διαρκέσαντος τέλος οὐδὲν πλέον ὁ τῶν Σαρακηνῶν ἤνυσε στόλος, ἀλλὰ πολλούς τε ἄνδρας μαχίμους ἀποβαλόντες καὶ δεινῶς τραυματισθέντες καὶ χαλεπῶς ἡττημένοι ὑπενόστουν πρὸς τὰ οἰκεῖα καταίροντες. πρὸς δὲ τοῖς πελάζουσι τοῦ Συλλαίου γενόμενοι ὑπὸ σκληρῶν πνευμάτων καὶ θαλασσίου κλύδωνος καταληφθέντες πανστρατιᾷ διώλοντο. ὁ δὲ τῶν Σαρακηνῶν βασιλεὺς τὸ τοῦ στόλου ἀκούσας δυστύχημα πρέσβεις ἀποστέλλει πρὸς Κωνσταντῖνον

This is the first such account in the *Short History* that carries specific and explicit literary elements in the description of the event, unlike and contrary to the general and concise reference to the Byzantines in the account of Herakleios's reign and his unsuccessful policy against the Arabs. This was a policy that Constantine IV also managed to accomplish by successfully defending Constantinople from the Arabs, thus in a way successfully accomplishing the otherwise negative consequences of Herakleios's unsuccessful war against the Arabs, and finally introducing peace between the Romans and the Arabs. Since the reign of his father, Emperor Constans II, was portrayed in a very concise manner in the *Short History*, with no attention to his policy toward the Arabs, in the narratological sequence of the *Short History* – from Herakleios to Constantine IV – his peace with the Arabs was actually the first introduction of order in the policy of Byzantium towards the Arabs from the beginning of the work. Thus, here for the first time peace with the Arabs assumed its proper context, which was crucial for Nikephoros to stress.

In contrast, Nikephoros did not consider it impossible to attach to such a concept of Constantine IV's reign the account of the emperor's, or rather Byzantium's, defeat against the Bulgarians in 681. When the emperor was informed about Bulgarian intrusions on the territories of the Empire, a fleet and a maritime army were prepared to fend off 'this nation'. The Bulgarians were surprised by the suddenness of the Byzantine expedition, which failed due to the disorganization in the Byzantine army. Namely, being ill the emperor left the battleground to receive medical treatment, and then news spread through the military ranks that the emperor had fled. The entire army then started retreating in panic, being followed and attacked by the Bulgarians, and thus finally defeated. The result was that the Bulgarians inhabited the regions around Varna, and continued to pillage areas in Thrace. 'Seeing this, the emperor was forced to pay them tribute.'[2]

ὡς σπεισόμενος πρὸς αὐτὸν ἐπὶ τελέσμασιν ἐνιαυσίοις. ὁ δὲ τούτους δεξάμενος καὶ τὰ δηλωθέντα ἀκηκοὼς συνεκπέμπει αὐτοῖς Ἰωάννην τὸν πατρίκιον, τὸ ἐπίκλην Πιτζιγαύδιον, πολυπειρίᾳ καὶ φρονήσει διαφέροντα, ὡς τὰ ἐπὶ τῇ εἰρήνῃ διαλεχθησόμενον· ὃς πρὸς τὰ τῶν Σαρακηνῶν γενόμενος ἤθη συμβαίνει τε αὐτοῖς ὅρκοις τὴν εἰρήνην βεβαιωσάμενος ἐπὶ τριάκοντα ἔτεσιν, ὥστε παρέχεσθαι Ῥωμαίοις ὑπὸ τῶν Σαρακηνῶν ἀνὰ ἔτος ποσότητα χρυσίου τρεῖς χιλιάδας ἄνδρας τε αἰχμαλώτους πεντήκοντα καὶ ἵππους πεντήκοντα. ταῦτα ἀκηκοότες καὶ οἱ πρὸς τὰ ἑσπέρια οἰκοῦντες μέρη, τουτέστιν ὁ τῶν Ἀβάρων ἡγεμὼν καὶ οἱ ἐπέκεινα ἄρχοντες τῶν πρὸς δύσιν παρακειμένων ἐθνῶν διὰ πρέσβεων δῶρα τῷ βασιλεῖ στείλαντες εἰρήνην ἐζήτησαν· ἐφ' οἷς εἴξαντος τοῦ βασιλέως εἰρήνη τὸ λοιπὸν καὶ γαλήνη ἔν τε τοῖς ἑῴοις ἔν τε τοῖς ἑσπερίοις ἐβραβεύετο.'
2    Nikephoros, *Short History*, § 36.1-29.

With this Nikephoros ended his narration of § 36, and in the next section, which was the last in his account of Constantine IV's reign, Nikephoros wrote about the Sixth Ecumenical Council and the emperor's merits for introducing peace in the Church, which was divided by the schism of the Monothelites:

> The Roman Empire being thus at peace on all sides, the ungodly heresy of the Monothelites, which had begun in the days of Emperor Herakleios, was gaining in strength and a schism prevailed in the Catholic Church.[3]

The emperor's readiness to make even a somewhat humiliating peace with the Bulgarians, which was caused by the failed military campaign, presented – in the interpretation of the writer of the *Short History* – a positive ideal, since peace prevailed in the state. Justinian II, leading the Byzantine Empire into an unstable twenty-year period of internal strife and disastrous wars with both the Bulgarians and the Arabs, later broke that peace.

In light of this evaluation of the structure of the chapters dedicated to Emperor Constantine IV, and given that they preceded the account of Justinian II's reign, it is possible to demonstrate that (at least in these parts of the *Short History*) Nikephoros's main preoccupation was to present the ideal of peace and order in the Empire. A particular emperor received a final evaluation either as negative or as positive – as an accepted role model of the emperor – in the pages of the *Short History* depending on whether he was able to introduce these ideals of peace and order during the course of his reign or, on the contrary, whether he acted to weaken these ideals. However, as we have seen, the elements which comprised such an ideal, and which led to the fulfilling of such ideas, could vary and were not exclusively dependent on the elements of the political processes and the outcomes of military acts. For example, Herakleios's personal downfall and sin had affected his position as emperor, causing his illness, and this may have been linked by Nikephoros to his unsuccessful military campaign against the Arabs.

In contrast to Herakleios's personal sin and his adherence to the doctrines of the Monothelites, which was only vaguely mentioned in the account of Constantine IV's reign, Nikephoros highlighted the virtue of Constantine IV, who convoked the council that solved the schism in the Church. Theophanes, who was firmly committed to doctrinal context in his narration,

---

3    Nikephoros, *Short History*, § 37.1-3: 'Οὕτω τοιγαροῦν εἰρηνευούσης πάντοθεν τῆς Ῥωμαίων βασιλείας ἡ τῶν Μονοθελητῶν δυσσεβὴς αἵρεσις ἐκρατύνετο, ἤδη τῶν ἀφ' Ἡρακλείου τοῦ βασιλέως χρόνων λαβοῦσα τὴν ἀρχήν· καὶ σχίσμα ἦν περὶ τὴν καθολικὴν ἐκκλησίαν.'

emphasized this virtue of Constantine IV even more strongly and set the entire account of his reign in a religious context. According to Theophanes, the Arabs, enemies of the Empire, were 'enemies of God' and 'renouncers of Christ', while the defeat by the Bulgarians was a consequence of the *sins* of the Byzantines (διὰ πλῆθος πταισμάτων).[4]

This is one aspect of the narration of the reign of Constantine IV. The second is of a political nature and deals with the governance of the state. Namely, the establishment of peace with the enemies of the Empire after defeat on the battlefield, and the ending of the schism in the Orthodox Church, brings society to a state of order in terms of both ecclesiastical and lay political relations. Theophanes developed a similar idea in his *Chronicle*, partly due to the mutual sources which both authors utilized in the course of making their works, although it is evident that Theophanes marked his narrative with literary details which enveloped his storytelling, and the episodes he described, in a religious context – from which he then gave his historical judgement about the causes and consequences of events. The later extensive and detailed account of Justinian II's harsh and tempestuous reign accentuated the reign of Constantine IV and its character as a peaceful and accomplished reign. The description of Constantine IV's reign in the *Short History* is quite similar to the one in the *Chronicle* of Theophanes. However, certain details point to a clear difference in his approach to making this narrative. Theophanes tended to invest his description in theological details and contexts, while Nikephoros avoided following this specific path. For Theophanes, Constantine IV was 'the most pious Constantine'. Although Nikephoros did not avoid discussing Constantine's personal adherence to the Chalcedonian definition of faith (contrary to the Monothelites), he did not resort to such qualifications of the emperor's personality, at least not openly. In his treatment of a hypothetical shared source, Nikephoros possibly worked with this source more objectively, transmitting the history of Constantine IV more realistically. Theophanes, in contrast, inserted specific terms and phrases such as *enemies of God* or *most pious*, which reshaped the narrative into an Orthodox manner of expression. Nikephoros obviously followed a more unbiased and realistic approach in developing his narrative. The image of Emperor Constantine IV in the *Short History* is an accomplished representation of a successful and competent ruler.

The reign of Constantine IV and its account in the *Short History* ended with a somewhat unusual case: the imperial burial which took place in

---

4    Cf. Theophanes, *Chronicle*, 353.25: 'τῶν θεομάχων στόλος, and οἱ ἀρνηταὶ τοῦ Χριστοῦ' (also 353.14 and 359.19-21).

the church of the Holy Apostles. This story was placed immediately after the description of the Sixth Ecumenical Council and the emperor's merits for the overcoming of the schism that had prevailed in the Church from Herakleios's time. Theophanes neglected to mention the church of the Holy Apostles as the burial place of Constantine IV. Nikephoros also did not insist in naming the places where Byzantine emperors were buried, but only in this case did he make an exception. The only example where he also mentioned the burial place of an emperor is the case of Herakleios, and now his grandson, Constantine IV, which might have a deeper sense in connecting these two rulers of the same dynasty, with some features of their rule being similar and present in their accounts, foremost being the idea of *peace*.[5]


## Peace Destroyed: Emperor Justinian II

A hypothesis exists in relation to the character of the reign of Emperor Justinian II, as it was described in the *Chronicle* of Theophanes and the *Short History* of Nikephoros.[6] These two histories presented a distorted image of Justinian II and his reign, mostly due to the sources they both utilized. However, the image of Justinian in the *Short History* is somewhat more balanced than the one presented by Theophanes, who probably had at his disposal additional sources from the epoch of Leo III, unknown to Nikephoros.[7] From such an understanding of the *Short History* and the *Chronicle*, it seems that certain details were more emphasized, and that several others were deliberately formed with a specific purpose to further distort the image of this emperor, and then to utilize the character of his rule to present the reign of Leo III as both legitimate and in a better light. Thus, we might suppose that, on the basis of the two accounts of Justinian II's reign, there were two different sources: the *History* of Trajan the Patrician, and a source from the epoch of Leo III, a propagandistic document created for the practical political intention of eulogizing the founder of the new dynasty.

5    Cf. Downey, 'The Tombs'; also Grierson, 'The Tombs'.
6    Cf. Head, *Justinian II*, pp. 14-18, and Head, 'Towards a Reinterpretation'. A new hypothesis was given that both Nikephoros and Theophanes transmitted the now lost *History* of Trajan the Patrician, which was a first hand report of a contemporary witness to Justinian II's reign. See Howard-Johnston, *Witnesses to a World Crisis*, pp. 256-259 and 299-307; Treadgold, 'Trajan the Patrician, Nicephorus, and Theophanes'.
7    This slight difference in the two accounts was noticed early; cf. Head, *Justinian II*, p. 16, and Tinnefeld, *Kategorien der Kaiserkritik*, p. 58.

Interpreting Theophanes's and Nikephoros's similar accounts of Justinian II's reign in such a manner brings a justifiable and rightful presumption that they both used the same source, which is corroborated by the fact that Nikephoros presented some details of Justinian's reign almost in the same manner as Theophanes. At other places, he evidently reworked his material in order to shape it in accordance with his narrative aims. However, the relationship between the two Iconophile historians and the source of supposed Iconophile provenance remains an open question, given that it was favourably disposed towards Leo III and most probably in the service of his imperial propaganda in order to confer legitimacy to his rule. The only explanation in favour of such a hypothesis would be that such a text was indeed produced in the epoch of Leo III, but prior to his open Iconoclastic policy in the Empire – it was, thus, unburdened by any Iconoclast motifs and acceptable for utilization by Theophanes and Nikephoros. A motif for producing such a history, which was so strongly opposed to Justinian II and intended to discredit his reign, could have been found almost exclusively in the early years of Leo III's reign. If we proceed to consider the issue of the unknown source, we must take into consideration the fact that Justinian II was not a precursor to Emperor Leo III, since in the six years between his death and Leo's accession to the imperial throne three more emperors ruled in Byzantium. In that sense, it is reasonable to ask: why would Leo III have particular interest in discrediting only the reign of one among last four of his predecessors in power?

In light of this investigation into the sources for the late seventh and early eighth centuries which were utilized by Nikephoros and Theophanes, an answer to these doubts can be found in the assumption that there existed a history which covered the period until 720 credited to Trajan the Patrician, which included the reign of Constantine IV.[8] As a result of this assumption, a brief passage in the *Short History* – about how the usurper Leontios spared Justinian II's life out of respect for his father Constantine IV – becomes understandable. In other words, is it possible that the negative image of Justinian II was created already during the rule of his two successors and enemies, emperors Leontios and Tiberius Apsimar? Their reigns were relatively short, however, and other details are lacking, except for those which relate to Justinian II, whom they managed to overthrow and whom Justinian II later succeeded in executing. At the same time, a question arises about the origins of the narrative concerning the reigns of these two emperors as given in the *Short History*. Were their rules a part of

8    Howard-Johnston, *Witnesses to a World Crisis*, pp. 299-307.

one history about Justinian II? In that case, their image had to be fitted into the context of their reaction against Justinian II's indecent rule.[9] At last, a logical presumption and a hypothesis remain, that the two, as usurpers against a legitimate but a cruel Emperor Justinian II, had an interest in creating legitimacy for themselves by pursuing several tasks: creating a negative image of Justinian II, praising his father (from whose ideal rule he had fallen), and undermining all of its benefits for the Byzantine state – while Leontios and Tiberius connected themselves to the traditions of the successful reign of Constantine IV. Eventually, such a propagandistic history was only continued in the epoch of Leo III, attaching to its content the narration about Justinian's exile and the reign of Tiberius Apsimar, and Justinian's subsequent return to Constantinople. This continuation would then basically adopt and widen the already established main motifs, the emperor's cruelty and his neglect of the state affairs, and thus finish and complete the already-created image of the last emperor from Herakleios's dynasty.[10]

The account of Justinian II's reign in the historical works of Theophanes and Nikephoros has common features, with a general characteristic that the former's work was more thorough, while Nikephoros left out some details – which again created a specific narration, and point of his own, in connection to the personality of the emperor. However, the place and the role of Justinian II in the context of the composition of the *Short History*, its structure, and the message it promoted, is one that deserves to be addressed, and especially in connection with the overall image of the emperor in Nikephoros's work.

The account of Justinian II's reign is among the lengthier ones in the work, along with those of Herakleios and Constantine V. The account of his reign is, however, most dynamic in its narration and presents almost an exception to the way other emperors were presented in the *Short History*. It focused entirely on Justinian II and his actions in his various endeavours during both his first and second reign (on the internal political level, and his relations with the Arabs and other nations in Byzantium's surroundings), and during his attempt to regain the lost throne. In that sense, only in Nikephoros's description do we encounter phrases which point to the emperor's mood and the character of a vicious ruler. Thus, in several places Nikephoros

---

9   Cf. Stratos, *Byzantium*, V, 75-101.
10   Stratos, *Byzantium*, V, 69-74, had already noticed that the entire account is in fact an awkward report lacking logic and with an uncertain and confusing descriptions of events, which asks far more questions than it offers clarifications.

mentioned the emperor's *anger* (θύμωμα) caused by the news about the citizens of Cherson having proclaimed Philippikos Bardanes emperor,[11] then Justinian's absurd *joy* (οὐ λυπηθεὶς ἀλλὰ καὶ λίαν περιχαρὴς) after receiving news that the navy fleet, which he had sent to punish the city of Cherson, had been shipwrecked and was destroyed at sea.[12] Moreover, a similar destruction of the imperial fleet was presented in the reign of Constantine V, but with a different commentary, from which consequently a different image of the emperor was shaped. Namely, Constantine V ordered that sailors should be buried with honour.

A certain contradiction appeared in this aspect of Nikephoros's overall stance in his *Short History* towards certain views which one would expect to be expressed in a different way, more in accordance with the general Orthodox mode of narration, as it appeared in the work of Theophanes. Namely, besides the surprisingly favourable display of Pyrrhos's image, and the positive depiction of the Iconoclast emperor's policy towards the Arabs and Bulgarians, Nikephoros painted different images of the two emperors, Justinian II and the heretical Emperor Constantine V. The Orthodoxy of Justinian II was not emphasized in the *Short History*. However, if we assume that both the author and his readers knew the details of Justinian's ecclesiastical policy, at least in convoking the Quinisext Council in the Thrulo palace, it appears strange to portray such an emperor in a less favourable light than the openly heretical Constantine V.[13] Unlike Justinian II, Constantine V was sincerely distressed by the event of his fleet being totally destroyed at sea, when a significant amount of men had suffered death. This image presented by Nikephoros later on in his work directly confronted the image of Justinian in a similar situation. Similar features of an emperor in the *Short History*, which can point to his personal feelings, are unique and present only in the account of Justinian's reign. However, their number is significantly lesser in amount compared to the descriptions of his reign in the *Chronicle* of Theophanes, pointing to the conclusion that Nikephoros rearranged his source's narration to suit his ambitions in presenting the imperial reigns in the *Short History*.

As an example of Nikephoros's shortening or even excluding of several narrative elements from his account that accent the negative image of the

---

11   Nikephoros, *Short History*, § 45.50-56.
12   Nikephoros, *Short History*, § 45.32.
13   One should bear in mind that it was during the Quinisext Council that the Church of Constantinople for the first time openly legitimated the practice of icon painting and veneration, which would later become a cornerstone of Iconophile apologetics against Iconoclastic doctrine.

emperor, but that correlate with the broader content found in the *Chronicle* of Theophanes, is a description of an unsuccessful military expedition against the Bulgarians which was led by the emperor himself. Namely, Nikephoros wrote in § 43 that Justinian 'destroyed peace' with the Bulgarians by leading a great army towards Anchialos. However, being surprised due to their lack of prudence, the Byzantines were forced to withdraw into the fortress, since the Bulgarians had killed many of them in a sudden attack. Nikephoros then narrated: 'Then for three days they besieged Justinian, who had remained in the city of Anchialos. Embarking on a ship at night, he fled from there and returned to Byzantium.'[14] In contrast, the account of the same event provided by Theophanes was more negative in relation to the emperor's action: 'Boarding a boat secretly at night, he returned to the City with shame (*μετ' αἰσχύνης*).'[15]

In Theophanes's narrative about Justinian's retaking of Constantinople and his throne, after he had successfully returned from exile, there exist details which point to the emperor's cruelty but which also display a deliberately constructed literary motif, predetermining his actions in his second rule. Namely, in the description of a storm which had overtaken the emperor and his retinue while they were sailing towards Constantinople, the emperor was presented in his words as a cruelly disposed avenger. Being admonished by one of his servants:

'Behold O Lord, we are about to die! Make a promise to God for the sake of your salvation, that you shall not make revenge towards your enemies if he gives back to you your empire!' And he replied angrily: 'If I spare any one of them, may God drown me right here.'[16]

In Nikephoros's account of Justinian's retaking of the throne, there is no such a story, probably because of the hindsight of the later historian that is evident in this scene. This might point towards his more nuanced and

---

14   Nikephoros, *Short History*, § 43.1-10: 'μετὰ τοῦτο λύει τὴν πρὸς τοὺς Βουλγάρους εἰρήνην, καὶ στρατεύματα πλεῖστα διά τε γῆς καὶ θαλάσσης πρὸς τοῖς Θρακῴοις μέρεσι διαγαγὼν πρὸς τῇ Ἀγχιάλῳ πόλει ὡς πολεμήσων αὐτοὺς παραγίνεται. ἀφυλάκτως δὲ τοῦ λαοῦ πρὸς τὰ ἐκεῖσε πεδία ἐπὶ κομιδῇ χόρτου σκεδαννυμένου ἐπιπίπτουσιν ἀθρόως οἱ Βούλγαροι καὶ πολλοὺς αὐτῶν διαφθείρουσι, πολλοὺς δὲ καὶ αἰχμαλώτους εἷλον. καὶ Ἰουστινιανῷ ἐν τῇ πόλει Ἀγχιάλῳ ἀπολειφθέντι ἐπὶ τρισὶν ἡμέραις προσεδρεύουσιν. ὁ δὲ νυκτὸς ναυσὶν ἐπιβὰς φυγῇ ἐκεῖθεν ἀπέπλευσε καὶ εἰς Βυζάντιον ἐπανάγεται.'
15   Theophanes, *Chronicle*, 376.13-29: 'τρόπαια δὲ ἐπὶ τῶν τειχῶν θέμενος διὰ νυκτὸς εἰς τὰ σκάφη ἐπιβὰς λαθραίως ἀπέπλευσε καὶ μετ' αἰσχύνης τῇ πόλει παραγέγονεν.'
16   Theophanes, *Chronicle*, 373.21-28: '"ἰδοὺ ἀποθνήσκομεν, δέσποτα, τάξαι τῷ θεῷ περὶ τῆς σωτηρίας σου, ἵνα, ἐὰν ὁ θεὸς ἀποδώσῃ σοι τὴν βασιλείαν σου, μηδένα ἀμύνεσθαι τῶν ἐχθρῶν σου." ὁ δὲ ἀποκριθεὶς ἐν θυμῷ λέγει αὐτῷ· "ἐὰν φείσωμαί τινος ἐξ αὐτῶν, ὁ θεὸς ἐνταῦθά με καταποντίσῃ".'

moderate approach in depicting the personality of Justinian – an approach which obviously involved his choosing of the material and content which he decided to include in his work. Thus, Nikephoros emphasized Justinian II's esteem for the Bulgarian Khan Terbelis, who helped him regain the imperial throne. Nikephoros told a more detailed story than Theophanes. While they both agree that Justinian had rewarded the Bulgarian archon with many gifts and dismissed him to his abode with peace, Nikephoros additionally depicted this relationship by stressing that Justinian II had invested Terbelis with an imperial mantle and proclaimed him *caesar*. Nikephoros added as well that Justinian II had Terbelis seated by his side while the people expressed homage.[17] This at least pointed towards one positive aspect of Justinian's government: his appreciation of his personal allies. Peace with Terbelis thus established a positive feature of Justinian II's reign, although Nikephoros later pointed out that the emperor broke this peace and was defeated at Anchialos.[18]

The reign of Justinian II was presented in seven chapters, among which several are of considerable length – a feature otherwise not characteristic of Nikephoros's work. These chapters are, in fact, the lengthiest in the *Short History*, and this is yet another feature of which the account of Justinian's reign is original in relation to other reigns described by Nikephoros.[19]

Both Nikephoros and Theophanes agree concerning the age of young Justinian at the time when he succeeded Constantine IV on the imperial throne. Unlike Theophanes, who set out his characterization at the very beginning of this account by stressing that the young emperor was 'thoughtless' (Ἰουστινιανὸς δὲ νεώτερος ὤν καὶ ἀβούλως), Nikephoros chose to remain restrained in presenting a forthright evaluation of his personality at the very beginning. He depicted the character of his reign by stressing in a more profound manner that he had annulled all those measures taken by his father in order to accomplish the peace and good order in the Byzantine state (τὰ ὑπὸ τοῦ πατρὸς τῆς εἰρήνης ἕνεκεν καὶ τῆς ἄλλης πολιτικῆς εὐταξίας βραβευθέντα διέστρεφε). Nikephoros also added that he even abolished peace with the Bulgarians and the Arabs.[20] While describing his second accession to imperial throne, after giving an account about many executions, Nikephoros gave this remark: 'He treated his subjects with great cruelty and

---

17   Nikephoros, *Short History*, § 42.58-64.
18   Nikephoros, *Short History*, § 43.
19   Introductory § 38; § 40 (the coup of Leontios); § 42 (Justinian in exile and taking of the throne); § 45 (Justinian's second reign).
20   Nikephoros, *Short History*, § 38.1-6.

a savage disposition' (ὠμότητι πολλῇ καὶ θηριώδει γνώμῃ), yet this is another qualification of his personality – not of his reign in a broader sense – which Nikephoros linked instead to the accusation of breaking peace treaties with the Bulgarians and the Arabs.[21] So in a literary context, an antithesis clearly emerged here – a contrast to what was described in the reign of Constantine IV and the results of his reign. Can this remark serve as the basis for an attempt to give an answer to the question of why and how the entire story of Justinian's reign fit into the narration of the *Short History*?

The assumption that a source of a propagandistic nature existed during the reign of Leo III, which was utilized later, is clearly challenged by the proposed reading of Nikephoros's description of Justinian's reign and its relation to the achievements of his father's policies. Even more than Theophanes, Nikephoros linked the reign of Justinian II with Constantine IV, comparing them and thus promoting the achievements of Constantine IV even more, consequently associating this with his praise for the good rule of the dynasty of Herakleios. This would not be the desired option for a source that had promoted the legitimacy of Leo III, if he intended to build his credibility by slandering Justinian II. Theophanes did not mention the detail which stands highlighted in the *Short History*, that Leontios spared Justinian's life out of respect for his father, the late Emperor Constantine IV. Nikephoros might have at least reworked the source which he utilized to promote the desired image of the dynasty of Herakleios by commending the reign of Constantine IV, and by shaping the account of the reign of his son and successor in the desired manner. Theophanes mentioned the peace agreement between Constantine IV and the Bulgarians. However, Nikephoros's judgement about the nature of Justinian's reign, emphasizing Constantine IV's measures for the sake of state welfare, implied a generally successful reign and carried in itself a more profound and a deeper message, which Theophanes's short discussion could not display by mentioning just one of several peace agreements which were later canceled.[22]

In contrast, in favour of the hypothesis about a source from the time of Leo III which Nikephoros might have used to describe the reign of Justinian II stands the fact that the narrative about his reign, when not relating to the image of the emperor himself and his cruelty towards his subjects, lists all the unsuccessful military endeavours of the Byzantines, blaming Justinian for these failures. The first such report is the account of the defeat of the Byzantine army against the Arabs, who had carried with them the peace

21   Nikephoros, *Short History*, § 42.73-75.
22   Theophanes, *Chronicle*, 363.5-7.

agreement which was concluded with Constantine IV, to which Nikephoros referred as being ruined by Justinian II, who consequently suffered the defeat on the battlefield.[23] The next mention of defeat appeared in the account of Justinian's second reign and the story about the Byzantine defeat near Anchialos. Nikephoros described the fall of the fortress Tyana, adding that, as a consequence of this defeat, the enemy could freely devastate the Roman lands, since there was no one who could prevent them from doing so.[24]

It is evident that Nikephoros additionally shaped the image of Constantine IV in his account of the reign of Justinian II. His policy in governing the Empire was confirmed in the description of Justinian's unsuccessful attempts to demonstrate Byzantine authority before the Bulgarians and Arabs. And he was explicitly mentioned when the usurper Leontios spared Justinian's life 'because of his affection for Justinian's father Constantine' ($\delta\iota\grave{\alpha}$ $\pi\rho\grave{o}\varsigma\ K\omega\nu\sigma\tau\alpha\nu\tau\hat{\iota}\nu o\nu\ \tau\grave{o}\nu\ \pi\alpha\tau\acute{\epsilon}\rho\alpha\ \alpha\grave{\upsilon}\tau o\hat{\upsilon}\ \grave{\alpha}\gamma\acute{\alpha}\pi\eta\nu$).[25] This detail was not mentioned in Theophanes's description of his first downfall, which corresponds to the story presented in the *Short History* in its other elements, apart from several parts where Theophanes brought in more particulars. Nikephoros for his part did not include the information added by Theophanes, that the coup of Leontios emerged after it became known that the emperor intended to indulge in a mass killing of the citizens of Constantinople.[26] In fact, he began his narration of Justinian's downfall by bringing Leontios into the storytelling right after his short description of Justinian's neglect of state affairs and his evil counsellors with whom he surrounded himself. He did not mention what Theophanes had included into his work, that the citizens had disliked the emperor due to the cruelty of his associates. Nikephoros portrayed the downfall of Justinian as a consequence of Leontios's coup, which was one among several similar examples of state officials who rose against imperial power, all in the turbulent period between Justinian II and Leo III, when the real causes for such actions are not well known except for the general downfall of state order (of which frequent shifts on the imperial throne were a regular event). Leontios acted out of fear, which is presented as his motif, both in the *Short History* and in Theophanes's *Chronicle*, and

23  Nikephoros, *Short History*, § 38.17-27.
24  Nikephoros, *Short History*, § 44.1-24.
25  Nikephoros, *Short History*, 40.32-35.
26  Theophanes, *Chronicle*, 368.15-18: 'The same year [694/695] Justinian was expelled from the imperial office in the following manner. He directed Stephen surnamed Rousios, the patrician and *strategos*, to kill at night the people of Constantinople, starting with the patriarch.'

by the advice of his close associates, whose significant role both authors confirm.[27]

> At a late hour of the night his friends – a certain monk Paul of the monastery of Kallistratos, who was an expert astronomer, and the monk Gregory, a Cappadocian by origin, who was abbot of the monastery of Florus – came to see him off. On seeing them, he rebuked them, saying: 'In vain have you predicted that I would become emperor, for now, as I depart hence, I shall be overtaken by a cruel death.'[28]

Such building of a story about the first downfall of Justinian, as it is presented in relation to Leontios's coup, fits into a pattern of later descriptions of several rebellions which lead towards instability of the imperial office, and as a result, and towards a decline in state and military organization as well as of cultural decline – a tribulation which shall be overcome only with a new dynasty of Leo III. Maybe this is the main reason why in Nikephoros's narrative there is no information about Justinian II which exist in Theophanes's Chronicle and which were directed towards a personal discreditation of the emperor. Such is the information of Justinian's absurd intention of executing the patriarch of Constantinople and its citizens, which was displayed by Theophanes with a clear intention towards discrediting Justinian himself, and only in a broader sense his rule as well.

Nikephoros continued his narration with his description of Leontios's coup and Justinian's fall, and he later proceeded to present a lengthy and complex narrative about Justinian's actions in his exile, which were directed towards assuming imperial power again and the overthrow of the usurpers who took the throne. This storytelling represents a unique

27   Theophanes, *Chronicle*, 375.20-21, which described the events in Constantinople after the fall of Emperor Tiberius Apsimar and the execution of Leontios and Tiberius. Theophanes added: 'everyone was overtaken by great fear.' Cf. Nikephoros, *Short History*, 45.63-65, where Nikephoros also placed fear as a main motif for anti-imperial action against Justinian. So a certain patrician, Mauros, was motivated by fear when he escaped to Cherson, which he previously had orders from the emperor to destroy due to its favourable disposition towards the usurper Philipikos Bardanes.

28   Nikephoros, *Short History*, 40.7-14: 'πρὸς ὃν γίνονται φίλοι τυγχάνοντες ἄωρι τῆς νυκτὸς Παῦλός τις μοναχὸς τῆς Καλλιστράτου μονῆς ὑπάρχων, ἀστρονόμος τὴν ἐπιστήμην, καὶ Γρηγόριος μοναχὸς καὶ ἡγούμενος ἐν τῇ Φλώρου μονῇ, Καππαδόκης τὸ γένος, ὡς προπέμψοντες. αὐτὸς δὲ ἰδὼν ἐνεκάλει λέγων ὡς "μάτην μοι τὰ τῆς βασιλείας προεμαντεύσασθε· νῦν γὰρ ἐνθένδε ἀποχωροῦντα τὸ τέλος με τῆς ζωῆς πικρὸν καταλήψεται".' Cf. Stratos, *Byzantium*, V, 71 and 73. Kaegi, *Byzantine Military Unrest*, p. 188, regarded the rebellion of Leontios, the former *strategos* of the Theme of Anatolica, as a result of Justinian's purge of the Byzantine military aristocracy.

entry in the *Short History* in terms of its structure, type of narration, and verbosity, and also due to the space given to the image of Justinian's return to the imperial office. It provides his account of the emperor's entire reign with a prominent and a stirring tone, which is not customary and characteristic for thematically similar descriptions that are displayed in the *Short History*.

Between the presentation of the two reigns of the Emperor Justinian II, two emperors, Leontios and Tiberius, found their place alongside a description of their role in the events which marked the two reigns of Justinian II. The focus on their reigns, however, only related to the main narrative line which described Justinian's reign; their reigns were thus part of a unique story in which the main focus remained on the Emperor Justinian II. Both Leontios and Tiberius came to power through rebellion against Justinian II and in a way acted against the state order. But they were also forced to action by Justinian's negative internal and foreign policy. Their rebellious motifs thus linked in a causal manner to the features of Justinian's reign and its negative characteristics.

Overall, this section of the *Short History* presented a narrative of the decline in state organization, with its coups and usurpers, who rose to power only to be deposed by the 'legitimate' emperor – an offspring of the Herakleios dynasty. While Nikephoros emphasized all the negative features of Justinian's imperial office during his first reign (including his breaking of the peace with the Arabs and the Bulgarians, which lead to his downfall), he showed a certain favourable attitude towards the actions of the emperor in his account of Justinian's exile and return to power. Namely, Nikephoros did not hesitate to mention that the 'Lord of the Bulgarians', the Khan Terbelis, had received the emperor 'with great honour' (σὺν τιμῇ μεγάλῃ) when he introduced him to the citizens of Constantinople and promoted him with the title of *ceasar*.[29]

The strong description which dominates the account of Justinian's adventurous residence in the regions of the Black Sea, and the sections in the narrative which were introduced by interpolating Constantinople – or rather the Emperor Tiberius Apsimar, who demanded the killing of Justinian II – and the consent to Tiberius's wish by the citizens of Cherson (Justinian's hosts), provided this part of Justinian's *history* with a meaningful and multileveled presentation of his personality. This is especially evident in the introduction of a strange turn of events, when the former emperor escaped his death by the sympathy and favour of a

---

29  Nikephoros, *Short History*, § 42.35-44.

Khazar princess, who later became a Byzantine empress. Such a composition of the material provided the account of Justinian II's reign with a
distinctly literary aspect, which made this phase in his second reign more
complex than previously considered. A simple remark – that Nikephoros
and Theophanes, the only two Byzantine narrative sources relevant to the
reign of Justinian II, transmit the bias and subjectivity of their sources
– does not reflect the essential understanding of the literary process of
these writers, nor their true intentions, and the place which this strange
but important historical account assumed within their histories.

These features of the Justinian narrative are already evident in
Nikephoros's reduction and even exclusion of the content which Theophanes decided to introduce in his narrative. These characteristics are
discernible through identifying small inconsistencies in the stories as
displayed both by Nikephoros and Theophanes, which had a significant
role in emphasizing the features of Justinian as a ruler and as a person,
which both historiographers had included in their works. Additionally,
Nikephoros accentuated those ideas which were crucial for him as an
author and which are rooted in his work, regarding the *eutaxia* in the state
of the Romans, as governed by their emperors. In that sense, Nikephoros
passed over certain details which Theophanes considered important
and of significance in the shaping of *his* Justinian – a vicious and stern,
imprudent ruler. Nikephoros portrayed Justinian with significant balance,
although there exist descriptions of the emperor which correspond with
the one given by Theophanes, especially in his second reign. However,
Nikephoros evidently left out certain literary elements which emphasized
Justinian's unbalanced cruelty, and which presented a clear intention in
Theophanes's storytelling to show this emperor in an entirely distorted
manner, or rather, his adoption of the source he used and its attitude
towards Justinian II.

## Incompetent Emperors

As part of the *Short History*, which portrayed the disorder and crumbling
of state organization during and after the two reigns of Justinian II, Nikephoros introduced a specific image of an incompetent emperor, who was
overwhelmed by inactivity and seemingly determined to conduct his reign
in an unskilled manner. Justinian II's reign was the opening scene for such a
narrative. However, unlike several emperors who reigned after him, Justinian II could hardly be blamed as an inactive emperor. He could be blamed

for rashness and recklessness in his political decisions, and Nikephoros openly accused him of such conduct. In contrast, several emperors who succeeded him introduced a specific image of inactivity and incompetence in state matters, which all pointed towards the further crumbling of state organization. As opposed to the picture of a bold Emperor Herakleios, stood the inactive Emperor Philippikos Bardanes. His was an image of complete inactivity regarding state matters, and even his deposition was portrayed as a result of his idleness. Namely, Nikephoros gave a remark on his reign in the very beginning, as he had done previously in the case of Justinian II, stating explicitly that 'he appeared to administer the empire in an indecorous and negligent manner' – a remark slightly stronger than the one given in regard to the reign of Justinian, who *undid* the measures of his father.[30] In the case of Philippikos Bardanes, Nikephoros utilized the terms ἀσέμνως καὶ ῥᾳθύμως intending to describe the manner of Philippikos's reign. The term ῥᾴθυμος can carry a meaning of negligence but also a deeper meaning of disinterest and lack of concern, which is more probable in the context of the entire account of his reign. The same term in the form of a verb (ῥᾳθυμέω) can also carry a meaning of entertainment, which was indeed presented in the case of the Emperor Philippikos in the account of his downfall, when Nikephoros emphasized the emperor's care for celebrating the anniversary of the dedication of Constantinople, pointing out that the emperor was deprived of his imperial office while he slept. This would not be such an interesting manner of description of an emperor's downfall if it was not preceded by a story about a Bulgarian raid against Byzantine territories in Thrace. Nikephoros stressed that these raiding companies, in fact, reached the Long Walls of Constantinople, and that even the Arabs, as a consequence, took several Byzantine towns in Asia Minor (τήν τε Μισθίαν καὶ ἕτερα πολίσματα συμπαραλαμβάνουσι). Such a description of events, which were concluded by the account of Philippikos's downfall, omitted any mention of the emperor's reaction to these hostile actions towards his Empire:

> At this juncture, an armed Bulgarian band suddenly fell upon the inhabitants of the Thracian Bosporus. They killed a great many people both among the local population and among those who had crossed over from Byzantium for the sake of pleasure and recreation; others they took captive and robbed of much silver and a considerable number of utensils.

---

30  Nikephoros, *Short History*, § 46.1-2 *passim*.

Having such freedom of action,[31] they fanned out towards the land walls of the City and advanced as far as the so-called Golden Gate.[32]

Nikephoros displayed the emperor's idleness in the context of a significant loss of both territory and towns as a result of Bulgarian and Arab raids. Such an image of the political situation that had occurred under Philippikos's reign was further developed in the next chapter in the account of the celebration of the City's birthday:

Now Philippikos, after celebrating the birthday of the City and putting on an equestrian contest, banqueted with his friends and lay to sleep at midday. At this juncture a plot was hatched against him.[33]

By combining both the terminology which alluded to Bardanes's inactivity in face of the raids by Bulgarians and Arabs, and the image of an emperor who sleeps at noon, after participating in a banquet, Nikephoros displayed a tendency to highlight the emperor's unworthiness to rule the Empire, a point which was accented in the very beginning of the story about his reign.

Nikephoros also stressed incompetence in relation to Emperor Theodosios III, who succeeded a somewhat capable Emperor Anastasios II.[34] Based on the manner of storytelling about the reign of Anastasios II, it seems that Nikephoros demonstrated a certain favour towards his reign. Such a conclusion can be based mainly upon the introductory statement: 'Anastasios bestowed care on military affairs and appointed capable commanders

---

31  'Taking advantage of this opportunity', according to the translation of C. Mango. Nikephoros here utilized the term ἄδεια, which can be translated as *chance*, but also as *freedom of action* in the context of a lack of any kind of retribution for action, which is supported by the manner in which Nikephoros further on presented and evaluated the reign of Philippikos Bardanes.

32  Nikephoros, *Short History*, § 47.1-9: 'Ἐν τούτοις τῶν Βουλγάρων ὁπλίτης ὅμιλος ἀθρόως τοὺς ἐν τῷ Θρακικῷ Βοσπόρῳ οἰκοῦντας ἐπεισπίπτει· καὶ λαὸν πλεῖστον τῶν ἐγχωρίων καὶ τῶν ἐκ Βυζαντίου διαπερώντων τέρψεως καὶ ἡδυπαθείας ἕνεκεν ἀναιροῦσιν, ἄλλους τε ἠχμαλώτευσαν καὶ ἄργυρον ὡς πλεῖστον καὶ σκεύη οὐκ ὀλίγα παρ' αὐτῶν προσκτησάμενοι· ἀδείας δὲ αὐτοῖς προσγενομένης καὶ πρὸς τῷ χερσαίῳ τείχει τῆς πόλεως σκεδάννυνται, ἄχρι καὶ τῆς Χρυσῆς καλουμένης πύλης προεκδραμόντες.' Cf. Herrin, 'Philippikos', pp. 141-142.

33  Nikephoros, *Short History*, § 48.1-5: 'Φιλιππικὸς δὲ γενέθλιον τῆς πόλεως ἡμέραν ἐπιτελέσας καὶ ἀμιλλητήριον τῶν ἵππων ἀγῶνα ἐπιδειξάμενος, εἶτα τοῖς φίλοις συμποσιάσας εἰς ὕπνον κατὰ τὸν μεσημβρινὸν τῆς ἡμέρας καιρὸν ἐτράπετο. συμβαίνει δέ γε αὐτῷ τὰ τῆς ἐπιβουλῆς ἐντεῦθεν.' For a different view on this part of Nikephoros's *Short History*, and compared to the narrative of Theophanes in regard to the plot against Emperor Philippikos Bardanes, cf. Abrahamse, 'Religion, Heresy', pp. 396-397.

34  For the dating of their reigns, cf. Sumner, 'Philippicus', and Speck, *Kaiser Leon III*, p. 79.

to take charge of them.'[35] Furthermore, Nikephoros proceeded to elaborate such a policy by stating that Anastasios, having known that the Arabs were preparing an attack on Roman territories, had sent the city prefect Daniel with the main task to negotiate *peace*, but actually to reveal the extent of the enemy's preparations against the Byzantines. In regard to this, the emperor had prepared Constantinople for a forthcoming siege:

> He restored carefully the walls of the City and refurbished the military engines. He also stored a great quantity of provisions in the City and fortified it by such other means as befitted a hostile attack.[36]

Maybe such remarks would not be so unusual if they did not appear after lengthy descriptions of neglected state affairs, which were presented in the reigns of Justinian II and Philippikos Bardanes. Only in contrast to these accounts did the news about Anastasios II's preparations to meet the challenge of an Arabs attack receive a positive sense in the *Short History*. Thus it is not strange that Nikephoros accentuated the fact that the emperor had appointed 'a prudent and experienced man' (ἔμφρονα τε καὶ ἔμπειρον) to lead the Roman army against the Arabs in Rhodes. But then a familiar occasion occurred which cancelled these measures implemented by the emperor: the emperor's preparations were hindered by a rebellion in the army, which had chosen 'an ordinary man uninvolved in politics (ἀπράγμονά τινα καὶ ἰδιώτην τυγχάνοντα), whom they urged to assume the imperial policy'.[37] Nikephoros obviously accentuated the defects of the new emperor, Theodosios III, in contrast to Anastasios II – defects which were not able to meet the requirements of the situation in which the Empire had fallen, in the wake of the Arab attack on Constantinople. The Empire was in need of a ruler of a different character. The message here was clear. Only in the following narration will we see in what manner Nikephoros described Leo III's accession to power. In his historical presentation of Leo III's reign, Nikephoros developed this narrative to which he had previously set down foundations in the earlier chapters of his work.

---

35  Nikephoros, *Short History*, § 49.1-3: 'Ἀναστάσιος δὲ δι' ἐπιμελείας τὰ πολεμικὰ πράγματα εἶχε καὶ ἄρχοντας ἱκανοὺς πρὸς τὰς τούτων διοικήσεις καθίστη.'
36  Nikephoros, *Short History*, § 49.9-17: 'τὰ δὲ τείχη τῆς πόλεως ἐπιμελέστερον καινίζει καὶ τὰ πολεμητήρια ὄργανα διασκευάζει, πλεῖστα δαπανήματα τῇ πόλει ἀποθέμενος καὶ ἑτέροις οἷς ἀνῆκε πρὸς πολεμίων ἔφοδον ταύτην κατοχυρώσας.'
37  Nikephoros, *Short History*, § 50.1-25.

# 5    Iconoclasts Restoring Order

## The *Peace* of the Emperor Leo III

The same chapter which introduced the Emperor Leo III in its narration began with a distinctive conclusion regarding the epoch that followed the reign of Justinian II, when tempestuous shifts in the imperial throne shook Byzantium. This note, interpolated by Nikephoros into this part of his work, is unique in the sense that it is the only instance of the author offering an open expression of thought, regardless whether these were his own or from his source:

> On account of the frequent assumptions of imperial power and the preva-
> lence of usurpation, the affairs of the Empire and of the City were being
> neglected and declined; furthermore, education was being destroyed
> and military organization crumbled. As a result, the enemy was able to
> overrun the Roman state with impunity [and to cause] much slaughter,
> abduction, and the capture of cities.[1]

It is both interesting and very indicative that Theophanes, in a similar but not quite the same manner, mentioned the decline in culture and education in the Empire. However, unlike Nikephoros, who judged that such a decline was a consequence of the decrease of the state order and imperial office, Theophanes connected these events to the Emperor Leo III and his Iconoclasm, placing this narrative in the tenth year of his rule.[2] Further, Nikephoros elaborated his conclusion by pointing to the fact that, as a result of such state of affairs, those who were enemies of the Romans (τοὺς πολεμίους τῶν Ῥωμαίων) were capable of overrunning the Empire. Nikephoros here actually repeated the same motifs which were predominant in both Justinian II's rule and the rule of Philippikos Bardanes in the scenes of Bulgarian and Arab raids on Thrace and Asia Minor. Then, with more details, Nikephoros passed to the description of the main consequence of

---

1    Nikephoros, *Short History*, § 52.1-4: 'Ἐπεὶ οὖν πυκναὶ τῶν βασιλέων ἐπαναστάσεις ἐγένοντο καὶ ἡ τυραννὶς ἐκράτει τά τε τῆς βασιλείας καὶ τῆς πόλεως κατημελεῖτο καὶ διέπιπτε πράγματα, ἔτι μὴν καὶ ἡ τῶν λόγων ἠφανίζετο παίδευσις καὶ τὰ τακτικὰ διελύετο.'
2    Cf. Theophanes, *Chronicle*, 405.10-14. Cf. Lemerle, *Le premier humanisme byzantin*, pp. 105-108, according to whom the first ideological protagonists of Iconoclasm had already emerged in the last decades of Herakleios's rule, when the Empire lost its regions in the East, which later had its negative influence on the decline of culture.

such affairs in the state of the Romans, which ultimately brought to the forefront the future Emperor Leo III. Namely, the Arabs were preparing to launch a siege of Constantinople, which was previously already mentioned in connection with the Emperor Anastasios II's defence preparations and the proper measures which he implemented to prepare the City for the coming siege. Nikephoros then emphasized an important aspect of the story, namely, that the Emperor Theodosios III could not meet the requirements of the hard situation for the state, and that as a consequence, the military and civil dignitaries in such circumstances asked him to abdicate.

> Thereupon they held a ballot of who was to become emperor (εἶτα εἰς ψῆφον ἐληλυθότων τοῦ βασιλεύσοντος) and elected the Patrician Leo, who was at that time *strategos* of the so-called Anatolic army. According to imperial custom, he was received in procession as he entered Byzantium through the Golden Gate and, having come to the Great Church, was invested with the imperial crown.[3]

Such a description of Leo's imperial advent and the making of an emperor who later provoked the Iconoclastic dispute sharply contrasts the account presented by Theophanes. This divergence can be seen in full light in Theophanes's description where he managed to avoid explicitly mentioning Leo's coronation and his assuming of the imperial office. Further, no implications can be found in Theophanes's narrative about the Emperor Theodosios III's incompetence in facing the critical events which were rapidly unfolding and threatening the Byzantine Empire. In other words, no admittance of Leo's capabilities both political and military in relation to the imperial government can be traced in Theophanes's account, while these do exists, at least indirectly, in Nikephoros's manner of storytelling. Namely, Theophanes began his narration about Leo III's first reigning year with a lengthy account of his endeavours as *strategos* in the remote regions of the Caucasus. This story is probably based on an eyewitness account which at its end mentioned Leo as the one who supported Anastasios II against the usurper Theodosios III, adding that he had the support of the then *strategos* Artabazos of the Armeniakon theme, whom he made his

---

3    Nikephoros, *Short History*, § 52.18-21: 'εἶτα εἰς ψῆφον ἐληλυθότων τοῦ βασιλεύσοντος ἡρέθη Λέων ὁ πατρίκιος, τηνικαῦτα στρατηγὸς ὢν τοῦ τῶν ἀνατολικῶν λεγομένου στρατοῦ. καὶ ὡς ἦν ἔθος βασιλεῦσι, διὰ προπομπίου δοχῆς διὰ τῆς Χρυσῆς καλουμένης πύλης εἰς τὸ Βυζάντιον εἰσελαύνει, καὶ ἐν τῇ μεγάλῃ ἐκκλησίᾳ γενόμενος ἐκεῖσε τὸν τῆς βασιλείας ἀνεδήσατο στέφανον.' For Leo's background and his origins cf. Theophanes, *Chronicle*, 386.28-395.12.

son-in-law after assuming the imperial office.[4] In this way, Theophanes managed to avoid explicit mention of Leo's imperial proclamation in the account of the first year of his reign. In contrast, he mentioned the 'pious emperor' (ὁ δὲ εὐσεβὴς βασιλεὺς) in the story about the great and victorious defence of Constantinople against the Arabs in 717. Such a display of events in the manner as it is written in the *Chronicle* of Theophanes remains vague regarding the issue of which emperor is credited for such a display of imperial success. The characteristically hazy account of Leo's first year as emperor, which lacks a clear description of his accession to power, made it possible to further displace Leo III from the account of the Byzantine victory over Arabs. Later in his account of the siege of Constantinople, Theophanes mentioned in two instances the 'pious emperor', with no direct connection to Leo III, while at the same time naming the Arab leader 'enemy of Christ', thus displaying a specific idea that the emperor's piousness is only regarded in relation to the Arab's non-Christian faith. In contrast, in the entire story about the siege, the emperor was mentioned four times, but with no mention of the name *Leo*. Even a stronger notion of evasion which drove Theophanes in making of such an account is presented by his conclusion at the end of this story, namely, that it was due to the help provided by God and the Theotokos that the City and the whole of Christianity were saved. From such a construction it follows that the emperor was only God's accomplice in his *oikonomia* of liberating the Byzantines from the hands of the Arabs – in essence, an argument typical for Iconodule ideology about the place and role of the emperor in the hierarchy of Byzantine society and his relation to divine power.[5]

In relation to such Theophanes's approach in the literary shaping of the account of the first year of Leo III's reign, Nikephoros presented his report about the same events in a diverse manner, with an entirely different image of Leo III. Namely, his role in Nikephoros's storytelling is a central one, dominating the entire narrative, where the emperor is in the centre of the events:

> At this point there arrived a Saracen fleet under the command of Soliman, as he was called in the Arab tongue. As they were sailing up the straits next to Byzantium, the ships that were guarding the rear, being heavily laden with a great number of soldiers and arms, met with a light contrary wind and were forced back by the current, thus falling behind. On seeing

4 Theophanes, *Chronicle*, 395.2-12, with C. Mango's n. 4 on p. 547.
5 Theophanes, *Chronicle*, 397.31-398.4.

them, the emperor embarked on biremes and, after breaking the enemy's line, burned twenty of their ships.[6]

It is notable that Nikephoros did not insert the motif of God's interruption on behalf of the Byzantines. Unlike Theophanes, his image of Leo III is that of an active and bold emperor, similar to the boldness – *parrhesia* – previously demonstrated and displayed by Herakleios. Nikephoros then concluded this episode with a new image of the emperor being set in the centre of the narrative about the successful raid on the Arabic fleet which was harboured in Bithynia in two locations:

> Now the Egyptian sailors entered at night the skiffs that were on their ships, came to Byzantium, and acclaimed the emperor. Taking courage at this, the emperor sent out fire-bearing ships against those fleets and burned all their vessels. They made much booty and, after loading the weapons and provisions that were in them, came back to the emperor.[7]

We can see that Nikephoros here demonstrated an image of Leo III in compliance with what he previously displayed as the positive and praiseworthy activity of Anastasios II's preparations for the defence of Constantinople. In fact, Nikephoros emphasized the point which he previously connected to Leo's imperial acclamation, namely, that he was elected emperor due to Theodosios III's incapability to meet the challenges which had befallen the Empire. In that sense, these scenes of Leo's first imperial actions had justified his imperial office which was offered to him.

In comparison with Theophanes, who mentioned the emperor in his account five times, in his more brief story about the siege of Constantinople, Nikephoros mentioned Leo III four times, without the term εὐσεβὴς. So he gave more emphasis to the emperor in the events he portrayed, especially since his victories were clearly presented as his

---

6    Nikephoros, *Short History*, § 54.7-15: 'ἐν τούτῳ καταλαμβάνει καὶ ὁ τῶν Σαρακηνῶν στόλος, οὗ ἡγεῖτο Σολιμὰν ὀνόματι Ἀράβων φωνῇ καλούμενος. ἐν ᾧ δὲ τῶν ὑπὸ τὸ Βυζάντιον πόρων ἀνήγοντο, αἱ κατόπιν ἰοῦσαι ναῦς, οἵαπερ νωτοφυλακοῦσαι καὶ φόρτῳ πολλῷ βεβαρημέναι ἔκ τε στρατιωτῶν πλήθους καὶ ὅπλων, καὶ ἅμα μικροῦ πνεύματος ἀντιπνεύσαντος καὶ τοῦ ῥείθρου εἰς τοὐπίσω ἄγεσθαι βιαζομένου, σχολαιότερον ὑπέπλεον. ταύτας ὁ βασιλεὺς θεασάμενος διήρεσιν ἐπιβὰς καὶ διέκπλους ποιησάμενος πυρὶ κατέφλεξεν, οὔσας τὸν ἀριθμὸν εἴκοσι.'
7    Nikephoros, *Short History*, § 54.32-39: 'οἱ δὲ ἐν αὐτοῖς εἰσπλέοντες Αἰγύπτιοι νυκτὸς τοὺς ἐνεστηκότας λέμβους τῶν νηῶν εἰσβάντες πρὸς τὸ Βυζάντιον ἧκον καὶ τὸν βασιλέα εὐφήμουν. ἐφ' οἷς ἀναθαρσήσας ὁ βασιλεὺς πυρφόρους ναῦς κατὰ τῶν τοιούτων στόλων ἐξέπεμψε καὶ πάσας αὐτῶν τὰς ναῦς ἐνέπρησεν. ἐκεῖθεν λαφυραγωγήσαντες καὶ ἐκ τῶν ὑπαρχόντων αὐτοῖς ὅπλων καὶ δαπανημάτων καταφορτισθέντες πρὸς βασιλέα ὑπέστρεφον.'

own capabilities, with no relation to divine interference into the faith of the City, which was saved due to Leo III's boldness in action, rather than due to divine intervention.

Such difference in the portrayal of the emperor's personality in the descriptions of the two almost contemporary historical works can even be seen in Theophanes's different description of the battle in defence of Constantinople and the sinking of Iezidos's fleet on the shores of Bithynia. We have already seen that the Egyptians who had acclaimed Leo III gave him the courage to act against the Arabs, which consequently brought victory and great spoils to the Byzantines. Theophanes mentioned the same events, but with a different arrangement of his narrative and thus with a different outcome, which shifted the main role and credits for this victory from the emperor to divine interference:

> When the emperor had been informed by them (the Egyptians from the Arab fleet) of the two fleets hidden in the bay, he constructed fire-bearing siphons which he placed in dromones and biremes and sent these against the fleets. With God's help, thanks to the intercession of the all-pure Theotokos, the enemies were sunk on the spot. Our men took the enemy's supplies as booty and returned in joyous victory.[8]

It appears that, while adhering to icon worship, Theophanes restrained himself from connecting Leo's victory (which he could not pass over completely) to divine intervention. Thus he managed not to produce an argument for the later persecution of icons conducted by Leo III, which might be utilized by Iconoclasts in their polemics with the Iconodules.[9] He rather chose to portray the Byzantine victory over the Arabs as the result of divine protection, not mentioning the emperor at all in this story. However, Nikephoros avoided mentioning any divine intercession in his descriptions of previous sieges of Constantinople, in the time of Herakleios and his grandson, Emperor Constantine IV, as well. Thus he displayed a developed literary approach toward describing these events, without any fear that he

---

8    Theophanes, *Chronicle*, 397.9-15: 'μαθὼν δὲ δι' αὐτῶν ὁ βασιλεὺς περὶ τῶν κρυπτομένων δύο στόλων ἐν τῷ κόλπῳ, σίφωνας πυρσοφόρους κατασκευάσας εἰς δρόμωνάς τε καὶ διήρεις τούτους ἐμβαλὼν κατὰ τῶν δύο στόλων ἐξέπεμψεν. τοῦ δὲ θεοῦ συνεργήσαντος διὰ τῶν πρεσβειῶν τῆς παναχράντου θεοτόκου ἐπιτοπίως ἐβυθίσθησαν οἱ ἐχθροί· καὶ λαβόντες τὰ σκῦλα οἱ ἡμέτεροι καὶ τὰς δαπάνας αὐτῶν μετὰ χαρᾶς καὶ νίκης ὑπέστρεψαν.' Cf. Gero, *Byzantine Iconoclasm during the Reign of Leo III*, pp. 34-36.

9    Cf. Gero, *Byzantine Iconoclasm during the Reign of Leo III*, pp. 34-36.

might lend an argument to the Iconoclasts in the case of Leo III's successful defence of Constantinople with God's help.[10]

The image of Leo III in the *Short History* covered almost thirteen chapters, which is a relatively large account similar to the ones dedicated to the emperors Herakleios, Justinian II, and Constantine V. The account of his reign began with the emphasis on his readiness and worthiness to succeed the incompetent Theodosios III. Such an image was then developed by placing the emperor in the centre of narration regarding the successful defence of Constantinople. A victorious, bold, and acclaimed emperor was portrayed in the lines of such a narrative. Such an image of Leo III completely contrasts the image Theophanes displayed on the pages of his *Chronicle*. Thus, Theophanes's treatment of Leo's character in the opening sequences of his reign can be summarized as such: Leo's ascension to the imperial throne was placed in the first year of Emperor Theodosios III's reign. With such a layout of his material, Theophanes managed to blur the emperor's character in the account of the siege of 717 by positioning this story immediately after the account of Theodosios III's reign, and additionally, by placing a short review on the reigns of Justinian II, Philippikos Bardanes, Anastasios II, and Theodosios III between the two accounts of Theodosios III's reign and the account of the successful defence of Constantinople under Leo III. In such an arrangement of material, Leo's imperial character was not eliminated, but it dwelled in a secondary narrative plan, outside the focus of Theophanes's storytelling.[11] The mere mention of the *basileus* in the story about the defence of Constantinople in 717 left the personality of Leo III by the side of the main course of events, and especially regarding his merits for the successful war against the Arabs. As presented by Nikephoros, Leo III was placed in the centre of the narration about the events described. Thus the beginning of Leo III's reign in the *Short History* is entirely different in its main account from the one given by Nikephoros's younger contemporary.

---

10    Regarding the nature of the source which both Theophanes and Nikephoros might had used to make their account of the siege of 717, see Alexander, *The Patriarch Nicephorus*, pp. 158 and 162 (in favour of a hypothesis of a source of Iconophile provenance); and also Gero, *Byzantine Iconoclasm during the Reign of Leo III*, p. 34, n. 8, proposing a badly processed source of Iconoclast provenance.

11    Such an arrangement of material is characteristic for Theophanes, and is not reserved only for the treatment of Leo's character in the *Chronicle* or the Iconoclastic theme in the work. On the contrary, a similar treatment of historical material can be traced in the pictures of other emperors. See Чичуров, *Место Хронографий Феофана*, pp. 41-53; Любарский, 'Феофан Исповедник'; Ljubarskij, 'Concerning the Literary Techniques', pp. 319-322; and also the comments of Mango and Scott in their edition of the *Chronicle* of Theophanes, pp. 51-65.

Further on Nikephoros continued to develop such an idea by emphasizing the motif of *peace and tranquillity* which settled in the western parts of the Empire (ἐν εἰρήνῃ καὶ ἡσυχίᾳ κατέστη), in Sicily, when during the reign of Leo III a plot against the emperor was successfully resolved. This is a story told in almost identical form as in the narration about the *peace* of Constantine IV.

At this time the Patrician Sergios, who was *strategos* of Sicily, along with the inhabitants of the West, gave up hope for Byzantium and the emperor himself on account of the enemy attack against them, and crowned their own emperor, one of the adjutants of Sergios, called Basil, the son of Gregory surnamed Onomagoulos, and renamed him Tiberius. On being informed of this, the emperor appointed the Patrician Paul *strategos* of Sicily, inasmuch as he was a faithful friend and experienced in military matters, and dispatched him to Sicily. When he had arrived there, Sergios fled to the Lombards. As for Paul, he gathered together the inhabitants of the island and read to them the imperial letters. Being reassured by them, they acclaimed the emperor and surrendered both Basil and the magistrates who had been appointed by him as prisoners to (Paul). Taking hold of them, he executed a certain George and others, and sent their heads to the emperor, while the rest (he punished) with blows and torments, cut off the noses of some, and sent them into exile. After requesting an assurance of his safety, Sergios, too, was brought to Paul. As a consequence, the affairs of the West returned to peace and tranquillity.[12]

---

12 Nikephoros, *Short History*, § 55.1-21: 'Τούτῳ τῷ χρόνῳ Σέργιος ὁ πατρίκιος ὁ τῆς Σικελίας στρατηγὸς καὶ οἱ τὰ ἑσπέρια οἰκοῦντες, τὰ περὶ τὸ Βυζάντιον καὶ τὸν βασιλέα αὐτὸν ἀπογνόντες τῆς γενομένης τῶν πολεμίων χάριν κατ' αὐτῶν ἐφόδου, ἴδιον στέφουσι βασιλέα τῶν ὑπηρετῶν τινα Σεργίου, Βασίλειον τοὔνομα, υἱὸν γεγονότα Γρηγορίου τὸ ἐπίκλην Ὀνομαγούλου, Τιβέριον αὐτὸν ὀνομάσαντες. τοῦτο ἀκηκοὼς ὁ βασιλεὺς Παῦλον τὸν πατρίκιον στρατηγὸν Σικελίας προβάλλεται ἅτε πιστὸν καὶ οἰκεῖον ὑπάρχοντα καὶ τακτικῶν ἔμπειρον, καὶ πρὸς Σικελίαν ἐκπέμπει. οὗ τινος ἐκεῖσε καταλαβόντος Σέργιος φυγὰς ἐκεῖθεν οἴχεται καὶ πρὸς Λογγουβάρδους γίνεται, Παῦλος δὲ ἐν τῇ νήσῳ λαὸν περιαθροίσας τὰ βασιλέως ὑπαναγινώσκει γράμματα, δι' ὧν εἰς πίστωσιν ἐλθόντες τόν τε βασιλέα εὐφήμησαν καὶ Βασίλειον καὶ τοὺς ὑπ' αὐτοῦ προχειρισθέντας ἄρχοντας δεσμίους αὐτῷ παρεδώκασιν. ὁ δὲ τούτους παραλαβὼν Γεώργιόν τινα καὶ ἑτέρους ἀνεῖλε καὶ τούτων τὰς κεφαλὰς πρὸς τὸν βασιλέα ἀνέπεμψε, τοὺς δὲ ἄλλους σὺν πληγαῖς καὶ αἰκίαις πολλαῖς, ὧν δὲ καὶ τὰς ῥῖνας ἐκτεμών, ὑπερορίαις παρέπεμψε. Σέργιος δὲ τῆς ἑαυτοῦ σωτηρίας λόγον αἰτήσας πρὸς τὸν Παῦλον ἐκομίσθη. ἐντεῦθεν τὰ τῆς ἑσπέρας πράγματα ἐν εἰρήνῃ καὶ ἡσυχίᾳ κατέστη.' Several interesting facts should be observed in this narrative. Namely, first the *strategos* Sergios 'gave up hope for Byzantium', that is, the besieged Constantinople, but he also gave up hope 'for the emperor himself on account of the enemy', which Leo III successfully managed to defeat. This is a rather interesting depiction of the significance of the personality of Leo III, which Nikephoros clearly embedded into his narrative. The other significant detail is the mention of the Patrician Paul, whom Nikephoros designated

The idea of peace, which obviously assumed a central place and role in the overall concept of narration which Nikephoros dedicated to Leo III, emerged anew in the chapter which dealt with the description of Anastasios's attempt to lead a coup against Leo with the help of the Bulgarians and several Byzantine dignitaries who were loyal to him. It should be noted that both the former Emperor Anastasios II, and his Byzantine adherents were devoted to Orthodoxy, yet Nikephoros did not introduce the religious issue of Leo III's reign. Thus, this specific account is based strictly on political premises and stands in relation to the good order of the state.

Thus, § 57 can be summarized as follows. After Leo III had assumed imperial office, the former Emperor Anastasios II, who had been banished to Thessalonica, once more attempted to take the Empire. He made contact with the Patrician Sisinnios whom Leo III had previously sent among the Bulgars with the task of concluding a military alliance against the Arabs. This Sisinnios also managed to compel the Bulgarians to join this conspiracy lead by the former emperor. The plotters managed to find supporters among several Byzantine officials who resided in Constantinople, Magister Niketas, Patrician Isoes (commander of the imperial Opsikion), the former emperor's first imperial secretary Theoktistos, and the commander of the Walls, Niketas. The former emperor sent letters reminding these men of their old friendship, asked for their support and to be received as emperor. Having in mind previous remarks by Nikephoros on the instability of imperial power and the frequent changes in the imperial throne, which led to the fall of order, both military and political, such actions described in this chapter, after the successful defence of Constantinople in 717 by Leo III, suggest a revival of disorder, an undesirable state of affairs. However, the narrative then took a turn: the emperor became aware of the preparations by the plotters and acted accordingly, restoring peace with the Bulgarians and consolidating his power.[13]

> The emperor, however, wrote to the Bulgarians that they should embrace peace and surrender his enemies. They apologized and asked his forgiveness, promising to bring about peace. Accordingly, they sent Artemios

as a trustworthy and a loyal official to the emperor, calling him a 'faithful friend' of Leo III and 'experienced in military affairs', which together indicate a general acceptance of the emperor among his more experienced officials. That the authority of the Byzantine state under Leo III might have indeed been present in the Western parts of the Empire, and in the Balkan coast of the Adriatic as well, is suggested by an Iconoclastic era ciborium from Ulcinj (Montenegro). Cf. Stević, 'Emperor in the Altar', p. 62 *passim*.

13    Nikephoros, *Short History*, § 57.16-21.

along with the archpriest of Thessalonica and many others as captives to the emperor. They also cut off the head of the Patrician Sisinnios and sent it likewise, and so departed to their own country.[14]

Leo's reaction to the plot against him in Constantinople, Thessalonica, and in Bulgaria cannot be equated with the harsh measures described in the account of Justinian II, since Leo's action was directed towards introducing peace in his state, while Justinian's measures managed to introduce the opposite.

Nikephoros's approach to making of Leo III's image is quite obvious in this story. Until now we have read that the Egyptians which were in the Arabic fleet acclaimed Leo III and that the Bulgarians expressed their apologies to the emperor for participating in a plot against his imperial office. The result in both scenes was *peace*, which was introduced in the Byzantine state under Leo III. In remaining six chapters dedicated to Leo III and his reign, only one was dedicated to his secular politics, and it was a short reference to an unsuccessful siege of Nicaea, led by the Arab leaders Ameros and Mauias, which they left without having accomplished their intention. Thus, it can be said that in the entire account of Leo III's reign, there is not one story of his unsuccessful military enterprise. In contrast, significant terms, such as *peace* and *calm*, which set in the Byzantine empire within his reign after a long period of anarchy and inappropriate government by the previous emperors, dominate the narrative of this part of the history of Leo III.

However, in Nikephoros's work there exists a second part of Leo's history dedicated to his ecclesiastical policies and his relationship with the Patriarch Germanos of Constantinople. In these sections, important ideas were embedded in the narrative. These sections emphasized both the authority and autonomy of the institution of the patriarch of Constantinople and the authority of the ecumenical councils in matters of doctrine and ecclesiology, in opposition to the emperor and his possible intentions to interfere in these affairs of the Church. In that sense, Nikephoros clearly separated the Iconoclasm of Leo III from his secular, military, and imperial successes in matters of state government. These two narratives were, as we shall see, separated rather than interwoven in Nikephoros's entire depiction of Leo

---

14   Nikephoros, *Short History*, § 57.24-31: 'γράφει δὲ Βουλγάροις ὁ βασιλεὺς ὡς τὴν εἰρήνην μᾶλλον ἀσπάσοιντο καὶ τοὺς ἐχθροὺς προδοῖεν. οἱ δὲ εἰς ἀπολογίαν κατέστησαν συγγνώμην αἰτήσαντες καὶ τὰ πρὸς εἰρήνην ὑπισχνούμενοι. καὶ τὸν μὲν Ἀρτέμιον σὺν τῷ ἀρχιερεῖ Θεσσαλονίκης καὶ ἄλλους πλείστους δεσμώτας πρὸς βασιλέα πέμπουσι, καὶ Σισιννίου τοῦ πατρικίου τὴν κεφαλὴν ἐκτεμόντες ὡσαύτως στέλλουσιν οὕτω τε πρὸς τὴν ἑαυτῶν ἀπεχώρουν.'

III's reign, and thus they presented a more objective and nuanced approach to the literary and historical shaping of his image.

## The Iconoclasm of Leo III?

Is the image of Leo III in the *Short History* an image of an Iconoclast emperor, or did Nikephoros preserve such a picture exclusively for his son and successor, Emperor Constantine V?[15]

Nikephoros emphasized the emperor's link to the Iconoclastic heresy in certain narrative elements which constitute the second part of his account in the *Short History*. Nikephoros even gave the causes that motivated the emperor to promote such an understanding of icon worship. These causes were, however, of an external character, events which had no direct relation to the emperor himself, and did not originate from him directly. Nikephoros concluded the account on Leo III's reign with reference to the illness which ended his twenty-four-year reign, which is a motif with extremely negative connotations in Theophanes's narrative and always linked with the heretical beliefs of a particular emperor. In his presentation, it was God who trampled the heretical emperor, who was similar to Diocletian since he also spilled Christian blood. His illness befell him during his campaign against the Bulgarians. The emperor died in the vicinity of Constantinople. Theophanes transmitted the alleged words of Leo, that being alive he was submitted to the unquenchable flames.[16] In contrast, Nikephoros did not connect the illness of any emperor directly to the character and nature of his imperial office. However, he did promote an idea of a *good death* in the case of Constantine IV, who spent the rest of his life in *peace and tranquillity* after he had repelled the Arab raids on Constantinople, and concluded peace with the Avars, while he also managed to calm the heretical storm in the Church of Constantinople. Such a description might carry in itself a certain evaluation of this emperor's career, but the only explicitly negative description of one emperor's death which stood in relation both to his illness and to his conduct as emperor, is the death of Herakleios.[17]

---

15   Cf. Gero, *Byzantine Iconoclasm during the Reign of Leo III*, pp. 94-112.

16   Cf. Theophanes, *Chronicle*, 448.12-449.3.

17   For the descriptions of physical features of Byzantine emperors, among them Phokas and Herakleios, see Head, 'Physical Descriptions', pp. 230-231, who pointed out that for the period between the reigns of Herakleios and Michael Rangabe there exists a big gap in sources in conection to this topic.

   The elements which could be characterized according to their content
as a part of a specific narrative about Leo III as an Iconoclast emperor are
the mention of a volcanic eruption in the sea near the islands of Thera and
Therasia, which led the emperor astray in his understanding of icon worship.
Nevertheless, it is significant that Nikephoros did not point explicitly to the
emperor's impiety as a reason for his heresy, which is the case with his son,
Emperor Constantine V. On the contrary, a misjudgement of the volcanic
eruption event was a naïve and superficial cause for the emperor's decision
to proclaim icon veneration an unorthodox practice. Nikephoros mentioned
that the citizens of the Helladic region and of the Cyclades revolted, since
they were against 'this impiety' (τὸ δυσσέβημα). Then he wrote that they in fact
rebelled against the emperor (πρὸς τὸν βασιλέα διαστασιάζουσιν). It was a new
exposition of faith which was contrary to the traditions of the Church that
introduced the revolt.[18] Contrary to Nikephoros, Theophanes mentioned
the 'impious Leo' (ὁ δυσσεβὴς βασιλεὺς Λέων) when he narrated about his edict
against icons and placed this part before he had written about the volcanic
eruption.[19] In a slightly different form, Nikephoros wrote that the emperor
tried to expound his doctrine to the people, who had, however, lamented
the insult (τὴν ὕβριν) which had been done to the Church.[20] Nikephoros
placed this entire episode into the broader context of the relations with
the Church, which is significant since it shifted the context from a strictly
Iconodule narrative towards issues of broader significance for the relations
between the Empire and the Church.
   The relation to the volcanic eruption in the context of Leo's Iconoclasm
is somewhat different between the two Iconodule writers.[21] Namely,
Theophanes placed the official promotion of Iconoclasm by Leo *before*
the volcanic eruption, thus giving his personal evaluation and interpretation of both events, pointing out in a rhetorical manner that the emperor
misunderstood the strange eruption to be a sign that God's wrath was in

18   Nikephoros, *Short History*, § 60.8-14.
19   For the reconstruction of the lost *Edict*, see Gero, *Byzantine Iconoclasm during the Reign
of Leo III*, pp. 106-111; Anastos, 'Leo III'. Theophanes, *Chronicle*, 404.3-4: 'This year the impious
Emperor Leo started making pronouncements about the removal of the holy and venerable
icons.' He then promoted the pope's authority in the matter, mentioning that it was Gregory of
Rome who had reprimanded the emperor for altering the doctrines of the Church, contrary to
the traditions of the Holy Fathers.
20   Nikephoros, *Short History*, § 60.
21   Cf. Gero, *Byzantine Iconoclasm during the Reign of Leo III*, p. 94, who noticed these diver-
gences between Nikephoros and Theophanes, but who did not evaluate the basic difference in
making an image of the emperor and the crucial divergence in making the final remark on the
emperor's Iconoclasm, particularly in Theophanes's *Chronicle*.

his favour, or rather, according to Theophanes, in favour of his heretical belief. Theophanes then proceeded to insist that these events should have been understood in a different way – as a sign of God's disapproval of the Iconoclasm of the emperor, whose impiety Theophanes had emphasized already in the text. He thus prepared and directed this particular narrative towards the conclusion that the emperor was contagious with heresy before the ominous eruptions. Consequently, Theophanes developed Leo's heretical image in the following manner. Leo appeared as impious emperor in the entry about his ninth regnal year,[22] while the volcanic eruption and Theophanes's rhetorical interpretation of a natural phenomenon in an Iconodule manner was given in the entry about Leo's tenth regnal year.[23] After such an arrangement, the episode about the volcanic eruption conformed to Theophanes's interpretation of God's fury towards the new heresy professed by Leo III. After all, according to Theophanes, the emperor's heresy appeared as an independent feature of Leo's impiety, and the natural phenomenon of the volcanic eruption in the sea was then transformed into a sign, or rather a consequence and result, of the emperor's failure in religious judgement. Later, as the patriarch of Constantinople, Nikephoros assumed such argumentation and utilized it in his theological writings. However, in his *Short History*, the cause of Leo's heresy appeared from without, caused by a misinterpretation of a natural phenomenon, which led the emperor astray, and into impiety.

Unlike Theophanes, Nikephoros presented a different course of events, since Leo, 'when he heard of these things considered them to be signs of divine wrath, and was pondering what cause might have brought them about. On this account, he took up a position contrary to the true faith and planned the removal of the holy icons, mistakenly believing that the portent had occurred because they were set up and adored.'[24]

The same technical terms ἐυσέβεια / δυσσέβημα were used by both authors. However, Nikephoros never attached them to the name of Leo III, whereas Theophanes made them almost an integral part of Leo's name: ὁ δυσσεβὴς βασιλεὺς Λέων. Thus, it would appear that Nikephoros relatively mitigated the weight of a negative description which can be found in Theophanes's work, mostly by separating the impiety from the name of the emperor. Thus,

---

22  Theophanes, *Chronicle*, 404.3-9.

23  Theophanes, *Chronicle*, 405.1-2.

24  Nikephoros, *Short History*, § 60.1-6: 'Ταῦτά φασιν ἀκούσαντα τὸν βασιλέα ὑπολαμβάνειν θείας ὀργῆς εἶναι μηνύματα, καὶ ἥτις αἰτία ταῦτα κεκίνηκε διασκέπτεσθαι. ἐντεῦθεν λοιπὸν κατὰ τῆς εὐσεβείας ἵσταται καὶ τῶν ἱερῶν εἰκονισμάτων μελετᾷ τὴν καθαίρεσιν ὡς ἐκ τῆς τούτων ἱδρύσεώς τε καὶ προσκυνήσεως γεγονέναι οἰόμενος τὸ τεράστιον, κακῶς εἰδώς.'

according to Nikephoros, Leo III assumed a position contrary to the true faith, while the Iconodule rebels against the emperor were presented as being motivated by his δυσσέβημα. It cannot be concluded that Nikephoros totally absolved Leo III from the guilt of promoting heresy. Later on, he wrote that the emperor pressed Germanos of Constantinople to accept Iconoclasm, and earlier, that he tried to expound *his* dogma (ἐκδιδάσκειν [...] τὸ οἰκεῖον ἐπεχείρει δόγμα).[25] There is no indication that Nikephoros attempted to interpret the odd natural phenomenon in an Iconodule manner – as a sign of divine wrath against the emperor and his heretical persecution of icons. However, placed immediately after the mention of Constantine V's coronation for his father's co-ruler, a question can be asked whether the mention of the volcanic eruption had the role of an allusion to the reign of Emperor Constantine V and his heresy, which was emphasized more openly than in the case of Leo III. Later, in connection to Leo's successor, Nikephoros linked the appearance of a plague in Constantinople with the *impious* emperor and with all those who dared to raise their hands against the holy icons, that is, in connection to the Iconoclasm in the days of Constantine V.

The section of the account about Leo's pressure upon the Patriarch Germanos of Constantinople to accept Iconoclasm fit into the same picture with the chapter about the casual connection of the volcanic eruption and the emperor's shift from Orthodoxy to impiety. This account was followed by the mention of the patriarch's voluntary abdication and the statement that, from that time the *pious* had suffered many punishments by refusing to accept the imperial dogma.

In such a context, a fact should be considered, namely that, already in the description of Leo's reign, Nikephoros introduced into his narrative the personality of the future Emperor Constantine V, placing in these chapters two omens which had happened in the time when the events from the life of the future Constantine V had taken place. Such arrangement of the material might have the function of an allusion about his later heretical strife against the Church of Constantinople – allusions which bear a significant meaning of the destruction of the peace which was mentioned several times in the reign of Leo III as having been in the Byzantine empire. In relation to such places in the *Short History*, it appears as if the personality of Emperor Leo

---

25   In the further course of narration, Nikephoros utilized a distinctive term, more characteristic of Theophanes (so probably utilized from the common source), which he put in the context of Constantine V, who was mentioned as 'enemy of Christ and new Midas' (ὁ μισόχριστος νέος Μίδας Κωνσταντῖνος).

III was emphasized more in relation to his successful lay policy, while his Iconoclasm was mentioned almost indifferently, and in the account of his reign was presented as a characteristic feature of the reign of his son and successor.

The amount of attention directed towards Leo's successful defence of Constantinople and the Empire, and in general towards his military successes, when compared to the relatively lesser amount of chapters dedicated to his Iconoclasm, points to the fact that Nikephoros was more directed towards the emperor's deeds from the secular sector, rather than towards his deviations in Orthodoxy and Church dogma.

## Patriarchs and the Authority of the Ecumenical Councils

The overall narration about the patriarchs in the *Short History* shifted after Herakleios's reign and the significant mention of patriarchs Sergios and Pyrrhos in the time of the emperors Leo III and Constantine V. The Iconoclast era with its controversy brought a new and a different direction in the narration about the patriarchs in Nikephoros's work, in which the idea of the authority of the ecumenical councils assumed a significant place in the authors overall idea. The descriptions of the patriarchs of Constantinople in their relations to the emperors received a new turn towards a description of the imperial persecutions of the Church. These are the accounts which are barren of and clearly emphasized dogmatic differences between an Orthodox patriarch, as was Germanos of Constantinople at the time of Leo III, and the Patriarch Constantine II of Constantinople from the reign of Constantine V. On the contrary, Nikephoros did not hesitate to mention Germanos's participation in anathematizing the fathers of the Sixth Ecumenical Council under the Monothelite emperor Philippikos Bardanes. This feature of the patriarchs Sergios, Pyrrhos, and Kyros, mentioned earlier in the *Short History*, was not highlighted at all, when he portrayed the emperor-patriarch relations in a somewhat idealized manner. In contrast, in the *Chronicle* of Theophanes, these patriarchs received a strict evaluation from the point of Christian dogma and the doctrinal disputes of the seventh century, and thus carried the label of heretics in Theophanes's narrative. Nikephoros rather shifted such a characterization of these patriarchs in the *Short History* into the secondary narrative plan.

Nikephoros's approach is evident in the narration about Constantine IV's reign, where Sergios and Pyrrhos were mentioned only as 'leaders of the heresy' (τῆς αἱρέσεως ἄρξαντας):

Constantine convened an ecumenical council which confirmed the five preceding ecumenical synods as well as the dogma of the two wills and two natural energies of our Lord Christ, whom it proclaimed perfect in His divinity and in His manhood, while condemning to anathema the leaders of the heresy.[26]

Of course, both Pyrrhos and Sergios were Monothelites and heretics, which is the main point of emphasis in Theophanes's portrayal of these figures. After he had mentioned Pyrrhos as Sergios's successor, but in the context of their heresy, Theophanes proceeded to present a short historical account of condemnation of Monothelitism in the Church which was out of Constantinople's reach, in Carthage and Rome, an account far more detailed than anything Nikephoros presented.[27] Unlike Theophanes, Nikephoros had rather remained silent regarding the Monothelitism of these patriarchs. We would not agree that Nikephoros was not aware of the main events from the history of the Monothelite disputations. On the contrary, the Christological dogma regarding the two wills and energies of Christ – the two pivotal issues in the controversy – was indeed present and mentioned in the *Short History* and in a manner which left no doubt about Nikephoros personal adherence. This topic was, however, displaced from the main narrative of the *Short History*. After abdication, Pyrrhos left for Carthage, as Nikephoros tells us, where he met St. Maximos the Confessor, who interrogated him concerning the *Exposition* which was made by the former Emperor Herakleios and Patriarch Sergios of Constantinople.

---

26   Nikephoros, *Short History*, § 37.5-10: 'ταῦτα διαγνοὺς Κωνσταντῖνος σύνοδον οἰκουμενικὴν συγκροτεῖ, ἣ τὰς μὲν προλαβούσας πέντε ἁγίας οἰκουμενικὰς συνόδους ἐκύρωσε καὶ τὰ δύο ἐπὶ τοῦ σωτῆρος Χριστοῦ θελήματα καὶ δύο φυσικὰς ἐνεργείας, τέλειον αὐτὸν ἐν θεότητι καὶ τέλειον ἐν ἀνθρωπότητι διατρανώσασα καὶ τῷ ἀναθέματι τοὺς τῆς αἱρέσεως ἄρξαντας παραπέμψασα.'

27   Theophanes, *Chronicle*, 331.6-15: 'As for John, bishop of Rome, he convened a council of bishops and anathematized the Monothelite heresy. Likewise, various bishops of Africa, Byzakion, Numidia, and Mauritania gathered together and anathematized the Monophisites. Now when Pyrrhos had come to Africa, he met the most holy father Maximos, who was venerable by reason of his monastic achievements, as well as the godly bishops who were there, who reproved and converted him and so sent him to pope Theodore in Rome.' ("Ἰωάννης δέ, ὁ Ῥώμης ἐπίσκοπος, συναθροίσας σύνοδον ἐπισκόπων τὴν τῶν Μονοθελητῶν αἵρεσιν ἀνεθεμάτισεν. ὁμοίως καὶ ἐν Ἀφρικῇ καὶ Βυζακίῳ καὶ Νουμιδίᾳ καὶ Μαυριτανίᾳ διάφοροι ἐπίσκοποι συναθροισθέντες τοὺς Μονοφυσίτας ἀνεθεμάτισαν. Ἰωάννου δὲ τοῦ Ῥώμης κοιμηθέντος, Θεόδωρος χειροτονεῖται πάπας ἀντ᾽ αὐτοῦ. Πύρρος δὲ τὴν Ἀφρικὴν καταλαβὼν συνοψίζεται τῷ ἁγιωτάτῳ ἀββᾷ Μαξίμῳ, τῷ αἰδεσίμῳ ἐν μοναχικοῖς κατορθώμασιν, καὶ τοῖς ἐκεῖσε ἐνθέοις ἱεράρχαις, οἵ τινες τοῦτον ἐλέγξαντες καὶ πείσαντες πρὸς τὸν πάπαν Θεόδωρον ἀπέστειλαν ἐν Ῥώμῃ'). Both Nikephoros and Theophanes refer to the *Disputation between Pyrrhos and Maximos*.

It is interesting to note that this scene is dated to the year 645 by the anonymous author of the *Disputation between Pyrrhos and Maximos*, who narrated in detail this meeting and debate which took place at a council in Carthage:

> A record of a discussion about controversial questions in church dogmas, between Pyrrhos the former patriarch of Constantinople and the most pious monk Maximos which was held in the presence of the most famous Patrician Gregorios and with him most holy bishops and other God loving and glorious men, in July of the third indiction. Whereas Pyrrhos was defending the innovation, that is, one will, which he and his predecessors introduced in Byzantium, Maximos advocated the teaching of the fathers and apostles coming to us from old times.[28]

In his account of the same event, Nikephoros introduced some of the main elements from the introduction of the *Disputation between Pyrrhos and Maximos*, namely, the mention of the *Exposition* about the one will, which was made by Sergios and introduced by Emperor Herakleios in Byzantium.[29] The interrogation of Pyrrhos, mentioned by Nikephoros was, in fact, a council which took place in Carthage in 645, in the presence of the Patrician Gregorios and 'the most holy bishops and God-loving men'. According to Theophanes, and the writer of the *Disputation*, Pyrrhos was converted to Orthodoxy and sent to Pope Theodore in Rome to confirm his confession of faith. Nikephoros followed most of these moments in his account of Pyrrhos's abdication, but he was concise, rather adhering to his own idea in narration. He puts forward Emperor Herakleios as the one who proclaimed the *Exposition*, while he failed to mention the patriarch's responsibility, since Sergios was the one who wrote it. Later, when writing about the Sixth Ecumenical Council, Nikephoros stressed that the heresy appeared in the time of Herakleios, while the patriarch was not mentioned

---

28  *Disputation between Pyrrhos and Maximos*, col. 288A: 'Παρασημείωσις τῆς γενομένης ζητήσεως χάριν τῶν κεκινημένων περὶ τῶν ἐκκλησιαστικῶν δογμάτων, παρουσίᾳ Γρηγορίου τοῦ εὐκλεεστάτου πατρικίου, καὶ τῶν συνευρεθέντων αὐτῷ ὁσιωτάτων ἐπισκόπων, καὶ λοιπῶν θεοφιλῶν καὶ ἐνδόξων ἀνδρῶν, παρὰ Πύρρου, τοῦ γενομένου πατριάρχου Κωνσταντινουπόλεως, καὶ Μαξίμου τοῦ εὐλαβεστάτου μοναχοῦ, μηνὶ Ἰουλίῳ, ἰνδικτίωνος γʹ. Πύρρου μὲν συμμαχοῦντος τῇ παρεισαχθείσῃ παρ᾽ αὐτοῦ τε, καὶ τοῦ πρὸ αὐτοῦ ἐν τῷ Βυζαντίῳ καινοτομίᾳ· τουτέστιν τοῦ ἑνὸς θελήματος· Μαξίμου δὲ συνηγοροῦντος τῇ ἄνωθεν εἰς ἡμᾶς ἐλθούσῃ πατρικῇ τε καὶ ἀποστολικῇ διδασκαλίᾳ.'
29  Nikephoros, *Short History*, § 31.28-33: 'When some of the monks there heard of his arrival, their leaders were Maximos and Theodosios, who dwelt in Africa, they interrogated him concerning the Exposition made by the former Emperor Herakleios and by Sergios, archpriest of the City, regarding the two wills and energies of Christ our Saviour.'

in this context. Thus, Nikephoros seems to have shifted the responsibility for the heresy from the patriarch to the emperor, although in reality the emperor was the one who even wanted to distance himself from it at one point, especially in regard to the Roman church and the pope.[30] In such a way, Nikephoros managed to promote a general idea that it was always the Byzantine emperors who had promoted heresy, not only in the time of Iconoclasm. In a way, this could be a strong argument in the contemporary struggle of the Orthodox party to define the place of the emperor in his relation to the doctrines of the Church.

Although mentioning the *Exposition* of faith by Sergios in the account of the meeting between Pyrrhos and Maximos the Confessor in Africa, Nikephoros seems to have refrained from offering a dogmatic evaluation from the Orthodox perspective, and the perspective of the definition of faith by the Sixth Ecumenical Council regarding the two energies and wills in Christ. Nikephoros offered his evaluation of the entire Monothelite dispute elsewhere, in the account of Emperor Constantine IV's reign.[31]

If we return to the issue of the ecumenical councils and the idea of its authority in the *Short History*, it appears that Nikephoros followed a definite plan in portraying events and individuals in such a context where the theme of his narration was of ecclesiastical provenance. Thus, in the reign of Emperor Philippikos Bardanes, we encounter a new image of the authority of the Sixth Ecumenical Council, although from a specifically negative portrayal of Philippikos's rule:

> As for Philippikos, he appeared to administer the empire in an indecorous and negligent manner. He subjected to anathema the Fathers of the Sixth Ecumenical Synod because he did not accept the two wills and energies of Our Saviour that had been piously defined by them. In this, he was supported by John, who was at the time archpriest of the City, Germanos, metropolitan of Kyzikos, as well as other priests and many senators.[32]

First of all, it is evident that Nikephoros gives a qualitative and final remark about the reign of Philippikos in the very beginning of the quoted passage,

---

30  Hovorun, *Will, Action and Freedom*, p. 58, n. 28.
31  Nikephoros, *Short History*, § 37.1-10.
32  Nikephoros, *Short History*, § 46.1-7: 'Φιλιππικὸς δὲ ἀσέμνως καὶ ῥαθύμως τὰ βασίλεια διέπων ἐφαίνετο, τοὺς δὲ ἐν τῇ ἕκτῃ οἰκουμενικῇ συνόδῳ πατέρας ἀναθέματι καθυπέβαλε, τὰ παρ' αὐτῶν ἐνθέως δογματισθέντα δύο τοῦ σωτῆρος θελήματα καὶ ἐνεργείας μὴ ἀποδεχόμενος, συλλήπτορα εὑρίσκων Ἰωάννην τὸν τηνικαῦτα τῆς πόλεως ἀρχιερέα καὶ Γερμανὸν τὸν Κυζίκου μητροπολίτην καὶ ἑτέρους ἱερεῖς καὶ συγκλητικοὺς πλείστους.'

pointing towards his negligent reign, and proceeding to explain what was the main issue, which was the subjection to anathema of the fathers of the Sixth Ecumenical Council. It was the emperor who did not accept the Orthodox definition of the Council about the two wills and energies in Christ. Patriarch John of Constantinople and Germanos, metropolitan of Kyzikos, were presented as supporting the imperial policy and making it the policy of the Church of Constantinople. It is hard to deduce whether Nikephoros here actually accepted their responsibility for participating in such an imperial policy or rather shifted their fault to a secondary plan, since they were referred to as accomplices, or rather supporters (συλλήπτορας) of the emperor, thus leaving Philippikos at the forefront of the blame for the heresy.

Unlike Nikephoros, Theophanes gave a rather detailed account of the same event with more protagonists, describing Philippikos's policy against the Sixth Council and for the renovation of Monothelitism in his Empire. Theophanes portrayed the emperor as the one who furiously attacked the Sixth Council and 'subverted the divine doctrines' which were confirmed by it. The emperor had, in fact, convoked a false council. However, Theophanes accented more the role of the Patriarch John and Germanos, emphasizing that the later was, in fact, the future patriarch of Constantinople, which Nikephoros did not underline in his account. Theophanes also called them the emperor's 'allies', also adding that Bishop Andrew of Crete, a certain Quaestor Nicholas, Deacon Elpidios of St. Sophia, and *Chartophylax* Antiochos were also involved in this action, as well as other men 'of the same ilk'.[33]

---

33  Theophanes, *Chronicle*, 382.10-21: 'Philippikos was not ashamed to make a furious attack on the holy Sixth Ecumenical Council, hastening to subvert the divine doctrines that had been confirmed by it. He found allies (ὁμόφρονας, likeminded) in John, whom he made bishop of Constantinople after deposing its bishop Kyros, whom he confined in the monastery of the Chora; in Germanos, who later occupied the see of Constantinople, but was then bishop of Kyzikos; Andrew, who was bishop of Crete; Nicholas, who, from being a servant in charge of cups, became a professor of medicine and was at the time a quaestor; Elpidios, deacon of the Great Church; Antiochos the chartophylax; and other men of the same ilk who anathematized in writing the holy Sixth Council.' ('Φιλιππικὸς δὲ οὐκ ᾐσχύνθη ἐκμανῶς κινηθῆναι κατὰ τῆς ἁγίας καὶ οἰκουμενικῆς ἕκτης συνόδου, ἀνατρέπειν σπεύδων τὰ ὑπ' αὐτῆς βεβαιωθέντα θεῖα δόγματα. εὗρε δὲ ὁμόφρονας αὐτοῦ Ἰωάννην, ὃν ἐπίσκοπον Κωνσταντινουπόλεως πεποίηκε καθελὼν Κῦρον, τὸν ταύτης πρόεδρον, ὃν καὶ περιώρισεν ἐν τῷ τῆς Χώρας μοναστηρίῳ· Γερμανόν τε τὸν μετὰ ταῦτα τὸν θρόνον Κωνσταντινουπόλεως κατασχόντα, ἐπίσκοπον τὸ τηνικαῦτα ὑπάρχοντα Κυζίκου, καὶ Ἀνδρέαν καὶ αὐτὸν ἐπίσκοπον Κρήτης ὄντα, Νικόλαόν τε τὸν ἀπὸ καυκοδιακόνων σοφιστὴν γεγονότα τῆς ἰατρικῆς ἐπιστήμης κυέστορά τε τότε ὑπάρχοντα, Ἐλπίδιόν τε διάκονον τῆς μεγάλης ἐκκλησίας, Ἀντίοχόν τε τὸν χαρτοφύλακα καὶ ἑτέρους τούτων ὁμοιοτρόπους.') Cf. *Synodicon Vetus*, 145.1-6, where no mention was given of later saints or the holy fathers Germanos of Constantinopple and Andrew of Crete and their participation at the pro-Monothelite council of Emperor Philippikos.

As Nikephoros's assessment of Constantine IV's reign generally stood in connection to his convocation of the Sixth Council, so did the critique of the reign of Philippikos stand in relation to his anathematization of the same council and negation of a positive aspect of Constantine IV's reign. Nikephoros pointed out that the Sixth Council confirmed all the previous five councils.[34] Such a statement then emphasized that Philippikos convoked a council which as a consequence refuted the previous five Ecumenical Councils as well.[35] Patriarch Nikephoros had dealt with the place and significance of the Sixth Ecumenical Council in his *Synodika* addressed to Pope Leo III.[36] He accepted the Sixth Council, which had proclaimed two wills and two energies in Christ (*καὶ τῶν κατὰ Χριστὸν φύσεων τάς τε ἰδιότητας καὶ φυσικάς, ἐνεργείας καὶ θελήσεις κηρύξασαν*) and which had anathematized, among others, the patriarchs of Constantinople: Sergios, Pyrrhos, Paul, and Peter, as well as the pope of Rome, Honorius, and the Patriarch Kyros of Alexandria. Nikephoros added that these patriarchs of Rome, Constantinople, and Alexandria received their patriarchal office according to God's dispensation, but their office was, in fact, their perdition since they were 'teaching about one will and energy in Christ, God, and Saviour'.

In the context of the Sixth Council and the heresy of the Monothelites, the significance of the council was that it brought the Empire a long lost unity, peace, and tranquillity. Two emperors were characterized exclusively in connection to this Council – Constantine IV in a positive manner for convoking it, and Philippikos Bardanes for anathematizing it. However, although mentioned in such a specific context, all the key aspects of the Orthodox dogma as professed at that council were referred to in a concise manner, and the authority of the Ecumenical Council was clearly accented.

In light of Nikephoros's deliberate exemption of the patriarchs Sergios and Pyrrhos of Constantinople from their heresy, it is important to closely identify the development of the image of Germanos of Constantinople in

---

34 Nikephoros, *Short History*, § 37.5-14 (*πέντε ἁγίας οἰκουμενικὰς συνόδους ἐκύρωσε*).

35 Cf. Nikephoros, *Antirrheticus* I, cols. 209D-212C, where Nikephoros the patriarch developed this particular idea when analysing and refuting the teaching of the Iconoclasts, which negated and refuted the decisions of previous Ecumenical councils and finished with a rhetorical question: why is it necessary to speak about the refutation of the councils which the Iconoclasts provoke with their teaching since they actually destroy the entire *oikonomia of salvation* of the Saviour (*τοῦ μυστηρίου τῆς τοῦ Σωτῆρος οἰκονομίας περιθεσμοὺς καὶ σεβάσματα*).

36 Nikephoros, *Ad Leonem*, col. 193AB.

the *Short History*. Germanos of Constantinople[37] is portrayed in the *Short History* in three episodes:

1. Under the Emperor Philippikos Bardanes, he participated in the restoration of the Monothelite doctrines and, together with the Patriarch John of Constantinople, took part in anathematizing the Sixth Ecumenical Council, as *Germanos metropolitan of Kyzikos*.

2. Under Leo III, Germanos (now the patriarch of Constantinople) refused to change the definition of faith concerning the veneration of images contrary to and without the convocation of an ecumenical council, and he thus withdrew from the patriarchal see of Constantinople.

3. And finally, under Constantine V he was anathematized by the First Iconoclastic Council of 754, which aspired to be *ecumenical* in its nature but failed to accomplish the required needs.

Thus, the image of Germanos of Constantinople was shaped and transformed, from a bishop who was actively involved in the heretical policies of the Emperor Philippikos Bardanes against the traditions of the Sixth Ecumenical Council, to the image of a confessor of faith and the defender of the authority of ecumenical councils as an institution of the Church under Leo III. Moreover, he was subjected to anathema, together with John of Damascus and George of Cyprus, by the false bishops of the false ecumenical council of Hiereia in 754, under Emperor Constantine V, and thus his Orthodoxy was confirmed in a specific manner.[38]

The next significant mention of Germanos of Constantinople, now as the bishop of the City, is in connection with the first description of imperial Iconoclasm in the *Short History*:

---

37   Cf. Stein, 'Germanos I'.

38   The absence of ecumenical authority concerning the First Iconoclastic Council is a significant argument and holds a significant place in Nikephoros's theological writings as an idea that confirms the legitimacy of the Seventh Ecumenical Council of 787 and the restored Orthodox identity of the Church of Constantinople. Cf. O'Connell, *The Ecclesiology of St. Nicephorus*, pp. 117-119, who offered an overview of corresponding places in Nikephoros's theological writings. This thought about the authority of the Ecumenical Councils as supreme keepers of Orthodoxy, and also its formation and expression, is encountered in Nikephoros's letter to the Pope Leo III, or rather in his confession of faith. Cf. Nikephoros, *Ad Leonem*, cols. 192B-193C. In this part of the Creed, Nikephoros's main motif is the divine inspiration of the numerous council fathers, who by the agency of the Holy Spirit defined all the crucial dogmas of the Christian faith and Church, confirming the preceding ones, and so they remain within the boundraries of the Orthodox tradition and the Church itself. Contrary to them, the Iconoclast emperor Constantine V 'was driven by the evil spirit' and, making war on piety, he convened a Council against icon worship and the Orthodox fathers. Cf. Nikephoros, *Short History*, § 72.3-17.

After this, the emperor convened to the palace a great throng of people from the City and summoned Germanos, who was then archpriest of Constantinople, whom he pressed to subscribe to the suppression of the holy icons. The latter declined to do so and laid aside his priesthood, saying: 'Without an ecumenical synod I cannot make a written declaration of faith.' Retiring thence to his ancestral house, he spent in it the remainder of his life.[39]

Anastasios, who was a cleric of the Great Church, succeeded Germanos on the patriarchal throne. Nikephoros immediately added: 'from that time onward many pious men who would not accept the imperial doctrine suffered many punishments and tortures.' A certain distinction should be pointed out in this description about the outbreak of Iconoclasm, although this rather appears to be more of a short notice about the roots of Iconoclasm, while Nikephoros reserved the main account of active Iconoclasm for Emperor Constantine V. Namely, the martyrdom for icon worship, persecutions, and tortures fell upon the pious who would not accept the *imperial dogma*. Germanos was portrayed as a patriarch who refused changes in the definition of faith and rejected Iconoclasm, while the faithful were persecuted for being loyal to icon worship. So basically, their Orthodoxy was of a different type. The patriarch was the one who defended not only icon veneration, but also the entire Orthodoxy and the general principle of the Church, that an ecumenical council was the only institution that could define matters of faith, contrary to the emperor. As a result of the patriarch's reply, he was pressed to abdicate.

Theophanes, in contrast, presented the story in more detail by introducing other protagonists of the Orthodox defence such as John of Damascus and the Roman Pontiff. He also emphasized Germanos's likeness to Christ through the motif of betrayal, which was committed from inside the Church, from the side of the patriarch's close associate, the future patriarch Anastasios, who acted in agreement with the emperor. Theophanes explicitly compared Patriarch Anastasios with Judas and thus equated Emperor Leo III with the Judean high priests of the Sanhedrin. He thus managed to promulgate the imperial idea about the connection between the priestly and imperial office into a negative context of the betrayal of Christ, which

---

39  Nikephoros, *Short History*, § 62.1-6: 'Μετὰ δὲ ταῦτα ὁ βασιλεὺς ἀθροίζει πλεῖστον λαὸν τῆς πόλεως περὶ τὰ βασίλεια, καὶ συγκαλεῖ τὸν τότε τῆς πόλεως ἀρχιερέα Γερμανόν, καὶ συγγράφειν κατὰ τῆς καθαιρέσεως τῶν εἰκόνων τῶν ἁγίων ἠνάγκαζεν. ὁ δὲ παρῃτεῖτο καὶ τὴν ἱερωσύνην ἀπέβαλε, λέγων ὡς ἄνευ οἰκουμενικῆς συνόδου ἔγγραφον πίστιν οὐκ ἐκτίθεμαι.'

in fact was the essence of the Iconophile theology of icon worship, the Iconoclasts being the foremost deniers of Christ's incarnation through the persecution of his images in his human likeness.[40] The greatest difference between Nikephoros's and Theophanes's portrayal of Germanos and his attitude towards the emperor is Theophanes's description of the patriarch's stand for the holy icons, which resulted in his deposition by the orders of the emperor. However, Theophanes had included the motif of the authority of the ecumenical council as well, and that it was impossible for the patriarch to proclaim the *new* faith without the council.[41]

Such a portrayal of both emperors and patriarchs in relation to the ecumenical councils has been accepted in research as a process which was evident especially after the Seventh Ecumenical Council, when the authority of the councils and the Church was being restored in Byzantium after the first wave of Iconoclasm. Both Tarasios and Nikephoros as patriarchs were promoters of such ecclesiastical policies, even facing significant opposition from the Studites led by their *hegumenos* Theodore.[42]

Germanos of Constantinople will be mentioned once more in connection to the First Iconoclastic Council of Hiereia in 754, during the reign of Constantine V. This mention of Germanos is placed in a context of the reign of Constantine V, where the persecution of monks, faithful men and the martyrdom of St. Stephen the Younger are dominant topics in Nikephoros's narration. This mention of the Patriarch Germanos places him among the first Iconodule defenders of images who were anathematized by the Iconoclastic council, John of Damascus and George of Cyprus, whose Orthodoxy is even more stressed by this mention in its contrast to the council which is named as heretical and ungodly by Nikephoros.[43]

---

40  Cf. Theophanes, *Chronicle*, 407.15-408.6, which concluded: 'The blessed man was not unaware that Anastasios was holding such a perverse position: imitating his own Lord, he wisely and gently kept bringing to his attention, as to another Judas Iscariot, the circumstances of betrayal.' ('ὃν ὁ μακάριος οὐκ ἀγνοῶν οὕτω στρεβλῶς διακείμενον, μιμούμενος τὸν ἑαυτοῦ δεσπότην, ὡς πρὸς ἄλλον Ἰσκαριώτην, σοφῶς καὶ πράως τὰ περὶ προδοσίας ἀνεμίμνησκεν.')

41  Theophanes, *Chronicle*, 409.7-9: 'χωρὶς γὰρ οἰκουμενικῆς συνόδου καινοτομῆσαι πίστιν ἀδύνατόν μοι, ὦ βασιλεῦ.'

42  Cf. Афиногенов, *Константинополский патриархат*, p. 16, who called attention to this process and, among other sources, to this particular part of the *Short History*.

43  Nikephoros, *Short History*, § 72.11-17: 'ὅρον δὲ πίστεως ἐκτίθενται, ἐν ᾧ ὑπεσημήναντο ἅπαντες κακῶς καὶ δυσσεβῶς συμφρονήσαντες, τὴν τῶν ἱερῶν εἰκονισμάτων καθαίρεσιν ἐκφωνήσαντες, καὶ ὥσπερ νηπιώδεις ἐπ᾽ ἀγορᾶς ταῦτα ἀνεθεμάτιζον. μεθ᾽ ὧν καὶ Γερμανὸν τὸν ἀρχιερέα τοῦ Βυζαντίου γεγονότα Γεώργιόν τε τὸν ἐκ Κύπρου τῆς νήσου ὁρμώμενον καὶ Ἰωάννην τὸν ἀπὸ Δαμασκοῦ τῆς Συρίας τὸ ἐπίκλην Μανσούρ'. Cf. Mansi XIII, 356CD.

If we proceed to analyse this story, we can conclude that it carried a message about the nature of the emperor's violence towards the Church of Constantinople. The freedom and the tradition of the Church were already denied and compromised by the convocation of the false council, which had no ecumenical characteristics. Here it is interesting to note that Nikephoros referred to the Iconoclast bishops as ἱερέων, which can also mean *priests*, and, in the context of the later procedure of admittance of such bishops into the Church, it was possible that some of them might not have been admitted as bishops but as priests. Such choice of terms highlighted the false character of the council. This was an idea which Nikephoros more thoroughly described in his theological writings. This thought was mentioned in his *Apologeticus Minor* more explicitly.[44] In this work, the Patriarch Nikephoros gave an introduction by mentioning Iconoclasm in the time of Leo III and adding that the Patriarch Germanos of Constantinople was a victim of emperor's heresy and violence. This led to his downfall from the patriarchal see, since Germanos opposed the 'evil plans' of the emperor. Considering the circumstances in which Patriarch Nikephoros had delivered his apology, after his own deposition from the patriarchal office in 815, the parallel with his personal struggle for icon worship as portrayed in the image of Germanos is more than obvious.

Nikephoros then proceeded to deny the validity of the First Iconoclastic Council in 754. His arguments in refutation of the proclaimed Orthodoxy of this council are typical of later Iconodule argumentation. The Council was not convened with the participation of the patriarch of Constantinople or the pope of Rome, and the patriarchs of the great eastern sees – Alexandria, Antioch, and Jerusalem – were not summoned. Constantine V had followed his own impiety and, by the cruelty of a tyrant, despising the divine laws, he gathered 'unholy priests' (ἀνιέρων ἱερέων).[45] From such an image of the emperor's ecclesiastical policy and the portrayal of the council of 754, Nikephoros's own ecclesiology and his understanding of the significance of ecumenical councils is clear. His stance was that there could be no ecumenical council without the participation of the five patriarchal sees of Christendom, and especially not when the imperial power interfered in the internal matters of the Church, as in the case of Constantine V, who defined the Iconoclastic dogma of the Church. His duty was to guide the

---

44  Cf. Alexander, *The Patriarch Nicephorus*, pp. 163-165.
45  Nikephoros, *Apologeticus Minor*, cols. 836C-837A. However, Nikephoros might have chosen the term ἱερέων in order to construct a word play with the idea of the unholy nature of the Council of 754: ἀνιέρων ἱερέων.

Council towards an Orthodox resolution. This is the basic thought of all the apologetics from the period of Iconoclasm.[46] According to the *Life of Stephen the Younger*, the monk Stephen refused to accept the definition of the Iconoclast Council from 754 and its designation as holy and ecumenical. His main argument for such a refusal was that the patriarchs of the five patriarchal sees did not approve the decrees.[47]

Although writing from the political and secular milieu of the imperial palace from where he rose to become patriarch, Nikephoros included in his *Short History* the issue of the authority of ecumenical councils, a theme which he later elaborated upon during the second phase of Iconoclasm. This narration about the place of the Church of Constantinople under the Iconoclast emperors of the Isaurian dynasty, which began with the portrayal of Patriarch Germanos of Constantinople and his views on the ecumenical council in relation to the matters of faith, will be continued in the description of the ecclesiastical policy of Emperor Constantine V and his relationship with the Patriarch Constantine II of Constantinople. The image of the emperor, which was twofold – of a strong ruler but also an impious emperor in his relationship towards the Church and Christian theology – resulted in a specific portrayal of the three patriarchs who presided upon the patriarchal see of Constantinople in the time of his reign.

## Constantine V and the Destruction of the Church of St. Eirene

If viewed strictly, the amount of attention towards Constantine V spanned twenty-six chapters of the entire work. However, Nikephoros already introduced him in the text where he narrated the reign of Emperor Leo III. In such a way, it could be said that Nikephoros started building the image of Constantine V already by mentioning his birth during Leo III's reign, and his coronation. Nikephoros placed these episodes in close relation to the anecdotes about the natural catastrophes and omens which had appeared during the reign of his father, but also coincided, according to Nikephoros's arrangement of his material, in close relation with Constantine's birth and coronation. In this way, it might be suggested that a subtle allusion to Constantine's later persecution of Iconophiles and the patriarchs of the Church was introduced into the

46   O'Connell, *The Ecclesiology of St. Nicephorus*, pp. 112-115 and 117-119.
47   Stephen, *Life of Stephen the Younger*, § 44, 144.9-145.11.

narrative. In this context, two facts are interesting: namely, the absence of the anecdote about Constantine's baptism by the Patriarch Germanos and his prophesy that the newborn infant would desecrate the Church and its doctrines, and the fact which was mentioned in Theophanes's *Chronicle*, that his wife was named Eirene, alluding to the peace which was obviously desecrated during his reign in the context of ecclesiastical relations with the emperor.[48]

Compared to the amount of space dedicated to the reign of Herakleios (twenty-seven chapters), the account of Constantine V's reign, with its twenty-six chapters (with an additional three from the account of Leo III's reign about his birth, coronation, and marriage, and keeping in mind that Nikephoros did not finish the account of his entire reign) seems to present a plan to implement the significant notions and messages which could best be highlighted in the reigns of the two emperor's who opened and ended the narrative of the entire work.

It can hardly be a coincidence that Nikephoros decided to merge several events in close relation, and thus point to their mutual similarity, through the display and arrangement of the text. These include the natural phenomenon of the volcanic eruption, which led Leo III to judge icon worship falsely, and came immediately after Nikephoros mentioned Constantine's coronation as Leo's co-emperor. Even more significant is the mention of an earthquake which shook Constantinople. In this account, one might think that while describing this event Nikephoros also alluded to the reign of Emperor Constantine V, whose violent impiety was later revealed. In the case of the fierce earthquake, which destroyed the church of St. Eirene, Constantine was linked to these events in Constantinople by the mentioning of his marriage to the Khazar princess in the same chapter. After he had narrated about Leo III pressuring the Patriarch Germanos to adhere to his Iconoclast doctrines, Nikephoros brought up the event of Constantine's marriage and the violent earthquake:

> While these things were being done, the emperor sent to the chief of the Khazar nation and fetched the latter's daughter, whom he betrothed in marriage to his son Constantine. After a lapse of time an earthquake occurred at Byzantium and likewise shook violently other towns and regions. In addition to many buildings, holy churches, and porticoes which it caused to fall down at once, some of them being overturned

---

48    Cf. Gero, *Byzantine Iconoclasm during the Reign of Constantine V*, p. 13, n. 15.

from their very foundation, it also threw down the sacred church which bears the name of St. Eirene and stands very close to the Great Church.[49]

Theophanes provided a more detailed list of destroyed churches, while Nikephoros mentioned only the church of St. Eirene, which in fact bore the name of *peace*. Nikephoros pointed out that the earthquake violently shook not only Constantinople, but other regions of the Empire as well, but then focused his attention on Constantinople, where the emperor resided and from where in fact the heresy of Iconoclasm originated and spread throughout the Empire. Thus the peace of the Church in its relation to the state, but also in connection to its doctrines, was shaken and violently overturned from its very foundation in Constantinople by the emperor and his Iconoclastic beliefs. Mentioning exclusively St. Eirene in this context is more than coincidental, and we believe that it stands with Nikephoros's specific and deliberate intention to promulgate certain views and messages in a literary form in his work. In such context, it is not without significance that, earlier in § 50, Nikephoros mentioned that peace prevailed in the West, during Leo III's reign, as a result of executing anti-imperial *strategoi* who had restored Sicily to the Empire. Nikephoros, unlike Theophanes, avoided mentioning the name of Constantine V's wife, Eirene of Khazaria, since the accounts of the marriage and the earthquake were in the same chapter. It would obviously be awkward to mention both Eirenes in the same passage, so Nikephoros decided to accentuate the destruction of St. Eirene rather than to emphasize that Constantine V was married to Eirene. Clearly, he followed a specific idea in creating the narrative about Constantine.

The emphasis that St. Eirene was close to the Great Church points to a deliberate allusion by the author that it was Constantine V who destroyed a very specific type of peace, namely, the ecclesiastical peace of the entire Church of Constantinople. By provoking Iconoclasm, and disgracing patriarchs and the pious Iconophiles, such as the monk Stephen the Younger, and several other notable imperial dignitaries, all of which Nikephoros

---

49  Nikephoros, *Short History*, § 63.1-10: ῾Εν ᾧ δὲ οὕτω ταῦτα ἐπράττετο, ἐκπέμπει ὁ βασιλεὺς πρὸς τὸν τοῦ ἔθνους τῶν Χαζάρων ἡγούμενον, καὶ τὴν αὐτοῦ θυγατέρα μεταπέμπεται καὶ τῷ υἱῷ Κωνσταντίνῳ εἰς γυναῖκα κατηγγύησε. χρόνου δὲ μεταξὺ παρελθόντος σεισμὸς ἐνσκήπτει κατὰ τὸ Βυζάντιον, μεθ᾽ οὗ καὶ πόλεσιν ἑτέραις καὶ χώραις ἰσχυρῶς ἐπιφύεται. καὶ ἤδη ἄλλους τε πολλοὺς οἴκους καὶ ἱεροὺς ναοὺς καὶ στοὰς ἀθρόον ἐπικαταβάλλει, ἐκ πρώτων βάθρων αὐτῶν ἔστιν οὓς τούτων ἀνατρέψας, καὶ τὸν θεῖον νεὼν ὃν τῆς ἁγίας Εἰρήνης ἐπώνυμον καλοῦσι κατέσεισεν, ὃς πλησιαίτατα τῆς μεγάλης ἐκκλησίας ἵδρυται.᾽

proceeded to narrate in the main section of his account of Constantine V's reign, the emperor failed to demonstrate competent rule.

By coincidence or not, which again depends on whether the *Short History* in its § 88 ended due to unknown circumstances or by the author's deliberate intention, Nikephoros concluded his history with the mention of the marriage between the future Emperor Leo IV and the future Empress Eirene the Athenian. It is obvious that Eirene had restored icons and icon worship and through such activity also introduced and restored peace in the Church of Constantinople by convoking the Seventh Ecumenical Council, in which Nikephoros himself actively participated as a lay official of the imperial court and Patriarch Tarasios's close associate. However, did Nikephoros suggest this role of the future Empress Eirene in his *Short History* by making a complex image of the idea of peace, subtly but firmly embedded in his entire work? Did the allusion of the destruction of the church of St. Eirene in Constantinople during the reign of Leo III, but attached also to the image of Constantine V, in the *Short History* and in its entire rich and meaningful context (which reveals itself in Nikephoros's authorial method) actually have an additional allusion to the reign of Eirene? On a more basic level, there exist dendochronological evidence which might suggest that the restoration of the church of St. Eirene happened indeed in the reign of the Empress Eirene in 796,[50] while at a later period, during the patriarchate of Methodios of Constantinople in the *Life* of Theophanes the Confessor, she was praised for introducing peace in the Empire (and a complex idea of *peace* which fully pervaded Byzantine society was elaborated).[51] Nikephoros did not elaborate these ideas in his *Short History*, but it seems that he did lay the foundation for such an image of Empress Eirene, which later developed to its full extent, probably inspired by her building activities and her support for the Orthodox definition of icon veneration.

Constantine's victories were described by Nikephoros in a objective and unbiased manner, who showed no hesitation to display the emperor's military capability to its full extent. This contrasts Theophanes, whose account, when compared with the other material which Nikephoros placed in his account of Constantine V, granted more space to the descriptions of the emperor's heretical policy – the convocation of the First Iconoclast Council in 754 and his persecution of the pious: monks, lay officials, and the Patriarch Constantine II. In contrast to Constantine V's military successes

---

50   Kuniholm and others, 'Of Harbors and Trees', p. 62.
51   Methodios, *Life of Theophanes*, § 19.

which were displayed in six descriptions of battles against the Arabs and Bulgarians, and with an image of one unsuccessful campaign against the Bulgarians in 766, stand the relatively numerous accounts of natural calamities and heavenly omens, which were all quite indicatively placed in close relation to the emperor's victories over his enemies.

The first of these three mentions of the future Constantine V in the account of Leo III's reign was the story of his birth, after which followed the story about the final withdrawal of the Arabs underneath the walls of Constantinople and the information that their entire fleet was shipwrecked. This link, which appeared more from the way that Nikephoros arranged his material than from the thematic context, again promoted a feature of his apparent objectivity and ability to separate religious issues from the strictly political events and deeds of the emperors. Even in the account of the Emperor Constantine V's reign, Nikephoros, unlike Theophanes, did not pass over in silence Constantine's military successes against Bulgarians and the Arabs. Thus it can be said that, even in the three allusions he told about Constantine in the narrative about Leo III's reign, Nikephoros managed to maintain such a conception in his narration and presentation of the image of emperors. Constantine V was presented as a successful emperor in his political and military feats, but as an Iconoclast, more decisive than his father was.

If we summarize the facts from our analysis of the first three mentions of the future Emperor Constantine V, his birth, marriage, and coronation for co-emperor, and the events to which Nikephoros linked him with by a proper arrangement of his historical material, we can conclude that the image of Constantine V was multi-layered. Even more importantly, Nikephoros managed to form and summarize at the beginning of his portrayal of Constantine V an image of him as an emperor who was a successful ruler of the Byzantine empire, but of heretical provenance when it came to his relations with the Church of Constantinople and its patriarchs. In that aspect, Constantine V was an emperor who destroyed a specific type of peace, through introducing heresy by convoking the First Iconoclast Council of 754, and through an aggressive attack on the Patriarch Constantine II. Nikephoros presented these stories more in relation to the institution of the patriarchal office than directly in relation to the people who occupied these ecclesiastical positions at that time. In this sense, even the Iconoclast Constantine V was placed into a specific role in the account about his war against the imperial pretender Artabazos, where Nikephoros seemingly set aside his Iconoclasm in order to promote the idea of order in the state, contrary to the misfortunes which might befall the Empire in a civil war among Christians.

## War among Christians

After he had narrated Leo III's death, Nikephoros turned his attention to the first years of Constantine V's reign.[52] The beginning of Nikephoros's account corresponds with Theophanes, but he avoided or did not know via his source the appropriate introduction which can be read in the *Chronicle*, which in summary presented the moral character of the new emperor as that of a man who was subjected to every iniquity.[53] However, the entire description of the civil war between the legitimate emperor Constantine V and the pretender Artabazos, his brother-in-law, significantly differs between the two historians, mostly in finding and promoting the reasons for their initial conflict. In the very beginning, Theophanes pointed out that it was due to God's dispensation and due to the sins of the Romans that Constantine had ruled in the first place, creating in such a way a very negative image of the new emperor which stands exclusively in connection to his heresy.[54] The cause of the conflict between the two brothers-in-law, Constantine V and Artabazos, was set in the same milieu. The Orthodoxy of Artabazos and the emperor's heresy were the main causes for the conflict that arose among them. In other words, according to Theophanes, it was Constantine V who carried the guilt for such strife, while Artabazos was to a certain extent provoked to act accordingly, or rather to act as if in self-defence, since the vile emperor intended to imprison his sons.[55]

In contrast, in Nikephoros's account of the same events there are no traces of such causes for the civil war. Nikephoros presented a different description of the events which led to war. Nikephoros offered a different image of the Emperor Constantine V, in which there was no place for Theophanes's reasons based on strict Iconodule ideals which he set up as criteria of a just ruler. Nikephoros's account was not embedded in a common Iconophile discourse. Namely, even the restoration of icons in Constantinople during Artabazos's short reign in the capital was mentioned only in one instance, in a short sentence, which left no reason to suspect that Nikephoros might

---

52 Theophanes, *Chronicle*, 413.2-3: 'in that same year of the ninth indiction, on 18 June, Leo died the death not only of his soul, but also of his body' (τῷ αὐτῷ ἔτει τῆς θ' ἰνδικτιῶνος μηνὶ Ἰουνίῳ ιη' τέθνηκε Λέων σὺν τῷ ψυχικῷ καὶ τὸν σωματικὸν θάνατον) not mentioning illness as a reason. Theophanes then proceeded to evaluate his entire reign by evoking the many misfortunes which had befallen the Empire due to the emperor's heresy.

53 Cf. Theophanes, *Chronicle*, 413.10-25.

54 Cf. Theophanes, *Chronicle*, 414.16-17.

55 Cf. Theophanes, *Chronicle*, 414.17-28.

have had any bias in portraying these events. This mention is certainly not casual or marginal, but there is a striking lack of intention towards building a more complex idea of icon worship during this phase and in relation to the Emperor Constantine V.[56]

Contrary to Nikephoros, Theophanes's account has a different context first of all due to the introductory note about Constantine V which was given in advance of the other details of his reign, in which his heresy was placed at forefront. As for Nikephoros, although he mentioned Constantine V already three times before the main account of his reign, the link between the emperor and his Iconoclasm in these opening chapters dedicated to his reign was not presented in a direct and precise manner. In such arrangement of the material, a short mention of Artabazos's adherence to icons does not seem to fit entirely into this strictly political context of the mutual struggle for power which the two brothers-in-law began at the outset of Constantine V's reign. Only later did Nikephoros proceed to present Constantine's Iconoclasm. However, in the account of his clash with Artabazos, who was obviously Orthodox, or used Orthodoxy as a mean of propaganda against his opponent, such a narrative remains outside Nikephoros's depiction of this political event.

Theophanes blamed the Iconoclast emperor for this conflict, obviously being motivated by his Iconophile posture. However, Nikephoros wrote that it was Artabazos who was ready in advance to overthrow Constantine from the throne.

> Now Artabazos, who was Constantine's brother-in-law [...] together with his army, for he was commander of the Opsikian host and his two sons [...], was encamped in the plain of Dorylaion as it is called. Immediately on being informed of the death of his father-in-law, he planned usurpation against [Constantine], and he imposed an oath on the army under his command that they would remain loyal to him and not accept another emperor.[57]

---

56  In the entire *Short History*, icons are mentioned only eight times: § 60.4: 'τῶν ἱερῶν εἰκονισμάτων'; § 62.4: 'τῶν εἰκόνων τῶν ἁγίων'; § 64.37: 'τῶν ἁγίων τὰ ἱερὰ ἀπεικονίσματα'; § 67.41-42: 'τῶν ἁγίων ἀπεικονισμάτων'; § 72.13: 'τῶν ἱερῶν εἰκονισμάτων'; § 81.18: 'ἱεραῖς εἰκόσι' – for this last mention, it is interesting that it is linked with the persecution of several individuals who were close to the emperor, and lay officials of the Empire, and not to the martyrdom of St. Stephen the Younger, which is mentioned and portrayed in the same chapter (§ 81.23: 'εἰκόνι ἁγίων'); 86.8: 'εἰκονογραφίας'.

57  Nikephoros, *Short History*, § 64.4-11: 'Ἀρτάβαζος δέ, ὃς γαμβρὸς Κωνσταντίνου [...], ἅμα τῷ περιόντι λαῷ (στρατηγὸς δὲ τοῦ Ὀψικίου λαοῦ ἐτύγχανεν) καὶ τοῖς δυσὶν υἱέσιν [...], κατὰ τὸ λεγόμενον

When Constantine became aware of this rebellion (τῆς τυραννίδος), he went to the country of the Anatolics, where he was received with favour while Artabazos was cursed with rough insults.[58] Such details, since they are totally in contrast to the negative image of the Iconoclast emperor, are absent from the *Chronicle* of Theophanes.[59] Theophanes highlighted the Orthodoxy of Artabazos and the anathema which was cast on Constantine V by the citizens of Constantinople, who received news about the emperor's suspected death with great joy – elements absent from Nikephoros's narrative.[60]

It seems that, in his making of the report of the civil war between Constantine V and Artabazos, a substantially different idea inspired Nikephoros and defined the nature of his account. Thus, his disagreement with Theophanes becomes more comprehensible.[61] Namely, Nikephoros introduced a reflection on the nature of friction and discord and the negative consequences they bring, a consideration that was already given in a similar manner at the beginning of his account of Leo III's accession to power. However, now a new motif was added, namely, the idea of 'war among Christians', τὸν ἐμφύλιον Χριστιανοῖς πόλεμον:

> Under these circumstances, the Roman state was in extreme distress, inasmuch as the struggle for power among those men aroused an internecine war among Christians. What terrible things are wont to happen in such conditions – so much that [human] nature is neglected and made to oppose herself, not to say anymore – is, indeed, known to many from experience.[62]

---

τοῦ Δορυλαίου πεδίον ηὐλίζετο. καὶ δὴ τυραννίδα εὐθὺς κατ᾽ αὐτοῦ μελετᾷ, τὸν τοῦ πενθεροῦ θάνατον πυθόμενος· καὶ ὅρκοις τὸν ὑπὸ χεῖρα κατεδέσμει λαὸν αὐτῷ μὲν εὔνουν ἔσεσθαι, ἕτερον δὲ εἰς βασιλέα μὴ δέχεσθαι.'

58   Nikephoros, *Short History*, § 64.20-25: 'καὶ Ἀρτάβαζον αἰσχρῶς δυσφημοῦντες καθύβριζον.'

59   Cf. Gero, *Byzantine Iconoclasm during the Reign of Constantine V*, pp. 15-21, noticed that the eastern sources are more in compliance with Nikephoros's narration than with the account made by Theophanes. There is no mention about the restoration of icons in Constantinople under Artabazos's rule who remains a usurper (p. 16, nn. 28-29).

60   Theophanes, *Chronicle*, 415.8-12.

61   Gero, *Byzantine Iconoclasm during the Reign of Constantine V*, p. 21, n. 49.

62   Nikephoros, *Short History*, § 65.14-20: 'ἐντεῦθεν ἐν μεγίσταις συμφοραῖς τὰ Ῥωμαίων διέκειτο, ὁπηνίκα ἡ παρ᾽ ἐκείνοις περὶ τῆς ἀρχῆς ἅμιλλα τὸν ἐμφύλιον Χριστιανοῖς ἀνερρίπισε πόλεμον. οἷα γὰρ καὶ ὅσα συμβαίνειν τοῖς τοιούτοις εἴωθε τὰ δεινότατα, ὡς καὶ τὴν φύσιν ἑαυτὴν ἐπιλανθάνεσθαι καὶ καθ᾽ ἑαυτῆς ἵστασθαι (καὶ τί γὰρ δεῖ τἆλλα λέγειν;), πολλοὺς ἂν ἐν πείρᾳ καθεστηκέναι.'

Nikephoros here reapplied his basic idea which marked both the beginning of the *Short History*, about the damage Phokas's rule had brought
to the Christians and the Roman state, and which resonated with the
ideas promoted in the oration of Shahin, where war was presented as an
action that could bring much distress and damage to the state. In a unique
discourse, Theophanes offered a different portrayal of the event, promoting envy of the devil against Christians as the main cause of the civil
war, while Nikephoros had the fate of the Roman empire in his primary
focus.[63] In the context of such ideas which he introduced into his work,
Nikephoros turned his attention again to his basic idea, namely, that rebellions and frequent civil wars caused internal distress. It is interesting that
Nikephoros in the quoted passage defined the war between Constantine
V and Artabazos, who obviously supported icon worship, as a 'war among
Christians', thus implying Constantine's Christianity in a context which
would not be suitable for a heretical emperor. However, he had not yet
begun to portray Constantine V in his role of an Iconoclast, which he
developed only later.

This undoing of civic peace and the introduction of disorder and civil
war resulted in the overturning of peace. It can be understood alongside
the previously displayed image of the ruins of St. Eirene in Constantinople,
which in fact had a more ecclesiastical character. Nevertheless, the idea of
peace, εἰρήνη, was present in the account of Constantine V's reign and was
frequently mentioned in relation to his victories over the Bulgarians.[64] In all
these descriptions of Constantine's successful military campaigns against
the Bulgarians, peace appeared as a result of the emperor's victories, after
which the enemies of the Empire were forced to appeal for peace. Nikephoros then provided several references to natural calamities and omens
and in general disturbance of nature which, by their close connection, in
terms of their structure, to the commentary on emperor's victories, seem
to allude to and predict Constantine's heresy and 'war against piety' (πρὸς
τὴν εὐσέβειαν ἤδη ἀπομαχόμενος). Later, in his *Apologeticus Minor*, Nikephoros
placed these motifs in the proper theological context of his evaluation of the
Iconoclastic heresy by asking, in a rhetorical manner: why doesn't nature
by God's dispensation expose the impiety of the enemies of Christ – the
Iconoclasts.[65]

---

63  Theophanes, *Chronicle*, 418.7-11.
64  Nikephoros, *Short History*, § 73.18-20; 77, 4-5, 16-18.
65  Nikephoros, *Apologeticus Maior*, col. 549A: 'Why does he bind the substances from its fast
and furious reprisal over the audaciousness of the enemies of Christ? Why does not he allow the

In this sense, the allusion present in the mention of the destruction of St. Eirene has a profound and precise message. It related the narration about Constantine's destruction of peace to a meaning of spiritual peace which was lost by the persecution of the patriarchs, but also due to war between Christians, where Constantine was included in such a role but without his own responsibility, rather as the one who strove for the legitimate order in the state of the Romans.

With such an arrangement of his material, Nikephoros managed to attach to every one of Constantine's successful campaigns a story about strange occurrences in nature, for which we have seen that, in his theological discourse, this might carry notions of God's disapproval of the emperor's actions on account of the Church and his war against piety. In relation to this, it should be stressed that the account of Constantine's war against *eusebeia* in the *Short History* does not form a coherent narrative, but rather it forms a divided account of his relations with the Church and towards the Orthodox faith, which always shifts to images of his victorious military campaigns against the enemies of the Empire. Sitting in opposition to the five descriptions of Constantine's victories over the Bulgarians and Arabs is a description of the plague which appeared in Constantinople during Constantine's reign, about which Nikephoros wrote that it connected to the emperor's ungodliness and his impiety, or rather his Iconoclasm.[66] To this he added the mention of a strong earthquake which shook regions in Syria, which in its structure contained additional reference to spectacular omens that were predicting victories over Arabs.[67] Then, Nikephoros mentions a heavenly spectacle 'worthy of remembrance' (μνήμης ἄξιον), but also a 'frightfully and miraculous sign' (φοβερὸν καὶ τεράστιον ξένον),[68] and a harsh winter in the year 763/764.[69]

---

worldly substances to come to such a state of a righteous revealing?' ('πῶς τὴν κτίσιν μαιμῶσαν καὶ βρέμουσαν τῶν Χριστομαχούντων ἐπεξιέναι τὴν τόλμαν. πεδήσας οὐκ ἠνέσχετο; πῶς παθεῖν ἃ παθεῖν δίκαιον, τὰ στοιχεῖα τὰ περικόσμια οὐδαμῶς συνεχώρησε;')

66  Nikephoros, *Short History*, § 67.38-43: 'Those who were able to think aright judged that these [misfortunes] were inflicted by God's wrath inasmuch as the godless and impious ruler of the day, and those who concurred with his lawless purpose, dared to lay their hands on the holy images to the disgrace of Christ's Church.' ('ταῦτα ἐκρίνετο τοῖς ὀρθὰ φρονεῖν εἰδόσιν ἐκ θείας ἐπισκήπτειν ὀργῆς, ἡνίκα ὁ τότε ἀθέως καὶ δυσσεβῶς κρατῶν, καὶ ὅσοι αὐτῷ συνήνουν τῷ ἀθέσμῳ φρονήματι, τὰς χεῖρας ἐπαφεῖναι κατὰ τῶν ἁγίων ἀπεικονισμάτων εἰς ὕβριν τῆς τοῦ Χριστοῦ ἐκκλησίας τετολμήκασιν.')

67  Nikephoros, *Short History*, § 69.1-13.

68  Nikephoros, *Short History*, § 71.

69  Nikephoros, *Short History*, § 74.

All of these descriptions were arranged in close relation one to another, with only one chapter dividing them (between the mention of the heavenly signs and a great winter there are only two chapters) which consisted of narratives about the great plague in Constantinople that was linked to the emperor's heresy. This was preceded by the account of Constantine's final victory over Artabazos and the victory of the Byzantine fleet over the Arabs, after which the victors 'returned to Constantine'.[70] Afterward, the story about an earthquake in Syria followed, which was preceded at the beginning of the chapter with the mention of Leo IV's birth, followed by the mention of his coronation in the next chapter and Constantine's successful siege of Melitene under the Arabs.[71] Then followed a mention of a 'terrible sight and a strange prodigy' in the sky[72] preceding the description of the Patriarch Anastasios's death and the account of the First Iconoclast Council of 754.[73] Then followed a story about a successful war against the Bulgarians in 758/759,[74] which was succeeded by the image of a great winter in 763/764.[75]

Nikephoros's arrangement of his material and shaping of an appropriate narrative is presented in the table below (Table 1).

**Table 1      Nikephoros's arrangement of material in the account of Constantine V's reign**

| War Campaigns | Natural Portents | War on Piety |
|---|---|---|
|  | After Constantine V's coronation for co-emperor (§ 58) follows the description of the volcanic eruption in the Aegean sea in § 59. |  |
|  | § 63: Constantine's marriage with the Khazar princess and the earthquake which destroyed St. Eirene in Constantinople. |  |
| § 64-§ 66. The account of the civil war between Constantine V and Artabazos. | § 67. Plague in Constantinople caused by Constantine's *godlessness* and *impiety*. |  |

70   Nikephoros, *Short History*, § 66 and § 68.
71   Nikephoros, *Short History*, § 70.
72   Nikephoros, *Short History*, § 71.
73   Nikephoros, *Short History*, § 72.
74   Nikephoros, *Short History*, § 73.
75   Nikephoros, *Short History*, § 74.

| War Campaigns | Natural Portents | War on Piety |
| --- | --- | --- |
| § 68. The victory of the Byzantine fleet over the Arabs near Cyprus. | § 69. The birth of the future emperor Leo IV and the mention of the earthquake in Syria and destruction of nearby cities. | |
| § 70. Coronation of Leo IV, successful siege of Melitene. | § 71. 'A memorable event [...] Indeed a terrible sight and a strange prodigy [...].' | § 72. The death of the Iconoclast patriarch Anastasios. Constantine V, 'who was completely determined to insult the Church, and was [...] making war on piety' convokes the First Iconoclastic Council in 754. |
| § 73. Constantine V defeats the Bulgarians at Markellai. | § 74. A detailed and a long description of severe winter. | |
| § 75-§ 79. Descriptions of: Slavic tribes are moved, the battle at Anchialos in 763, Constantine's policy towards the Bulgarians and the establishment of peace, an unsuccessful attempt by the Arabs to attack Sicily, and a campaign on Bulgaria in 765. | | § 80. Description of the emperor's ungodliness (ἡ ἀσέβεια τοῦ κρατοῦντος),[76] further persecution of the pious Christians, and the insults done to the Church. |
| | | § 81. Description of St. Stephen the Younger's martyrdom and the persecution of lay officials of the Empire by Constantine V, but both accounts not explicitly connected to Iconoclasm. |
| § 82. Constantine's only unsuccessful military campaign in the *Short History*, against the Bulgarians in 766 and the sinking of the Byzantine fleet. | | § 83. A new description of the persecution of monks and lay officials, deposition of the Iconoclast patriarch Constantine II. |

76 Ševčenko, 'Was there Totalitarianism', p. 97, n. 17, pointed towards this particular term in the Byzantine literature of the ninth century as a negative characterization of a ruler. Nikephoros himself utilized this term several times in his *Short History*, two times in connection to Constantine V and once in connection to the Emperor Herakleios's attempt to leave Constantinople in the face of great distress in the Empire, when Patriarch Sergios managed to persuade him to remain in the City.

| War Campaigns | Natural Portents | War on Piety |
|---|---|---|
| | | § 84. Execution of the Patriarch Constantine II, which by its character fit the previously proclaimed 'insult to the Church' done by Constantine V. |
| | | § 85. 'Christ's enemy Constantine – New Midas.' (ὁ μισόχριστος νέος Μίδας Κωνσταντῖνος).[77] |

Based on such analysis of the structure and arrangement as well as of the character of the material which Nikephoros utilized in connection to Constantine V, and taking into consideration the news which Nikephoros presented in his account of Leo III's reign, it seems that the relation between the information linked to the miraculous omens and allusions, as well as to Constantine's heresy as it is presented in the work – with considerable attention to his successful wars – was significantly altered by these stories about natural catastrophes, which almost dominate equally the narrative of Constantine's reign, as do his imperial acts, which seemingly built the main narrative about his reign.

Many of the topics which dominate the account regarding the reign of Constantine V can also be read in the patriarch's third refutation of the emperor's Iconoclasm.[78] Thus, in this patriarch's work, several similar details can be found: the mention of the monastery of Florus and Calistratus,[79] which were mentioned in the account about Leontios's coup against

---

77   Nikephoros introduced an additional characteristic of Constantine V as *avaricious*, naming him an *enemy of Christ*, or rather as one who hated Christ by his Iconoclastic and avaricious deeds. Nikephoros here applied additional accusations on behalf of Constantine V that he governed with oppression, being avaricious as a result of human sickness. A similar image of the emperor can be seen in Nikephoros's *Antirrheticus* I, col. 276AB: 'Drunk with adoration of gold, and subjected to gold, you who heed to the ancient Midas, you who had painted your image on the golden plates, do you know your teaching?' Here we have in both of Nikephoros's works the same idea connected to Constantine V, and in the *Short History* it recurred also in the negative image of the Persian emperor Chosroes II, when Nikephoros painted an appropriate image of Herakleios as a bold and devoted emperor, contrary to Chosroes, who was also obsessive with his love towards gold.

78   Both Alexander, *The Patriarch Nicephorus*, and Mango, *Short History*, pp. 9-11, pointed to these similarities and parallels between the *Short History* and Nikephoros's *Antirrheticus* III, trying to resolve the mutual dependence of these two patriarchs' works.

79   Nikephoros, *Antirrheticus* III, col. 493D.

Justinian II, the plague in Constantinople,[80] strange heavenly portents,[81] and earthquakes (although not the destruction of St. Eirene).[82] Also mentioned were the Byzantine intrusions into the regions of Armenia and the false abundance of food, where Nikephoros again compared Constantine V to the mythical King Midas.[83] All these mentions which are present in the *Antirrheticus* III also formed part of the patriarch's argumentation in his act of suppressing the main ideas of Iconoclasm, where a severely negative image of Emperor Constantine V and his entire reign dominated the text in a unconcealed and visible manner. In contrast, their presence in the narrative of the *Short History* at the appropriate place, without Nikephoros's additional commenting, had a literary function: to allude to the emperor's irreligion and at the same time to allow the author to appear as an unbiased historian, according to the requirement of the historical genre. When writing a theological work with polemical pretensions, however, such places in the text could serve their main purpose in a more open manner: to emphasize the emperor's heresy and to affirm the patriarch's Iconodule argumentation.

Nikephoros turned towards these in the portrayal of Constantine V's reign in his *Antirrheticus* III, which is a negative evaluation of the emperor's wars against the Arabs and Bulgarians. While these same accounts were described in an unbiased and positive manner in the *Short History* so as to present Constantine V as an accomplished and successful emperor, the same events received a negative characterization in the patriarch's theological apology against Constantine's Iconoclasm. Namely, Nikephoros asserted that Constantine exclusively waged war against Christians, although earlier he noticed his defeat in battle against the Scythians at Anchialos.[84] Additionally, he added an observation about the emperor's fear of facing Arabs, thus giving a different account of the siege of Melitene, adding that he even ran from a minor army of the Arabs,[85] contrary to the concise but clear account in the *Short History*, where Nikephoros admitted the emperor's victory in the siege of Melitene.[86]

---

80  Nikephoros, *Antirrheticus* III, cols. 496AD-497A.

81  Nikephoros, *Antirrheticus* III, col. 497AC.

82  Nikephoros, *Antirrheticus* III, cols. 496D-497A. See also col. 500AB.

83  Nikephoros, *Antirrheticus* III, cols. 500B-501A.

84  Interestingly, aside from the main difference in describing the outcome of this battle (cf. Nikephoros, *Short History*, § 76.1-21), where he explicitly stated that the emperor won the war, Nikephoros named the Bulgarians in a more classicizing manner as Scythians.

85  Cf. Nikephoros, *Antirrheticus* III, cols. 508C-509A.

86  Cf. Nikephoros, *Short History*, § 70.1-5.

Evaluating this *historical* section of Nikephoros's theological work, the *Antirrheticus* III, another aspect of the author's literary and authorial approach reveals itself, carrying as well a force of argument in the frame of a wider apology of icons. Namely, at the very end of this work, Nikephoros made a comparison of Constantine V's reign, in its historical aspect and its duration, with the reigns of earlier notable Byzantine emperors, naming the most distinguished ones: Constantine the Great, Theodosios the Great, and Justinian I. At the end of this list, Nikephoros also mentioned the long reign of Emperor Herakleios, at the same time placing him in a clear Iconophile context of the *Antirrheticus* by noting several *Iconophile* acts or events from his reign. Thus, in a manner already known from his *Short History*, Nikephoros the patriarch managed to reshape and modify his characters in order to accomplish the preconceived idea for the purpose of his work. In a similar manner, he managed to utilize the pictures of the patriarchs in the *Short History*, although heretical, as Sergios and Pyrrhos, in order to emphasize particular and prevailing ecclesiastical ideas around the year 787.[87]

Somewhat earlier, Nikephoros even pronounced a conclusion – as a part of an exclusively theological argumentation which emphasized several Old Testament examples – that the painting of sacred vessels, contrary to the prohibition of Prophet Moses concerning adoration of images, was possible when placed into a proper context of the events and the history of the Israelites. Giving a certain conclusion, Nikephoros pronounced an interesting reflection, which might serve our analysis of a similar authorial method which he demonstrated in particular when he portrayed the heretical Constantinopolitan patriarchs of the seventh and eighth centuries in his *Short History* in a predominantly positive manner. This thought expressed by Nikephoros in his *Antirrheticus* III, and which allowed him as an author the possibility to relativize and to present personalities, processes, and events differently, seem to reveal something of his historical outlook.

> After everything said, it appears as a conclusion that, on one side, not everything should simply be renounced which is in connection with the commandment, nor should it be accepted, since not everything is cursed and worthy of contempt, nor is everything sacred and worthy of reverence.[88]

---

87  Cf. Nikephoros, *Antirrheticus* III, cols. 524C-525A.

88  Nikephoros, *Antirrheticus* III, col. 456C: ʽΕκ τούτων δὲ πάντων συνάγεται, ὡς οὔτε πάντα τὰ γεγραμμένα περὶ τῶν ὄντω νομοθετουμένων ἀποπεμπτέον ἁπλῶς, οὔτε πάντα προσδεκτέον· οὔτε γὰρ πάντα ἐναγῆ καὶ ἀπόπτυστα, οὔτε πάντα ἅγια καὶ σεβασμία.ʼ

If we would utilize this remark on the method of polemics in the Iconoclastic disputation, and apply it to the *Short History*, and especially when it comes to Nikephoros's presentation of the reign of Emperor Constantine V, it can be said that Nikephoros actually portrayed two different sides of his imperial personality, as is also the case with Leo III. One is an image of a successful ruler who provided victories for his Empire over its enemies. But it is the image of his impiety, which is portrayed as well, that prevented this emperor from embodying in his reign an ideal type of the Roman *basileus*. This exemplary model of a governor of the state, who had the dual responsibility to govern both secular and sacred spheres of his power properly, and to take care of *eutaxia* and *peace* both towards his external enemies and towards the internal order of his realm, seems to be reserved for his predecessor – Emperor Constantine IV.

It is clear that such a portrayal of the imperial persona of Constantine V in its basic elements corresponds to the image of Emperor Herakleios, with whose reign Nikephoros opened the narration. Thus, concerning the image of emperors in the *Short History*, Nikephoros began and finished his history with the same narrative messages about the role of the emperors in the history of the Roman Empire from the beginning of the seventh century until the second half of the eighth century. His portrayal of imperial reigns represents a closed entity, beginning its narration with the description of a powerful personality at the imperial throne as Herakleios was, but who was not without certain personal flaws. Later such an ideal, which was pronounced mostly in the portrayal of Herakleios's victorious war against Persia, was violated by the reigns of a certain number of emperors due to which both the state and order – peace and tranquillity – were brought to the lowest condition and faced the ultimate downfall. However, his narration ended with the portrayal of the generally successful reigns of the first two Iconoclast emperors, who were not completely ideal rulers only due to their heresy. It was Constantine V who earned a complete conviction for the heresy of Iconoclasm.

But regarding the assessment of the image of emperors in Nikephoros's *Short History*, this image oddly corresponds and matches the portrayal of Nikephoros's attitude towards Leo V, which was transmitted by the latter historian Joseph Genesios, who portrayed Patriarch Nikephoros's character and his relation towards the Iconoclast emperor Leo V, with whom he had later on struggled for the true faith and suffered banishment.

> This Emperor Leo, even though he was impious in religious matters, was a
> highly competent administrator of public affairs. He overlooked nothing

that could benefit the State, and after his death, even the Patriarch Nike-phoros said that the government of the Romans had lost a great provider, even though he was impious.[89]

Such attitude corresponds with the manner of portrayal of the image of emperors by Nikephoros in his *Short History*. On the other hand, this alleged opinion given by the Patriarch Nikephoros could rather be understood as an echo of a proper understanding of his authorial method in his historical work and of his literary and ideological approach in portraying emperors as successful rulers, unbiased and with no personal approach due to their heresy. Joseph Genesios, after all, used the *Life of Nikephoros* by Ignatios the Deacon in the course of the writing of his own historical work. Could it be possible that he even read his *Short History*, or that he simply formed his own image of Nikephoros as a learned cleric both in theological and secular matters borrowing these ideas from Ignatios?[90]

### Patriarchs of Constantinople – *Iconoclasts by Oppression?*

Since Nikephoros had enjoyed the reputation of a defender of holy icons already during his lifetime, and especially after the final victory of Orthodoxy, it would be expected that the image of the few Iconoclast patriarchs of Constantinople in his *Short History* would be portrayed in a uniform manner and a biased form in terms of criticizing of their heresy. In such a context, the image of the three Iconoclast patriarchs – Anastasios, Constantine II, and Niketas – is not blatantly adverse. Nowhere in the work does there exist an explicit condemnation of their Iconoclasm. The patriarchs were rather portrayed as submitted to the emperor, who always held the initiative for the impiety of Iconoclasm. However, as in previous cases, the mention of these patriarchs was limited to accompanying comments – episodic appearances as parts of a larger narration about

---

89　Joseph Genesios, *Four Books about Kings*, I, § 16.11-15: 'Οὗτος δὲ Λέων ὁ βασιλεύς, κἂν δυσσεβής, ἀλλὰ τῶν δημοσίων πραγμάτων ἦν ἀντιληπτικώτατος, ὡς μηδὲν τῶν ὀνησιφόρων παραλιμπάνειν ἀπρόοπτον, ὡς καὶ μετὰ τὴν αὐτοῦ τελευτὴν Νικηφόρον τὸν πατριάρχην τοιαῦτα ἐρεῖν, ὡς ἄρα ἡ πολιτεία Ῥωμαίων κἂν δυσσεβῇ, ἀλλ᾽ οὖν γε μέγαν προμηθευτὴν διαπολώλεκεν.' Genesios referred to Patriarch Nikephoros in yet three more episodes, narrating his exile and the mutual respect which Theophanes and Nikephoros exchanged during the patriarch's sail to banishment (I, § 14.60-82), his attempt to enforce an oath upon Leo V during his imperial coronation (I, § 22.1-7), and in connection to the futer Patriarch Methodios's mission to the city of Rome (IV, § 4.55-64).
90　See Treadgold, *The Middle Byzantine Historians*, p. 180 *passim*.

the political deeds of the Iconoclast Constantine V and his treatment of the Church.

Patriarch Anastasios, who succeeded Germanos and who was patriarch for quarter of a century, was presented in a brief account of his ascension to the patriarchal throne.[91] Nikephoros then attached to this news a sentence which related to the outbreak of Iconoclasm under Leo III, in which it is not clear whether Nikephoros intended to blame the emperor or the patriarch for the persecution of Iconophiles: 'From that time onward many pious men who would not accept the imperial doctrine suffered many punishments and tortures.'[92] Due to the demonstrative pronoun ἐκεῖνος, it seems possible that Nikephoros might have alluded to the Patriarch Anastasios, although the Emperor Leo III was presented in the chapter as the initiator of the heresy. Nikephoros might have implied that, when the new pro-Iconoclast patriarch was imposed, the emperor began his full-scale promotion of heresy against the Orthodox. This would fit the general pattern of the idea that the imperial violence against the Church only burst out after the patriarchal office was usurped, either by the emperor's direct interference (like in the case of Germanos) or by the patriarch's abdication.[93] Depending on the answer to this question, a proper understanding of the image of Anastasios in the *Short History* can be reached. His character could then be attached to the persecution of the faithful Iconophiles, in which case this patriarch would share the blame for heresy with the Iconoclast emperor and his *imperial dogma*. Iconoclasm certainly found its beginning during the patriarchate of Anastasios, and Nikephoros was aware of this fact but displayed it in a rather vague manner.

The account by Theophanes about the deposition of Germanos of Constantinople is radically different. Theophanes called Germanos 'most holy patriarch', and in his description of Anastasios's ascension to the patriarchal see – who was referred to as a false disciple of the former patriarch and 'a false bishop' who accepted the emperor's impiety – no indication about Anastasios's participation in the persecution of Iconophiles was presented. It was Leo III who received all the guilt and responsibility for such conduct.[94]

---

91   Nikephoros, *Short History*, § 62. 8-9. Cf. Rochow, 'Anastasios'.
92   Nikephoros, *Short History*, § 62.9-12: 'ἐξ ἐκείνου τοίνυν πολλοὶ τῶν εὐσεβούντων, ὅσοι τῷ βασιλείῳ οὐ συνετίθεντο δόγματι, τιμωρίας πλείστας καὶ αἰκισμοὺς ὑπέμενον.'
93   Cf. Mango, *Short History*, p. 131 n. 45.
94   Cf. Theophanes, *Chronicle*, 409.11-14: 'On the twenty-second of the same month of January, Anastasios, the spurious pupil and *synkellos* of the blessed Germanos, who had adopted Leo's impiety, was ordained and appointed false bishop of Constantinople on account of his worldly ambition.'

In Nikephoros's account, the qualification of Anastasios the patriarch as a pupil of Germanos and the false bishop was left out. Also, Nikephoros did not explicitly emphasize that Anastasios accepted the emperor's impiety. In contrast, Theophanes himself did not ascribe the persecutions of Iconophiles to the Patriarch Anastasios, but to the emperor's tyranny.[95] Theophanes did point out Anastasios's one-mindedness with the Emperor Constantine V.[96]

Nikephoros only added to this image of Anastasios a short passage regarding the end of his patriarchal office, referring to his passing before the First Iconoclastic Council was convened. In the narration by Nikephoros, such a portrayal of him as a 'false pupil' of Germanos and a 'false bishop of Constantinople', which was sharply emphasized by Theophanes, was left out. In such a way, Patriarch Anastasios received almost a neutral presentation in the pages of the *Short History*, with virtually no clear indication of his like-mindedness with the Iconoclast emperor.

However, it was the Patriarch Constantine II who received much more attention from Nikephoros, who told a complete story about the disgrace of the patriarch. In such terms, the patriarch resembled the account of Pyrrhos's abdication in the time after Herakleios's death.[97] After this account of Patriarch Constantine II's downfall followed a short review about the Iconoclasm of his successor, the Patriarch Niketas, which is the only such instance in the work.[98] Niketas's active Iconoclasm was explicitly mentioned by Nikephoros:

> At the same time Niketas, the bishop of the City, restored certain structures of the cathedral church that had fallen into decay with time. He also scraped off the images of the Saviour and of the saints done in golden mosaic and in encaustic, which were in the ceremonial halls that stand

---

95  Theophanes, *Chronicle*, 409.18-21: 'In his anger the tyrant intensified the assault on the holy icons. Many clerics, monks, and pious laymen faced danger on behalf of the true faith and won the crown of martyrdom.'

96  Theophanes, *Chronicle*, 426.27-29: 'ἔστεψε Κωνσταντῖνος ὁ δυσσεβὴς βασιλεὺς τὸν ἑαυτοῦ υἱὸν Λέοντα εἰς βασιλέα δι' Ἀναστασίου, τοῦ ψευδωνύμου πατριάρχου καὶ σύμφρονος αὐτοῦ.'

97  Cf. Rochow, 'Konstantinos II'.

98  Cf. Nikephoros, *Short History*, § 83.28-30: 'Νικήταν δὲ πρεσβύτερον τῆς τῶν ἁγίων ἀποστόλων ἐκκλησίας εὐνοῦχον προχειρίζεται ἀρχιερέα.' Also Theophanes, *Chronicle*, 440.12-13: 'Νικήτας ὁ ἀπὸ Σκλάβων εὐνοῦχος ἀθέσμως πατριάρχης Κωνσταντινουπόλεως.' Once again here we encounter a difference in the description of the patriarch in the two almost contemporary sources, where Theophanes did not miss the opportunity to emphasize that Niketas was enthroned in a irregular manner.

there; these are called *secreta* by the Romans, both in the small one and
in the big one.[99]

In such a sequence of information, Constantine II appeared almost as an
Orthodox patriarch, since there was no explicit mention of his Iconoclasm.
Even his oath of Iconoclasm was presented as being forced upon him by
the emperor, who later ordered his execution, which Nikephoros described
in considerable detail.

The portrayal of Patriarch Constantine II began with the introductory
notice that he succeeded Anastasios to the patriarchal throne. It was the
emperor who was guided by the evil spirit, and who convened the council
under the presidency of Archbishop Theodosios of Ephesus and thus,
among other things, proclaimed this Constantine to be the new patriarch
of Constantinople:

> After some time Anastasios, the archpriest of Byzantium, died. Now
> Constantine, who was completely determined to insult the Church and
> was, by now, making war on piety, driven as he was by the evil spirit that
> directed him, convened a council of 338 priests under the presidency of
> Theodosios, archbishop of Ephesus, and appointed to be archpriest of
> the City a certain Constantine, who wore the monastic habit and had
> been bishop of Syllaion. They drew up a definition of the faith in which
> all of them, by an evil and impious agreement, set down a proclamation
> of the destruction of the holy icons. These they childishly anathematized
> in public and, along them, Germanos, who had been archpriest of By-
> zantium, George, a native of the island of Cyprus, and John of Damascus
> in Syria, surnamed Mansour.[100]

---

99  Nikephoros, *Short History*, § 86.2-8: 'ὑπὸ δὲ τὸν αὐτὸν καιρὸν Νικήτας ὁ τῆς πόλεως πρόεδρος
τινὰ μὲν τῶν ἐκ χρόνου διαφθαρέντα τῆς καθολικῆς ἐκκλησίας ἀνακαινίζει κτίσματα, τὰς δὲ ἐν τοῖς
ἐκεῖσε ἱδρυμένοις τῶν προόδων οἴκοις, ἃς Ῥωμαῖοι σέκρετα καλοῦσι, τό τε μικρὸν δόμημα καὶ τὸ μέγα,
τοῦ σωτῆρος καὶ τῶν ἁγίων οὔσας διὰ ψηφίδων χρυσῶν καὶ κηροχύτου ὕλης εἰκονογραφίας ἀπέξυσε.'
100  Nikephoros, *Short History*, § 72.1-17: 'χρόνου δέ τινος διῳχηκότος Ἀναστάσιος ὁ τοῦ Βυζαντίου
ἐτελεύτα ἱεράρχης. Κωνσταντῖνος δὲ καθ' ἅπαξ πρὸς τὴν ὕβριν τῆς ἐκκλησίας ἰδὼν καὶ πρὸς τὴν
εὐσέβειαν ἤδη ἀπομαχόμενος, ὡς ὑπὸ τοῦ ἄγοντος αὐτὸν ἐναντίου πνεύματος κινούμενος, σύνοδον
ἱερέων ἀθροίζει ὀκτὼ καὶ τριάκοντα καὶ τριακοσίους τὸν ἀριθμὸν τυγχάνουσαν (ταύτης ἐξῆρχε
Θεοδόσιος ὁ τῆς Ἐφεσίων πόλεως ἀρχιεπίσκοπος), ἀρχιερέα τε τῆς πόλεως ἀνακηρύσσει Κωνσταντῖνόν
τινα τὸ τῶν μοναχῶν σχῆμα περιβεβλημένον, ἐπίσκοπον δὲ τῆς τοῦ Συλλαίου πόλεως γεγονότα. ὅρον
δὲ πίστεως ἐκτίθενται, ἐν ᾧ ὑπεσημήναντο ἅπαντες κακῶς καὶ δυσσεβῶς συμφρονήσαντες, τὴν τῶν
ἱερῶν εἰκονισμάτων καθαίρεσιν ἐκφωνήσαντες· καὶ ὥσπερ νηπιωδεῖς ἐπ' ἀγορᾶς ταῦτα ἀνεθεμάτιζον.
μεθ' ὧν καὶ Γερμανὸν τὸν ἀρχιερέα τοῦ Βυζαντίου γεγονότα Γεώργιόν τε τὸν ἐκ Κύπρου τῆς νήσου
ὁρμώμενον καὶ Ἰωάννην τὸν ἀπὸ Δαμασκοῦ τῆς Συρίας τὸ ἐπίκλην Μανσούρ.'

Although the wording of this part of the account about Constantine II seemed to be a strong rebuke of the Iconoclastic measures of the council, where Nikephoros clearly stated that *they*, the Archbishop Theodosios, 338 priests, and Constantine the new patriarch, drew up a definition of Iconoclasm as official doctrine of the Church, such presentation of the event, at least when dealing with the image of the new patriarch, was in fact far from critical. However, when compared to the manner of his portrayal by Theophanes concerning the same event of his election, there exists one significant difference, namely, Theophanes placed Constantine's election for patriarch at the end of the council, while Nikephoros only noted that it took place during the council:

> In this year Anastasios, who had held in unholy fashion the episcopal throne of Constantinople, died a spiritual as well as a bodily death of a dreadful disease of the guts after vomiting dung through his mouth, a just punishment for his daring deeds against God and his teacher. In the same year, the impious Constantine convened in the palace of Hiereia an illegal assembly of 338 bishops against the holy and venerable icons under the leadership of Theodosios of Ephesus, son of Apsimaros, and of Pastillas of Perge. These men by themselves decreed whatever came into their heads, though none of the universal sees was represented, namely those of Rome, Alexandria, Antioch, and Jerusalem. Starting on 10 February, they went on until 8 August of the same 7th indiction. On the latter day the enemies of the Theotokos having come to Blachernai, Constantine ascended the ambo holding the monk Constantine, former bishop of Syllaion, and, after reciting a prayer, said in a loud voice 'Long live Constantine, the ecumenical patriarch!' On the 27th of the same month the emperor went up to the Forum together with the unholy bishop Constantine and the other bishops and they proclaimed their misguided heresy in front of all the people after anathematizing the most holy Germanos, George of Cyprus, and John Damascene of the Golden Stream, son of Mansour, holy men and venerable teachers.[101]

101 Theophanes, *Chronicle*, 427.25-428.12: 'Τούτῳ τῷ ἔτει Ἀναστάσιος ὁ ἀνιέρως τοῦ θρόνου Κωνσταντινουπόλεως ἡγησάμενος τέθνηκε σὺν τῇ ψυχῇ καὶ τῷ σώματι οἰκτίστῳ πάθει, τῷ λεγομένῳ χορδαψῷ, κόπρον διὰ στόματος ἐμέσας, ἀξίαν ἔτισε δίκην ὑπὲρ τῆς κατὰ θεοῦ καὶ τοῦ διδασκάλου τόλμης. τῷ δ' αὐτῷ ἔτει καὶ Κωνσταντῖνος ὁ δυσσεβὴς κατὰ τῶν ἁγίων καὶ σεπτῶν εἰκόνων παράνομον συνέδριον τλη' ἐπισκόπων συνέλεξεν ἐν τῷ τῆς Ἱερείας παλατίῳ, ὧν ἐξῆρχε Θεοδόσιος ὁ Ἐφέσου, υἱὸς Ἀψιμάρου, καὶ Παστιλλᾶς ὁ Πέργης· οἳ καθ' ἑαυτοὺς τὰ δόξαντα δογματίσαντες, μηδενὸς παρόντος ἐκ τῶν καθολικῶν θρόνων, Ῥώμης, φημί, καὶ Ἀλεξανδρείας καὶ Ἀντιοχείας καὶ Ἱεροσολύμων, ἀπὸ ι' τοῦ Φεβρουαρίου μηνὸς ἀρξάμενοι διήρκεσαν ἕως η' τοῦ Αὐγούστου τῆς αὐτῆς ζ' ἰνδικτιῶνος. καθ'

Aside from the fact that Theophanes's account offers more detail in general about the council in Hiereia in 754, his portrayal of Constantine II is completely in accordance with the idea that he was the successor to the *unholy* Patriarch Anastasios, thus naming him 'unholy Bishop Constantine' as well. Such an open negation of the patriarchal legitimacy by Nikephoros is absent in the *Short History*, although he was implicated as a participator in the council which anathematized icons and the holy fathers, Germanos, George, and John of Damascus. It is significant to note that Nikephoros and Theophanes both agree that the Iconophiles were publicly anathematized by the emperor and the patriarch. Nikephoros, however, did not separate the patriarch from the other participants at the Council, thus creating a somewhat hazy image of Constantine II, not so in relation to Iconoclasm as Theophanes had done in his *Chronicle*.

Thus, the image of the Patriarch Constantine II was significantly generalized and deprived of any remark on account of his person alone. The patriarch was actually placed in such a context where the emperor dominated the scene as the one who made war on piety by convening the *priests* and proclaiming Constantine of Syllaion patriarch of Constantinople. All the patriarch's actions were connected to the emperor; together they publicly anathematized the icons.

Further mention of the patriarch was placed in the account of the emperor's *impiety* and his persecution of Iconophiles, in the narration about the martyrdom of St. Stephen the Younger, and of the monks and laymen who were loyal to the doctrines of icon worship. The emperor's impiety was the main cause of the passions of the faithful, and in such a description of the emperor's deeds, we read about the patriarch's oath that he would not propagate icon worship. In these chapters Nikephoros also placed the account of the patriarch's execution by the orders of the emperor, which was listed as an additional sin of Constantine V. The portrayal of the patriarch's execution is the only such description (besides the description of the martyrdom of St. Stephen the Younger, which is also placed in thematically same chapters which narrate the emperor's irreligion). This motif is more evident when compared to Theophanes's account of Patriarch Constantine's death,

ἣν ἐν Βλαχέρναις ἐλθόντες οἱ τῆς θεοτόκου πολέμιοι, ἀνῆλθε Κωνσταντῖνος ἐν τῷ ἄμβωνι κρατῶν Κωνσταντῖνον μοναχόν, ἐπίσκοπον γενόμενον τοῦ Συλλαίου, καὶ ἐπευξάμενος ἔφη μεγάλη τῇ φωνῇ· 'Κωνσταντίνου οἰκουμενικοῦ πατριάρχου πολλὰ τὰ ἔτη.' καὶ τῇ κζ' τοῦ αὐτοῦ μηνὸς ἀνῆλθεν ὁ βασιλεὺς ἐν τῷ Φόρῳ σὺν Κωνσταντίνῳ τῷ ἀνιέρῳ προέδρῳ καὶ τοῖς λοιποῖς ἐπισκόποις, καὶ ἐξεφώνησαν τὴν ἑαυτῶν κακόδοξον αἵρεσιν ἐνώπιον παντὸς τοῦ λαοῦ ἀναθεματίσαντες Γερμανὸν τὸν ἁγιώτατον καὶ Γεώργιον τὸν Κύπριον καὶ Ἰωάννην τὸν Χρυσορρόαν Δαμασκηνὸν τὸν Μανσούρ, ἄνδρας ἁγίους καὶ αἰδεσίμους διδασκάλους.'

where his death was characterized as deserved due to his participation in the imperial heresy.

## The Humiliation and Execution of the 'Iconoclast' Patriarch Constantine II and St. Stephen the Younger

Nikephoros placed the section of the *Short History* in which his account of the patriarch's abasement and death by the direct influence of imperial power within a group of chapters that portrayed the nature of the emperor's Iconoclasm. In these chapters, the persecution of Iconophiles and the martyrdom of St. Stephen the Younger were described in considerable detail. § 80 began with an introductory sentence that also revealed the character and purpose of such a narration, namely, that 'the emperor's irreligion was by now freely expressed: every avenue leading to piety was brought into discredit, the manner of life of the pious and those devoted to God was ridiculed and mocked; and, in particular, the holy regiment of monks was lawlessly persecuted.'[102] Nikephoros clearly emphasized what would be the main theme of his narration in the next three chapters. He seems to have had a specific interest in the persecution of the monastic order in general, since he deemed it relevant to mention that even the Iconoclast Patriarch Constantine II 'wore a monastic habit'. And he later placed the account of his disgrace in the chapters where he narrated the persecution of monks. Thus on yet another level, Nikephoros equated the patriarch with Stephen the Younger, placing them on the same line and at the same level of narration.

Both martyrdoms, of the patriarch and the monk Stephen, were depicted in the context of public disgrace. Stephen the Younger also endured a public abasement, while the humiliation and the death penalty for the patriarch were also placed in the public sphere. In both events, individuals and a crowd of people took part in the execution of both the monk Stephen and the Patriarch Constantine, himself a former monk. The only difference between the two scenes is that the disgrace of the patriarch received a depiction of a juridical trial in which the indictment was read by the representatives of the emperor. In contrast, the martyrdom of Stephen the Younger was placed in a context of absolute lawlessness, where the crowd

---

102 Nikephoros, *Short History*, § 80.1-5: ''Ηδη δὲ ἡ ἀσέβεια τοῦ κρατοῦντος ἐπαρρησιάζετο, καὶ πᾶσα εὐσεβείας ὁδὸς διεβάλλετο καὶ τῶν εὐσεβούντων καὶ θεῷ προσανακειμένων ὁ βίος ἐχλευάζετο καὶ διεσκώπτετο, μάλιστα δὲ τῶν μοναζόντων τὸ ἱερὸν ἐκθέσμως ἐδιώκετο τάγμα.'

participated in the saint's execution on the streets of Constantinople. This description was later developed further in the *Life of Stephen the Younger*, written during the first years of Nikephoros's patriarchal office by a deacon of the Hagia Sophia, who appears to have been a member of the patriarchal court.[103]

Chapter 83 began with the introductory remark that the emperor, breathing hatred against the holy faith, insulted the sacred habit of the monks.[104] Then the narration turned towards a familiar portrayal of the humiliation of the entire monastic order in the scene of their public display at the Hippodrome in Constantinople. Nikephoros proceeded to narrate the emperor's false accusation on behalf of certain lay officials for their alleged participation in a conspiracy against him. In the end, the patriarch himself was accused of taking part in the plot, which was the main reason of his deposition:

> And the next day he contrived that some friends of Constantine, archpriest of the City, should concoct a sworn accusation against him, proving clearly that they had heard from him all the designs of the companions of Antiochos and Theophylaktos. Straightaway he exiled Constantine to Hiereia, this is the name of an imperial palace that

---

103  See Auzépy's introduction to the edition of Stephen's *Life of Stephen the Younger*, pp. 6-9. On the basis of such reasoning, the author of the *Life*, a patriarchal deacon, appears to have been familiar with both the patriarch and the history of the Church of Constantinople. We can suggest several parts of the *Life*, which might suggest an ideological compliance with the views of Nikephoros as they were expressed in his *Short History*. First, the reverence expressed towards the Patriarch Germanos of Constantinople might suggest an awareness about a succession of Orthodox patriarchs in the tradition of the Constantinopolitan patriarchate. Stephen the Deacon naturally did not share Nikephoros's methods of depicting past heretical patriarchs, Sergios and Pyrrhos of Constantinople among others, but the idea of *peace* in the Church is expressed in the *Life* (§ 22, 118.26-27). Further, we have already noted the same adherence towards the authority of the Ecumenical Councils (Cf. § 9, 6-22). The consecration of Constantine II as patriarch of Constantinople by the will of the Iconoclast emperor is depicted as a scene of extreme humiliation of the Church (§ 25). The idea of war amongst Christians as members of the body of Church is also present in the *Life*, but it appears as a consequence of Constantine V's malignity (§ 27, 123.3-23). Finally, several references to secular learning and the writing of books (a very interesting interpretation of books as icons which elevate the mind of the reader towards the archetype – possibly the ideal image of the past, as created and displayed in the *Short History* by Nikephoros) make the *Life of Stephen the Younger* a crucial narrative source for the reconstruction of secular and ecclesiastical notions of the past, history writing, and ecclesiastical ideology in early ninth-century Constantinople (Cf. 2, 5-15)

104  Nikephoros, *Short History*, § 83.1-2. Stephen, *Life of Stephen the Younger*, § 24, 119.20-120.12, mentioned an oath imposed by the emperor upon his subjects which was directed against the monastic order.

lies across the water from Byzantium in an easterly direction, and appointed as archpriest the eunuch Niketas, who was a presbyter of the church of the Holy Apostles.[105] Shortly thereafter he had Constantine fetched and sent him to the church riding in a cart. He had him accompanied by one of the imperial secretaries bearing the written charges against him, these [the secretary] read out before the gathered people, striking him in the face for every item of the accusation. In this way, they brought him up to the ambo and deposed him, while the new patriarch read out these same charges in front of the sanctuary in a low voice. The next day [the emperor] conducted the customary hippodrome games and directed that [Constantine] should be pulled along, seated on a donkey, facing towards the rear of the animal, and should be cursed and spat upon by the whole people. Not long thereafter he commanded that his head should be cut off in the Kynegion of the City and exposed aloft at the so-called Milion, while his body was dragged by a rope through the streets of the City and cast in the tombs known as those of Pelagios.[106]

The narrative about Patriarch Constantine's degradation and of his violent death, as it was portrayed here, and of the possible message of such an account, needs to be explained in the context of the author's literary method, and to offer a clarification about its possible purpose. Does such an image fit Nikephoros's conception of defending the authority of the patriarchal office as it was defined in the cases of patriarchs from Sergios to Germanos of Constantinople? Can such an account of Patriarch Constantine's cruel deposition and execution be understood in the context of a narrative about the degradation of the patriarchal office in general, regardless of the fact that the executed patriarch was an Iconoclast, but nevertheless forced into Iconoclasm by the emperor? The fate of the patriarch, as it was portrayed

105 Nikephoros, *Short History*, § 83, 21-31.
106 Nikephoros, *Short History*, § 84, 2-18: 'μετ' οὐ πολὺ δὲ μεταπέμπεται Κωνσταντῖνον καὶ ἀποστέλλει πρὸς τὸ ἱερὸν φορείῳ ἐποχούμενον. συνεκπέμπει δέ τινα αὐτῷ τῶν βασιλικῶν γραμματέων κομίζοντα ἐν γραμματίῳ ὅσα κατ' αὐτοῦ· ἅπερ εἰς ὑπήκοον τοῦ ἀθροισθέντος ἐκεῖσε λαοῦ ἀνέγνω, παίων αὐτὸν κατὰ κόρρης ἐφ' ἑνὶ ἑκάστῳ τῶν κατηγορουμένων. καὶ οὕτως ἐπὶ τοῦ ἄμβωνος ἀνενέγκαντες καθαιροῦσι, τοῦ νέου πατριάρχου πρὸς τῷ θυσιαστηρίῳ τὰ τοιαῦτα αἰτιάματα ὑπαναγινώσκοντος. καὶ τῇ ἑξῆς τὴν συνήθη αὐτῷ ἱππικὴν ἀγωνίαν ἐπιτελῶν ἐπιτρέπει αὐτὸν ἐπ' ὄνου προσιζηκότα, τῆς καθέδρας αὐτῷ πρὸς τοῖς ὀπισθίοις τοῦ ζῴου περιτραπείσης, καὶ ἐκεῖσε διέλκεσθαι καὶ ὑπὸ τοῦ λαοῦ παντὸς δυσφημεῖσθαί τε καὶ καταπτύεσθαι. εἶτα μετ' οὐ πολὺ ἐν τῷ τῆς πόλεως κυνηγίῳ τὴν κεφαλὴν αὐτοῦ ἀποτμηθῆναι προστέταχε, καὶ τὴν μὲν ἐν τῷ καλουμένῳ Μιλίῳ ἐξαρτηθεῖσαν μετέωρον φέρεσθαι, τὸ δ' αὐτοῦ σῶμα σχοινίοις διασύρουσιν ἀνὰ τὰς λεωφόρους τῆς πόλεως εἰς τοὺς τῶν Πελαγίων καλουμένους τάφους ἐξέρριπτον.'

in the text, seems to fit such a manner and concept of Nikephoros's history writing, and also explains why more space was given to Constantine II than to Patriarch Anastasios, whose final image remained somewhat ambiguous.

In addition, it is important to evaluate the choice of the content in relation to what was included concerning the Patriarch Constantine II and to take into consideration in the outcome of the analysis of his account. As in the case with the Patriarch Pyrrhos, where thematic emphasis was put on his forceful abdication, and not to his Monothelite heresy, the narrative of Patriarch Constantine II could probably have been more eventful, or at least it could have given a broader perspective in relation to doctrinal issues of the time, or of when the author himself lived and wrote. However, Nikephoros avoided such an approach and emphasized instead the patriarch's humiliation by the emperor, and his consequent death. In such a way, he emphasized the specific circumstances of his patriarchal office, which could well be applied to the general issue of Church-State relations in his own day, and in the specific context of the monastic opposition to the patriarchs of Constantinople. The result was a presentation of a specific image of the authority of patriarchal power – as the one which also endured persecution and suffering in a specific manner, parallel to the monastic order. Therefore, the close relation in the text between the two accounts – that of Patriarch Constantine II's death and the martyrdom of St. Stephen the Younger – may stress such an idea in a more profound way. In the epoch of the Seventh Ecumenical Council, such a message could have had a profound role in accenting the significance and the power of the Church of Constantinople in general, but also, in a more precise manner, the status and the authority of the patriarchs in their relation to imperial power, and to the internal opposition which had appeared, and which might reappear in the future. The emphasis on the need for greater autonomy and freedom for the patriarchs in such an account is the obvious conclusion. Almost at the same time, in the *Life of Stephen the Younger*, the first hagiographical appraisals of Germanos of Constantinople were created and embedded into the narrative about Iconodule resistance against the imperial impiety of Leo III and Constantine V.[107]

Patriarch Constantine's Iconoclasm was significantly milder in its portrayal in the *Short History* than in the *Chronicle* of Theophanes. Iconoclasm was related to the patriarch only in the story about the oath which the patriarch was forced to swear by the persuasion and pressure

---

107  Cf. Stephen, *Life of Stephen the Younger*, § 5 (Germanos, 'celebrant of mysteries'), § 7 ('blessed beacon'), § 9 ('herald of piety'), § 29 ('divine and orthodox patriarch of the Church').

of the emperor. This was, in fact, an image of the patriarch's submission to the *imperial dogma* of the emperor, more than a picture of the patriarch's true Iconoclasm. This image came in a group of chapters, beginning with § 80 where Nikephoros displayed the emperor's irreligion, where 'every avenue leading to piety was brought into discredit, and every form of piety was, so to speak, rejected and driven away and, as though a second paganism had grown up among Christians.'[108] The invocation of a *second paganism* here obviously related to the Iconoclast accusations of pagan idolatry lurking in the acts of icon worship, thus indicating that Nikephoros was not unfamiliar with the subtle literary shaping of his narrative. He then shifted his narration from the emperor with whom he had opened this chapter and the specific narration about his Iconoclasm to *them* – those who had participated in the persecution of monks and Iconodules – thus beginning this section of narration with Constantine V but continuing to display the *irreligion* of an impersonal multitude of those who had complied with imperial policy. These *unholy* men martyred St. Stephen the Younger, and they also 'resolved that all the subjects should affirm under oath that henceforth none of them would worship the icon of a saint. It is even said by eyewitnesses that the then archpriest of the City elevated the life-giving Cross and swore that he, too, was not a worshiper of the holy icons. Concluding: such were the daring deeds of the impious.'[109]

In such a narration, first it is clear that in § 80 to § 81 Nikephoros opened his commentary with the explicit mention of the emperor's irreligion, but then shifted to the general remark of the *unholy* multitude who led the persecutions and imposed Iconoclasm on the whole of Byzantine society and the Church as well, mentioning Patriarch Constantine II, who sworn an oath. From such an account it is not clear whether the patriarch freely consented to such an oath, or that he was pressured by the emperor instead. The atmosphere in Constantinople under Constantine V was presented as fervently Iconoclastic, which corresponds to the imagery displayed in the *Life of Stephen the Younger*.[110] We will later note that, unlike such descriptions

---

108 Nikephoros, *Short History*, § 80.1 *passim*: "Ἤδη δὲ ἡ ἀσέβεια τοῦ κρατοῦντος ἐπαρρησιάζετο, καὶ πᾶσα εὐσεβείας ὁδὸς διεβάλλετο καὶ τῶν εὐσεβούντων καὶ θεῷ προσανακειμένων ὁ βίος ἐχλευάζετο καὶ διεσκώπτετο, μάλιστα δὲ τῶν μοναζόντων τὸ ἱερὸν ἐκθέσμως ἐδιώκετο τάγμα.'

109 Nikephoros, *Short History*, § 81.23-27: 'ἐφ' οἷς ὅρκοις βεβαιοῦν ἐβουλεύσαντο ἅπαν αὐτοῖς τὸ ὑπήκοον ὡς τὸ λοιπὸν εἰκόνι μὴ προσκυνεῖν ἁγίων τινά. φασὶ δὲ ὡς καὶ τὸν τηνικαῦτα τῆς πόλεως ἀρχιερέα θεασάμενοι ὑψώσαντα τὰ ζωοποιὰ ξύλα ὁμωμοκέναι μηδ' αὐτὸν εἶναι τῶν προσκυνούντων τὰς ἱερὰς εἰκόνας. τοιαῦτα τῶν ἀσεβούντων τὰ τολμήματα.'

110 Stephen, *Life of Stephen the Younger*, § 39-§ 40.

displayed in § 80-§ 81, Nikephoros directly mentioned the emperor who persecuted the Patriarch Constantine.

In contrast, while the Iconoclast council of Hiereia and its promulgations were mentioned with no explicit reference to the new patriarch, except that he was elected at the council, the statement that the emperor and bishops had proclaimed the destruction of holy icons and anathematized Orthodoxy was quite vague in its relation to the patriarch. In other words, the patriarch's responsibility for such a council and its regulations was significantly less, and presented in a much reduced way compared to the *Chronicle* of Theophanes. Such details were absent from the *Short History*. However, Iconoclasm was attached to the other patriarch – Niketas of Constantinople –, while the account of Patriarch Constantine's 'martyrdom' was incorporated into a negative image of the emperor and the persecution of Stephen the Younger. Any explicit remark about the patriarch's execution as a deserved fate of an Iconoclastic patriarch was left out.

The mention of the patriarch's oath, in which he swore not to revere holy icons, points to his acceptance of imperial dogma and policy. In this context, the presentation that emphasized his passivity in the face of Iconoclasm can be contrasted with the story about the destruction of icons in Hagia Sophia by Niketas, who attacked the holy images in a passage without reference to the emperor or any imperial pressure. It seems that a detail from the account of Patriarch Constantine's 'martyrdom', as presented in the *Chronicle*, supports such view on these matters. Namely, the emperor asked the patriarch to confirm his loyalty to the 'imperial dogma' and to the Council of Hiereia. This detail negated the previously-described personal oath by the patriarch in favour of Iconoclasm, as well as his anathematization of the holy icons at the council itself, which was mentioned by Nikephoros.[111] And just as in the case of the previously portrayed patriarchs Sergios and Pyrrhos of Constantinople, so it was now done in the case of Patriarch Constantine II. His Iconoclasm was vaguely mentioned, while

---

111 Theophanes's account is more detailed. Nikephoros's narration is more concise and thus ensures that the patriarch and emperor are in the centre of events. Theophanes, however, added this dialogue between the patriarch and the imperial envoys (*Chronicle*, 441.30-442.8): 'On the fifteenth of the same month the emperor sent his patricians to him with this message: "What do you say concerning our faith and the synod we have held?" His mind made vain, he replied: "You believe rightly and you have held the synod rightly," thinking that he would thereby win the emperor's mercy once again. But they immediately replied: "This is just what we wanted to hear from your foul mouth. Henceforth depart into the darkness and under anathema." Having thus received the verdict, he was beheaded at the Kynegion.'

Constantine V was saddled with the full blame for introducing the heresy, which was labeled 'imperial dogma', and pressed upon the Church as well as the monastic order and the lay officials of the Empire. In the case of Constantine II, a far greater emphasis was placed upon his tribulation and execution by the orders of the heretical emperor than on his possible adherence to the official Iconoclasm propagated from the imperial palace.

Nikephoros portrayed the deposition and execution of Patriarch Constantine II in connection with the trial over a plot against the emperor which was directed by several lay officials accused of acting against Constantine V. The patriarch's guilt was in relation to these persons. Both Nikephoros and Theophanes emphasized that the accusations against these officials were false, made by the emperor himself – and they portrayed this event in the same manner. It is significant to note that the place and arrangement of this story assumed a significant position in the overall narrative of Constantine V, where he was portrayed as a cruel and impious ruler who persecuted all who were devoted to faith. Note also that faith in general, and not icon worship explicitly, was here highlighted as a criterion of the emperor's irreligion, and that Patriarch Constantine II was mentioned, and his deposition was portrayed in such a context. However, this section of Nikephoros's narration and Patriarch Constantine II's image was placed in the part of the *Short History* that presented the persecutions of the monks and lay officials and of the martyrdom of St. Stephen the Younger. So it can righteously be asked whether these lay officials accused of plotting against the emperor were in fact icon worshipers. Theophanes explicitly mentioned that some of the accused dignitaries were pious and that they were persecuted by the emperor rather because of their piety and beauty.[112]

By placing the patriarch in this group of people fallen into disfavour, and by further building up of the story about the patriarch's involvement in the plot of the lay officials, for which both Nikephoros and Theophanes pointed out the emperor's fabrication, the patriarch was seemingly relieved of his responsibility for participating in the Iconoclastic heresy. Namely, if the aforementioned imperial officials were accused of plotting against the emperor, which could easily be understood as their adherence to the Iconophile doctrines against the 'imperial dogma' (while Theophanes emphasized that several of them were followers of St. Stephen the Younger – possibly under the influence of the *Life* itself), then placing the patriarch

---

112 Theophanes, *Chronicle*, 443.7-18. Unlike Theophanes, Nikephoros did not mention the ἀνδρομανής of the emperor.

in connection with these persons may have had deeper and more realistic grounds. In that sense, the question directed to the patriarch by the emperor's envoys, as portrayed by Theophanes – whether he remained firm in Iconoclasm – might point to the possibility that the plot against Constantine V had certain Iconodule motifs, and that the patriarch might have even conceded to their Iconophile views. After all, Paul of Constantinople, the last official Iconoclast patriarch from the reign of Leo IV, had publicly renounced Iconoclasm.

In this respect, it could be suggested that Theophanes and Nikephoros had different intentions when they shaped the image of Patriarch Constantine II, since Nikephoros did not mention the dialogue between the accused patriarch and the imperial envoys. Theophanes definitely portrayed the patriarch as an Iconoclast who remained loyal to the Iconoclastic policy of Constantine V. He accepted and confirmed such a policy in three instances – after the Council of 754, through his public oath, and before his execution, which befell him as a deserved punishment for his adherence to Iconoclasm. This is how Theophanes shaped the image of Patriarch Constantine II. In contrast, by failing to mention the two confessions of the patriarch about the alleged accuracy of the emperor's Iconoclastic policy, especially the one which was presented by Theophanes in his account of the patriarch's execution (although this last one could be considered the result of extortion in the face of imminent death), Nikephoros offered a considerably nuanced image of Patriarch Constantine II.

Since the author of the *Short History* was designated as patriarch of Constantinople in the very title of his work, and since he was the leader of the Iconophile party at the outset of the second Iconoclasm in 815 (and thus he connected to a long sequence of Orthodox patriarchs), one would expect that due attention would be expressed towards the Orthodox patriarchs who held their ecclesiastical office in the chronological frame of the *Short History*. However, the content of the *Short History*, its structure, and the author's attention directed towards specific topics, leads towards a different conclusion.

As part of the narration about political events which had shaped the history of the Empire from 610 to 769, Nikephoros mentioned a total of twelve patriarchs, ten of whom were patriarchs of Constantinople, while two were holding other patriarchal sees: one of Alexandria, Patriarch Kyros, and the other Jerusalem, Patriarch Modestos (see Table 2). However, these two patriarchs were mentioned in the *Short History* in the narration about the deeds of Emperor Herakleios in the account of the Arab intrusion into Egypt, and the return of the Cross from Persia, after a successful and victorious campaign. Other patriarchal sees, those of Antioch and Rome, were not mentioned in the *Short History* and we can thus conclude that the patriarchs who had entered Nikephoros's literary interest were those whose patriarchate stood in some relation to the aspects of imperial power and governance over the Empire. (Both exceptions confirm the rule: the mention of Kyros of Alexandria and Modestos of Jerusalem stand in relation to the narration about Herakleios's Persian campaign, and his struggle to preserve Egypt under Byzantine rule.)

**Table 2   The patriarchs mentioned in the *Short History***

| Constantinople | Alexandria | Jerusalem | Antioch | Rome |
|---|---|---|---|---|
| Sergios 610-638 | Kyros 631-644 | Modestos 630-631 | | |
| Pyrrhos 638-641; 654 | | | | |
| Paul 641-653 | | | | |
| Kalinikos 694-706 | | | | |
| Kyros 706-712 | | | | |
| John 712-715 | | | | |
| Germanos 715-730 | | | | |
| Anastasios 730-754 | | | | |
| Constantine 754-766 | | | | |
| Niketas 766-780 | | | | |

As for the patriarchs of Constantinople, the most prominent group mentioned in the entire work, it is evident that seven out of ten were in fact heretical patriarchs according to the tradition of the Church of Constantinople that was already established during the time when Nikephoros depicted them in his work, while only three other patriarchs mentioned fall into the group of Orthodox patriarchs of Constantinople. Modestos of Jerusalem should be added to this Constantinopolitan group of Orthodox patriarchs. In the context of the Orthodoxy of patriarchs, the number of instances when heretical patriarchs were mentioned exceeded the occasions when Orthodox patriarchs were mentioned, while several heretical patriarchs dominated the narration in both a patriarchal and a political context in the work (see Table 3).

**Table 3    An overview of heretical and Orthodox patriarchs mentioned in the *Short History***

| Heretical Patriarchs | Orthodox Patriarchs |
| --- | --- |
| **Sergios of Constantinople:** Portrayed as a close associate of the emperor in governing the Empire.<br>§ 2.1-3: together with the citizens of Constantinople accepted Herakleios into the city during the overthrow of Emperor Phokas.<br>§ 2.6-9: crowned Herakleios.<br>§ 2.31-47: participated in a staged play in which the emperor unmasked Priscus's disloyalty.<br>§ 5.1-4: Herakleios's son baptized.<br>§ 7.1-5: together with imperial officials supported the emperor's decision to send envoys to the court of Chosroes II.<br>§ 8.13-16: imposed an oath on Herakleios in order to persuade him not to leave Constantinople for Libya.<br>§ 11.16-18: opposed the emperor's incestuous marriage.<br>§ 11.19-21: the emperor addressed the patriarch as 'high priest and friend'.<br>§ 12.6-14: Herakleios proclaimed the patriarch guardian of his young son, Emperor Herakleios New Constantine.<br>§ 14.37-41: Sergios offered thanksgiving prayers in Blachernai after the successful defence of Constantinople in 626.<br>§ 18.17-21: elevated the Cross brought by Herakleios from Jerusalem to Constantinople.<br>§ 26.1-2: a short notice about Sergios's death.<br>§ 31.28-33: Dialogue of Pyrrhos and Maximos concerning the Monothelitism of Herakleios and Sergios. | **Modestos of Jerusalem:**[113]<br>§ 12.3-6: Persians captured the Cross at the time of his patriarchate.<br>§ 18.8-12 Herakleios returned the Cross to Jerusalem and the Patriarch Modestos confirmed that it was not desecrated by the Persians. |

113   Mango, Short History, pp. 180 and 185, pointed out that both mentions of Modestos are chronologically wrong since he did not occupy the see of Jerusalem at the time of Persian raids nor at the time of Herakleios's triumphal return of the Cross.

| Heretical Patriarchs | Orthodox Patriarchs |
|---|---|
| **Pyrrhos of Constantinople:** A favourable account of his person in the portrayal of his abdication.<br>§ 26.1-6: Herakleios made Pyrrhos the new patriarch of Constantinople, considered him his 'brother'. Pyrrhos's close ties with Patriarch Sergios.<br>§ 28.1-4: Martina proclaimed her imperial rights in the presence of Pyrrhos.<br>§ 29.1-9: Pyrrhos pressed to hand over money to Herakleios's successor, Emperor Herakleios New Constantine.<br>§ 30.20-23: Heraklonas swore an oath before the Patriarch Pyrrhos.<br>§ 31.1-34: A detailed account of the events which lead to Pyrrhos's abdication. His meeting with Maximos in Carthage. | **Kalinikos of Constantinople:**<br>§ 40.26-29: During the coup against Justinian II, Leontios pressed the patriarch to support the deposition of the legitimate emperor. The patriarch shouted: "αὕτη ἡ ἡμέρα ἥν ἐποίησεν ὁ κύριος."<br>§ 42.64-66: He was deposed and blinded for participating in the plot against Justinian II. |
| **Kyros of Alexandria:**<br>§ 23.6-21: Kyros assumed a significant position in the narration about Arabs in Egypt. Kyros's correspondence with Herakleios, the proposition of paying tribute to the Arabs. He proposed to Herakleios that his daughter Eudokia be married to the leader of the Arabs in Egypt. Kyros enjoyed sympathy from the Arabs, but Herakleios refuted his policy.<br>§ 26.6-22: Herakleios summoned Kyros to Constantinople; Kyros accused by the emperor that he gave Egypt to the Arabs. Kyros was called a pagan and God's enemy and enemy of Christians.<br>§ 30.6-7: Kyros returned to his patriarchal see in Alexandria. | **Kyros of Constantinople:**[114]<br>§ 42.66-69: Raised to the priesthood after Kalinikos. He foresaw Justinian II's second rise to power. Prior to his patriarchal office, he was a hermit near Amastris. |
| **Paul of Constantinople:**<br>§ 32.9-12: The former *oikonomos* of Hagia Sophia, Paul elected patriarch of Constantinople. A gap in the narration about twenty-seven years during Constans II's reign makes it unclear whether more attention was given to Paul's patriarchal office. | **Germanos of Constantinople:**<br>§ 46.1-7: Together with John, patriarch of Constantinople, he supported the Monothelitism of Philippikos Bardanes and anathematized the Sixth Ecumenical Council. |

---

114   Cf. Theophanes, Chronicle, 381.31-32. Emperor Philippikos Bardanes deposed the Patriarch Kyros and elected for patriarch: 'Ἰωάννην τὸν ἀυτοῦ συμμύστην καὶ συναιρετικόν.'

| Heretical Patriarchs | Orthodox Patriarchs |
| --- | --- |
| | § 58.1-5: Crowned the future Emperor Constantine V.<br>§ 62.1-8: Pressed by the Emperor Leo III to promote Iconoclast doctrine. Refused and abdicated his patriarchal see.<br>§ 72.11-15: Posthumously anathematized by the First Iconoclastic Council together with John of Damascus and George of Cyprus. |
| **John of Constantinople:**<br>§ 46.1-7: supported the Monothelite policy of the Emperor Philippikos Bardanes, anathematized the fathers of the Sixth Council together with the future patriarch Germanos. | |
| **Anastasios of Constantinople:**<br>§ 62.8-12: Succeeded Germanos at the Constantinopolitan see, a former clergyman of Hagia Sophia. An ambiguous remark that from then/him persecutions of the pious began, or by the Emperor Leo III?<br>§ 72.1-3: The death of Anastasios and convocation of the Iconoclast council in 754. | |
| **Constantine II of Constantinople:**<br>§ 72.3-11: A former monk and bishop of Syllaion. Made patriarch of Constantinople by the choice of Emperor Constantine V at the end of the council.<br>§ 81.24-26: He gave an oath of Iconoclasm.<br>§ 83.21-28: Accusation against the patriarch for alleged participation in a plot against the emperor. His deposition and exile to Hiereia.<br>§ 84.1-18: Continued the previous chapter in giving an account of the patriarch's execution. | |
| **Niketas of Constantinople:**<br>§ 83.28-30: Eunuch and presbyter of the church of the Holy Apostles, made patriarch after Constantine II was defrocked.<br>§ 84.7-9: Took part in the former patriarch Constantine's deposition and public degradation. He read the accusations against Constantine II 'in a low voice' in the church.<br>§ 86.2-8: Restored fallen parts of Hagia Sophia but also destroyed holy images of Christ and the saints. | |

## Past Events Resounding in the Present: Empress Eirene in the *Short History*

Finally, possible references to the rule of Eirene and Constantine VI in the *Short History* need to be dealt with in this study. If Nikephoros wrote his work in order to present a specific image of the past so as to apply it to the events of his own time and provide them with a special historicity or a tradition of past Byzantine history, could he also have shaped his narrative in order to implicate Eirene's and Constantine VI's rule in a positive or a critical manner? If peace was the dominant motif attached to Eirene's reign in the *Life of Theophanes Confessor* by Methodios of Constantinople, how much does the idea of 'peace and tranquillity' in the *Short History* comply with such an idea which could be promoted during Eirene's reign? This would certainly be a positive assessment of Eirene's rule, since Nikephoros gave a positive evaluation of Constantine IV's peace agreements with the Bulgarians in 680, which were in fact at the expense of the Empire. Eirene's rule knows of several such peace treaties after the disastrous defeats of the Byzantine armies in Asia Minor and the Balkans. The first was the disaster of the Byzantine army in 781 in the Thrakesian *thema*, where, according to Theophanes, the Byzantines lost a significant number of men, and Eirene was forced to plead for peace to the Abbasid Caliphate by paying an annual tribute which did not prevent the Arabs in their future raids of Byzantine territories in Asia Minor.[115] Equally unsuccessful were the Byzantine actions in the Balkans. From 789 to 791, the Byzantine troops endured several defeats against Bulgarians.[116] Finally, in 792 came a grave defeat near the fortress of Markellai, when the Bulgarians managed to seize the emperor's tent along with his possessions, and to kill many Byzantine dignitaries on the battlefield. Such a defeat then provoked a rebellion of the *tagmata*, who attempted to proclaim *caesar* Nikephoros as emperor. Eirene seized the opportunity presented by the military defeat and subsequent disorder in Constantinople to remove her son from imperial power.[117]

In contrast to such a state of affairs in Byzantine foreign and domestic policy under Eirene and Constantine VI stands the equally shameful defeat of the Byzantine army under Constantine IV against the Bulgarians, but Nikephoros provided a specific context of this event, setting it in the ideal

---

115   Theophanes, *Chronicle*, 456.2-22. Cf. Lilie, *Eirene und Konstantin VI.*, pp. 146-155.

116   Theophanes, *Chronicle*, 463.28-464.2; 467.6-12. Cf. Lilie, *Byzanz unter Eirene*, pp. 165-187.

117   Theophanes, *Chronicle*, 467.27-468.21. According to Theophanes, Constantine VI's blinding by Eirene came as a consequence of this defeat. Cf. Lilie, *Byzanz unter Eirene*, pp. 87-99.

of peace which had prevailed in the Empire. It is hard to definitively answer whether Nikephoros might have used the account of Constantine IV's reign to criticize Eirene and her manner of imperial government. The high appraisal of Eirene's rule and the idea of *peace* as displayed by the Patriarch Methodios in the *Life of Theophanes* marks the final victory over Iconoclasm, which thus forms a sort of recapitulation of the past battles for Orthodoxy, to the victory of which Eirene had contributed.

The proposed restoration of the church of St. Eirene during the reign of Eirene might also stand in close connection to Nikephoros's literary shaping of his historical account of Constantine V's reign and his comparison between the results of Iconoclast policies and those of Eirene's Orthodox rule. Eirene abolished the Iconoclastic policies of the Isaurian dynasty – to which she was connected by her marriage with Leo IV, an event with which the *Short History* ended its narration. Nikephoros certainly deemed it fit that his historical account could finish with the mention of Eirene being included into a dynasty of rulers who had violently shaken the established ecclesiastical traditions of Byzantine Orthodoxy. Whatever might be the reason that Nikephoros was compelled to end his historical depiction of Constantine V's rule in 769, it seems that the last chapter in which he mentioned Leo IV's marriage to Eirene might have been his last literary attempt to provide his historical work with at least a seemingly fitting ending, which would stand in correlation to his main ideas which he pronounced in his history. Peace was certainly emphasized in his work, and Eirene's introduction into the narrative at its very ending alluded to the suppression of the Iconoclastic policies of the Isaurian dynasty, to which she largely contributed. Thus, Nikephoros might have attempted to at least suggest that peace and order were finally established in her rule. This is certainly one aspect of an assessment of Eirene's place in the *Short History*, though it was only faintly expressed in the narrative.

However, several aforementioned events strongly allude to opposition towards Eirene's independent rule, after she managed to oust her son – the legitimate heir to Leo IV's throne – and to govern the Empire by herself after 797. This issue stands in connection to the dating of the *Short History* and several known events from Nikephoros's secular career. If Nikephoros might have decided to blame Eirene for the blinding of her son, then it would seem fit to conclude that he was forced to leave his secular office and Constantinople due to his opposition to Eirene's independent rule. The refusal of the Constantinopolitans to accept Empress Martina's pretensions to rule the Empire after Herakleios could be seen as a direct attack on Eirene's ambitions. In such a context, it becomes clearer why the Emperor

Nikephoros I demonstrated such respect towards Nikephoros's 'secular writings', his *Short History*, as Ignatios the Deacon informs us in the *Life of Nikephoros*. This could mean that he might have suggested to Nikephoros to write a history of Byzantium, after which he deemed him fit to assume the patriarchal dignity following Tarasios's death. Does the abrupt ending of the narrative in 769 suggest that the future patriarch was interrupted in his writing by the emperor after Tarasios had died in 806 and Nikephoros I chose Nikephoros the *ptochotrophos* to succeed him at the patriarchal see? Nikephoros did shape an ideal image of the Constantinopolitan patriarch in his *Short History*, as if he was preparing to advance to such an office. He demonstrated firm character in relation to the monastic opposition and he seems to have been supported, rather than pressured, by the Emperor Nikephoros I during his patriarchal office. The Emperor Nikephoros I could have been satisfied with the image of Eirene the Athenian displayed in the *Short History* – as an empress connected with the Iconoclast Isaurian dynasty, with no further elaboration of her later contribution to the downfall of Iconoclasm.

There were several rebellions that Nikephoros witnessed prior to his patriarchal career which could have motivated him to give a specific remark in his work about the frequent assumption of imperial power and war amongst Christians, which resulted in decline of state organization. His remark that such a state of affairs was indeed known to many might imply that he had in his mind several of these rebellions, one of which was Nikephoros I's deposition of Eirene, but during Eirene and Constantine VI's rule as well. Such were the rebellions of *caesar* Nikephoros in 780,[118] and of Iconoclastic troops in 786 against the attempted Ecumenical Council in Constantinople,[119] and the first attempted coup of Eirene against Constantine VI in 790 which resulted in many dignitaries of the Empire being slain.[120] Nikephoros might have supported Constantine VI's legal right to the throne against Eirene's pretensions, and due to such an attitude he might have been forced to abandon the capital. Ignatios the Deacon compared this part of his biography to the Prophet Elijah and his seclusion on Mt. Carmel, which implies his clash with the empress. Conversely, the account of Herakleios's *unlawful* marriage to Martina could allude to Constantine VI's *illicit* marriage to Theodote, which was strongly opposed by Plato of Sacudion and his nephew Theodore, an issue which burdened

---

118  Theophanes, *Chronicle*, 454.6-23.
119  Theophanes, *Chronicle*, 461.12-462.3.
120  Theophanes, *Chronicle*, 464.10 *passim*.

Nikephoros's patriarchal office even before 815. While Patriarch Sergios had repudiated Herakleios's connection with Martina in the *Short History*, Nikephoros's superior, Patriarch Tarasios, had appointed the *hegumenos* Joseph of Cathara to officiate the unlawful marriage of the emperor. It seems unlikely to us that Nikephoros could in such a manner criticize Constantine VI's second marriage, which was approved by Patriarch Tarasios, while at the same time creating a complex image of Herakleios and Sergios of Constantinople as *friends* in his historical work. Thus, the words of the citizens of Constantinople directed to Martina after Herakleios's death suggest that this passage in the *Short History* might have been directed towards acclaiming the imperial rights of Constantine VI:

> But some of the people presented to her: 'You have the honour due to the mother of the emperors, but they [e.g. Constantine III and Heraklonas] that of our emperors and lords!' They paid particular respect to Constantine because, by reason of his seniority, he was the first to have been appointed emperor when he was still a child. 'Nor can you, O Lady,' they said, 'receive barbarian or other foreign emissaries who come to the palace or hold converse with them. May God forbid that the Roman state should come to such a pass'.[121]

Several aspects of this narrative are worth emphasizing and analysing in the context of its possible relation to the Empress Eirene and Constantine VI. First, it is evident that Nikephoros here referred to Constantine III, son of Herakleios, and placed strong emphasis on his imperial rights and the fact that he was appointed emperor while still a child. The very name here conveniently might reshape the account into an allusion about Constantine VI and his relationship with Eirene, as well as to his young age when he became his father's successor to the imperial throne. The entire passage dealt with Constantine III's imperial rights contrary to the aspirations of his stepmother, aspirations which Eirene also had towards imperial power after Leo IV's death as the mother of Constantine VI. Furthermore, the mention of barbarians which Martina had received in the palace is especially similar to Eirene's policy of developing a relationship with the Empire of Charlemagne

---

121  Nikephoros, *Short History*, § 28.8-17: 'τινὲς δὲ τοῦ συνεστῶτος λαοῦ ἀνεφώνουν πρὸς αὐτὴν ὅτι "σὺ μὲν τιμὴν ἔχεις ὡς μήτηρ βασιλέων, οὗτοι δὲ ὡς βασιλεῖς καὶ δεσπόται." ἐξαίρετον δὲ ἐδίδουν γέρας Κωνσταντίνῳ ὡς πρώτῳ εἰς τὴν βασιλείαν κατὰ τὴν ἡλικίαν ἐκ παιδὸς προχειρισθέντι. "οὐδὲ γὰρ βαρβάρων ἢ ἀλλοφύλων πρὸς τὰ βασίλεια εἰσερχομένων, ὦ δέσποινα," ἔφασκον, "δύνασαι ὑποδέχεσθαι ἢ λόγοις ἀμείβεσθαι· μηδὲ δοίη θεὸς ἐν τούτῳ τάξεως τὴν Ῥωμαϊκὴν ἐλθεῖν πολιτείαν".'

(which at one point involved the exchange of ambassadors).[122] Thus, we would place the most emphasis on the name Constantine in this account and the mentioning of Empress Martinas's relations with the barbarians, an account which is only known from Nikephoros's *Short History* and which might have been his own invention, written to stress the policies of Eirene the Athenian in the eighth century. Finally, by protecting Constantine VI's imperial rights, Nikephoros in a more personal way protected the role of Patriarch Tarasios, who had been forced to accept the second marriage of Constantine VI in the same way Sergios of Constantinople had been forced to officiate the *unlawful* marriage of Herakleios.

All these examples might or might not allude to the contemporary events after 780 in Constantinople. There is no clear evidence which might point specifically to Nikephoros's display of contemporary political developments through the shaping of the Byzantive past. The image of Empress Martina and her unlawful marriage, as well as the issue of the legitimate imperial rights of Constantine III, are the most specific references which could possibly echo the struggle between Eirene and her son. The mention of the barbarians with which Martina made connections additionally points to the time of Eirene's reign, when the empress attempted to connect with the the Franks, who could be recognized as *barbarians* from Nikephoros's narrative. Thus in this specific account of the *Short History*, three 'arguments' might point towards a veiled allusion to the events after 780 in Constantinople.

122 Theophanes, *Chronicle*, 455.19-25.

# Conclusion: In Search of an Ideal Image of an Emperor

In the context of narrativity, the *Short History* of Nikephoros of Constantinople is a multi-layered work. Our analysis was determined by our aim to explain its content in relation to the context in which it was written, given that Nikephoros himself had taken part in the events that shaped this very context. In the end, it seems to us that Nikephoros's work could offer additional new directions in research, depending on the ability of the researcher to ask new and original questions with regard to this significant source of Byzantine history writing at the end of the eighth and beginning of the ninth century.

The *Short History* of Nikephoros, with its specific content, manner of narration, and appropriate arrangement (which gives the text its particular structure), actually presents a specific source for the author's own epoch – the time of Nikephoros. Such a work equally tells us about the reigns of emperors Herakleios and Constantine V, and about Nikephoros's own understanding of the nature and role of the imperial office and its relationship to the institution of the patriarch. Nikephoros's personal ideas can be read in his portrayal of past events and historical personalities of the seventh and eighth centuries. As much as it might seem contradictory, by choosing to write about distant events, Nikephoros actually told us much about his own epoch and about history writing at the end of the eighth century. Strongly resounding in this work are those ideas which related to the events and processes that led the Church and the State into a new period after 787 – especially the ideas of the renewed autonomy and freedom of the Church. In such a cultural and political atmosphere, which the restored Orthodoxy established both in the Church and in the imperial palace – and Nikephoros was in position to observe these events from both perspectives – the *Short History* developed its specific content. Thus, the *Short History* took a nuanced and twofold glance at the position of the patriarch and his relation to the emperor, and looked also towards the character of successive imperial reigns, which had a direct effect on the state and the condition of the Roman empire.

Thus, Nikephoros's attitude towards the patriarchs of the *Short History* is rather multifaceted. His historical perspective is mostly directed towards the patriarchs of Constantinople, although they are incorporated into his narration of the imperial reigns of the period specified. Through various descriptions of emperors and patriarchs, Nikephoros created a specific image of the Church of Constantinople, or rather of the idea he wished to promote, although such an approach is not in the foreground of the narration of the work. The issue of Nikephoros's relation to the personalities of the patriarchs which he mentioned in his work only becomes more understandable when observed separately, and can be interpreted and explained exclusively in the context of the epoch in which the work was created and for which it was written. Only after a contextualized reading do certain parts of the *Short History* – such as the account of Pyrrhos's abdication, Germanos's reply to Emperor Leo III concerning the authority of the Ecumenical Councils, or the description of Patriarch Constantine II's execution together with the martyrdom of St. Stephen the Younger – become meaningful in their full extent and receive their important place in the structure of the work.

Nikephoros's shaping of the image of patriarchs, who were more often heretics than Orthodox hierarchs, points towards an original and creative approach in his writing of history. Such an approach is different when compared with the predominant literary manner of later Iconophile writers, and especially when compared with the images of heretical patriarchs portrayed by Theophanes the Confessor and the author of the *Life of St. Stephen the Younger.* In this respect we point to the fact that Nikephoros did not hesitate to mention one of the most prominent Iconophile figures, the Patriarch Germanos of Constantinople, as a former Monothelite who as a metropolitan participated in the rehabilitation of the Monothelite heresy, under the pressure of imperial power.

Everything mentioned points to a complex approach in the forming of a work such as the *Short History*, which was by no means a passive work that merely compiled source material. Nikephoros, as undoubtedly an Iconophile and later even a patriarch of Constantinople, managed to use the historical processes which he portrayed to create an idea about the place and role of the Church, its patriarch, and their multifaceted relations with both the Empire and the emperor himself. In such a literary approach, favourable portrayals of several heretical patriarchs were possible, since Nikephoros was guided by his intention to highlight the dignity of the very institution of the patriarchal office, rather than to analyse the dogmatic features and preferences of these patriarchs. Thus, these heretical identities were shifted into a secondary narrative and remained muted.

In its main narrative, the *Short History* offered an account of the reigns of the Byzantine emperors who governed the Empire from 602 to 769, with the images of Herakleios and Constantine V being the most characteristic and, in a literary sense, the two most complex characters in the entire work. Their portraits are in fact models according to which Nikephoros later portrayed and evaluated the reigns of other emperors which filled the space between these two reigns. Also, certain common elements in the description of these two emperors can be identified, which point towards Nikephoros's approach in the shaping of the overall image of an emperor on the pages of the *Short History*. In this respect, we can talk about a specific idea which the author introduced in his work, and which is probably the main motif of the characteristic structure of the *Short History*. Nikephoros's secular education and his political career, through which he was involved in all the political events that marked the Byzantine society of his time, left traces in his work as well. His intention to promote the positive aspects of the reigns of such emperors as Herakleios, Constantine IV, Leo III, and even some aspects of the reign of Constantine V, is also an indicator of the specific milieu and environment from which he originated.

This returns us to the question of dating the *Short History*. The *Life of Nikephoros* by Ignatios the Deacon is helpful since it mentions *secular writings* before Nikephoros's election as patriarch and alludes to a possible conflict with the Empress Eirene, which might be embedded in the comparison of Nikephoros to the Prophet Elijah (and his withdrawal from the capital to the prophet's escape to Mount Carmel after his dispute with the Empress Jezebel). The accentuated idea of *peace and tranquillity* which extends throughout the entire work, and especially dominates the narration in a positive manner in the account of Emperor Constantine IV, and in a negative manner in the portrayal of the destruction of the church of St. Eirene attached in narration to Constantine V, in fact presents an unspoken but dominant motif with which the *Short History* even ends – through the final mention of the marriage between the future emperor Leo IV and the future empress Eirene, who will largely contribute to the restoration of Orthodoxy and the renewal of a specific peace in the Church of Constantinople through the convocation of the Seventh Ecumenical Council.

The reign of Herakleios as portrayed in the *Short History* is of significance from several points of view, but it does not present the completely fulfilled ideal of a proper reign as presented in his account. In context of his mode of narration, it seems that Nikephoros set all the ideal features of a Byzantine emperor in the chapters dedicated to Herakleios, even though the emperor was portrayed as not being completely successful in accomplishing all of these principles. The idea of peace and good state order imposed itself as the main topic in the description of his reign. However, his unlawful marriage with his niece Martina and his Monothelitism were some of his faults. But he established a better rule than the previous emperor, Phokas. He had shown great disregard for his own life for the sake of the Empire during his campaigning in Persia. And, significantly, his relationship with the patriarchs Sergios and Pyrrhos was portrayed as a friendly and brotherly relationship. In the context of Iconophile ecclesiastical argumentation, these are very important messages. Conversely, Constantine V, as well as all the other emperors, to some extent failed to promote such a rule. Philippikos Bardanes deposed the Patriarch John of Constantinople and anathematized the Sixth Ecumenical Council, while the reigns of the subsequent emperors Anastasios II and Theodosios III were a time when the state and military organization of the Empire crumbled, as Nikephoros made sure to stress in his work. Leo III and his son, Constantine V, were victorious emperors against the Arabs and Bulgarians, but their Iconoclasm and persecution of the patriarchs, unlike the model established in the account of Herakleios's reign, made them not so much a worthy role model in the *Short History*.

So the only emperor who did not receive any kind of blame in the entire *Short History* was Constantine IV, who managed to restore both political peace with the enemies of the Empire and the ecclesiastical peace of the Church through the convocation of the Sixth Ecumenical Council. This was the reason that, in Constantine IV's reign only, Nikephoros displayed a perfect and a complete definition of order as established in the oration of Shahin – an idea of *peace and tranquillity* which pervaded the entire Empire as a result of the emperor's government. This political aspect of peace was later disrupted during the reign of Emperor Justinian II, and the ecclesiastical peace during the reign of Philippikos Bardanes, when the doctrines of Monothelitism were reaffirmed and the Sixth Ecumenical Council anathematized. In the further course of his narration, Nikephoros tended to present the renewal of the political aspects of peace and good state order in the reigns of the two Iconoclast emperors, while the ecclesiastical peace and order continued to be destroyed even further by the persecutions of monks, patriarchs, and pious Christians. These achievements were accomplished by none of the other emperors mentioned in the *Short History*. Neither Herakleios nor Constantine V managed to achieve these ideals.

In the end, why would such an image of Constantine IV, as a specific *hero* in the *Short History*, be relevant at all for Nikephoros and his possible audience in the late eighth and early ninth century? In a time when the Seventh Ecumenical Council was convened and propagated the renewal of the Orthodoxy of the Church of Constantinople and proper relations between patriarchs and emperors, contrary to the pressure placed upon the Church by the previous Iconoclast emperor Constantine V, an image of Constantine IV who convened the Sixth Ecumenical Council a century earlier could possibly be very plausible and appealing to the educated Byzantines of the eighth century. Since Constantine IV managed to introduce peace not only in the political sphere of his rule but in ecclesiastical matters as well, confirming Orthodoxy against Monothelitism just as Tarasios and his party (to which Nikephoros obviously adhered on many levels) had restored Orthodoxy after the first wave of Iconoclasm, his rule is the one with which Iconophiles could associate. And it is an interesting fact that the Seventh Ecumenical Council was held almost at the precise centenary of the previous Sixth Council, which might or might not have had a certain value and importance for the Byzantines at the end of the eighth century. In such a context, his image is the most positive one in the entire work of Nikephoros, and as such he might be viewed as a role model, a specific hero to which the Byzantines could refer as a desired type of an emperor in the turbulent times of the first Iconoclasm and around the year 787, when Nikephoros was active both in secular and ecclesiastical events, and as a historian as well.

# Glossary

*Akribeia*, exactness, precision and stricktness, among other things, in adhering to ecclesiastical rules and canon law. See Liddell and Scott, *A Greek-English Lexicon*, p. 55.

*Asekretis*, from Latin *a secretis*, an imperial secretary. See ODB I, 204.

*Apocrisiarius*, a messenger of a bishop or a patriarch to other church officials and representatives at the imperial court. See ODB I, 136.

*Caesar*, originally a dignity applied to the emperor; later, until the eleventh century, a dignity most often bestowed upon the sons of the emperor. Several exceptions are known, as the case of the Bulgarian Khan Terbelis, who received this title from the Emperor Justinian II. See ODB I, 363.

*Chartophylax*, lit.: *the one who safeguards the documents*, an archivist in the patriarchal archive, a member of the Constantinopolitan clergy, usually a deacon. A person who could assume a prominent ecclesiastical role, as evident in the case of the *chartophylax* Antiochos, who supported the revival of Monothelitism under Philippikos Bardanes. See ODB I, 415-416.

*Cubicularios*, a term designating eunuchs of the imperial palace in the service of the emperor. Often of noble descent, they performed various duties at the court, as governors and army commanders or envoys in diplomatic missions. See ODB II, 1154.

*Enkyklios paideia* (Ἐγκύκλιος παιδεία), encircled education. Often a technical term, as in the *Life of Nikephoros* by Ignatios the Deacon, referring to a higher level of secular education. See ODB III, 1552.

*Eusebeia*, in Nikephoros's narrative this term mainly points to the correct faith, or piousness of the emperor in regard to his personal devotion to the Church of Constantinople and icon worship. Standing in contrast is the term δυσσέβημα, as a negative attribute of impiousness of the iconoclast emperors. See Liddell and Scott, *A Greek-English Lexicon*, pp. 460-461, 731.

*Eutaxia*, lit.: *good arrangement*. See Liddell and Scott, *A Greek-English Lexicon*, p. 734. See also *Taxis*.

*Grammatikos* (Γραμματικός), in its ancient meaning, a teacher or a scholar. Later also utilized in the meaning of a scribe or a secretary. See ODB II, 866.

*Hypographeus*, lit. *one who writes under another's orders*; See Liddell and Scott, *A Greek-English Lexicon*, p. 1887. A secretary, thus in Nikephoros's *Synodika* to Pope Leo III the term points to the function of *asekretis* at the imperial court.

*Kopronymos* (Κοπρώνιμος). A nickname attached to the Emperor Constantine V by later iconophile circles. Lit.: *dung-named*. See ODB I, 501.

*Logothetes*, the term was used in the sixth century to designate fiscal controllers on various levels of state administration. In the seventh century the title was used to designate chiefs (*logothetai*) of various state departments (*dromos, genikon, stratiotikon*) which had become independent after the office of the praetorian prefect had lost its importance. See ODB II, 1247.

*Oikonomia*, lit. *managing a household*. In addition, the term could refer to the divine providence of the salvation of humankind through Christ's Incarnation, as narrated in the Gospels. Finally, *oikonomia* may refer to a deliberate moral concession or loosening of strict regulations of ecclesiastical rules in order to affirm the unity of the Church. See ODB III, 1516-1517.

*Oikonomos*, lit. *one who manages the household*. A priest or a monk who administers the financial income, expenditures, and the goods or properties of a church, monastery, or a bishopric. Some *oikonomoi* were appointed patriarchs of Constantinople. See ODB III, 1517.

*Oros*, a definition of true faith – Orthodoxy – as proclaimed at an ecumenical council. See Liddell and Scott, *A Greek-English Lexicon*, pp. 1255-1256.

*Parrhesia*, lit. *freedom of speech*. Nikephoros used it to portray Herakleios's boldness in action against the Persians. The term is mostly designated to explain a saint's boldness in his relation to God. See ODB III, 1591.

*Proedros*, the term might designate both a civilian and ecclesiastical title and function. Since its basic meaning alludes to the one who presides, Nikephoros utilized it to designate the patriarchs of Constantinople. See ODB III, 1727-1728.

*Protasekretis*, head of the imperial college of *asekretis*. See ODB III, 1742.

*Ptochotrophos*, lit. *one who feeds the poor*. A title of ambigous nature in relation to its exact place and role in the Byzantine sociopolitical and even ecclesiastical practice and tradition. A semi-ecclesiastical title as refered to by Alexander, *The Patriarch Nicephorus*. *Ptochotrophos* was the head of a *ptochotropheion* – a poor house (see ODB III, 1756). The function and title stems from the well-developed Byzantine notion of philantropy. Before becoming patriarch, Nikephoros of Constantinople was appointed to the position of *ptochotrophos* by the Emperor Nikephoros I, according to Ignatios the Deacon.

*Spatharios*, lit. *sword-bearer*. A dignity which in the Late Roman Empire designated an imperial bodyguard. Emperor Justinian II appointed the future Emperor Leo III as a *spatarios*. See ODB III, 1935-1936.

*Strategos*, an ancient term designating a general. In the *Short History*, *strategoi* most often appear as prominent military and government officials in their relation to the emperor. See ODB III, 1964.

*Synkellos*, lit. *living in the same cell*. A patriarch's or a bishop's confidant who shared his residence. From the sixth century the *synkelloi* became influential ecclesiastical officials, frequently succeeding the vacant patriarchal see. See ODB III, 1993-1994.

*Synkletos*, a state institution descending from the old Roman senate. In the imperial period it was transformed into an advisory board of the emperor. See ODB III, 1868-1869.

*Synodika*, an enthronement letter with a definition of correct faith sent by the patriarchs of Constantinople to the popes of Rome informing them about their election and consecration to the patriarchal office, and confirming the unity of the two Church sees. See ODB III, 1994.

*Tagmata*, plural of *tagma*. A classical term used to designate a regiment. Constantine V created a professional army of *tagmata* under the direct comand of the emperor, when the term becomes a techincal one. See ODB III, 2007.

*Taxis*, order. In Byzantine society *taxis* can express notions of both ecclesiastical or political order. Disorder (*ataxia*) in Byzantine society presents the gravest departure of ideal notions of government or church organization. See ODB III, 2018.

# Abbreviations

Mansi        *Sacrorum conciliorum nova et amplissima colectio, XII-XIII*, ed. by J.D. Mansi (Florence, 1766; repr. Paris: H. Welter, 1901)

ODB I-III    *The Oxford Dictionary of Byzantium*, ed. by A. Kazhdan, 3 vols. (New York and Oxford: Oxford University Press, 1991)

PG           *Patrologiae Cursus Completus, Series Graeca*, ed. by J.P. Migne, 166 vols. (Paris, 1857-1866)

PL           *Patrologiae Cursus Completus, Series Latina*, ed. by J.P. Migne, 217 vols. (Paris, 1841-1855)

# Bibliography

## Primary Sources

Aristotle, *Politics*, ed. by T.E. Page and others, trans. by H. Rackham (Cambridge, MA: Harvard University Press, 1959).

*Chronicon Paschale*, ed. by L. Dindorf, Corpus Scriptorum Historiae Byzantine, 1 (Bonn: Weber, 1832).

*Concise Chronicle* (Χρονογραφικὸν σύντομον), ed. by C. de Boor, *Nicephori archiepiscopi Constantinopolitani opuscula historica* (Leipzig: B.G. Teubner, 1830), pp. 79-135.

*Disputation between Pyrrhos and Maximos*, ed. by J.P. Migne, PG 91 (Paris: Garnier Fratres), cols. 288-353.

Grumel, V., *Les Regestes des actes du patriarcat de Constantinople*, vol. I.2: *Les actes des patriarches, 715-1043* (Istanbul: Assumptionists of Chalcedon, 1935).

Ignatios the Deacon, *Correspondence*, ed. by C. Mango, *The Correspondence of Ignatios the Deacon: Text, Translation, and Commentary* (Washington, DC: Dumbarton Oaks, 1997).

—, *Life of Nikephoros*, ed. by C. de Boor, *Nicephori archiepiscopi Constantinopolitani opuscula historica* (Leipzig: B.G. Teubner, 1830), pp. 139-217. Translation: *Byzantine Defenders of Images: Eight Saints' Lives in English Translation*, ed. by A.M. Talbot and trans. by E. Fisher (Washington, DC: Harvard University Press, 1998), pp. 25-142.

—, *Life of Tarasios*, ed. by S. Efthymiadis, *The Life of the Patriarch Tarasios by Ignatios the Deacon (BHG 1698): Introduction, Text, Translation, and Commentary* (Birmingham: Ashgate, 1998).

John Skylitzes, *Synopsis of Histories*, ed. by H. Thurn, *Ioannis Scylitzae Synopsis Historiarum* (Berlin: Walter De Gruyter, 1973).

Joseph Genesios, *Four Books about Kings*, ed. by A. Lesmueller and H. Thurn, *Iosephii Genesii Regum Libri Quattuor* (Berlin: Walter De Gruyter, 1978).

Methodios of Constantinople, *Life of Theophanes the Confessor*, ed. by B. Latyšev, *Methodii Patriarchae Constantinopolitani: Vita S. Theophanis Confessoris* (Petrograd: Russian Academy of Science, 1818).

Nikephoros of Constantinople, *Ad Leonem*, PG 100, cols. 169-200.

—, *Antirrheticus* I-III, PG 100, cols. 205-534.

—, *Apologeticus Maior*, PG 100, cols. 534-832.

—, *Apologeticus Minor*, PG 100, cols. 833-849.

—, *Refutatio et eversio*, ed. by J.M. Featherstone, *Nicephori patriarchae Constantinopolitani refutatio et eversio definitionis synodalis anni 815*, Corpus Christianorum, Series Graeca, 33 (Turnhout and Leuven: Brepols, 1997).

—, *Short History*, ed. by C. Mango, *Nikephoros Patriarch of Constantinople: Short History. Text, Translation and Commentary* (Washington, DC: Dumbarton Oaks, 1990).

Oikonomidès, N., *Les listes de préséance byzantines des IXᵉ et Xᵉ siècles: Introduction, texte, traduction et commentaire* (Paris: Centre National de la Recherche Scientifique, 1972).

Photius, *Bibliotheca*, ed. by R. Henry, *Photius, Bibliothèque, texte établi et traduit*, vol. I ("codices" 1-84) (Paris: Société d'Editions Les Belles Lettres, 1959).

—, *Epistulae*, ed. by B. Laourdas and L.G. Westernik, *Photii patriarchae Constantinopolitani epistulae et amphilochia III* (Leipzig: B.G. Teubner, 1985).

Rabanus Maurus, *Reversio sanctae atque glorissime Crucis Domini nostri Jesu Christi*, PL 110, cols. 131-134.

Stephen the Deacon, *Life of Stephen the Younger*, ed. by M.F. Auzépy, *La vie d'Étienne le Jeune par Étienne le Diacre: Intorduction, édition et traduction* (Birmingham: Centre for Byzantine, Ottoman, and Modern Greek Studies – Variourum, 1997).

*Suidae Lexicon II*, ed. by A. Adler (Leipzig: B.G. Teubner, 1931).

*Synaxarium ecclesiae Constantinopolitanae*, ed. by H. Delehaye (Brussels: Société des Bollandistes, 1902).

*Synodicon Vetus*, ed. by J. Duffy and J. Parker, *The Synodicon Vetus: Text, Translation, and Notes* (Washington, DC: Dumbarton Oaks, 1979).

*Synodikon*, ed. by J. Gouillard, 'Le synodikon de l'orthodoxie: Edition et commentaire', *Travaux et Mémoires*, 2 (1967), 1-136.

Theodore Studites, *Epistulae*, ed. by G. Fatouros, *Theodori Studitae Epistulae*, Corpus Fontium Historiae Byzantinae, 31.1-2 (Berlin and New York: Walter De Gruyter, 1992).

Theophanes, *Chronicle*, ed. by C. de Boor, *Chronographia* (Leipzig: B.G. Teubner, 1883). Translation: *The Chronicle of Theophanes Confessor: Byzantine and Near Eastern History, AD 284-813*, ed. and trans. by C. Mango and R. Scott with G. Greatrex (Oxford: Oxford University Press, 1997).

Theophylact Simocatta, *History*, ed. by I. Bekker, *Theophylacti Simocattae Historiarum*, Corpus Scriptorum Historiae Byzantine (Bonn: Weber, 1834).

*Three Byzantine Saints: Contemporary Biographies of St. Daniel the Stylite, St. Theodore of Sykeon and St. John the Almsgiver*, trans. by E. Dawes, intro. and notes by N.H. Baynes (London: Blackwell, 1948).

# Literature

Abrahamse, D. de F., 'Religion, Heresy, and Popular Prophesy in the Reign of Philippikos Bardanios (717-713)', *East European Quarterly*, 13 (1979), 395-408.

Afinogenov, D.E., 'Patriarch Photius as Literary Theorist, Aspects of Innovation', *Byzantinoslavica*, 56.2 (1995), 339-345.

—, *Константинопольский патриархат и иконоборческий кризис в Византии (784-843)* (Moscow: Indrik, 1997).

Alexander, P.J., *The Patriarch Nicephorus of Constantinople, Ecclesiastical Policy and Image Worship in the Byzantine Empire* (Oxford: Clarendon Press, 1958).

Alexander, S.S., 'Heraclius, Byzantine Imperial Ideology, and the David Plates', *Speculum*, 52.2 (1977), 217-237.

Anastos, M., 'Leo III's Edict Against Images in the Year 726-727 and Italo-Byzantine Relations Between 726 and 730', *Byzantinische Forschungen*, 3 (1968), 5-41.

Brubaker, L., and J. Haldon, *Byzantium in the Iconoclast Era c. 680-850: A History* (Cambridge: Cambridge University Press, 2011).

Bryer, A., and D. Winfield, *The Byzantine Monuments and Topography of the Pontos I* (Washington, DC: Dumbarton Oaks, 1985).

Bury, J.B., *A History of the Later Roman Empire from Arcadius to Irene (395 AD to 800 AD)*, vol. II (London: Macmillan, 1889).

Butler, A.J., *The Arab Conquest of Egypt and the Last Thirty Years of the Roman Dominion* (Oxford: Clarendon Press, 1902).

Болотов, В., 'Къ исторіи императора Ираклія', *Византийский Временик*, 14 (1907), 68-124.

Codoñer, J.S., *The Emperor Theophilos and the East, 829-842: Court and Frontier in Byzantium During the Last Phase of Iconoclasm* (Birmingham: Ashgate, 2014).

Chryssostalis, A., *Recherches sur la tradition manuscrite du contra Eusebium de Nicéphore de Constantinople* (Paris: CNRS Editions, 2012).

Чичуров, И.С., *Место Хронографии Феофана в ранневизантийской исторической традиции (IV-начало IX в.)*, Древнейшие государства на територии СССР. Материали и последования (Moscow: Наука, 1981).

Constantelos, D.J., *Byzantine Philanthropy and Social Welfare* (New Brunswick: Rutgers University Press, 1968).

Da Costa-Louillet, G., 'Saints de Constantinople aux VIII$^e$, IX$^e$ et X$^e$ siècles', *Byzantion*, 24.1 (1954), 247-248.

*Dictionary of Greek and Roman Geography*, vol. II, ed. by W. Smith (London: John Murray, 1872).

van Dieten, J.L., *Geschichte der Patriarchen von Sergios I. bis Johannes VI. (610-715)* (Amsterdam: Adolf M. Hakkert, 1972).

Downey, G., 'The Tombs of the Byzantine Emperors at the Church of the Holy Apostles in Constantinople', *Journal of Hellenic Studies*, 79 (1959), 27-51.

Drijvers, J.W., 'Heraclius and the *Restitutio Crucis*: Notes on Symbolism and Ideology', in *The Reign of Heraclius (610-640): Crisis and Confrontation*, ed. by G.J. Reinink and B. Stolte (Leuven: Peeters, 2002), pp. 175-190.

Dvornik, F., *Byzantium and the Roman Primacy* (New York: Fordham University Press, 1979).

Efthymiadis, S., 'On the Hagiographical Work of Ignatius the Deacon', *Jahrbuch der Österreichischen Byzantinistik*, 41 (1991), 73-83.

Фрейберг, Л.А., *Традиционное и новое в исторической литературе и в агиографии*, Византийская литература эпохи расцвета, ур. Л.А. Фрейберг, Т.В. Попова (Moscow: Наука, 1978).

Garland, L., *Byzantine Empresses: Women and Power in Byzantium, AD 527-1204* (London and New York: Routledge, 2002).

Gero, S., *Byzantine Iconoclasm during the Reign of Constantine V with Particular Attention to the Oriental Sources* (Louvain: Corpus Scriptorum Christianorum Orientalium, 1977).

—, *Byzantine Iconoclasm during the Reign of Leo III with Particular Attention to the Oriental Sources* (Louvain: Corpus Scriptorum Christianorum Orientalium, 1973).

Golden, P.B., *An Introduction to the History of the Turkic Peoples: Ethnogenesis and State-Formation in Medieval and Early Modern Eurasia and the Middle East* (Wiesbaden: Otto Harrassowitz, 1992).

—, *Khazar Studies: An Historico- Philological Inquiry into the Origins of the Khazars*, vol. I (Budapest: Akadémiai Kiadó, 1980).

Grierson, P., 'The Tombs and Obits of the Byzantine Emperors (337-1042)', *Dumbarton Oaks Papers*, 16 (1962), 3-65.

Haldon, J., *Byzantium in the Seventh Century: The Transformation of a Culture* (Cambridge: Cambridge University Press, 1990).

—, 'The Reign of Heraclius: A Context for a Change?', in *The Reign of Heraclius (610-640): Crisis and Confrontation*, ed. by G. J. Reinink and B. Stolte (Leuven: Peeters, 2002), pp. 1-16.

Hatlie, P., *The Monks and Monasteries of Constantinople, ca. 350-850* (Cambridge: Cambridge University Press, 2007).

Head, C., *Justinian II of Byzantium* (Madison: University of Wisconsin Press, 1972).

—, 'Physical Descriptions of the Emperors in Byzantine Historical Writing', *Byzantion*, 50 (1980), 226-240.

—, 'Towards a Reinterpretation of the Second Reign of Justinian II', *Byzantion*, 40 (1970), 14-32.

Herrin, J., 'Philippikos and the Greens', in *Novum Millenium: Studies on Byzantine History and Culture Dedicated to Paul Speck*, ed. by C. Sode and S. Takács (Aldershot: Ashgate, 2001), pp. 137-146.

Hovorun, C., *Will, Action and Freedom: Christological Controversies in the Seventh Centuries* (Leiden and Boston: Brill, 2008).

Howard-Johnston, J., 'Byzantine Sources for Khazar History', in *The World of the Khazars: New Perspectives. Selected Papers from the Jerusalem 1999 International Khazar Colloquium*, ed. by P.B. Golden and others (Leiden and Boston: Brill, 2007), pp. 163-194.

—, *Witnesses to a World Crisis: Historians and Histories of the Middle East in the Seventh Century* (Oxford: Oxford University Press, 2010).

Irigoin, J., 'Survie et renouveau de la littérature antique a Constantinople (IX siècle)', *Cahiers de Civilisation Médiévale*, 5.3 (1962), 287-302.

Janin, R., *Constantinople Byzantin: Développement urbain et répertoire topographique* (Paris: Institut français d'études byzantines, 1950).

—, 'L'Église Byzantine sur les rives du Bosphore (côte asiatique)', *Revue des études byzantines*, 12 (1954), 69-99.

Kaegi, W.E., *Byzantine Military Unrest 471-843: An Interpretation* (Amsterdam: Adolf M. Hakkert, 1981).

—, *Byzantium and the Early Islamic Conquest* (Cambridge: Cambridge University Press, 1992).

—, *Heraclius Emperor of Byzantium* (Cambridge, Cambridge University Press, 2003).

Kalogeras, N.M., *Byzantine Childhood Education and its Social Role from the Sixth Century to the End of Iconoclasm* (PhD Thesis, University of Chicago, 2000).

Kazhdan, A., '"Constantine Imaginaire": Byzantine Legends of the Ninth Century about Constantine the Great', *Byzantion*, 57 (1987) 196-250.

—, *A History of Byzantine Literature (650-850)* (Athens: The National Hellenic Research Foundation Institute for Byzantine Research, 1999).

Komatina, P., *Church Policy of Byzantium from the End of Iconoclasm to the Death of Emperor Basil I (843-886)* (Belgrade: The Institute for Byzantine Studies Serbian Academy of Sciences and Arts, 2014). In Serbian with an English summary.

Kompa, A., 'In Search of Syncellus' and Theophanes' own Words: The Authorship of the Chronographia Revisited', *Travaux et Mémoires*, 19 (2015), 73-92.

Kuniholm, P.I. and others, 'Of Harbors and Trees: The Marmary Contribution to a 2367-Year Oak-Tree-Ring Chronology from 97 Sites for the Aegean, East Mediterranean, and Black Seas', *Istanbul and Water*, ed. by P. Magdalino and N. Ergin (Leuven: Peeters, 2015).

Lardiero, C.J., *The Critical Patriarchate of Nikephoros of Constantinople (806-815): Religious and Secular Controversies* (PhD Thesis, Catholic University of America, 1993).

Leader, R.E., 'The David Plates Revisited: Transforming the Secular in Early Byzantium', *The Art Bulletin*, 82.3 (2000), 407-427.

Lemerle, P., *Le premier humanisme byzantin: Notes et remarques sur enseignement et culture à Byzance des origines au X<sup>e</sup> siècle* (Paris: Presses universitaires de France, 1971).

Liddell, H.G., and R. Scott, *A Greek-English Lexicon* (Oxford: Clarendon Press, 1843-1940; repr. 1996).

Lilie, R.J., *Byzanz unter Eirene und Konstantin VI. (780-802)* (Frankfurt am Main: Peter Lang, 1996).

Липшиц, Е.Э., 'Никифор и его исторический труд', *Византийский Временик*, 3 (1950), 85-105.

Ljubarskij, J.N., 'Concerning the Literary Techniques of Theophanes the Confessor', *Byzantinoslavica*, 56.2 (1995), 317-322.

—, 'Man in Byzantine Historiography from John Malalas to Michael Psellos', *Dumbarton Oaks Papers*, 46 (1992), 177-186.

—, 'Феофан Исповедник и источники его Хронографии (К вопросу о методах их освоения)', *Византийский Временик*, 45 (1984), 72-86.

Macrides, R., ed., *History as Literature in Byzantium: Papers from the Fortieth Spring Symposium of Byzantine Studies* (Birmingham, 2007).

Mango, C., 'The Breviarium of the Patriarch Nikephoros', in *Byzance: Hommage à A.N. Stratos*, vol. II (Athens, 1986), 539-552.

—, 'Deux études sur Byzance et la Perse Sassanide', *Travaux et Mémoires*, 9 (1985), 91-118.

—, *Short History*; see under Primary Sources: Nikephoros, *Short History*.

Marjanović, D., 'Seventh Ecumenical Council and Historical Representations of Patriarchal Successions in Literature of the Late 8th and Early 9th Century Byzantium', *Belgrade Historical Review*, 6 (2015), 49-67.

McCarthy, M.F., 'Rabanus Maurus', *New Catholic Encyclopedia*, 11 (1967), 881.

Niavis, P.E., *The Reign of the Byzantine Emperor Nicephorus I (AD 802-811)* (Athens: Historical Publications St. D. Basilopoulos, 1987).

O'Connell, P., *The Ecclesiology of St. Nicephorus I (758-828) Patriarch of Constantinople: Pentarchy and Primacy* (Rome: Pont. Institutum Studiorum Orientalium, 1972).

Ohnsorge, W., *Konstantinopel und der Okzident* (Darmstadt: Wissenschaftliche Buchges, 1966).

Pratsch, T., 'Ignatios the Deacon: Cleric of the Constantinopolitan Patriarchate, Metropolitan Bishop of Nicaea, Private Scholar, Teacher and Writer (a Life Reconsidered)', *Byzantine and Modern Greek Studies*, 24 (2000), 82-101.

Rapp, C., 'Old Testament Models for Emperors in Early Byzantium', *The Old Testament in Byzantium*, ed. by P. Magdalino and R. Nelson (Washington, DC: Dumbaton Oaks, 2010), 175-198.

Reinink, G.J., and B. Stolte, eds., *The Reign of Heraclius (610-640): Crisis and Confrontation* (Leuven: Peeters, 2002).

Ringrose, K.M., *Saints, Holy Men and Byzantine Society, 726 to 843* (PhD Thesis, Rutgers University, 1976).

Rochow, I., 'Anastasios (730-754)', in *Die Patriarchen der ikonokalstischen Zeit, Germanos I.-Methodios I. (715-847)*, ed. by R.J. Lilie (Frankfurt am Main: Peter Lang, 1999), pp. 22-29.

—, 'Konstantinos II (754-766)', in *Die Patriarchen der ikonokalstischen Zeit, Germanos I.-Methodios I. (715-847)*, ed. by R.J. Lilie (Frankfurt am Main: Peter Lang, 1999), pp. 30-44.

Ruggieri, V., *Byzantine Religious Architecture (582-867): Its History and Structural Elements* (Rome: Pont. Institutum Studiorum Orientalium, 1991).

Russell, J., 'The Persian Invasions on Syria/Palestine and Asia Minor in the Reign of Heraclius: Archaeological, Numismatic and Epigrafic Evidence', in *The Dark Centuries of Byzantium (7th-9th c.)*, ed. by E. Kountoura-Galake (Athens: The National Hellenic Research Foundation Institute for Byzantine Research, 2001), pp. 41-71.

Scott, R., '"The Events of Every Year, Arranged Without Confusion": Justinian and Others in the *Chronicle* of Theophanes Confessor', *Dosiers Byzantins*, 6 (2006), 49-66.

Ševčenko, I., 'The Search for the Past in Byzantium around the Year 800', *Dumbarton Oaks Papers*, 46 (1992), 279-293.

—, 'Was there Totalitarianism in Byzantium? Constantinople's Control over its Asiatic Hinterland in the Early Ninth Century', in *Constantinople and its Hinterland: Papers from the Twenty-Seventh Spring Symposium of Byzantine Studies*, ed. by C. Mango and G. Dagron (Aldershot: Ashgate, 1997), pp. 91-108.

Sophocles, E.A., *Greek Lexicon of the Roman and Byzantine Periods (from BC 146 to AD 1100)* (Cambridge: Cambridge University Press, 1914).

Speck, P., 'Byzantium: Cultural Suicide?', in *Byzantium in the Ninth Century: Dead or Alive*, ed. by L. Brubaker (Aldershot: Ashgate, 1998), pp. 73-84.

—, *Das geteilte Dossier: Beobachtungen zu den Nachrichten über die Regierung des Kaisers Herakleios und die seiner Söhne bei Theophanes und Nikephoros* (Bonn: Dr. Rudolf Habelt GmbH, 1988).

—, *Kaiser Konstantin VIII* (Munich: Wilhelm Fink, 1978).

—, *Kaiser Leon III: Die Geschichtswerke des Nikephoros und des Theophanes und der Liber Pontificalis, Teil I: Die Anfänge der Regierung Kaiser Leons III* (Bonn: Dr. Rudolf Habelt GmbH, 2002).

Stanković, V., 'The Path toward Michael Keroularios: The Power, Self-Presentation and Propaganda of the Patriarchs of Constantinople in the Late 10th and Early 11th Century', in *Zwei Sonnen am Goldenen Horn? Kaiserliche und patriarchale Macht im byzantinischen Mittelalter*, vol. II, ed. by M. Grünbart (Münster: LIT, 2013), 131-151.

Stein, D., 'Germanos I (715-730)', in *Die Patriarchen der ikonokalstischen Zeit, Germanos I.-Methodios I. (715-847)*, ed. by R.J. Lilie (Frankfurt am Main: Peter Lang, 1999), pp. 5-21.

Stevović, I., 'Emperor in the Altar: An Iconoclastic Era Ciborium from Ulcinj (Montenegro)', in *International Colloquium "Texts-Inscriptions-Images": Институт за изcведлане на изкуствата при БАН, София, Art Readings XIV*, ed. by E. Moutafov and J. Erdeljan (Sofia: Institute for the Study of Societies and Knowledge, BAS, 2016), pp. 49-67.

Stoyanov, Y., *Defenders and Enemies of the True Cross: The Sasanian Conquest of Jerusalem in 614 and Byzantine Ideology of Anti-Persian Warfare* (Vienna: Österreichische Akademie der Wissenschaften, 2011).

Stratos, A.N., *Byzantium in the Seventh Century*, vol. V: *Justinian II, Leontius and Tiberius 685-711* (Amsterdam: Adolf M. Hakkert, 1980).

Sumner, G.V., 'Philippicus, Anastasius II, and Theodosius III', *Greek Roman and Byzantine Studies*, 17 (1976), 287-294.

Tinnefeld, F., *Kategorien der Kaiserkritik in der byzantinischen Historiographie von Prokopios bis Niketas Choniates* (Munich: Wilhelm Fink, 1971).

Travis, J., *In Defense of the Faith: The Theology of Patriarch Nikephoros of Constantinople* (Brookline, MA: Hellenic College Press, 1984).

Treadgold, W., *The Early Byzantine Historians* (New York and Basingstoke: Palgrave Macmillan, 2007).

—, *A History of the Byzantine State and Society* (Stanford: Stanford University Press, 1977).

—, 'The Life and Wider Significance of George Syncellus', *Travaux et Mémoires*, 19 (2015), 9-30.

—, *The Middle Byzantine Historians* (New York and Basingstoke: Palgrave Macmillan, 2013).

—, 'The Revival of Byzantine Learning and the Revival of the Byzantine State', *American Historical Review*, 84.5 (1979), 1245-1266.

—, 'Trajan the Patrician, Nicephorus, and Theophanes', *Bibel, Byzanz und Christlicher Orient: Festschrift für Stephen Gerö zum 65. Geburtstag*, ed. by D. Bumazhnov and others, Orientalia Lovaniensia Analecta, 187 (Leuven: Peeters, 2011), pp. 589-621.

Zuckerman, C., 'The Khazars and Byzantium: The First Encounter', in *The World of the Khazars: New Perspectives. Selected Papers from the Jerusalem 1999 International Khazar Colloquium*, ed. by P.B. Golden and others (Leiden and Boston: Brill, 2007), pp. 399-432.

—, 'La petite augusta et le Turc: Epiphania-Eudocie sur les monnaies d'Héraclius', *Revue Numismatique*, 6 (1995), 113-126.

—, 'Theophanes the Confessor and Theophanes the Chronicler, or a Story of Square Brackets', *Travaux et Mémoires*, 19 (2015), 31-52.

# Index

## Personal names, ethnonyms and places

## Key-terms